Pacific Answers to Western Hegemony

EXPLORATIONS IN ANTHROPOLOGY
A University College London Series

Series Editors: Barbara Bender, John Gledhill and Bruce Kapferer

Daniel Miller, *Modernity – An Ethnographic Approach: Dualism and Mass Consumption in Trinidad*

Robert Pool, *Dialogue and the Interpretation of Illness: Conversations in a Cameroon Village*

Cécile Barraud, Daniel de Coppet, André Iteanu and Raymond Jamous (eds), *Of Relations and the Dead: Four Societies Viewed from the Angle of their Exchanges*

Christopher Tilley, *A Phenomenology of Landscape: Places, Paths and Monuments*

Victoria Goddard, Josep R. Llobera and Cris Shore (eds), *The Anthropology of Europe: Identity and Boundaries in Conflict*

Pat Caplan, *Understanding Disputes: The Politics of Argument*

Alisdair Rogers and Steven Vertovec (eds), *The Urban Context: Ethnicity, Social Networks and Situational Analysis*

Saskia Kersenboom, *Word, Sound, Image: The Life of the Tamil Text*

Daniel de Coppet and André Iteanu (eds), *Cosmos and Society in Oceania*

Roy Ellen and Katsuyoshi Fukui, *Redefining Nature: Ecology, Culture and Domestication*

William Washabaugh, *Flamenco: Passion, Politics and Popular Culture*

Bernard Juillerat, *Children of the Blood: Society, Reproduction and Imaginary Representations in New Guinea*

Karsten Paerregaard, *Linking Separate Worlds: Urban Migrants and Rural Lives in Peru*

Daniel Miller, *Capitalism: An Ethnographic Approach*

Nicole Rodriguez Toulis, *Believing Identity: Pentecostalism and the Mediation of Jamaican Ethnicity and Gender in England*

Jerome R. Mintz, *Carnival Song and Society: Gossip, Sexuality and Creativity in Andalusia*

Neil Jarman, *Material Conflicts, Parades and Visual Displays in Northern Ireland*

Gary Armstrong and Richard Giulianotti, *Entering the Field: New Perspectives on World Football*

Deborah Reed-Danahay, *Auto / Ethnography: Rewriting the Self and the Social*

Marianne Elisabeth Lien, *Marketing and Modernity*

R. D. Grillo and R. L. Stirrat (eds), *Discourses of Development: Anthropological Perspectives*

Simon Sinclair, *Making Doctors: An Institutional Apprenticeship*

Gary Armstrong, *Football Hooligans: Knowing the Score*

Mark Johnson, *Beauty and Power: Transgendering and Cultural Transformation in the Southern Philippines*

Pacific Answers to Western Hegemony

Cultural Practices of Identity Construction

Edited by Jürg Wassmann

Oxford • *New York*

First published in 1998 by
Berg
Editorial offices:
150 Cowley Road, Oxford, OX4 1JJ, UK
70 Washington Square South, New York, NY 10012, USA

Published with the aid of the Swiss Academy of Humanities and
Social Sciences in a hardcover edition of 400 copies.

Berg is the imprint of Oxford International Publishers Ltd.

Library of Congress Cataloging-in-Publication Data

A catalogue record for this book is available from the Library of
Congress.

British Library Cataloguing-in-Publication Data

A catalogue record for this book is available from the British
Library.

ISBN   1 85973 154 6 (Cloth)
       1 85973 159 7 (Paper)

Typeset by JS Typesetting, Wellingborough, Northants.
Printed in the United Kingdom by WBC Book Manufacturers,
Bridgend, Mid Glamorgan.

Contents

Introduction
Jürg Wassmann   1

Part I: Constituting Historical Knowledge

1   Knowing Oceania or Oceanian Knowing: Identifying
    Actors and Activating Identities in Turbulent Times
    Jonathan Friedman   37

2   Inventing Natives/Negotiating Local Identities:
    Postcolonial Readings of Colonial Texts on Island
    Melanesia
    Bronwen Douglas   67

3   Writing Local History in Solomon Islands
    Ben Burt   97

4   'Noble Savages' and the 'Islands of Love':
    Trobriand Islanders in 'Popular Publications'
    Gunter Senft   119

Part II: Ways of Constructing Identities

5   Contrasting Transcripts: Constructing Images and
    Identities in Mediations among the Wam People of Papua
    New Guinea
    Nigel A. Stephenson   143

6   The Identity Construction of Ethnic and Social Groups
    in Contemporary Papua New Guinea
    Berit Gustafsson   169

7   Reinventing Identities: Redefining Cultural Concepts
     in the Struggle between Villagers in Munda, Roviana
     Lagoon, New Georgia Island, Solomon Islands, for
     the Control of Land
     Gerhard Schneider   191

8   'Alas! And On We Go'
     Philippe Peltier   213

9   Resource Management in Lavongai and Tigak
     Islands: Changing Practices, Changing Identities
     Ton Otto   229

10   Metaphors, Media and Social Change:
     Second-generation Cook Islanders in New Zealand
     Thomas K. Fitzgerald   253

11   Identity Construction as a Cooperative Project:
     Anthropological Film-making with the Vaiakau and
     Fenualoa Peoples, Reef Islands, Temotu Province,
     Solomon Islands
     Jens Pinholt   269

Part III: Australia after Mabo

12   National Identity: Australia after Mabo
     Robert Tonkinson   287

13   Knowing the Country: Mabo, Native Title and
     'Traditional' Law in Aboriginal Australia
     Ad Borsboom   311

14   'All One but Different': Aboriginality: National
     Identity versus Local Diversification in Australia
     Barbara Glowczewski   335

15   Essentially Black, Essentially Australian, Essentially
     Opposed: Australian Anthropology and Its Uses of
     Aboriginal Identity
     John Morton   355

Part IV: Questioning Western Democracy?

16 Culture and Democracy among the Maori
    Toon van Meijl   389

17 Is Aristocracy Good for Democracy? A Contemporary
    Debate in Western Samoa
    Serge Tcherkézoff   417

Notes on the Contributors   435

Index   441

Introduction

Jürg Wassmann

I

Allow me to begin with a personal remark.

Having grown up in Southern Switzerland, I therefore spoke Italian with my friends and at school; at home, however, I spoke a Swiss German dialect – not becoming fluent in High German until much later, while studying in Basel (some of my colleagues question this fluency even today). I remember well how I had no school on Wednesday and Saturday afternoons and set out, first on foot, later with a small moped, to explore the surroundings: a rural area outside the city of Lugano (thus my subjective picture), with chestnut woods, open streams, clearly separated villages with old stone houses; the local dialect was spoken, there was no television. When I go back nowadays, I can see how my parental home has been swallowed up by suburbia, there are new buildings everywhere whose inhabitants for the most part did not grow up there (although my parents, after all, had also been newcomers), the streams are now running underground in pipes, there is a bus connection to the centre of town, a bank and two shopping centres; the language predominantly spoken now is a kind of 'television Italian'. And I myself am playing around with my identity: in Germany, where I now live, I present myself as an affable Southern Swiss; when I am visiting my family, however, I pretend to be more of a down-to-earth Northern Swiss (while strongly doubting that anybody believes this) – but, in every instance, I am trying to be 'different'.

My personal comment seems to me to point to nothing out of the ordinary since most of us have experienced something similar, we are 'uprooted', having grown up in rural areas, having lived for a long time in urban centres or moving back and forth, and we are guided by clichés, such as that of one's own past as a place which is specific, traditional and unchanging. The problem is that these patterns of thinking cannot function any more today since what was formerly thought of as autonomous and regional (without this being the truth even then) today is increasingly being levelled by a universal Western lifestyle, by a McDonaldization which (superficially and temporarily) appears to turn everything into a uniform suburbia. Pier Paolo Pasolini, the Italian writer who originated in the Friaul and was killed in a faceless suburb of Ostia near Rome, in 1975 described the state of his Italy where:

> The old cultural models are being denied. The people no longer want to have them. . . . With the help of television, the centre has assimilated the whole of the rest of the country to its image, a country, after all, which has been incredibly varied in the course of its history and rich in indigenous cultures. A levelling process has been started which is destroying everything authentic and special. The centre has carried through its plan: that plan that modern industrialization wanted . . . an industrialization that professes that ideologies other than that of consumption are absolutely inconceivable (1975:32).

'Globalization' is a key word of the present and, as such, a contested term. In the most general sense, 'globalization is a matter of increasing long-distance interconnectedness, at least across national boundaries, preferably between continents as well' (Hannerz 1996:17). Two aspects seem to be different today: the mobility of human beings themselves, and the mobility of meanings and meaningful forms through the media. These interconnections have many faces. We interfere in the environment of other nations, for instance by cutting down the rain forests, by dumping toxic waste, by global warming; the goods we buy may come from far away; the proliferation of media technologies allows for ideas and the tangible shapes which are given to them to circulate without much regard for distance. With this increasing interconnectedness in the world, it is assumed, there is also a threat to cultural diversity, or at least to certain cultural variations, as Pier Paolo Pasolini put it. Clifford Geertz is also affected by this sense of cultural loss: 'We may be faced with a world in which there simply aren't any more headhunters, matrilinealists, or people who predict the weather from the entrails of a pig' (1986:253). This is often linked to an uneasy feeling that Coca Cola can be sipped anywhere, that 'Dallas' can be watched, Barbie dolls can be played with; that we cannot recognize in the freely moving goods on the global market where and by whom they have been produced (the famous Swiss chocolate Toblerone is made by the American tobacco enterprise Philip Morris, and the ever-so-British After Eight mints, on the other hand, by the Swiss global player Nestlé).

The concept of globalization is so controversial because it has become a trendy word used by anyone, anywhere and for anything, with a tendency to resort to hyperbole and excessive generalization, which in most cases is connected with the dichotomies so typical for the European intellectual tradition. Thus globalization becomes associated with a dramatic shift between 'before' and 'after'. But of course the interconnectedness across great distances is not altogether new. The idea that each culture was to have a territorial entity with clear, sharp, enduring edges never really corresponded to reality. There have always been interactions, and diffusion of ideas, habits and things. And the objects of the anthropologist, such as tribes and chiefdoms, were frequently already products of the colonial system and not part of a traditional 'before' (Friedman 1994). In addition, globalization also implies the idea of a contrast between 'global' and 'local' associated with 'change' and 'continuity' whereby anthropologists in particular may show a tendency, caused by the tradition of their discipline which has focused on what is locally 'different', to think of the global as bad and to mystify the local. Finally, the context of 'centre' and 'periphery' also plays a role. At one end of the continuum, there is thus the culture of the centre, hence of the Western world, with greater although not always unambiguous prestige, at the other end are the cultural forms of the periphery, a creolized periphery more or less under constant pressure from the centre whilst itself creatively looking for autonomous answers.

One may reject the term globalization, ridicule it like Lila Abu-Lughod (1991) who speaks about 'globalbabble', one may wish to replace it by 'transnational', 'global village' or, as does Ulf Hannerz (1996), with a term he takes from Kroeber, i.e. 'ecumene'. The fact remains that our world is becoming increasingly interwoven and that this interconnectedness is notoriously uneven. The First World is the most strongly interwoven, in part with the Third World as well, but on unequal terms, which has made globalization appear to a large extent synonymous with Westernization. The phrasing 'on unequal terms' means that the flow of culture is asymmetrical, that the flow from the centre to the periphery is stronger than vice versa. It is a hegemonic process where culture becomes ideology. Cultural diversity, then, may be cultural resistance (Hannerz 1996).

This global interconnectedness is also a challenge to the intellectual traditions of our discipline yet it does not only affect the periphery, the Third World and the Fourth World (that of the Aboriginal people who are becoming more and more marginalized) but our own world as well – as I tried to point out at the beginning. We are still talking about the 'two-thirds society'; executives of the global players, however, talk of only twenty per cent of the working population being still needed. When leading politicians, economic leaders and scientists met in San Francisco in 1996 to discuss the future, an executive of the computer firm Sun Microsystems is reported to have said: 'We are hiring our people via computers, they work at computers and they are also fired by computers.' This is not just the consequence of the global economy with its transnational enterprises and unlocalized capital flows but also of political thinking that is tied to territories and that believes it is only possible to maintain a location for which it is responsible through the reduction of the welfare state, through the deregulation of all markets and through a lessening of government influence in general and thus also through the restriction of democracy. In this context, it is worth considering whether it is only a coincidence that, parallel to this, the so-called information society is expanding, most frequently in the form of the 'tittytainment', the provision of the (unemployed) population with entertainment spectacles. From the point of view of the economy, the world is becoming one; from the point of view of society, however, it seems to be falling apart. On the one hand, there is the hegemony of the centre over the periphery; on the other hand, however, the world is fragmenting. In order better to comprehend this, it might be useful to ask where, at which levels or in which 'organizational frames', as Hannerz calls them (1996), globalization is progressing and where resistance against it has formed.

II

The State Level

Today's world is spatially limited and separated into nation-states. However, the idea of the nation-state itself is a product of global cultural diffusion. The idea may have originated in Europe in the nineteenth century; in the twentieth century it exists almost everywhere. The states at the periphery are creations of the international system, built from the top rather than from the bottom up. In *Imagined Communities* (1983), Benedict Anderson describes how it was largely the commercialization of the printed word which led to more and more people recognizing that there were people much like themselves beyond the face-to-face community. We are citizens of one country and not of another and this is why we use a certain language and not another. Today, development goes beyond words, but the struggle of the new nation-states for internal homogenization continues. This becomes manifest for instance in the educational apparatus of schooling and in the production of one's own textbooks through which versions of the national past are authorized and disseminated. But these states are increasingly dominated by élites who are transnational cultural producers and consumers, forming a global class with few real cultural allegiances to the nation-state (Appadurai and Breckenridge 1988). Or in other words: many of these states promote messages of nationhood by themselves creolizing local cultures, they produce new cultures by inserting selected indigenous meanings and symbols into an imported matrix. More formal education tends to be synonymous with a greater involvement with metropolitan culture, as much of the knowledge involved is shared with the centre. Thus education creates differences – between educated and non-educated citizens.

The struggle for homogenization can not only be seen in the educational apparatus but also – which is often overlooked – in the legal system. Colonial powers like Great Britain, France, Germany, Holland or Portugal, enforced their own legal systems on the newly created countries everywhere. However, the precolonial regulations, social norms or local legal systems survived all the same, most frequently at the local level. But everywhere the traditional authorities were affected. They were either deliberately deprived of power because one wanted to introduce a uniform legal system, one wanted to 'modernize' the country, i.e. introduce new land rights and a new family law, once again from the top down in the sense of 'social engineering'. Or the old authorities were intentionally integrated into the new system ('indirect rule'), often there were simply not enough colonial administrators and hence the old authorities were left in their local positions but made dependent on the orders from above. As a rule, this resulted in a legal pluralism, most frequently in a dual system of jurisdiction: the colonial law applied at the national level, hence at the higher levels, and the traditional system of norms at the local level. But, in addition, transnational rules like for instance those of the World Bank or of the human rights organizations also play a role (Merry 1992). And here familiar concepts again play a part: that of the centre (city) and of the periphery (rural area) as well as the question in how far 'customary law' (if we remember the *kastom* debate) is in fact traditional or is itself already the result of colonialization (Ranger 1983; Chanock 1985). To be cautious, one could also talk about 'social fields', normative rules, including the national rules which are partially discrete, which overlap, being two-way rules (from the bottom up, from the top down), semi-autonomous rules (Moore 1986). Two competing models stand in the background: the 'customary' harmony model (which looks for the balance between the parties so the social injuries do not become too grave) versus the Western confrontational model (reference to abstract principles, i.e. dogmatics of law). The irony is apparent. In the USA, since the 1970s and 1980s, the Alternative Dispute Resolution (ADR) has been used, i.e. resolutions of conflicts outside the courts according to the harmony model.

The Market

The same T-shirt designs from Acapulco, Mallorca or Hawaii, the same watch and computer clones with different brand names, even Gucci clones: people are frequenting major department stores which offer similar products everywhere and are preferring foreign fast-food chains. Consumption thus becomes an aspect of broader cultural strategies of self-definition and self-maintenance. Products express what I am. I identify with a clearly defined set of products and activities, a lifestyle (Friedman 1994). The success of world globalization is probably based on these highly visible consumption patterns. In the terms of cultural flow, it is particularly the asymmetries of the market frames that create relatively unambiguous centre–periphery relationships. The market is the prime mover in globalization: goods, images and representations of the others (also via anthropologists) seem to diffuse most readily across national boundaries, thanks to new technologies of transport and media.

Where the media are concerned, Rupert Murdoch, who controls News International, BSkyB and the global parent company News Corporation, seems to be the prototype of the new world citizen. In the global village, media moguls like him call the tune. Nobody elected them, they owe their influence to technology and to the market and their only message is the Western culture of consumption: glittering, tempting, hedonistic, vulgar and at the same time violent and infantile. Above all, this culture is a prophet of the Americanization of the world – here Europe also becomes periphery. And it addresses itself directly to the youth – if formerly culture was something the older people handed down to the younger ones as the tradition of their society, now for the first time culture means that which can be sold or consumed. It is also remarkable that the key words used for these phenomena such as digital age, multimedia culture, data highways or information society seem to use the concepts of media and communication in a totally inadequate way. For television is not a medium, hence a mediator or exchanger (the reply of the television viewer will in no way influence what the television presenter on the screen has to say), so why talk of communication, meaning talking with each other, if one does not really communicate with another?

Behind the market stands the primacy of the economy. Many realms of life have been commodified and the individual, propagated as a socially detached individual, is in danger of degenerating into an opportunistic and lonely 'homo oeconomicus'. In the First World, these tendencies are especially tangible (and it is symptomatic that, in 1991, Amitai Etzioni, Robert Bellah and William Galston founded the communitarian platform). To list a few examples from Europe: many cultural productions which were formerly supported by patrons today have to survive with sponsoring; society demands of the universities that they change from being an educational institution into being a provider of professional, highly specialized knowledge; a deregulation has been suggested in the national churches so the religious goods like spiritual welfare, morals or sermons can be offered once more as customer-specific services against payment; in the end human labour will become an actual commodity and be commanded like a resource with reference to global practical constraints and made flexible 'just in time'.

Transnational Migrations

The postmodern era is characterized by a new time–space compression. The West is expanding and as a consequence the world is becoming smaller. Let me give you two typical examples of this reduction. Marshall McLuhan (1994) evoked the dramatic scenario of an implosion of the world into the global village with the image of the technological extension of the human organism. He distinguishes between a literate type of society, visually orientated and focused on the individual and a traditional, illiterate and oral, collectively organized tribal culture. In the course of the compression of the world thanks to the communication media, the auditive abilities of oral societies become necessary again, with radio taking on the role of the tribal drum. However, the expression 'global village' seems to be misleading since it suggests not only interconnectedness but also greater togetherness, a kind of large-scale idyll. David Harvey (1989) analysed the transition from the modern age to the postmodern age, from the end of the economic boom in the late 1970s to the present-day flexibility of production, labour markets and consumer behaviour, all of which are closely related to the technological innovations in the fields of transport and communication. The global (yet again) compression is caused by a process of acceleration which shortens the time-span within which money expenditure returns profit to the investor. As a reflex of this continuing global expansion of capital, postmodern thinking tries to emphasize transitoriness, insecurity, fragmentation, decentralization and eclecticism. The universal dominance of capital leads to a reduction of spatial separation; David Harvey depicts this shrinking of the world cartographically (1989:242). But this shrinking of the world is at the same time an enlargement of the Western world, implying the reduction of the rest of the world.

In 'Our Sea of Islands' (1994a), Epeli Hau'ofa contrasted this hegemonial point of view of the shrinking world to the border-crossing mobility of the inhabitants of the Pacific which results in an enlargement of the Oceanic world. The present island nations of Oceania are not isolated particles of land in the Pacific but an interlinked sea of islands. But migration is a worldwide phenomenon and increasingly affects the centres of the First World as well, such as (in the Pacific area) Auckland, Sydney or Los Angeles. This poses the question whether the bipolar imagery of space and time, the idea of the centre and the periphery do not have to be partly replaced by a multidimensional global space. For due to transnational migrations the peripheries implode into the centres. However, with over 100 million people living outside their natal countries this means not only that, increasingly, many people have no roots, but that they have no soil any more. Thus culture is becoming increasingly 'deterritorialized' (King 1991; Kearney 1995; Lavie and Swedenburg 1996; Kempf n.d.). Or in other words: the transnational migrants create transnational spaces, spaces which are mentally conceived as part of the original nation, as a tenth province or something similar, which leads to the paradoxical situation that people who live close to each other shield themselves against each other for reasons of identity but have close relationships with others living further away (in their own country of origin).

Local Actors

However, not only the shifting relationship between culture and territory poses a problem but also the assumption that the carrier of a culture is a people. We go one step further and ask: Where are the local actors within the globalization? The focus lies on the mobility of goods, images, ideas and people, and the potential consumers who follow their daily routine within their local context are forgotten. When, in the 1980s, the catchword of the 'just plain folks' was taken on by anthropology (Rogoff and Lave 1984; Lave 1988), this was a deliberate turning towards the everyday life of the actors and away from the traditional anthropological descriptions of structure, a conscious concentration on the 'average person' and away from the traditional omniscient informant or opinion leader who was seen as the carrier of the common culture of a group. These local actors have an everyday knowledge (of which they do not always have to be aware and which is not always linguistically encoded) which enables them to follow their everyday routine, a knowledge directly connected with the actions and also expressed by them, which thereby receives a definite structure and in addition prompts further actions, sets goals to them and directs them. This means less a conceptual but more a procedural knowledge associated with certain contexts. And while everyday knowledge was also being investigated in the West (Scribner 1984; Carraher, Carraher and Schliemann 1985), similarities became clear between a US woman out shopping and a Papua New Guinean woman at the market and thus the contrast of 'homo primitivus' versus 'homo logicus' as a construct, as a myth of 'Western' thinking, was exposed.

But there was a second point. The local exudes continuity exactly because it is highly repetitive, redundant, practical and often face-to-face, with a strongly emotional aspect. It is here in the local context that first experiences are made. At the same time, however, this local context is not autonomous but rather a kind of arena in which a variety of influences come together, are acted out, in a unique combination under those special conditions. Globalization may have a levelling influence, but the local contexts differ, just as the actors differ as well. And thus on the local level old, formerly more separate, currents of meaning and knowledge are blended together, and new, creolized, idiosyncratic cultures also come into existence. Two questions remain central in all this. What is the relationship of the local actors to the wider cultural entities? We cannot assume that wider cultural entities emerge simply through an aggregation of their activities; there is management of meaning by the state government or by the market. Zygmund Bauman (1992) proposes connecting the actor not to a system but to a flexible sense of habitat, to habitats of meaning; Jonathan Friedman (in his contribution to this volume) uses the term 'space of experience' coined by Mannheim. However, there seems to be scant research into this relationship. Associated with it is also the question of the access to this new knowledge, of its intelligibility. With ever more frequent national interference at the local level, with global commodities which can be bought at the village level, the spread of radio or even television at the village level, with increasing mobility, the exposure of the local actors to these goods is growing. In all this, the young men in particular seem to have the best access, at the expense of the women and the older people.

Thus it becomes understandable that, in tendency, the individual is growing more autonomous. Societies are drawn into larger commercial systems as peripheries, while commercialization, however, always has a tendency to disintegrate the traditional kinship and segmentary organization and small segments of the population are integrated into the dominant sector (Friedman 1994). This correlates with a move from culturally strong identity, from ethnicity, to weaker forms as lifestyles, which is the least ascriptive in so far as it refers to the practice of a culturally specific scheme which makes no claims to historical legitimacy and which can be freely chosen by the individual subject. Thus it is modernist in so far as it maintains the autonomy of the subject with respect to the culture in which he or she participates.

III

If all this is more or less accurate and if the interconnectedness becomes comprehensible at the level of the nation, of the market, in transnational migrations and in different local contexts, this has the consequence that our old concept of culture can no longer be applied. Today, culture is understood as a pastiche or a collage, as a hybrid or a creole form. There is much rhetoric involved. Our search for purity, homogeneity and boundedness of cultures is no longer appropriate although there is a deep longing everywhere for primordial meanings, which finds its expression in the interest in exhibitions or books on, for instance, the Celts or the Romans, an attempt to find in the past what anthropology finds in what is geographically distant.

> The view of an authentic culture as an autonomous internally coherent universe no longer seems tenable in a postcolonial world. Neither 'we' nor 'they' are as self-contained and homogeneous as we/they once appeared. All of us inhabit an interdependent late 20th century world, which is at once marked by borrowing and lending across porous cultural boundaries, and saturated with inequality, power, and domination (Rosaldo 1988:87).

The old culture concept grew out of romantic ideas regarding distinctive characteristics of peoples rooted in national territories; but this idea is not fitting for people, meanings and images moving all over the world (Barth 1969; Abu-Lughod 1991; Hannerz 1996). Nor did it fit in earlier times. Colonization of the Pacific did not start with Europeans; indeed the entire process of Austronesian expansion in the Pacific has been viewed as a colonizing process (Bellwood 1989). A sense of cultural difference doubtlessly predated European visits (Linnekin and Poyer 1990), a cultural insularity never existed but fragments of artefacts, dances, songs and rituals wandered and frequently the unfamiliar language of the songs was also adopted to emphasize the exotic – all this Boas (1927) already knew. But Europeans built up the extreme contrast between our ways and theirs, between civilized behaviour and heathen or barbaric behaviour (Jolly and Thomas 1992). Let us remember Christian missionaries who demanded that Pacific people detach themselves from their past practices and treat the past as a time of darkness. Cannibalism, warfare and sorcery became iconic of the whole (Jolly 1992). Thus custom became objectified – a thing that could be detached from indigenous actors and left behind. Moreover, colonialism not only brought Pacific people into contact with Europeans, but often extended and intensified their contact with other Pacific people, through the operations of missions, the processes of labour recruitment and the emergence of urban centres. A purposive accommodation of ancestral and introduced practices was effected, a process which continues today under the heading 'politics of tradition' (for example, see Keesing and Tonkinson 1982; Otto 1991, 1993; van Meijl and van der Grijp 1993).

In 1992, a handful of young men from the Finisterre Range in Papua New Guinea, all around twenty years of age, were discussing their future. Their own local Yupno culture and the one which had been imported are seen as two possibilities, as alternatives. But there is no consensus. The burden on the young men to find their own way could be felt. Let me quote a short passage (Keck 1993:77–85).

[A young man:] There have been many changes here, and I actually do not like it when the old and also the younger people walk around in bark-cloth belts and grass-skirts. After all, the station was built some years ago, and we have got independence so we give up this kind of clothing, bark-cloth belts, grass-skirts. It is good if we now have to buy shirts and trousers. The mission only brought us the message of God, but then the *gavman* [government] came ... [to us] and thus came corrugated iron houses, the airstrip, the health centre, the community school, the station, the bank, the market, all that. ... The *gavman* came and everything with it, tinned fish, salt, soap, rice. We are very happy that the *gavman* came and that airplanes land ... [here].

[Another young man:] We were ... all living in the bush and were completely behind the times, we had no idea about these things.

[A third young man:] It looks like we could now no longer live traditionally. Everybody wants to follow the traditions [*kastom*] from other regions. ...

[Yet another young man:] Those of the white people.

[A further young man added thoughtfully:] That is how it is. They are all starting now to follow the *kastom* from outside. And we will notice that our *kastom* does not work out. ... And some also say: We are now independent. Do not go back to a different level, to that of our ancestors. This is how many of them talk. But that is not true. Our *kastom* is very important. My father taught me to carve bows and arrows, to build fences, to pound bark-cloth, and he took me with him to the bush, to go hunting. Okay, so we are angry, but we do not imitate them.

[The first young man again]: You finished grade 10 at Karkar High School, but there was no place for you and they did not take you ...

[The thoughtful one again:] '*Sori, nogat wok* (sorry, we do not have work)!' You get raving mad when you hear that. I also went to town and tried to get a job, but it did not work out. But I had after all finished school and therefore it was very difficult for me to just make a garden (to live as a planter), and if I were to go to the market in front of the other people's eyes (to sell vegetables), then I would be ashamed as then some of them would say: This educated man here, why does he come to the market? I would hence be very ashamed, and this is how it is, and I and the young people in town of whom many have a school education, we wandered through town, we picked pockets, mugged people, things like that. We have left our parents, that hurt, we have spent a lot of money, we have left our village to go to a distant place, and we have used up our parents' money, and when shall we give the money back to them? This is the big worry I have and I often think about it. I am angry.

IV

The contributions[1] of this volume take up concerns of postcolonial politics in Oceania. They navigate uncharted waters, that wide sea between the classic ethnography of the Pacific and contemporary concerns in anthropological theory with global relations and transnational culture. Many of the authors tack across the expanse between what is already known about Pacific island societies and the new social forms that are emerging in these new states. Without exception, all the authors have done fieldwork in the Pacific region over many years. Despite all the topical or also regional limitations (thus examples from Micronesia are missing), despite all coincidences as well as the differing theoretical orientations and intellectual aims of the authors, and also despite the fundamental problem that Western scholars write about Pacific people, the contributions aim to represent some current Pacific answers to Western hegemony.

(1) Benedict Anderson's concept of 'imagined communities' has renewed a familiar Durkheimian question: how does a multitude of human beings come to think, feel and act as members of a single moral community? In a community or a nation-state introduced from outside and from above? Rites and symbols, but above all, the constitution of a national past, 'the continuous history of the community unfolding through homogenous, empty time' (Foster 1991:241; cf. Foster 1995), is a technique of integration to furnish a heterogeneous population with a sense of shared national identity. As was to be expected, this inscription of an official history by an élite nationalist discourse is highly controversial (Babadzan 1988; Hanson 1989; Keesing 1989; Linnekin 1991; Jolly 1992): some authors here talk about the 'invention of tradition' meaning not only the continuing manipulation of symbols to create new meanings in the sense of Roy Wagner (1975) but the *de novo* creation without continuity, or even with falsity and fabrication. This has been seen as an attack on the authenticity of indigenous political claims to land (see, for example, Fabian 1996 for related African historiographies). But Roger Keesing (1989:24) postulates:

> The present political contexts in which talk of custom and ancestral ways goes on are of course very different from precolonial contexts. Nonetheless, such mystification is inherent in political processes, in

all times and places. Spurious pasts and false histories were being promulgated in the Pacific long before the European arrived.

No other single event highlights this topic so much as the so-called 'Mabo decision'. Prior to 3 June 1992, Australia was the only former British colony that had failed to lawfully recognize the prior ownership of its indigenous inhabitants. On that day, in *Eddie Mabo and others* v. *the State of Queensland*, the High Court of Australia handed down a historic judgment (Robert Tonkinson's contribution in this volume). At that time, the argument was accepted that, under common law, the native title of Australia's indigenous inhabitants should be recognized. In so doing, the Court abandoned a 200-year-old legal fiction which held that, at the time of the first British settlement, the continent was *terra nullius* and without owners. (The bitter irony lies in the fact that a local group attained its traditional right by appealing successfully to 'imported' international law.) Considering this judgment, one easily overlooks the further finding that grants of freehold and some leasehold titles by the Crown extinguish native title. This extinguishment leaves most of Southern and Eastern Australia unclaimable. Also, most of Australia's quarter of a million Aboriginal people have been displaced from their ancestral lands and now live in urban areas and large country towns, so Mabo offers the potential for some security of tenure to only ten to thirty per cent of them. Two correlated problems seem to be contained in this.

First, there is the fact that, today, Aboriginal people of Australia are different from one another not only as a result of their cultural heritage but also because of their individual history of contact – reserves, separation of the children, mixed descent. Nevertheless, most of them claim the existence of an Aboriginality as a common identity, new affirmations of singular local identities which are only partly defined by tradition (Barbara Glowczewski's contribution). The foundations of the cohesion of each Aboriginal society are listed: indigenous theories of conception and kinship, social and marital organization, ways of economic survival and religious systems. Over the last decade, precisely this alignment of 'true' Aboriginality with the above-mentioned markers of 'authentic traditions' has been questioned as essentialism, hegemonic or (in Saidian terms) as 'Aboriginalist' (John Morton's contribution) – disregarding the fact that for many indigenous people the contrast between innate and acquired, just as between body and spirit, does not make sense. How this essentialism is indissoluble from a certain relation to the environment and therefore forms the basis for native title is shown in the contribution by Ad Borsboom with an example from Arnhemland. But there are not only Aboriginal 'nations' which are being formed, there is (secondly) also a nation-building of Australia as a whole. In this context, the nation as a whole must reimagine itself via a myth-making process in which the search for distinctively Australian national symbols may well include elements drawn from indigenous cultures (contribution by Robert Tonkinson). But how is the political system to look? Since democracy has become one of the most popular political ideologies in the world, many Pacific societies have in recent years become concerned with the introduction of political structures based not only on descent, ascribed rank and chieftainship, but also on political charisma, popular elections and representative government (see Serge Tcherkézoff's contribution on Western Samoa; cf. Hau'ofa 1994b; also Jonathan Friedman's contribution). Of course, Fourth World minorities like the Aborigines or the Maori (contribution by Toon van Meijl) have problems with the parliamentary form of government of First World states, since their internal politics are guided by the principles of consultation and consensus and not by those of majorities.

(2) From the early days of colonization in the fifteenth and sixteenth centuries, the contact has been characterized by the conviction of the dominant superiority of the Europeans with respect to the representatives of overseas cultures. This conviction manifests itself between two extremes. Pacific cultures experienced either intolerant damnation or pitiful recognition of their civilization, their people were either portrayed as 'savages' or, according to Bougainville's description of Tahiti (1772), also as 'noble savages' (contribution by Gunter Senft on the Trobriand Islands). This Western monopoly to portray others on the worldwide market of images and meanings is increasingly being questioned. With the myriad of emergent cultural identities and movements, the question of knowledge becomes a very important issue since it is related to the capacity to represent the world, not only for oneself but for others (contribution by Jonathan Friedman on Hawaii).

Let us remember Epeli Hau'ofa's 'counterimage' of the 'sea of islands' (see above) or his defence of Tonga's aristocracy:

> We still expect to see in our aristocracy ... the ideal faculties of our collective personality. In our hurly-burly free-for-all, dog-eat-dog modern society, we look to them for such qualities in social interaction as civility, graciousness, kindness, and that calming aura of a unifying presence in our midst (Hau'ofa 1994b:427; see, too, Friedman's contribution).

Here the changed condition of the production of anthropological knowledge becomes manifest. We have increasingly been faced with resistance by indigenous local actors and a series of what anthropologists feel are strangely alternative visions of local pasts, local culture, local traditions. But the *kastom* debate is not only a theoretical topic but also a political one. We have no longer a monopoly of cultural encompassment (Sahlins 1994) and the good old days of ethnographic authority are gone. Many Pacific islanders are engaged in reclaiming lands, cultural knowledge and political sovereignty. In so doing, they have also engaged in representing themselves, both for themselves and for the general public. This is an activity that was previously monopolized by the Western experts. But regardless of whether Western scholars or Pacific islanders claim the narrative authority for themselves, images of the past, whether mundane or professional, in memory, speech or written, are always constructed in the present, for present purposes (contribution by Bronwen Douglas on Kanaks). It goes without saying that the research by First/Worlders in a Third World region is always susceptible to accusations of exploitation or paternalism. This reputation is not improved by publications which pursue academic agendas more or less unintelligible to most ordinary islanders, sold at prices they cannot afford to pay. But the same problems seem to confront the Pacific authors with a Western education whose representations of culture and history may indeed be contradicted by their own rural people. With the example of Alasa'a's life history from the Solomon Islands, Ben Burt's contribution points out a fundamental contradiction between the oral traditions of a region, inherited as the local, often private, knowledge of families and clans and renewed with the life experience of succeeding generations and the conditions of publishing history for a wider audience.

(3) When people leave their village for the first time in order to, for instance, work on a plantation, this results in the emergence of a new perception of identity since they are forced to find their own place in a much wider world than the one they had formerly known. A case study from the Sepik River (contribution by Philippe Peltier) shows how landmarks are being used in this which are laid out in concentric circles. The first circle takes in the *wantok*, those who speak the same language, the second is comprised of adjacent groups (Arese and his comrades realized to their great surprise that there was no basic difference between their customs), the third circle is formed for each man by a 'mother' in the plantation area (Buka) who gives him food in exchange for presents, and finally the socially remote whites form the fourth circle. But more and more frequently the situation will arise where the parent-generation has left their island to settle once and for all in one of the big towns where they also raise their children. This second generation grows up without roots and without soil and yet they insist that they are at least symbolically distinct. Their identity, in large part due to mediated communicated influences, loses its place quality and acts independently of culture *per se* (Thomas Fitzgerald's contribution on second-generation Cook Islanders in New Zealand).

(4) It is certainly an advantage that anthropology has enlarged its perspective by taking into account the interconnectedness of the present-day world even though it concentrates mainly on the local actors in small contexts. For it is exactly one of the fundamental strengths of traditional fieldwork ethnography to focus on local details and the human dimension of social processes. A series of contributions makes this clear with the help of various topics which all show how in postcolonial times the local actors have to deal with new conditions prescribed from outside in order to preserve their own identity or to newly adapt it. The contributions not only describe the outcome but the actual process of this new creation and the procedural knowledge applied in it.

In the village discourses analysed in Nigel Stephenson's contribution on Papua New Guinea, *kastom* and *komuniti* (custom and community) are the two key terms. The two terms are antithetical and exclude each other. *Kastom* stands for the traditional culture and is negatively connoted since it implies ignorance, competition, jealousy, backwardness, superstition and strife. On the other hand, there stands *komuniti*, a concept associated with property, progress, truth, equality, peace, harmony and unity. However, both terms do not form clear concepts but are used as rhetorical plays by the factional leaders and political competitors of the village. But, between different villages as well, identities are newly constructed. Due to the migration into the centres, individuals meet who are not related through kinship, nor are they members of the same ethnic groups, and they might not even speak the same language. Yet they are expected to associate regularly through work as well as in their spare time. Berit Gustafsson's contribution from Manus shows how football teams are not organized along kinship lines but that there are villages whose teams are competing against each other. Yet modern developments may not only result in a weakening of kinship ties and matrilineal inheritance (remember Geertz's quotation above?) and a strengthening of the principle of the place of residence but also in social fission and individualization. Thus cultural concepts of the past may be modified in the present to validate claims to land ownership. In this process, social identities are reinvented in order to exclude related people from the control of land and, as a consequence, from the distribution of royalties from logging operations (Gerhard Schneider's contribution from the Solomon Islands). Something similar also happens in a case where, with the emergence of commercial fishing and, more importantly, the harvesting of sedentary marine products, concepts of boundaries and ownership gain more currency. The notion of identity has influenced this in four ways: the gradual decline of the central importance of clan identities, residence becoming a more important criterion for defining someone's identity, a trend towards linking one's identity with better-defined and smaller areas of sea or land, and a strengthening of the notion of individual identity and agency through the distribution of royalties to individuals and the possibility to register individual titles (Ton Otto's contribution from New Ireland). All these struggles of a reorientation may also lead to a growing interest in cultural matters, to a reflection which can not only be described but, in a different way, in cooperation with those concerned, also be shown: as a cooperative film project (Jens Pinholt's contribution on a tiny island in the Solomons).

V

The present contributions have been grouped under the following headings for the purpose of this volume and in order to form a plausible sequence. The first selection of papers on problems in 'Constituting Historical Knowledge' establishes the limits of the theoretical problems of entwining history and anthropology. The second selection, 'Ways of Constructing Identities', expands on the approaches to the problem: dialogic, discursive, ethnographic, each chapter re-posing the question of the interrelation of indigenous epistemology and ontology. The third section, 'Australia after Mabo', examines the issues of the previous section in the light of Aboriginal identity. The complexities of asserting an Aboriginal political citizenship in Australia lead into the final section. The volume draws to a conclusion with a section on 'Questioning Western Democracy?', in which the fundamental concepts of political participation are reworked. All the papers strongly represent the 'native point of view' except the last contribution in each section, which leads towards the topic, as it were, 'from outside'. A summary of the chapters in their order in this volume follows below.

I Constituting Historical Knowledge

The contribution by *Jonathan Friedman* deals with modes of knowing, anthropological and native, both in the plural sense. It begins with some of the more recent disagreements and conflicts between native activists and anthropologists and then moves on to investigate several examples of contrasting forms of knowledge production, both implicit and explicit in contemporary Oceania, concentrating on Hawaii. It argues that the confrontation between modes of knowledge can be understood in terms of changing global configurations of hegemony but that the content of the conflict can only be understood by grasping the very different senses of knowing in Western anthropology and among those that anthropologists study. Suggestions are offered as to the way anthropologists might deal constructively with this problem. Two recent articles (1994a, b) by Epeli Hau'ofa bring this issue home very clearly. The latter piece (1994b) deals with the democratization of Tonga, a process to which the author has made considerable contributions. Describing what might be called the decline of the monarchy and the aristocracy as a whole as wealth and power have become increasingly decentralized, Hau'ofa ends by affirming the value of the aristocracy for Tongan identity, as guardians of tradition and representatives of something more serious, the core of Tongan selfhood.

In a previous article in the same journal (1994a), Epeli Hau'ofa writes of a misconception by Westerners of Oceanic worlds. Whereas we conceive the Pacific as islands in a vast sea, he suggests that Pacific islanders conceive the same world as a 'sea of islands'. This implies a different view of resources, of possibilities of survival and of strategies of movement and living. The space occupied by a 'society' is not the island as such but the sea of islands, a sea of possibilities, a sea of wealth.

In both of these cases, we have an intellectual confrontation not just of ideas or intellectual products, but of strategies, of ways of going about engaging in the world. Now one might counter this by saying that the statement about Tongan royalty is simply wishful thinking, romantic respect, an attempt to avoid conflict, and similar to ordinary English attitudes to their royalty, and that, in the second case, the image of the encompassing Oceanic world is an ideological response to Western categorical truths. Hau'ofa does not believe that such is the case, but he does believe that it implies that we must investigate the matter intensively.

Invention of tradition/politics of identity are tropes for these postcolonial times, argues *Bronwen Douglas*: they condense central concerns of postmodern theorists, political activists and their respective opponents. The Pacific islands and Australia have recently provided contexts for significant theoretical, method-ological and substantive input on these related themes, much of it focused on the politics of representation and the issue of narrative authority: the authenticity and morality of competing images of the past constructed by engaged actors and analysts, variously claiming or challenging privileged access to objective knowledge. Imbedded in and crosscutting these contests is a debate about whether and to what extent objectification of culture might have been an indigenous experience or potential, rather than a colonial invention or a counterhegemonic reflex of the colonially dominated.

Bronwen Douglas provides a contribution to and reflection on that literature from overlapping, at times conflicting, perspectives.

She deconstructs a body of early colonial texts which named and represented native persons, places and identities in parts of island Melanesia – particularly New Caledonia. Ethnologically, these islands are sometimes depicted as extremes of 'Melanesian' hierarchy and its absence, which could translate as relative recognizability in terms of the political expectations of nineteenth-century European commentators. She considers processes of reciprocal mimesis by which indigenous nomenclatures, sociopolitical units and relationships were invented by colonial discourses attempting to register particular island settings, were often indigenized as useful strategies in altered, colonized contexts, and might ultimately be reinscribed as 'traditional' in modern political contests. The author reflects on the scope offered by dissonance and discrepancy between and within plural, unstable colonial discourses for an ethnographic historical narrative reconstructing indigenous enactment of identity and difference, and on the potential utility of such shadowy images in the toolkit of an anti/postcolonial nationalist project.

Ben Burt questions the role of written history and ethnography in the ongoing development of Pacific island culture, comparing the academic agenda of Western historical studies with those of the oral historical traditions which serve local interests within the communities they describe. While researchers have recognized the need to identify local historical agendas to give islanders a voice in the academic histories, there is also a need for histories written on these agendas. This might ensure that the inevitable process of transformation from oral to literate culture helps empower local people rather than simply promoting Western cultural hegemony, albeit mediated by local élites. Burt comments on selections from recorded stories, told by a Kwara'ae elder from Malaita in the Solomon Islands, to interpret the agenda of one particular local historical tradition concerned especially with the politics of cultural identity and land claims. His chapter considers the value of such history in the ongoing cultural reconstruction of Kwara'ae society, and the implications of documentation and publication for the development of an indigenous Pacific historical literature, which is by and for local people as well as about them.

Ever since the publication of Malinowski's ethnographic masterpieces on the Trobriand Islanders, novelists, psychologists, writers of travelogues and journalists have referred to the

Trobrianders, so *Gunter Senft* notes, as typical representatives of islanders living in a Pacific paradise. The references to the Trobrianders to be found in novels, 'reports', articles in journals, in newspapers and in other 'popular' publications in general revive the cliché of the 'noble savage'. They highlight either the Trobrianders' adaptability or their unwillingness to adapt to modern Western culture and emphasize – with many innuendoes about 'the sexual life of savages' – their carefree life on the 'Islands of Love'. After presenting some typical example of how the Trobriand Islanders are portrayed and 'sold' in such publications, Gunter Senft discusses from the point of view of the fieldworker and of fieldwork ethics what can and must be done to oppose these degrading and almost always sensation-seeking 'reports' based on a smattering of, or even completely false, 'knowledge' of the Trobriand Islanders, which we find not only in the rainbow press but also elsewhere.

II Ways of Constructing Identities

Nigel Stephenson reports that among the Wam peoples of the East Sepik Province (Papua New Guinea) mediations form an important instrument of conflict management. Mediations on a small scale are held frequently to settle altercations between individuals or families. Over a longer period of time, a distinct pattern becomes apparent which shows that at regular intervals of six to ten months large-scale mediations involving the whole village are convened. Invariably the issues at these meetings are sorcery accusations, but also the topics of the intermediate, minor mediations become woven into the fabric of the meeting in the course of the process. The sorcery accusations tend to build up as hidden transcripts and spread in the form of rumours in the weeks and months prior to the event. The full-size mediations are more than merely a forum for settling disputes. They constitute veritable 'state-of-the-village' debates, in which, firstly, an accountable version of the recent past is constructed from the diverse and contrastive transcripts (hidden and public), secondly, the effective relations of power in the nominally egalitarian polity are reified and made transparent, and, thirdly, the villagers' allegiance towards the at present dominant ideology of development and change is scrutinized and thus further substantiated.

Berit Gustafsson's chapter deals with sports and games, important occasions in modern societies through which ethnic and social groups, such as villages, may define their boundaries and thereby maintain their ethnic and social identity. In traditional Manus society, the clans were the basic foundations of sociality, not only within the village community, but also in relations with individual clans in other villages. Alliances therefore were not between villages as wholes, and the village did not constitute a social or political unit. Occasionally, however, the different clans living in the same village would define themselves as a unit, and create boundaries towards other groups. This happened in relation to warfare and more elaborate trade. The cultural practices of warfare and more elaborate trade have long since been officially discouraged and, nowadays, people are encouraged to associate freely across ethnic and social boundaries. Modernization has not, however, led to increased integration, but instead to a growing concern with ethnic identity. Still, people from different ethnic and social groups communicate and establish relations with each other. This happens mainly through sports meets and games, which are the only occasions that occur more regularly, and when the clans in a village constitute a unit. During sports meets and games, a number of people from different ethnic and social groups stay in the same village for several days to play against each other. The teams are chosen among the different clans in a village, and it is not the prestige of a particular clan but of the village as a whole that is at stake.

Today Munda (in the Solomon Islands), the former stronghold of the Roviana headhunters, is the focus of bitter disputes concerning land ownership, *Gerhard Schneider* writes. To justify their claims, people modify concepts of traditional culture in this process of arguments. Apart from abstractly dividing 'ownership' into 'primary' and 'secondary' rights, disputes then arise over the role of the chief, principles of descent (patrilineal vs. matrilineal), genealogy, aspects of traditional religion. Today's refined arguments developed from a 'landmark' High Court case decision in 1971 given by a European judge at a time when new economic policies (promotion of export of timber and fish) were formulated and had to be implemented. The Chief Justice awarded a small faction of people control over the vast, vaguely defined area of land on the grounds of their matrilineal descent from a founding tribal ancestor. Statements of Europeans were used (missionaries, administrators) to establish matrilineal descent as a principle of conferring superior land rights. Even an article in *Man* was used for this purpose. It is clear that descent in Kazukuru – the Munda tribe – is cognatic. Absolute concepts of 'ownership' developed over time with an individualization of social relations fostered by the prospects of money from timber and fish. Major lineage segments are cut out of the genealogy as a consequence to channel the money into few hands. Today the violation of rights is dealt with by the courts where formerly control over land was supernaturally sanctioned.

Philippe Peltier reports that, during fieldwork in 1991–2, Arese, one of the oldest men of an Adjirab village in the Porapora (East Sepik Province, Papua New Guinea), told his life story. Arese was born probably at the end of the 1920s, a few years before first contact with the European recruiters. He was drafted by the Japanese army during the Second World War before becoming a *doktaboi* and a worker on Buka's plantations. Arese never talks about his life or social changes in his society but about his relation to – and his position in – the outside world. After a brief discussion concerning the influence of forms of traditional oral history in his own narrative, Philippe Peltier tries to analyse, first, what have been, for Arese and the Adjirab, the most important historical events since first contact and, in consequence, how Arese and his society have managed to respond to those sometimes dramatic events; and, second, how the intrusion of the 'new world' and the new economic system (introduced by two different societies: the white colonial Australian and the other New Guinean from the Sepik or other islands such as Buka) have had a direct influence on the social organization of the community.

Ton Otto starts by saying that customary marine tenure is a classical but rather underdeveloped theme in Melanesian anthropology. Paradoxically, modern economic developments which transform and even threaten the continued existence of traditional systems of marine tenure have prompted the state and other organizations to fund research projects in this field. Anthropologists are asked to codify local customs in order to determine whether local people have a 'right' to compensation if the marine resources in their environment are exploited by modern industrial enterprises. The anthropologist is thus operating as a mediator between different cultural 'fields', namely national law, national and supranational economy and local traditions. Clearly the anthropologist is also operating in a context of diverse interests and unequal power relations. While producing 'knowledge', the anthropologist is involved in changing cultural realities. Ton Otto reflects on the role of the anthropologist as a cultural broker, using his own experience in a consultancy project as an example. In 1975, the Papua New Guinea Minister for Mineral Resources decided that tuna fishing companies had to pay royalties to the local 'owners' for the baitfish which they caught in coastal waters. Ever since, the just distribution of this money has proved to be a near-impossible task since 'traditional ownership' of baitfish was a largely undefined and hotly contested cultural proposition.

The research by *Thomas K. Fitzgerald* represents a case where identity is still alive and well in a modern, urban setting; but this identity does not necessarily involve the maintenance of a separate culture. There is today often a huge gap between everyday social realities and rhetoric about culture. Social change and cultural change are not identical, and to confuse the two leads to serious misinterpretations about communication. Identity – in large part, due to mediated communication influences – loses its 'place-defined' quality and begins to act independently of culture *per se*. The conclusion is that identity has important functions that transcend culture as such. Culture certainly is standardized by the media in many parts of the globe; at the same time, identities are being increasingly asserted. The paradox is cultural identity without a corresponding culture. This argument raises the question of how best to nurture a strong national identity and yet still recognize the psychological need of various minorities for symbolic 'cultural' identities. An ethnographic example from the South Pacific illustrates how the media further contribute to changes in both culture and identification, thus challenging the positive implications for 'cultural' revivals.

In his contribution, *Jens Pinholt* discusses problems relating to defining, interpreting and representing cultural 'traditions' from the anthropological fieldworker's point of view. In earlier days, a regional trading system used to integrate the Northern Santa Cruz Islands into a reproductive totality. Each local group played its specific part, which gave to a large extent form and meaning to its social and cultural reality. For the Vaiakau, living in the marginal, poor coral islands of the Outer Reefs, the Puke trading canoe was an all-important means of survival.

The demise of the regional trading system in the 1950s and 1960s has forced a major part of the Vaiakau to scatter widely or to live a highly mobile life in order to obtain alternative means of survival: land, education and contract work. Many of the social and cultural ways of the *puki* trading days have been given up as meaningless. Others live on in a changed guise or with a new content. However, lately some of the Vaiakau have become increasingly aware of the importance of these cultural ways.

The anthropologist is currently, together with a film crew, collaborating with the Vaiakau people to make a film about their cultural 'traditions'. Both parties agree on the importance of having a strong cultural identity as a survival kit in the modern world. But how far do we agree in our views on the nature of 'tradition'? Can we produce a film which takes into account the Vaiakau people's wish to have a true, authentic account to be used in their existential and political struggle, and which at the same time satisfies the anthropologist's commitment to truth and authenticity as he sees it?

III Australia after Mabo

Robert Tonkinson refers to the landmark decision in 1992 when Australia's High Court rejected the doctrine of *terra nullius* and conferred legal recognition on the Aboriginal people's claims to prior ownership of the continent. Despite the fact that many Aboriginal people will not be able to make native title claims, the 'Mabo decision' may provide a basis for a renewed call for Aboriginal sovereignty grounded in a pan-Aboriginal national identity. We can observe a process in which Aboriginal people are actively redefining themselves in multiple social fields. Notions of community and nation are being examined and sometimes contested, both among Aboriginal people and between them and society at large.

There is no consensus among Aboriginal people that they should aim for sovereignty or the creation of some state-like entity; and there is also real and potential conflict among groups seeking title to land. In addition, a large and mostly unsympathetic majority of Australians perceive Aboriginal claims to land as inimical to their interests, and are unlikely to support any moves towards the attainment of Aboriginal sovereignty. It is clear that the Mabo decision provides an unprecedented structural underpinning for pan-Aboriginal ethnogenesis. However, the problems of boundary creation and separation, and the realities of Aboriginal encapsulation and lack of access to significant resources, are among the serious obstacles to the realization of political autonomy within the Australian nation-state. Irrespective of the outcomes, the Mabo decision and the playing out of the legal issues it raises will have a number of important implications: for the way Aboriginal people define themselves, for inter-Aboriginal social and political action, and, at the level of the society as a whole, for inter-ethnic relations and the politics of identity.

Ad Borsboom also refers to the year 1992 when the High Court of Australia rewrote Australia's law on the impact of colonization, in the case of *Freddy Mabo and others* vs. *the State of Queensland* (*Aboriginal and Torres Strait Islanders Commission Bulletin* 1993). The Court held that Australia was not *terra nullius* ('empty land', or 'land belonging to no one') when settled by the British in 1788. Instead it was acknowledged that Australia was occupied by Aborigines and Torres Strait Islanders, who had their own laws and customs, and whose 'native title' to land survived the Crown's annexation of Australia. The Court's judgment has captured the public's attention like no other in recent times, and has been in the centre of public debate and controversy since then. For Aboriginals, the Mabo judgment is a milestone in their continuous struggle for land rights.

Ad Borsboom first explains the basic elements of the Court's decision and some of its major implications for both indigenous and non-indigenous Australians. He then explores the political and symbolic importance for Aboriginal and Torres Strait Islanders. To exemplify the importance of land, he finally presents a brief analysis, based on fieldwork, on the intense relationship between an Arnhemland clan (Northern Australia), its mythology, songs and rituals, and its 'country'.

Barbara Glowczewski starts out by stating that today Australian Aborigines are different from one another not only as a result of their cultural heritage (the continent used to have more than 500 languages) but also because of their individual history of contact – reserves, separation of the children from the parents, mixed descent, etc. Nevertheless, most of them claim the existence of an 'Aboriginality' as a common identity even though its definition is not unanimous. In fact, when claiming their Aboriginality many groups affirm themselves first as different from and eventually opposed to their other Aboriginal neighbours. It is as if pan-Aboriginality itself was creating the emergence of those identity singularities: as if the process of anthropological and social heterogenization were part and parcel of the creation of political uniformity.

Barbara Glowczewski presents some of the practices and discourses which oppose or draw together various government agencies and Aboriginal organizations (local, state or federal level). Gender relations, theories of kinship and ritual innovations are also considered. Aboriginality as a national identity is a construction of post-contact history in relation to non-Aborigines. But autochthonous status in terms of ethnic identity always existed as the foundation of the cohesion of each Aboriginal society. It included indigenous theories of conception and kinship, social and marital organization, ways of economic survival and religious systems. The affirmation of an Aboriginal 'spirituality' associated with land rights and its political relations with Christian Churches is discussed. Aboriginality as a melting-pot of collective traditions and militantism is undetachable from individual creations (art, literature, etc.) but also from conflicts of interests which seem to promote the identity of local groups when they are placed in opposition to one another.

The 1992 decision is the starting-point for *John Morton* as well. In 1992, the Australian High Court made a landmark decision which saw the end of the legal fiction of *terra nullius* in Australia. It found that, contrary to previous interpretations of the law, Australia had not been settled as 'unoccupied land' and that Australian Aborigines had by common law a form of 'native title' over certain lands. This decision, which effectively rewrote Australian history in favour of the Aboriginal people, has sparked and fed vigorous debate about the country's past and future. At the centre of this debate between Aborigines, politicians, economic interest groups and various intellectuals lies the complex question of the identity of Aboriginal Australians in relation to the development of the nation-state. John Morton's chapter examines this ongoing and contested narrative construction of Aboriginal and Australian history and identity, and situates it in the context of postcolonial relations in the Pacific region and in the world at large. It also suggests the terms (limits, opportunities and contradictions) by which Australia's indigenous peoples can continue to maintain a distinct and productive profile in the national consciousness.

IV Questioning Western Democracy?

Toon van Meijl writes that democracy has recently become one of the most popular political ideologies in the world, including the Pacific. But democracy is a multivalent concept which has different meanings in different cultural contexts while, at the same time, democracy may be used to legitimize widely divergent political practices within the same social situation. The conceptual confusion surrounding the discourse of democracy is further compounded by the fact that the articulation of a political ideology in terms of democracy does not necessarily bear on political practice, while, paradoxically, a discourse on democracy may be absent in areas where political developments are taking place which have been clearly influenced by the global dissemination of democracy. Toon van Meijl goes on to discuss several interpretations, usages and applications of democracy in Maori society. The focus lies on a multiplicity of conflicting meanings of democracy, on the one hand, in counterhegemonic discourse arguing against the dominance of the European majority within the New Zealand nation-state, and, on the other hand, on the rivalry between urban and rural factions within Maori society, or between regional (pan-tribal) and tribal organizations.

Serge Tcherkézoff concentrates on Western Samoa where a big debate is going on in this rather paradoxical way: is the *faamatai* (the system of representation through chiefs) better than universal suffrage for maintaining the *alofa* bond (social mutual help and gift-giving and sympathy) equally between all people? In Samoa, the traditional system of sacred chiefs has never been discontinued. At the time of independence (1962), the whole people of Samoa insisted on setting up a parliamentary system where the chiefs only would vote and be voted in. In 1990, another referendum broke up a part of that system and established the universal suffrage for electors, only the chiefs remaining as parliamentary candidates. Since the announcement of that referendum and up to this day, the debate remains very intense in the country. All sides have the same goals and values. All put forward that the way they propose is the only way to save and preserve forever the *faamatai*, the 'chief system', and all put forward that their way is more 'democratic' than the other. The answer to the paradox will be given in this chapter.

Regarding aristocracy: the so-called chief system is a kind of aristocracy where there are no families who would not be aristocratic. Actually, the chief – the *matai* – is the head of an extended family; the *matai* is elected by all the heirs of that name (i.e. all the people constituting the family, young and old, females and males) and he can be ousted from his office in the same way. Regarding democracy: the idea of democracy – which is taken as a value by the Samoans – can be approached and is being approached in the debate in two ways: one is the idea of representation, the other the idea of suffrage. Because the *matai* is elected and can be ousted by the same people, because the electors are all the members of the family, the election of the *matai* is said to be a strongly democratic system. People in favour of universal suffrage do not contest that view but consider that a direct democracy (universal suffrage: people elect parliament) instead of an indirect one (people elect *matai* who elect from among themselves) is still better. These aspects explain why all sides say they defend democracy.

Note

1. The contributions in this volume are a selection of revised papers held at the Conference of the European Society for Oceanists, in Basel, December 1994; another selection is edited by Verena Keck (1998). I wish to thank Ingrid Bell and Norma Stephenson for translating and shaping this introduction into proper English.

References

Abu-Lughod, L. (1991). Going beyond Global Babble. In: A.D. King (ed.), *Culture, Globalization and the World-System: Contemporary Conditions of the Representation of Identity*, pp. 131–8. London: Macmillan.

Anderson, B. (1983). *Imagined Communities: Reflections on the Origin and Spread of Nationalism*. London: Verso.

Appadurai, A. and Breckenridge, C.A. (1988). Why Public Culture? *Public Culture* 1(1):5–9.

Babadzan, A. (1988). Kastom and Nation Building in the South Pacific. In: R. Guidieri, F. Pellizzi and S. Tambiah (eds), *Ethnicities and Nations: Processes of Interethnic Relations in Latin America, Southeast Asia and the Pacific*, pp. 199–228. Austin: University of Texas Press.

Barth, F. (ed.) (1969). *Ethnic Groups and Boundaries: The Social Organization of Cultural Difference*. Boston: Little, Brown.

Bauman, Z. (1992). *Intimations of Postmodernity*. London: Routledge.

Bellwood, P. (1989). The Colonization of the Pacific. Some Current Hypotheses. In: A.V.S. Hill and S.W. Serjeantson (eds), *The Colonization of the Pacific: A Genetic Trial*, pp. 1–59. Oxford: Clarendon Press.

Boas. F. (1927). *Primitive Art*. Cambridge (Mass.): Harvard University Press.

Carraher, T.N., Carraher, D.W. and Schliemann, A.D. (1985). Mathematics in the Streets and in Schools. *British Journal of Developmental Psychology* 3:21–5.

Chanock, M. (1985). *Law, Custom, and Social Order. The Colonial Experience in Malawi and Zambia*. Cambridge: Cambridge University Press.

Fabian, J. (1996). *Remembering the Present. Painting and Popular History in Zaire*. Berkeley: University of California Press.

Foster, R. J. (1991). Making National Cultures in the Global Ecumene. *Annual Review of Anthropology* 20:235–60.

—— (1995). *Nation-Making. Emergent Identities in Postcolonial Melanesia*. Ann Arbor: University of Michigan Press.

Friedman, J. (1994). *Cultural Identity and Global Process*. London: Sage.

Geertz, C. (1986). The Uses of Diversity. In: S.M. McMurrin (ed.), *The Tanner Lectures on Human Values 7*, pp. 251–77. Cambridge: Cambridge University Press.

Hannerz, U. (1996). *Transnational Connections. Culture, People, Places*. London: Routledge.

Hanson, A. (1989). The Making of Maori. Culture Invention and its Logic. *American Anthropologist* 91:890–902.

Harvey, D. (1989). *The Conditions of Postmodernity*. Oxford: Blackwell.

Hau'ofa, E. (1994a). Our Sea of Islands. *The Contemporary Pacific* 6(1):147–61.

—— (1994b). Thy Kingdom Come. *The Contemporary Pacific* 6(2):414–28.

Jolly, M. (1992). Specters of Inauthenticity. *The Contemporary Pacific* 4(1):49–72.

Jolly, M. and Thomas, N. (eds). (1992). *The Politics of Tradition in the Pacific. Oceania* (special issue) 62(4):241–362.

Kearney, M. (1995). The Local and the Global. The Anthropology of Globalization and Transnationalism. *Annual Review of Anthropology* 24:547–65.

Keck, V. (1993). Talk about a Changing World. Young Yupno Men in Papua New Guinea Debate their Future. *Canberra Anthropology* 16(2):67–96.

—— (ed.) (1998). *Common Worlds and Single Lives. Constituting Knowledge in Pacific Societies.* Oxford: Berg.

Keesing, R.M. (1989). Creating the Past. Custom and Identity in the Contemporary Pacific. *The Contemporary Pacific* 1:19–42.

Keesing, R.M. and Tonkinson, R. (eds) (1982). *Reinventing Traditional Culture: The Politics of Kastom in Island Melanesia. Mankind* (special issue) 13(4):279–399.

Kempf, W. (n.d.). Cosmologies, Cities, and the Enlargement of the World. Manuscript.

King, A.D. (ed.) (1991). *Culture, Globalization and the World-System: Contemporary Conditions for the Representation of Identity.* London: Macmillan Education.

Lave, J. (1988). *Cognition in Practice. Mind, Mathematics and Culture in Everyday Life.* Cambridge (Mass.): Cambridge University Press.

Lavie, S., and Swedenburg, T. (eds) (1996). *Displacement, Diaspora, and Geographies of Identity.* Durham and London: Duke University Press.

Linnekin, J. (1991). Cultural Invention and the Dilemma of Authenticity. *American Anthropologist* 93:446–9.

Linnekin, J. and Poyer, L. (eds) (1990). *Cultural Identity and Ethnicity in the Pacific.* Honolulu: University of Hawaii Press.

McLuhan, M. (1994). *Understanding Media. The Extension of Man.* London and New York: Routledge. (First published in 1964.)

Merry, S.E. (1992). Anthropology, Law, and Transnational Processes. *Annual Review of Anthropology* 21:357–79.

Moore, S.F. (1986). *Social Facts and Fabrications. 'Customary' Law on Kilimanjaro, 1880–1980.* Cambridge: Cambridge University Press.

Otto, T. (1991). *The Politics of Tradition in Baluan. Social Change and the Construction of the Past in a Manus Society.* Canberra: Australian National University; Nijmegen: Centre for Pacific Studies.

—— (ed.) (1993). *Pacific Islands Trajectories: Five Personal Views.* Canberra: Australian National University, Department of Anthropology; Nijmegen: Centre for Pacific Studies.

Pasolini, P.P. (1975). *Scritti Corsari.* Milano: Aldo Garzanti.

Ranger, T. (1983). The Invention of Tradition in Colonial Africa. In: E. Hobsbawm and T. Ranger (eds), *The Invention of Tradition,* pp. 211–63. Cambridge: Cambridge University Press.

Rogoff, B. and Lave, J. (eds) (1984). *Everyday Cognition. Its Development in Social Context.* Cambridge (Mass.): Cambridge University Press.

Rosaldo, R. (1988). Ideology, Place and People without Culture. *Cultural Anthropology* 3:77–87.

Sahlins, M. (1994). Goodbye to Tristes tropes. Ethnography and the Context of Modern World History. In: R. Borofsky (ed.), *Assessing Cultural Anthropology,* pp. 377–94. New York: McGraw-Hill.

Scribner, S. (1984). Studying Working Intelligence. In: B. Rogoff and J. Lave (eds), *Everyday Cognition: Its Development in Social Context,* pp. 9–40. Cambridge (Mass.): Cambridge University Press.

van Meijl, T. and van der Grijp, P. (eds) (1993). *Politics, Tradition and Change in the Pacific. Bijdragen tot de Taal-, Land- en Volkenkunde* (special issue) 149(4):633–824.

Wagner, R. (1975). *The Invention of Culture.* Chicago: University of Chicago Press.

Part I

Constituting Historical Knowledge

Chapter 1

Knowing Oceania or Oceanian Knowing: Identifying Actors and Activating Identities in Turbulent Times

Jonathan Friedman

It ought to be obvious from many of the contributions that the world is undergoing considerable change. There is a clear tendency in certain quarters to an intensifying feeling of fragmentation, that the world is no longer coherent, that we are all discovering our hybrid nature at the same time as, in other quarters, people who have lived in a state of fragmentation under the weight of social marginalization are getting their acts together. Now this double process, and it is, of course more multiplex than simply double, is an area that has occupied my own research interests for a number of years (Friedman 1994). While some have feared an emergent world in homogenization, or celebrated a world creolization, I have suggested that the world may, in a more important way, be a world in balkanization and that this has its positive and negative sides, depending very much on one's position in the global arena. Any former tendencies to homogenization would seem today to be offset by a myriad of emergent cultural identities and movements, which can best be understood in relation to the fragmentation and reorganization of the global system. We have seen Hawaiians resurge and take their place on the cultural and political map, and grow at a rate defying the laws of biological reproduction, just as the North American Indian population more than doubled in a decade and several new tribes have made their appearance. Now in what I have understood as the cultural ramifications of the fragmentation of a formerly hegemonic world and an ensuing scramble for both identification and the empowerment that it implies, the question of modes of knowledge and their confrontation becomes a very important issue since it is related to the capacity to represent the world, not only for oneself but for others.

I might begin by noting the force of this change as it is expressed in the work of one of the most brilliant anthropologists of the Pacific. Epeli Hau'ofa, who has written such important satires of his own society and introduced class analysis into the understanding of cultural movements in the South Pacific, has for me been associated with a position that I would identify as modernist, arguing against a traditionalism that he saw as a tool of élite domination. More recently he has turned his acumen to a resurrection and defence of the specificity of Tongan, Polynesian and possibly pan-Pacific ways of going about understanding the world. This is coupled to a clear opposition to Western modernity at its worst. Discussing the declining aristocracy of his home country in a period of demands for democratization he enters an important caveat.

> We have travelled together with our aristocracy for over a thousand years, and their leadership has given us reasons to be proud of our history, our heritage, and ourselves as a nation . . . We still expect to see in our aristocracy, as in no other group in our society, the ideal faculties of our collective personality. In our hurly-burly free-for-all, dog-eat-dog modern society, we look to them for such qualities in social interaction as civility, graciousness, kindness, and that calming aura of a unifying presence in our midst (Hau'ofa 1994b:427).

This follows another important piece in which Hau'ofa attacks the Western understanding of Pacific civilization as consisting of relatively isolated islands separated by vast bodies of ocean. He opposes this to a view summarized by the title 'Our Sea of Islands', in which the sea is not a separator but where, on the contrary, it is the substance of a world of open connectivity (Hau'ofa 1994a:155). This in its turn helps to understand the ease with which people can move and settle throughout the globe without losing their homes. The return to, and defence and rehabilitation of, other forms of knowing is part of the global transformation sketched above. It necessitates a reconsideration of the constitution and confrontation of ways of knowing.

Rationale

The study of modes of knowledge constitution is especially important in Pacific anthropology today due to the changed conditions of production of anthropological knowledge itself. Anthropologists have been having trouble establishing their knowledge of the Pacific in these turbulent times. They have increasingly been faced with resistance and a series of what they feel are strangely alternative visions of local pasts, local cultures, local traditions. More often than not they seem to express dismay at this activity and they are often critical of what they feel are patent misrepresentations of the real cultures of the people that ought perhaps to remain anthropological objects as in the good old days of ethnographic authority. In social terms what has changed are the general conditions of representation and self-representation. Many native Pacific islanders, like other indigenous peoples, are engaged in reclaiming lands, cultural knowledge and political sovereignty. In doing so they have also engaged in representing themselves, both for themselves and for the general public. This is an activity that was previously monopolized by the experts. But something has happened in anthropology as well. There has been a shrinkage of the previous apparatus of scientific activity. Theoretical discourse has been eliminated or at least seriously curbed as a self-conscious realm of activity and has been absorbed or replaced by an expanded notion of ethnography. The latter is a documentary notion which in the absence of the notion of hypothesis, now replaced by interpretation, becomes a powerfully dogmatic discourse of its own, a way of defining other peoples worlds. Something between fact and interpretation has become ethnographic reality.

This change in the conditions of anthropological knowing has serious consequences. For a certain predominant discourse in the Pacific it has led to the importation of the 'invention of tradition' to characterize *kastom* movements and other similar cultural movements' construction of their identities. The approach is equally applicable to all forms of modern cultural corpuses in Oceania. While much back-tracking 'I didn't mean it that way' statements have attempted to modify the implications of this approach, surprisingly little research has been concentrated on the actual processes of knowledge production in such movements.

Rather there has been a tendency to study products, very much, by comparing them to our own forms, i.e. results, of knowledge. This occurs, I suggest, because it lies at the core of the way we produce our own knowledge, but, in the absence of a notion of hypothesis, it becomes an issue of the power and right to represent in which different modes of knowing are reduced to a single mode. The specificity of our kind of knowing is that it is decontextualized with respect to its own social conditions and goals (other than knowledge itself). In fact much argument is dedicated to clearing away such irrelevant, ideological, socially infected, factors from the pure issue at hand, establishing the truth about the world. If this is understood as a modernist form of science, it is certainly not the only one. Another problem involved here is the facility with which certain anthropologies have pretended to be able to gain access to other forms of knowledge in the guise of rejecting modernism and scientism. In the view argued here, there is no postmodern solution to this problem, simply because postmodern and related strategies of knowledge acquisition are just as much a part of our world as are the modernist strategies. All the problems of Lévy-Bruhlian and Léenhardtian constructions to the universalist rationalism of Keesing are at issue. I shall argue, if this is necessary, that this is not a question of the operations of what might formally be designated as rational discourse, but higher-order strategies of selection and combination of propositions that are themselves embedded in a socially specific constitution of experience of the world.

The Fragmentation of Modernism and the New Cosmopolitanism

This argument is part of an older one in anthropology, one that goes back to Sapir and even to Boas who argued that a culture is not comprehensible in terms of the origin of its elements but in terms of the way they are structured in relation to one another. This is an argument for an understanding of lived realities rather than *our* identification of the origin of cultural elements. The emergence of this latter interest, intriguingly diffusionist in nature, is part of a particular emergent cultural élite understanding of the world. What I have called the new cosmopolitanism refers to a somewhat complex phenomenon, part of the decomposition of modernism as the hegemonic identity of the real political-economic hegemony of the West. The latter was based on a striving for the rational as opposed to the concrete-cultural. The latter was understood in terms of an abhorred tradition, or at least a ranking of cultural specificities in relation to a developed civilization that had surpassed superstition and the filthy desires of the libido. There were, of course, romantic relativist visions as well but these were also based on a ranking in a temporal continuum of primitive to civilized. All of this, I have argued, is the result of the application of the self-understanding of the modernist subject to the world of which the latter is the centre.

Times have changed. The modern space of identity is fragmenting as it is polarizing. There is a surge of traditionalism in the form of a return to roots, fixed identities, religious securities, and to 'culture' in general. There is a primitivist reaction as well, not so much reflexive, but a visceral revolt against the iron cage: the surge of the demonic, the jungle, the libidinous, the famed pornotopia of Daniel Bell (1979:144), but also the urban Indians, the Marxist-Leninist, antifascist middle-class révoltés who have become an ethnic group of their own. There is a postmodernist, somewhat cynical and clearly contemplative enjoyment of what is referred to as wisdom (tradition) and nature (primitive) as opposed to the much despised figures of modernism. There are, of course, still plenty of modernists, somewhat beleaguered, often hysterically afraid of the approaching mob of non-modernists, but they are a dwindling minority to be found among a certain faction of the cultural élites of the centres of the global system. The general change is toward fixed identities, toward a celebration of cultural specificity as such in an era where rational modernism has lost its attraction, for very good systemic reasons (which I have explored elsewhere (Friedman 1994)).

It follows from this that this is also an era of explosive identifications, indigenous, ethnic, national, regional. It is an era of cultural fragmentation, following on the political-economic fragmentation of hegemony in the global system. It implies freedom and emotional well-being for many, just as it implies violent consequences implicit in a process best described as balkanization, not creolization.

Some anthropologists have been severely affected in their own identities by this process. The former ability to define the world of the other has begun to evaporate. Now this ability was the *minimal* function of an anthropology that at one time distinguished clearly between ethnographic interpretation and more general theory. But the latter, theoretical footing slipped as well in the process of social fragmentation, leaving only ethnography as such, i.e. propositions about other people's realities, or, in an even more minimalist sense, about our realities 'of them'. Intellectuals have been in a mad scramble to survive this situation rather than to try and struggle with its parameters. Among the major results of this scramble have been a family of related positional identities.

1 Some, indeed quite a few, have held to their modernism in the form of progressivist condemnations of mystified 'national-isms', not least in the Pacific. The tool of analysis in this has been the 'invention of tradition' in one form or another.
2 Some have relinquished modernism for a notion that the modern world consists of hybrid forms, the result of colonial and postcolonial globalizations of pre-existent cultural forms. In the dominant discourse of Bhabba and others, this hybrid mix represents a kind of (sub)alternative to modernity that has been suppressed by the latter and which is now on the upsurge. For others this mixture is simply the reality of the modern world, the amplification of what I have called the spaghetti principle, which is misunderstood by both ethnics and multicultural state machines.

Both of these positions are cosmopolitan, one old, one new. The first maintains that the modern world is non-cultural and that cultural identities are suspiciously unauthentic unless those who practise them can be classified as real 'traditionals'. The second comes to terms with the modern situation by focusing on origins alone. Both identities define themselves in relation to the 'others', either by negation or by encompassment. The former is cosmo-politanist modernism, the latter is cosmopolitanism without modernism. Both define the realities of the contemporary world as *essentially* different from traditional 'otherness'. They are modern and therefore not 'traditional', they are hybrid and therefore not traditional. The modernities of the Pacific are thus ranked with respect to a previous more substantial baseline of primitivity; this, in spite of official disclaimers, I would argue.

The Problem: Culture and the Experiential Substrate

A crucial problem in assessing different modes of knowledge, as with all cultural corpuses, is that our starting-point has tended to be a notion of culture as enumerable items, practices, beliefs, symbolic constructs, etc. and that the latter have not been referred back to the structures of experience that might have engendered them and in which they exist in people's lives. In this connection I would found my case on work such as that of Mannheim in the late 1910s and early 1920s, which engaged students such as Lukacs and Elias in real fieldwork. Mannheim distinguishes in his *Structures of Thinking* (1983) between the communicative and conjunctive. The former refers to context-free knowledge that can be freely transferred. The latter refers to the embedded forms of knowledge that are dependent upon context and which are not easily elicited. The latter knowledge is very much the basis of the former in the sense that communicative knowledge is elaborated out of experientially based knowledge. Mannheim refers here to what he calls *Erfahrungsraum*, the social space of experience, the shared field of tacit understandings embedded in social interaction. I have stressed a similar argument in a previous paper referring to Sapir's distinction between 'genuine' and 'spurious' culture and to Sartre's (1957) discussion of existential authenticity as opposed to that of the artefact (Friedman 1993).

Sahlins (1993) in a forceful argument against the 'invention of tradition' school stresses from a slightly different point of view that cultural invention can only be properly understood in terms of cultural continuity, and that its current usage implicitly denies any such continuity and therefore cultural/historical reality to those engaged in such invention. In the present argument I would suggest that this is not a mere question of the continuity of cultural form, of the application of old mythical or symbolic 'texts' to new situations, which is the kind of continuity usually argued from a culturalist standpoint. The latter approach is still based on the notion of culture as codes, artefacts, symbols, i.e. things, products whose meaning, furthermore, tends to be embedded in the objects themselves. While such 'things' are of course central, they are not dynamic in themselves. Rather we must begin to grasp the social structures of experience that engender and maintain such codes, symbolic forms, etc. and which enable us to understand the motivations involved in cultural production/creativity. In other words we must consider that, while cultural 'invention' is obviously motivated, the motivations themselves are not invented.

Experience and Embedded Knowledge

The following examples from Hawaii are attempts to relate social experience to cultural form. They deal with conjunctive knowledge, knowledge that is embedded in the immediacy of social relations, and not with context-free texts. The former can be abstracted, of course, and their properties can be clarified, as Hau'ofa has tried to do in the articles cited above. The examples are not of the same type. The first consists of stories while those that follow consist in various practices. In both cases I have attempted to reach what appears to me to be a unity of experience and a core mode of relating to the world, which is not made explicit but seems to connect the different examples. The stories or discourses produced by people express the same kinds of embedded forms of relatedness as the practical strategies of everyday existence, ways of transacting, of adopting, of relating to kin. The stories project such embedded forms onto imagined universes and mythical pasts. The structuration of these discourses through their variants can be accomplished with great virtuosity because they lie so close to the self-evident interpretations of the world that are generated by immediate social experience.

Captain Cook: the Real Story?

The apotheosis of Captain Cook has by now become an icon of Hawaiian studies and debate about the 'true' history of the islands. The version suggested by Sahlins (1981) is culled from a combination of the ships' reports and official mythology, recorded decades later, concerning the gods and their adventures. In the case of Sahlins the small-print paragraph at the start of *Historical Metaphors*, which recounts the story of the priest Pa'ao and the establishment of Lono from Kahiki in the islands, is reconstructed from a larger number of versions carefully noted in parentheses but not reported as whole texts. A number of variants disappear in this unified version. Even more interesting is the existence of a body of traditions from the area of Kealakekua Bay and the entirety of South Kona that recount a great variety of versions of the Spanish arrival in Hawaii almost 100 years earlier. Now Cook did use a Spanish map to locate the islands, which were called *Islas de la Mesa*, and it is the case that Hawaii island looks very much like a table stood on its end from far out at sea. The Spanish also claimed the islands in the United Nations after the Second World War. The geographer O. Spate (personal communication; Spate 1979) insists that the Spanish must have been in Hawaii before the English. The first curator of the Bishop Museum, Brigham, a natural scientist, wrote an extensive manuscript (typescript actually) history of Hawaii that makes rather much of the Spanish contact. The manuscript has never been published and it is not easy to gain access to it except piecemeal. It is said that there were remains of the great chief Keawe, who was apparently buried in a Spanish sail along with numerous Spanish items all kept at the Museum that suddenly disappeared during the Spanish American War and the expansion of the USA into the Pacific. It is following this, the overthrow of Queen Liliu'okalani, that official American discourse begins to deny the existence of any Spanish connection to the islands preceding Cook's arrival. Question? What are we to make of Western established knowledge about such facts? How are they constructed?

Local Hawaiians have maintained their own stories about the events. They have also elaborated upon them in their own ways, ways that have to do with the ways in which they construe their own identities. The following texts are based on recordings from a Hawaiian village. They are not presented verbatim here but have been converted into a rather reduced standard English form so as to make the analysis of their content easier. The local dialect of English would necessitate a preliminary analysis that does not really bear on the present goals. The first statement was collected earlier than the others.

Long before Captain Cook Jesus came to this place. Our ancestors came from the holy land. The tribes of Israel travelled east over India and into Oceania. That is why our religion is so much like Bible. You know about the City of Refuge in Honaunau. People who committed a crime could go there and be safe from their enemies, just like in the Bible (interview 1985).

Now one might say that this is simply a carry over from the missionaries, since the story is common throughout the Pacific and is central, for example, to Fornander's history of Polynesian origins (1969). Some anthropologists and historians would claim that the Hawaiians had been duped or tricked into a new Western mythology. I would argue that there is something else going on here that has to do with the mode in which Hawaiians have gone about making their constructions, whether or not they have used Western statements.

Kitchen-table *Bricolage*

The following stories are from a tape made in the kitchen of an elderly wise woman, a *kupuna* of a small fishing village. She and her distantly related niece set out to tell me the real story of Captain Cook at Hawaii. The several versions were the results of a rapid succession of interpretive discussions in which the story was elaborated upon. The entire session took about half an hour and displays a combinatorial virtuosity reminiscent of Lévi-Strauss but with the speed of a short-order cook (no pun intended). At each phase of the presentation it seemed to my interlocutors that they were filling in the story so that I would better understand it.

Version 1:   There was a Spanish shipwreck here in the eighteenth century [date]. Only two children survived and they were taken in. They were married to aristocrats. That is why some of us are more light skinned. You know that aristocrats are often lighter than commoners. That is also why some of us have Spanish names.

Version 2:   There was a Spanish shipwreck here before Captain Cook, up at Kealakekua Bay. Everyone died but two children who we saved. The boy was brought up by the *ali'i* and was adopted to Maui. The girl was brought up here as a high *kahuna*. They were brother and sister and each became great in their own realms. The boy became a great warrior and the woman a famed priestess. When Captain Cook came the people mistook his sails for the Makahiki cross and believed that he was a great chief descendent of Lono. But they discovered that he was no such person and so they killed him.

There is a more elaborate version of this story in which Jesus is combined with Captain Cook in an interesting way. The story envisions Cook's visit as a false repetition of the return of Jesus.

Version 3: The Makahiki cross you know came originally from Jesus who came to Hawaii with his teachings. Hawaiians awaited his return over the centuries. There was a Spanish shipwreck here in the eighteenth century, here at Kealakekua Bay. Everyone died but two children who we saved. The boy was brought up by the *ali'i* and was adopted to Maui. The girl was brought up here as a high *kahuna*. They were brother and sister and each became great in their own realms. The boy became a great warrior and the woman a famed priestess. When Captain Cook came the people mistook his sails for the cross and were ready to accept him as their god, as Jesus. But the priestess, who then lived on the upper slopes as did *kahuna* of high status, sent a message down to the Bay in which she warned the Hawaiians that this was not the real Jesus but an impostor. That is why he was mistrusted and eventually killed because he was an impostor, not the real Jesus.

In these stories there are two core versions, one dealing with the relation to Jesus and the other with the relation to the Spanish. Cook is a reference point and a point of contrast, i.e. before Captain Cook we had other visitors from afar. Not only that, we are descended in part from them, in good cognatic fashion. The story of the shipwreck is a common theme from the Big Island, especially from Ke'ei, the area just to the south of Kealakekua Bay where Cook met his death. Some versions of this story were collected early in the century by Kekahuna (n.d.) and they are considered part of the traditions of the Spanish in the islands. In the third variant of the story we have a more elaborate version of the way in which the Spaniards are incorporated into Hawaii. In all versions there is a brother–sister pair, who become part of Hawaiian society, either by marriage or by upbringing, in this case, clearly *hanai*, or adoption. They are lighter in complexion, and therefore of higher status, and their arrival explains the phenotypic difference among aristocrats and commoners. That this event also explains the occurrence of Spanish names in Hawaii is an interesting example of time compression, referred to below, in which the existence of Spanish at the end of the past century can be equated with centuries-old connections. The equation of male to female as warrior to priest is also part of the sibling dualism characteristic of Hawaiian mythology and kinship. Finally the arrival of Captain Cook is another event, a misunderstanding juxtaposed to the Spanish as the inversion of its circumstances. The Spanish children are saved by the Hawaiians while Cook arrives and is mistaken for the god Lono, a mistake that leads to his death. The Spanish children arrive by mistake as well, but the mistake is not one of misinformation in relation to the Hawaiians, rather a physical mistake or perhaps a mishap. The Spanish children are brought *up* by the Hawaiian aristocracy, while the false God, Cook, is brought *down* by the same aristocrats. The fourth version links all the previous versions of the story. Returning to version 1 and Jesus, for whose return the Hawaiians have waited for centuries, the arrival of the Spanish children follows and finally the arrival of Captain Cook. This time he is not mistaken for Lono but for Jesus, and for the same reason, i.e. his sails and the form of his mast. The connection to the Spanish *kahuna* enables the Hawaiians to realize that Cook is not Jesus, but an impostor. That is why he was mistrusted and eventually killed.

Now these four versions were told to me in the order presented in Figure 1.1, an order that establishes a playful process of elaboration on the core themes via a process of increasing inclusiveness. There are always innumerable openings to new interpretations and stories, loose ends so to speak, but in any one series we can appreciate the processes of combinatorial variation.

There is a structural consistency about the themes that is pertinent to understanding the nature of this local knowledge. The primary discourse, that of descent, organizes the relations between Hawaiians and both Jesus and the Spanish. Jesus does not merely come for a visit, although the transfer of his teachings is central. Jesus is clearly associated with the migration of the Tribes of Israel. The Spanish are also assimilated via marriage and adoption, which in Hawaii consists in the production of kin by means of 'feeding' *hanai*. The adoption aspect is reinforced by the taking up and then bringing up of the children from overseas. Here, of course, is the parallel theme of migration from overseas. This motif of assimilation via descent is present in much everyday talk about origins, as we shall see below. This is, of course, precisely the principle

The Spanish Connection

The Jesus Connection

1. Before Captain Cook there was Jesus.
2. We are from the Holy Land.
3. The Hebrews migrated over India to the Pacific and finally to Hawaii.
4. We are similar to the ancient Hebrews.

1. There was a Spanish shipwreck here in the 18th century.
2. Only two children survived who were saved by us.
3. They were married to aristocrats.
4. That is why some of us are more light skinned than others.
5. Aristocrats are lighter than commoners.
6. Some of us also have Spanish names.

Jesus Connection to the Spanish Connection to the Death of Cook

1. Jesus came originally to Hawaii with his teachings.
2. Hawaiians awaited his return.
3. Spanish shipwreck in 18th century.
4. Only two children survived:
   a. sister and brother;
   b. brother brought up by *ali'i* in Maui;
   c. sister brought up by *kahuna* in Hawaii.
5. Both became great in their own realms:
   a. brother became a great warrior;
   b. sister became a great priestess;
6. Captain Cook came later.
7. People mistook his sails for the Cross and believed he was their God, Jesus.
8. But the *kahuna* from Spain, who lived on the upper slopes as did all *kahuna* of high status, knew the truth and sent a message that this was not the real Jesus but an impostor.
9. That is why Cook was mistrusted and killed.

Spanish Connection to the Death of Cook

1. There was a Spanish shipwreck here in the 18th century.
2. Only two children survived:
   a. sister and brother;
   b. brother brought up by *ali'i* in Maui;
   c. sister brought up by *kahuna* in Hawaii.
3. Both became great in their own realms:
   a. brother became a great warrior;
   b. sister became a great priestess.
4. Captain Cook came later.
5. People mistook his sails for the Makahiki cross and believed that he was a great chief descendent of Lono.
6. They discovered that he was no such person and so they killed him.

Figure 1.1 Four variations on Captain Cook.

analysed by Sahlins (1981, 1985), whereby the god Lono or Cook
is incorporated into the identity of the chief Kalani'opu'u via his
sacrifice. It is expressed in the adoption, by the *ali'i*, of British
clothing, names and the association of Britain with Kahiki. The
appropriation of Cook, however, is negated in the village stories,
which represent in a certain sense a subaltern perspective that
might be more in line with a cosmological opposition between *ali'i*
and *maka'ainana*, one where Cook is a false image, not a true *kino
lau* of either Lono or Jesus and is, thus, a kind of impostor. This is
the same cosmology that divides the world into a pre- and post-
Tahitian period, the latter being associated with the coming of
warfare and human sacrifice, the latter with fertility and peace,
with chiefs who are of the people rather than opposed to the them.
Thus aristocratic identity pegs itself to Cook and Britain, while
commoner identity associates itself to a true Lono, to Jesus, even
to the Spanish, certainly not to violence and conquest. But this
opposition is partial at best in the stories. In a system of oppositions
of this sort the latter are always relative. It may be that Cook is
associated with the demise of Hawaiian society in this discourse
so that he cannot be treated as a true icon of the system. For
Hawaiians, who have lost their sovereignty, their lands and their
language, Cook may well represent a discontinuity, and is, thus,
no source of descent, except, perhaps, for the aristocracy. The
difference between the two models of incorporation is shown in
Table 1.1.

The models are united in their opposition within a larger
commoner scheme in which the entire aristocratic model is
identified as the foreigner scheme. Cook is on the side of the
invaders in a society split between the original Hawaiians and
the invaders from Tahiti, Brittanee, etc. This expresses the class
division of Hawaiian society, one which either emerges or is
accentuated after the Europeans' arrival, and which is reinforced
by status/class endogamy, so that commoners, by and large, are
not related to aristocrats.

The second consistency, already touched upon above, is the
theme of the coming of the overseas visitors, on a cyclical basis.
The annual cycle is thus extended to the repetition of the visit and
the incorporation of the visitor into the being of the Hawaiians.
Lono, Jesus, the Spanish and Cook constitute a series of substi-
tutions that either replicate, transform or negate the original visit.
Variations might be said to exist on a continuum from peaceful

Table 1.1 The Two Models of Incorporation.

Aristocratic Model: Sacrificial Appropriation	Commoner Model: Appropriation via Kinship
Captain Cook identified with the god Lono who comes from overseas. He is related to the high chiefs, but his real assimilation is by means of sacrifice, symbolic for Lono, real for Cook.	Jesus is Lono, the saviour and champion of the 'people'. He represents the Hebrews, who are the ancestors of the Hawaiians. This is a relation of common substance, real descent.
Cook-as-Lono represents Kahiki which is thus equated with England as the home of the gods.	Kahiki is the same as Ancient Israel, the original home of the people
Cook comes as a chief and as Lono, breaks the rules of the ritual Makahiki, by returning to Hawaii after the end of the ceremony, thus asserting his will to conquer. He is sacrificed as the result of destruction willed on another, the Hawaiian chiefs. He becomes a chiefly ancestor by sacrifice.	The Spanish chiefly pair are adopted by the Hawaiians, from a shipwreck. This is the inversion of a sacrifice. They are saved from death as the result of self-destruction. They are incorporated by adoption and then by marriage to Hawaiians. Their descent relation is one of cognation.
The act of incorporation is also an act distinguishing chiefs from commoners, identifying the relatively endogamous high chiefs with the foreign gods.	Cook is no Jesus and no Lono but an impostor. His death is thus no sacrifice, no act of incorporation for the commoners.

descent, via migration, marriage and/or adoption, to agonistic descent, via sacrifice to the negation of kinship.

The third consistency is the parallel dualism: brother/sister::warrior/priest(ess), which in the classical Cook story becomes the opposition Ku/Lono. The fact that the opposition is included within the sibling unity might also be interpreted as a statement of the specific form of the relation, its antagonistic intimacy, which is present in so much of the Hawaiian mythology of succession.

This play on the three themes of Jesus, the Spanish and Captain Cook was, as I indicated, communicated with a certain virtuosity. It was not the result of elaborate discussions. On the contrary, the versions were themselves elaborated much like music is improvised, the different versions being enunciated in rapid succession and in a kind of responsive dialectic, building up the final (for the time being) version. The structuralist appearance of this variation, its form, is dependent on the relation between the enunciators and the semantic field of the stories. This relation might be likened to the relation of the jazz musician to the thematic/harmonic substrate out of which he creates his musical variations. This is a relation of intimacy that permits the kind of non-reflexive virtuosity that characterizes the process of mythical variation. One might suggest here that these enunciated texts, like many mythical texts and music, are conjunctive. They cannot be unpacked on the basis of their content alone, dependent as they are on a set of implicit understandings that are thematized above and which strategically organize the episodes of the stories into a scheme of self-identification.

Underlying Logics of the Interpretation of Experience

There are certain interesting features in alternative versions of the Cook story. The apotheosis of Cook can be seen as a Western phenomenon that identifies Cook as the product of the godlike characteristics invoked in the apotheosis story. This is the version attributed by Europeans to Hawaiians as part of the European construal of their superstitions but which is pegged to a constant, the notion of the god-as-hero. Now it might be argued that the notion of god in Hawaiian schemes of the world is related to a continuum of effectivity, of power expressed in terms such as *mana* where there is no single individual but a broad spectrum of social effectivity identified in terms of potential or realized social ranking. This is not a particularly Polynesian understanding but is rather widespread in hierarchical kinship-based societies. If we return here to the question of Hawaiian Christianity we might suggest that it is in many an assimilation of Christian symbolism and interpretation to Hawaiian notions and experience of power. The conversion to Christianity that began in the 1820s was not a mere act of political identification on the part of the chiefs. The latter argument is partly true, but again for the same reasons, i.e. because of the nature of hierarchy itself; i.e. dependency on God was a function of dependency on all sacred power including that of the chiefs. There are manifold instances in the missionary records of individual conversion of a strikingly emotionally engaged nature which contradicts the more manipulative political interpretation of such acts. This is a period of political and social disintegration and of rampant fatal disease. Conversion is often directly related to healing.

> April 15: Kepaa, the woman who takes care of the house for me, in the absence of my dear wife, after prayers to night, remarked that she now could see the service of God is no drudgery – She said everything else in life was a wearisomeness but not so with the service of God. Poor creature, I can see a manifest change in her. She often sheds tears when talking of the love of Christ or of her former hardness of heart. She is very kind and faithful in all her duties (Forbes 1837).

Hawaiian assimilation reorganizes Christianity into the local organization of existence. 'The old Hawaiian gods were just Hina and Ku, the flat stone and the upright stone. They were the same as Eve and Adam. The Tahitians brought the other gods, the war gods' (interview 1985).

Church services in the village where we have worked for the past decade are not focused on questions of morality, but on questions of health and curing, on praying for renewed health and life. 'Church attendance for the purpose of obtaining solutions to specific problems led one minister to tell me in a joking manner, "My church could almost be viewed as a clinic". But before the individual turns to the church as a "clinic" he may try to solve his problems, specifically illnesses, with traditional treatments' (Heighton 1971:37).

The relation to Christianity is a relation of dependence on a higher power actively cultivated and with an array of expected consequences. It is also an identity with the ancient Hebrews and as such a project of genealogical identification with the source of *mana*. Lesser projects are equally dynamic, identification with the British, and even with the Vikings, which would seem to corroborate the migratory scheme of the myths. '[T]here is a person in the second generation that is called noliwai – meaning Norway,

and the Vikings come from there.' 'Hawaiians are really from the
Vikings. I have seen helmets that look just like ours, with horns
on the side. Where I came from in Napo'opo'o there was someone
named Noliwai (Norway). We had teachers from there.'

The association of Hawaiian traditions with the Old Testament
or the Vikings, with the outside, the dominant, the European, is
not unusual. It is true of course that many of these stories have
been transferred from missionaries and other Westerners, but there
assimilation to Hawaiian identity is not, I would argue, a mere
cognitive or intellectual phenomenon, a case of misinformation.
Rather it is part of the practice of identification itself, of the
identification of a space or world within which to place oneself.
In this sense, being a descendent of the Hebrews is an act of social/
cosmic mobility.

Hawaiians, and I imagine this might hold for Maori as well,
were not passive dupes of the strange tales of missionaries. They
were actively engaged in the construction of bodies of knowledge
founded upon their very real social experience and its structures.
Their knowledge is, if constructed on a different model, of the same
order as the construction of the French Revolution, a selective
process of reconstruction organized to establish modern French
identity as egalitarian and democratic.[1] Just as the migration stories
establish Hawaiian identity in the larger genealogical cosmos, so
the French Revolution establishes the terms of a new national
identity. But, while the former is based on the forging of continuity,
the latter is based on historical rupture.

Exchange?

The strategy of incorporation, of the transformation of outside to
inside, might even be extended to the domain of kinship and
exchange. Now the notion of exchange in anthropology is based
on the prior existence of distinct exchanging units and their
continued separate existence via the very processes of transaction
of goods, services, etc. This is part of our anthropological
knowledge and is usually said to exist independently of native or
folk models.[2] The model can be applied to all situations in which
visible transactions occur. But Hawaiians rarely speak of exchange
as such. To arrive with a gift for my informant was indeed what
Michael Agar (1986) refers to as a 'breakdown'. The gift was taken

without a word and placed aside and never again mentioned. On another occasion, a gift to a very good friend was examined and commented upon. 'What is it?' 'Strange thing. I can never use it' referring to a designer razor from Scandinavia. It too disappeared, never to be mentioned. Some relatives, however, told me that he had talked about the strange object and had it in his truck.

Sometimes when walking through the village we would hear, 'come in . . . come and eat . . . come and take', as we passed our neighbours. Children came to our house (shack) often and took our children's underwear, T-shirts and bathing-suits, and food that was available. 'I like' they would say before taking.

Other breakdowns accumulated over the years.

Going to Parties

We are invited to a huge fiftieth-year birthday party in Kona, Hawaii, as guests of a local Hawaiian. The man is known as one of the most knowledgeable of Hawaiians in the matters of tradition. He often lectures us on the 'real' history of Hawaii. He is well educated, with a college degree in engineering and has been engaged in Hawaiian struggles for many years. We arrive at the party. There are well over 100 people present. There is live music and a table filled with local delicacies such as stew of entrails and raw crab (just caught). We take our seats and then go to take our food and listen to speeches and music. But we don't stay more than an hour. Suddenly our friends produce several plastic bags and begin quickly to sweep in masses of food, after which we leave quite abruptly without saying much of anything. When we arrive home the food is stashed in the fridge. It was clearly acceptable to take in this way, a phenomenon that is documented from other areas of the Pacific.

Captain Cook and the Thieving Natives

Captain Cook's relations with Hawaiians ought not to be compared to modern Hawaiian practices, but some of the relations are so striking that it is worth the attempt. Reports from the voyages are consistent in their interpretation of Hawaiian acts of theft, of small trinkets, of knives, nails and even a ship's cutter. It is clear in the contact literature that a number of different relations are established between Cook's ships and the Hawaiians. There is ceremonial exchange among high-status individuals. There is what appears to be trade or barter between the ships and the canoes, where foodstuffs and pigs are exchanged for iron and nails. There is also a kind of generalized form of exchange in which Hawaiians provision the ships on a daily basis and received 'gifts' of various sorts, from iron to bracelets for the women and cloth. There are also many cases of what the ships' logs refer to as stealing, a phenomenon that occurs all over the Pacific according to the logs and which seems to indicate a lack of social control among the natives, i.e. crude desire leads to theft. It is this phenomenon that interests me here although the material is far from adequate to gain a purchase on its true motivation.

Cases

Samwell (Beaglehole 1967) reports of the first contact at Kauai the following sequence:

1 Hawaiians come out to the ship in their canoes
2 Cook gives them red cloth, nails about which they are very pleased. Hawaiians seem very pleased and reciprocate with 'some of the cloth they had about their waist in return' (Beaglehole 1967:1081).
3 Cook enquires about food and they say they have plenty of hogs.
4 Every canoe has stones (in case of battle) which are now thrown into the water.
5 They come aboard and express astonishment and the 'riches'.
6 Cook gives them some more presents.
7 He soon finds them 'thieving'.
8 One man covering himself with a sail attempts to loosen the clamp that holds the driver boom. 'He was detected on which he immediately left off seemingly as unconcerned as if he had been doing an indifferent action' (Beaglehole 1967:1082).
9 Further down the coast, they are presented with tiny pig, always given to strangers as token of friendship but not understood as such by the crew.

Later, on 20 January:

1   In a new location the boat is attacked by Hawaiians.
2   They attempt to pull the ship ashore, and the crew are 'obliged
    to shoot one' (Beaglehole 1967:1083).
3   The ship moves out to two miles, followed by canoes who then
    gave them pigs, fowls, sweet potatoes and plantains 'for which
    we gave them small nails and adzes' (Beaglehole 1967:1083).
4   Next day, on 21 January, Cook goes ashore with several boats
    and natives prostrate themselves and are most kind – 'the young
    women, who were in general exceeding beautiful, used all their
    arts to entice our people into their Houses . . . tried to force
    them . . . would take no denial' (Beaglehole 1967:1083).

Why do Hawaiians seem to steal? The phenomenon of taking
would seem to fall on a continuum from more to less aggressive
acts. There is a fundamental aggression in the fact that one is
invited in to take as one pleases. This implies a penetration of the
space of the domestic sphere at parties – 'come and take' is the
word of welcome. The word give is not used, as in 'here let me
give you this!' Within an already established network the taking
has the form of reciprocal access. At the negative end of this
continuum the act of saying, 'No, you can't come and take' is the
worst thing one can do to that person. It is to tell them that they
are excluded from the sharing group. The act of exclusion from
reciprocal taking is most serious and leads to great psychological
pain. This can occur in a situation where such reciprocity is
expected and it can occur in situations where the reciprocity is
broken. In both cases it is a violently painful experience that cannot
be repressed. In situations where the reciprocity is not part of the
everyday, the act of aggression appears more saliently, as when
invitees to a party fill their bags after several minutes of being
social and go home with as much as they can carry. In situations
of no relation, taking may be a test of the possibility of establishing
such a relation. It is aggression employed to make a relation and
it may be necessary to go through open violence to arrive at a
stable organization. Such violence is usually accepted in the
historical material, it doesn't lead to a breaking of the relation for
all time but to a continued attempt to establish a relation. Taking
is not the same as stealing since it is not bounded in terms of the
same moral context. Taking is saying to the 'victim', 'I am

impinging on your life space. What's yours is mine.' Exchange in a situation like this is a compromise in the true sense and takes the form of taking. In the early reports from Tonga, where Mariner spent four years in the first years of the nineteenth century, it seems as if the agonistic practice of taking is closely associated with a situation where the first missionaries appeared with their obvious wealth and did not make it available to the natives. The initial situation of taking was transformed into a very much more congenial situation when the missionaries consciously made a series of generous distributions. Taking is a violent inversion of giving but expresses the same kinds of social parameters. It is not a morally reprehensible act, but the expression of an agonistic assimilation of the other.

Hanai

Adoption seems to fall into the same category. It is often described normatively, i.e. in terms of what it is good for socially: allowing grandparents to raise their grandchildren so as to provide them with wisdom and knowledge of the old ways, stories, etc., spreading responsibility, weakening the family units as political units and creating larger webs of solidarity. There are interesting points in all of this, but there is little analysis of the actual practices of adoption in life-historical terms. Here the motives are striking and of a different nature from the supposed social functions involved. Now, of course, there is historical material that would indicate that *hanai*, 'to feed', refers to the hierarchical relation between people and chiefs, where the latter feed the former. Adoption in this sense retains a core of hierarchy, which is reciprocated, in usual hierarchical manner, by the fact that the chiefs 'take care' of their people. The term is also reversed to refer to children that are fed by their adoptive parents. 'Taking care' is a relation of hierarchy, and adoption, especially, between gener-ations, which is the most common form, is a practice that breaks up lower-order relations among nuclear family members by integrating the young into the larger kinship group, centred on the grandparents. This aspect of the relation does not often appear in normative discussions of adoption, or in the psychological reductionist arguments that represent adoption as a solution to an insecure psychological reality dominated by the failure to establish dependency relations among peers (Howard *et al.* 1970:47). In a recent study (Ekholm Friedman n.d.) the contrast between normative and life-history discourses reveals an often hidden drama of great proportions.[3] Levy reports from Tahiti that 'the relations between all parents and children are fragile and conditional' (1970:84). The expression often used by adopters is, 'I like take care . . . of children . . . got no more own.'

One need not have children or one might have children of one's own but who are somewhat older. Reciprocity in such a relation is about an engagement in the lives of other people, a sacrifice of self to other. This can be hierarchical as well as egalitarian, but in either case it results in a kind of fusion rather than a balanced exchange. 'I like take care' can be understood as an instance of 'I like take'.

The expression here is the establishment of a sociality based not on exchange in the sense of reciprocity between groups, but of a reciprocal taking, perhaps even an instance of Sahlins's (1974) generalized 'negative reciprocity', a domestication of the act of taking. Here it is not a question of balance but of practising a kind of group fusion, a negation of exchange itself. Of course there is always a limit of reciprocity involved, a threshold that marks the difference between good and evil, but it is not calculated in any clear-cut terms, and the existence of such a limit is not the same as the practice of exchanging, of in some way counting and balancing the immediate act itself.

Ohana

The *ohana* is represented by the Hawaiian movement as a basic form of social organization. It refers to the extended family, one that contained within it the entire subsistence base for the ancient *ahupua'a*. It is within the sphere of this organization that the reciprocity to which I refer takes place, a form of generalized reciprocity, of reciprocal taking in which the parties practise fusion rather than exchange. Anthropologists have taken upon themselves to disprove the age of this institution, arguing that under the kingdom there were no such solidary groups and that the latter were the result of the formation of corporate groups during the nineteenth century. I have myself argued that this may indeed be the case in terms of overt forms of social organization. The conjunctive basis of the *ohana* in our argument lies not in explicit institutional forms but in the way in which social relations are practised. Here we find a clear continuity in the use of the term as well as the underlying substrate of experience on which it is based. The notion that various products and services are made available to a larger group and that the entirety of the group's wealth belongs to the group and can be taken is the practice of fusion that characterizes the *ohana* as a form of relatedness.

The Disintegration of Fusion

> In the old days, i.e. the 1950s, when fishing was still done by canoe, the boats had to be taken in with the help of other people, often children of other families . . . they could take as much fish as they needed. Today with motor boats everyone keeps to himself.

The worst thing one can be is someone who breaks the relation of reciprocal taking by not enabling reciprocity. The story of a certain man in the village where we worked is exemplary of this rupture of the relation. E had worked outside the village for years. He had a friend for many years who was related to one of his neighbours in the village and thereby also kin by marriage. This man was a happy-go-lucky type that was used to living on what he could get, part-time fishing, building, etc. He was an excellent party-goer and a very charming individual. He often slept in E's house, often lived with him and often used his assets, house and goods in his own projects. E represented him as the essence of evil. The evil was the practice of taking without giving. Now this is complicated, since Hawaiians deny the act of exchange itself, making non-reciprocity a constant possibility. But it is a common understanding that giving is a total act of self-sacrifice whereby one gives oneself and not a particular good or service. When a partner to such a relation demonstrates a lack of generosity he shatters the fusion and wounds the other. This involves a great deal of pain and suffering. E recounted endless stories of this man's evil, which often had to do with what we would designate as the freeloader syndrome. This is partly compatible with Howard *et al.*'s description of adult male peer relations as 'intense and unstable' (1970:47). It is clear that the emotional investment in interpersonal relations produces great expectations as well as tragic outcomes, and that the latter can take on mythical proportions.

But Howard *et al.*'s psychological explanation couched in terms of 'powerful dependency needs which are inhibited as a consequence of punitive training' seems much too reductionist. In my own material, the dependency is clearly practised, but, while there are often conflicts, the latter seldom lead to broken relations. On the contrary, there seems to be a rather strong stability, at least in village peer groups.

Applying the Classic Model

It has often been assumed that the paradigm of exchange is a general property of 'traditional' or 'primitive' societies in the Pacific as elsewhere. Now, while one might, as certain ethnographers have done, complain of the modernity of Hawaiian rural society, this has not prevented research from aiming at ferreting out the traditional exchange patterns that are assumed to exist there. Thus, Linnekin, in her study of Keanae, has stated a specific variant of the Maussian model:

1. A gift must be repaid,
2. but not immediately;
3. different things must be given in exchange.

Now this is meant to account for certain discrepancies in Hawaiian transactional behaviour, not least of which is the fact that the act of exchange itself would seem to be denied and is certainly not calculated in terms of immediate balance. In numerous cases Linnekin attempts to apply the model with dubious success:

> Chauffeuring is a highly valued service for elderly Keanae residents who cannot drive. The sister expressly stated that she was giving the fish and crabs in return for the favor of transportation. Some villagers are expert at manipulating the protocol of exchange in order to obtain a high gift from a neighbor. A villager may perform a valued service for another, or make a series of small presentations, with the deliberate intent of provoking a higher return gift than would ordinarily pass between neighbors ... Finally the unwilling recipient of her favors angrily refused, cut off communication, and began to talk stink about the woman, whose calculating motives were too obvious to be tolerated: 'She only hoped to get more crabs and fish, see' (Linnekin 1985:161).

The relation is broken here because the woman under attack is not giving her services because she simply wants to, not out of *aloha*, love, but for gain of that which is to be expected from an act of exchange. The question is not even one of balance, but of motivation. One should not offer one's services in order to get something in return. There is no return as such. There is only a net effect of everyone offering themselves to one another, to the larger group. The woman in question is similar to an individual from my own field experience and sometimes the word *maha'oi*, impertinent, is used to describe her. Just as often she is accused of stealing, and generally of evil, i.e. selfish intentions. Now the exchange paradigm might be used to elucidate the breach of ultimate balance in the relations between people, but it does not clarify the enormous emotional crisis involved in such a breach. This is related to the implicit negation of exchange involved in interpersonal transactions among Hawaiians. The reference to the exchange paradigm highlights the centrality of the model of fusion. This is also a form of transfer of goods and services, but the latter are signs of the relation rather than their constituent elements. Linnekin finds it necessary to invoke the Trukese term *niffag*, a 'gift that embodies its own return' in order to gloss the Hawaiian situation. 'The rules of giving *niffag* are implicit in the protocol of Hawaiian gift giving and illustrate the paradigm of non-Western exchange: gifts are powerful and productive of further transactions' (Linnekin 1985:166–7).

The problem is that there are no such explicit objects in her material. The relation of balance exists and it might ultimately be understood in terms of relations or transactions that can in some way be calculated. But from my own work, and this is not contradicted by other people's work including that of Linnekin, who, while making explicit use of the exchange paradigm, provides no indication of a strategy of exchange in the sense of the explicit transfer of goods and services whose value must be recompensed by equivalents. On the contrary, she provides an example of the way in which the exchange strategy is refused by Hawaiians as a form evil. Rather the strategy of interpersonal relations is focused on offering oneself. This can be translated into active openness, which leads those involved into a kind of reciprocal feeding on one another, a kind of pooling or sharing of substance.

Conclusion

The point of these examples is to explore a set of conjunctive forms of knowledge, embedded in social experience, that have been lifted into the context-free space of anthropological discourse. In the case of the Cook stories the degree to which versions can be elaborated spontaneously ought to give some idea of the relation of substrate to cultural product. The capacity to produce variations on a set of themes in such short order implies an intimate relation to the themes, an ability to perform *bricolage* framed by a general set of implicit understandings. This ability is itself an expression of conjunctive knowledge. But there is also a question of content, i.e. the themes themselves, which I have tried to work out in the following examples. There are fundamental strategies of related-ness at work here that afford a consistency to disparate domains of activity and representation. These relate to the negation of exchange, to the incorporation of outsiders in myth via a strong practice of descent (in the case of Jesus, the Spanish, Norwegians and, in the classical myth, to Cook) and to the hierarchical incorporation of potential kin segments into higher generations (*hanai*). The decontextualization of the existence of transactions into the paradigm of exchange, the phenomenon of adoption into a particular strategy accountable by means of its functions and of myth-making as text production, is part of a strategy of knowledge production that easily misinterprets the reality of other worlds and of other ways of constructing knowledge. Anthropologists can be forced to take such modes of knowledge seriously and to grant them existence even where people seem to be hopelessly Westernized and thus mere 'inventors' of themselves rather than authentic representatives of a real pre-contact reality. Those who see 'natives' as false representatives of cultures that anthro-pologists thought they monopolized, as hybrids who don't recognize the fact, as would-be traditional peoples, do so from their own social experience and its cultural constructs, an experience of distance from any particular cultural reality. In this experience culture is reduced to text, script or object, and the experience of others is negated.

I have argued here for a historical continuity as well as a specificity of social experience that has not been destroyed by the massive onslaught on the entirety of the trappings of Hawaiian social life. Of course, Hawaiian society was virtually destroyed and its population mixed with immigrants. Hawaiians have lost their lands and their institutions and they have for the most part inhabited the margins of plantation- and then tourist-based and thoroughly modernized societies. But this does not mean that they are just another lower class trying today to be cultural by falsifying their past. There is a continuity, however transformed, that has become the source of a restoration of Hawaiian identity. That is what social and cultural transformation is all about, even where it contains a high degree of discontinuity. Epeli Hau'ofa provides an insight into the way in which the modern world is organized into the lives of Oceanic peoples, just as Oceanic peoples are integrated into the modern world. These are processes that are simultaneous but separate. It is the confusion or perhaps conflation of the two processes that leads to the sibling errors of hybrid ideology and inventionist anthropology since both deny the integrity of native populations, that is their capacity to integrate their experiences into coherent forms. And it is the confrontation between the anthropologist/culture expert's identity and that of indigenous populations that appears threatening and conflictual. This is not an error in thinking or an academic problem. It is a condition of the real world today. Anthropologists can solve their end of the problem by reversing a by now classic proposition.

Think locally, act globally.

Notes

1. There are of course numerous traditions of scholarship concerning the nature of the Revolution, but they all, as noted by François Furet, 'share a common ground: they are all histories in quest of identity' (1981:10).
2. This is the common assumption underlying approaches as opposed as Mauss (1925), Lévi-Strauss (1967) and Weiner (1992). The problem is brilliantly analysed in Derrida (1991).

3. Beaglehole's examples from the 1930s (Beaglehole 1939:58, 67–8), cited by Howard *et al.* (1970), involve the magical power of a grandmother over the health of a grandchild who is not given willingly in adoption. This is similar to the case analysed in Ekholm Friedman (n.d.). It is, of course, true that adoption can occur between siblings, but here too there is clearly a strong obligation at work.

References

Agar, M. (1986). *Speaking of Ethnography*. Beverly Hills: Sage.

Beaglehole, E. (1939). *Some Modern Hawaiians*. Honolulu: University of Hawaii Research Publications, 19.

Beaglehole, J.C. (1967). *The Journals of Captain James Cook on His Voyages of Discovery: The Voyage of the Resolution and Discovery*. Part II. Cambridge: Cambridge University Press.

Bell, D. (1979). *The Cultural Contradictions of Capitalism*. London: Heinemann.

Derrida, J. (1991). *Donner le temps: 1. La fausse monnaie*. Paris: Galilée.

Ekholm Friedman, K. (n.d.). *An African Tragedy: Magic and the Liberation of the State from the People in the Congo*. London: Zed Press (forthcoming).

Forbes, C. (1837). *The Journals of Cochran Forbes, Missionary to Hawaii 1831–1864*. Honolulu: Hawaiian Mission Children's Society.

Fornander, A. (1969). *An Account of the Polynesian Race*. 3 vols. Rutland, Vermont: Tuttle.

Friedman, J. (1993). Will the Real Hawaiian Please Stand: Anthropologists and Natives in the Global Struggle for Identity. In: P. van der Grijp and T. van Meijl (eds), *Politics, Tradition and Change in the Pacific*, pp. 737–67. Special issue of *Bijdragen Tot de Taal-, Land- en Volkenkunde* 149.

—— (1994). *Cultural Identity and Global Process*. London: Sage.

Furet, F. (1981). *Interpreting the French Revolution*. Cambridge: Cambridge University Press.

Hau'ofa, E. (1994a). Our Sea of Islands. *The Contemporary Pacific* 6(1):147–61.

—— (1994b). Thy Kingdom Come. *The Contemporary Pacific* 6(2):414–28.

Heighton, R.H. Jr (1971). Hawaiian Supernatural and Natural Strategies for Goal Attainment. PhD. Department of Anthropology, University of Hawaii at Manoa.

Howard, A., Heighton, R., Jourdan C. and Gallimore, R. (1970). Traditional and Modern Adoption Patterns in Hawaii. In: V. Carroll (ed.), *Adoption in Eastern Oceania,* pp. 21–51. Honolulu: University of Hawaii Press.

Kekahuna, H.E.P. (n.d.). Henry E.P. Collection. Hawaii State Archives.

Lévi-Strauss, C. (1967). *Les Structures elémentaires de la parenté.* Paris: Mouton.

Levy, R. (1970). Tahitian Adoption as a Psychological Message. In: V. Carroll (ed.), *Adoption in Eastern Oceania,* pp. 71–87. Honolulu: University of Hawaii Press.

Linnekin, J. (1985). *Children of the Land: Exchange and Status in a Hawaiian Community.* New Brunswick, NJ: Rutgers University Press.

Mannheim, K. (1983). *Structures of Thinking.* London: Routledge.

Mauss, M. (1925). Essai sur le don: Forme et raison de l'échange dans les sociétés archaïques. *L'Année Sociologique* Nouvelle Série, 1:30–186.

Sahlins, M. (1974). On the Sociology of Primitive Exchange. In: M. Sahlins, *Stone Age Economics,* pp. 185–276. Chicago: Aldine.

—— (1981). *Historical Metaphors and Mythical Realities.* Ann Arbor: University of Michigan Press.

—— (1985). *Islands of History.* Chicago: Chicago University Press.

—— (1993). Goodbye to Tristes Tropes: Ethnography in the Context of Modern World History. *Journal of Modern History* 65:1–25.

Sartre, J.P. (1957). *The Transcendance of the Ego: An Existentialist Theory of Consciousness.* New York: Octogon Books. (First published in 1936.)

Spate, O.H.K. (1979). *The Spanish Lake.* Minneapolis: University of Minnesota Press (The Pacific Since Magellan, Vol. I).

Weiner, A. (1992). *Inalienable Possessions: The Paradox of Keeping while Giving.* Berkeley: University of California Press.

Chapter 2

Inventing Natives/Negotiating Local Identities: Postcolonial Readings of Colonial Texts on Island Melanesia

Bronwen Douglas

Introduction

'Identity' and 'tradition' are metatropes for ambiguously post-colonial times – they condense central concerns of postmodernist scholars, political activists *and* their respective conventional/ conservative opponents. The 1983 publication of Hobsbawm and Ranger's *The Invention of Tradition* and Anderson's *Imagined Communities*, with, closer to home, Keesing and Tonkinson's 1982 special issue of *Mankind*, anticipated and stimulated an anthropological growth industry about a fraught political issue, with significant theoretical, substantive and polemical input – already too vast to cite here – on the Pacific Islands and Australia. Much of this literature concerns the politics of representation and the issue of narrative authority: the authenticity and morality of competing images of the past constructed by engaged actors and analysts, variously claiming or challenging privileged access to eternal truth/objective knowledge (e.g. Babadzan 1988; Keesing 1989, 1993; Trask 1991). But the notions of identity and tradition/ custom also resist objectivist analysis, because they display clearly how images of the past, whether mundane or professional, in memory, speech or written, are always constructed in a present, for present purposes (Linnekin 1990, 1992; Jolly 1992; Thomas 1992). My own engagement with this debate is inflected by an emancipatory discursive commitment: to a concept of indigenous agency, seen as multiplex, unstable, strategic and variously enabled and constrained; to a concept of locally motivated appropriation and domestication of the foreign and the novel, seen as inescapable and potentially transformative, though never static or uncontested. I regard Kanak in New Caledonia – the main subjects of my histories – as får more pluralist, relativist, tolerant of distinctions and pragmatically selective of meaningful innovations than most colonial Europeans, whose disposition to oppositional thinking, whether Manichaean or secular, was probably a condition for and a reflex of coloniality, at least in its formal guise.[1]

Recently many anthropologists – sensitive to accusations of essentialism, primitivism and Orientalism – have fervently embraced history, but their perspectives on the past tend to differ from historians'. Not only are they more theoretically inclined, but their typical analytic movement is from ethnographic present to motivating past. Historians ostensibly fix their gaze on the past and move linearly from prior cause to later effect, though there is sleight of hand in this seemingly innocent empiricism, since 'effects' are typically pre-identified to fit the teleological morality and aesthetics of narrative closure (White 1987: chs 1–2, 217). Both may universalize the present, but differently: anthropologists by assuming unbroken cultural continuity from precontact past to ethnographic present (Carrier 1992); historians, unconsciously ethnocentric, by projecting backwards present morality or utilitarian, rationalist, notions of common sense as if they applied everywhere and always (Philipp 1983:347).

Knowing Pasts, Doing Histories

This second introductory section sketches an antipositivist historical epistemology indebted mainly to Collingwood (1961), Barthes (1970) and White (1978, 1987). Its corollary, my major methodological concern, is this: given a conception of knowledge/ truth as constructed, plural, present and political; given displacement of the objectivist historian's metaphor of *the* fixed real past in favour of notions of real*ities* as multiple, contested and ephemeral, and of the believed-in real past as a present mental image and narrative artefact – how then are historical narratives feasible or valid? This seeming paradox is partly addressed by Jackson's reminder that 'the *world* is out there, to be sure, and deep within us too, *but not the truth*' (1989:182, emphasis in original).

Those whose truth claims are threatened by anti-objectivism may level a fervid charge of nihilistic relativism: that professional and moral standards are abandoned, anything goes and history is thereby conflated with fiction or propaganda. Histories, though, are not fictions, despite similar narrative form and discursive strategies, because their content differs: actual events in the past rather than possibly imaginary ones (White 1978:121–5; 1987:27, 44–5). Deliberate distortion or falsification of the past for present ends is best exposed by critique of the criteria of selection and evaluation on which it rests, rather than confronted via competing claims to absolute truth. Any refutation project gains legitimacy and force from reflexivity – taking moral and discursive responsibility for one's own knowing and telling, and leaving space for others to do so. All historical interpretations are thus *not* equally plausible or admirable. My criteria for narrative evaluation and construction are not so different from conventional historians', but they are empowered, not vitiated, by reflexivity and renunciation of History's claims to objectivity, unitary truth and mimetic realism (Barthes 1970:153–5; Stivers 1993:424; White 1987:24–5). They include intelligibility, credibility, aptness, meticulousness, honesty, morality – the latter always teetering between allowance for contextual and cultural relativities and assertion of personal and humanist values. I use them creatively and rigorously to assemble images out of words which most appropriately describe, label and classify the past actions and worlds I discern through reading texts. The project is best labelled as a severely qualified realism.

Because the past has gone, it is knowable only through the relics – 'texts'[2] – in which fleeting traces of past presents were randomly inscribed. Texts are neither neutral nor transparent: they have authors and readers, while their constituent terms, ideas and images cluster systemically in discourses. The partiality and biases of texts and authors are discursive characteristics to be recognized, deconstructed and exploited. An epistemology which conceives knowledge as know*ing* – a gerund rather than an abstract substantive – and denies the existence of a fixed real past makes texts and their politics of representation and reception irreducible elements in any process of narrative construction. By discrediting essentialist notions of 'traditional' societies as timeless, homogeneous and inert, such an epistemology also means we cannot take for granted that *later* sociocultural patterns – as recorded in formal ethnographies or oral histories – have unbroken genealogical links with earlier ones, particularly given transformations occurring with external contacts, colonialism, decolonization and modernization. Yet a narrative of indigenous naturalization of the novel logically presumes that meanings made of alien encounters are knowable, that there are lenses on those past worlds, albeit narrow and distorted. *Contemporary* colonial texts[3] (i.e. contemporaneous to the period studied) are therefore significant resources for exploring preliterate indigenous worlds and colonial engagements, despite ethnocentrism, racism, sexism and other biases, because they may, often inadvertently, register shadowy traces of local agency, relationships and settings. The intimacy and richer detail of later indigenous histories, both oral and written, and ethnographies provide crucial clues for identifying past ethnographic inscriptions, but they are not automatically salient.

Invention and Mimesis in Colonial New Caledonia

The body of this chapter has an archaeological relationship to literature on the present politics of identity: anthropologists ponder the identities people create, live, share and contest, but in so far as past identities and the criteria on which they were based were not necessarily present ones – if neither more nor less authentic – there is scope for historical expertise. I use the conceptual overburden outlined to unearth and read early traces of indigenous enactments of affiliation and difference in New Caledonia, lodged in a cluster of colonial texts which named and represented native places, groups and persons. 'Identity' in this context connotes presumed loci of linkages and distinctions between persons and groups. I argue that colonial tropes and classifications both invented and echoed particular indigenous settings, initiating serial processes of reciprocal mimesis: indigenous nomenclatures, sociopolitical units and relationships were invented by colonial authors *attempting to register specific island settings*; colonial categories were both contested by islanders and indigenized as useful local strategies in altered, colonized contexts; some naturalized colonial categories were ultimately reinscribed as 'customary' in later political contests, as were transformed or reinvented indigenous categories.

This chapter concentrates on the first phase – colonial invention of native names, groups and relationships in particular settings –

but exemplifies or alludes to the others. It does so via a body of early colonial – mainly Catholic – texts which refer to the northern region called Hoot ma Waap, centring on Balade and nearby Pouébo. As the focus of most French activity in New Caledonia from December 1843, when the Marist Fathers established a mission at Balade, until a year or so after French annexation in September 1853, Balade and Pouébo were textually – and hence historically – the epicentre of 'New Caledonia' for much of this decade. My argument moves between eyewitness action descriptions and more formal contemporary representations, including ethnographies by missionaries and naval officers, correlated with later ethnographies, linguistic works and oral texts. My general thesis is that formal nineteenth-century segmentary images of New Caledonian politics – largely contradicted in modern ethnographies – were often also implicitly belied in less consciously wrought contemporary observations and remarks on what people did. New Caledonia, then, might exemplify Linnekin and Poyer's contention that indigenous Oceanic 'theories of affiliation consistently emphasize context, situation, performance, and place over biological descent' (1990:11).

It seems clear now, as it did to the first European visitors, that the indigenous inhabitants of the large island – *la Grande Terre* – which Cook named New Caledonia in 1774 neither identified with politically nor named the whole island.[4] Population density was thin and in the north people mostly lived in small house clusters, dispersed over garden land. A naval officer who helped install the mission at Balade described the 'entire abode' of a local 'chief'[5] as comprising 'four or five huts; one is for the chief himself, two others for his men; the fourth serves to lodge visiting strangers, and the last, a little apart from the others, is meant for the women: that is what is called the village of Balade'. He further described 'what we call the village of Koko' as 'only the group of five or six huts belonging to the family of the chief of the region [*contrée*]; it is the same for all this part of New Caledonia, at least in the six or eight leagues we have covered, a space in which all abodes are separated one from the other' (Laferrière 1845:69, 92–3).[6] These two men had been quickly identified and fostered by the French as the most important chiefs in the vicinity of Balade – no doubt they presented themselves in some such terms – but the missionaries, who hoped to appropriate and channel chiefly authority to their own ends, deplored their ineffectuality: echoing and extending the officer's descriptions, one missionary complained: 'these kings are almost without influence, and one of the causes to which we must attribute this, is . . . their too great number; the smallest hamlet has its own' (Rougeyron to Supérieur-Général, 1 Oct. 1845, Archivio dei Padri Maristi [hereinafter APM], General Correspondence 1845–9).

Early hints of a nexus between the size of a 'chief's' following and the extent and effectiveness of his authority (or lack thereof) were recapitulated in subsequent colonial experience, which showed the Balade chiefs to be notably impotent. Such hints were elaborated in later ethnographic wisdom, which dissociated chiefly authority from direct control over territory and linked it to complex, unstable patterns of relative seniority/juniority, allegiance, exchange and identity between persons, small groups, their leaders and particular places (Guiart 1963; Bensa and Rivierre 1982; Douglas 1994). Mary Wallis, an American with lengthy experience in Fiji, who spent three months at or near Balade in 1852 with her trader husband, described chiefs acutely as severely constrained by a norm of reciprocity:

> We learn that there had been a battle at Balade . . . It appears that the difficulty was caused by the chief of Balade taking some shell-fish from the women who collected them. The chiefs of Caledonia have no right to claim anything belonging to others. If they beg, it is expected that an equivalent will be returned. If they take by force what does not belong to them, there is war (Journal, 5 Aug. 1852 – Wallis 1994:124).[7]

Anthropologist Alban Bensa echoed this impression in depicting the modern *daame*, 'chief', in the *cèmuhî*-speaking zone: 'subject to the rules of gift and obligatory counter-gift, [he] possesses . . . no specific power of coercion' (1986:255). Acquaintance with places other than Balade introduced Europeans to seemingly more chiefly chiefs, but indigenous politics remained vexingly ambiguous to them until some Kanak began for largely local reasons to reinvent themselves in more familiar and congenial guises, in line with newly contrived colonial offices which cast chiefs as colonial 'agents' (La Hautière 1869:70; Douglas 1985:61–4). There were early such instances at Pouébo and Belep, engineered by able Christian chiefs and charismatic missionaries, who sought in tandem to subvert indigenous constraints on chiefly power by concentrating settlement and centralizing production and distribution (Douglas 1982:404–7; 1995).

Residential patterns sketched in the early texts eventually altered with conversion to Christianity and the official policy of *cantonnement*, which from the 1860s gradually confined mainland Kanak to small and diminishing reserves (Saussol 1979:155–330).[8] Missionaries and Christian chiefs encouraged or bullied converts into orderly villages centred on the new churches. Missionary motives were as much ideological as practical: at Belep in the 1850s Lambert sought 'to have a little regularity in our village and give a few ideas of order to our savages'. He read abhorrent spatial and mental connotations of savagery in their narrow, twisting footpaths, which told him that 'as much physically as morally these poor people seem not to know the right path [*le chemin droit*], and it is not an easy thing to familiarize them with the [concept of the] straight line [*la ligne droite*]'. But as well as ethnocentric primitivism, his diary also registered traces of local equivocation and resistance to the new modes of settlement (1855–75:38, 41). In a later ethnography the same missionary allowed that Kanak reinscribed pre-existing spatial arrangements in the novel, concentrated landscape of the mission village: 'The whole tribe is composed of an aggregation of small tribes, mixing their huts in the same village without ever intermingling' (1900:82).[9] At Balade, too, the mission was the focus of a growing Christian settlement: in marked variation from the previous pattern of dispersion, it comprised two parallel lines of native-style houses extending to the foot of the church.[10] This layout none the less recapitulated elements of the indigenous habitat, with its avenue(s) flanked by trees and houses culminating in the house of the master of the site, adorned with sacred objects, with altar and sacred places close by (Leenhardt 1930:1–25; Bensa and Rivierre 1982:42; Douglas 1982). The actual site of the Balade church was known locally as 'Pouivoué' (Douarre, 14 Oct. 1845, 4 Mar. 1852), or *Pwiyiwe*, identified by anthropologist Jean Guiart as the original house mound of the holders of the *Tea Bweoon* title, high chiefs at Balade; it was located underneath the present church (1974:98; n.d.:2). In 1844, as the site of the house of a defunct high chief, it was protected by a taboo which the then high chief formally transferred to Douarre (Douarre, Journal, 1, 9 Feb. 1844).

In formal descriptions of native polities, contemporary Europeans invoked a tidy geopolitical schema, which took for granted a permanent segmentary structure of bounded, mutually hostile, sociopolitical entities, constituted by common descent and neatly mapped on to discrete territories. Cook 'got the names of several [districts] with the Name of the King or Cheif of each; hence I conclude that the Country is divided into several districts, each governed by a Cheif, but we know nothing of the extent of his power' (1961:544). Leconte, a naval captain who published a treatise on native 'customs' after a two-month sojourn at Balade in 1846, thought that 'the peoples of New Caledonia form a great number of tribes'; their 'wars' took place 'between neighbours of the same village', 'from village to village [of the same tribe]', and, 'the most terrible', 'between tribes' (1847:822, 834). Montravel, senior naval officer in New Caledonia during 1854, used classic segmentary terminology: 'divided into an infinite number of tribes, subdivided themselves into villages, . . . [it is the] general rule that each of the tribes is the enemy of those adjacent to it' (Montravel to Ministre, 27 Apr. 1854, ANOM, Carton 40; see note 10 for definition of Ministre and ANOM). Two naval surgeons with several years' service in the new French colony described 'the population of New Caledonia . . . [as] divided into a certain number of tribes almost all independent' (Vieillard and Deplanche 1863:20). Another referred to 'tribes' as 'so many little nations', subdivided into 'villages' and in a state of 'perpetual war' (Rochas 1862:240–2). For a colonial functionary in the 1860s:

> the native population . . . is divided into an infinite number of tribes, more or less powerful, each having their chief, their interests, often even a different dialect . . . Each tribe . . . is subdivided into a certain number of little tribes or families; the whole tribe submits to a sovereign chief, to whom are responsible petty chiefs [*petits chefs*] commanding the subordinate tribes (La Hautière 1869:69, 71).

Such descriptions registered an emphasis on structure and entity – an 'assumption that cultural units coincide with geographically defined political units' – characteristic of post-Enlightenment Western political theory (Linnekin and Poyer 1990:14; Segal 1988:306, 318). It became colonial reality in New Caledonia via the officially taken-for-granted existence of *tribus*, 'tribes': the 'declarations' of 'recognition and acceptance of the sovereignty of His Majesty Napoléon III', which Montravel thought he had negotiated with 'chiefs' at seven places around the coast during

1854, included a reference to 'the territory of my [the chief's] tribe' (ANOM, Carton 67). The *tribu* was subsequently enshrined in colonial legislation, beginning with 'codes of law' promulgated in 1854 at Balade and Pouébo at the instigation of Christian chiefs and missionaries. The 'tribe's' legal status was formalized during the 1860s, when, in a typical yoking of science to expediency (cf. France 1969:102–28), the concept was deemed at once ethnographically true, apt in evolutionary terms and hierarchically needful to colonial administration. The key 1867 act decreed that 'the native tribe has been and continues to be constituted in New Caledonia; it forms there a legal aggregation having attributes of ownership and organized under the only form which was and still is appropriate to the state of the native population'.[11] The governor had earlier opined that 'where [colonial] authority has no representatives, tribal chiefs . . . [are] naturally responsible to it for what happens in the locality and for the execution of the Governor's orders'.[12]

Formal European images of New Caledonia as a politically atomized world of opposed, hierarchically structured 'tribes' attached to discrete, coterminous 'territories' were probably not inappropriate to indigenous ideological representations – especially, one presumes, those conveyed by the Marists' chiefly associates, whose influence on missionary constructions was surely marked, as they sought to inflate their own group's solidarity, manipulate alliances with Europeans and consolidate their authority (e.g. Douglas 1982, 1995). Such images were, however, often at odds with the import of Europeans' action descriptions, casual remarks and inadvertent ethnographic inscriptions, which provide glimpses of the countervailing pull of widely dispersed individual and small group relationships and allegiances – a reflex of high mobility – and of marked mutability in political practice. Indeed, the most discerning of the naval ethnographers qualified his essentialist, evolutionary model of 'the tribe' as a form of 'patriarchal government' derived from 'the primitive family' by acknowledging that, in practice, 'conquest, migration, benevolent or forced fusion of foreign elements' and 'indefinite multiplication of families' had produced a 'very mixed' population (Rochas 1862:240–1).[13] I sample four such glimpses: two, reasonably transparent, in empirical mode; two requiring adversarial reading, against the grain of their authors' interested ethnocentrism. Bishop Douarre reported:

Lately, we asked a woman from Arindo why she had left this place to
live at Bouelate; 'It is', she told us, 'Because I am afraid of the spirit of
that woman who died at Mahamata'; in fact, a woman died as a result
of wounds she had received at Pouépo, and Arindo[,] which is two
minutes from Mahamata, had no residents, since a voyage to
Hienghène of the Diemène family (Journal, 28 July 1845).

Leconte remarked: 'As this people often changes residence, one
notices, in almost every part of the island [i.e. the limited part of
the north-east known to him and the missionaries], those little
circular hillocks on which they build their houses, without doubt,
the bases of those abandoned' (1847:832–3).[14] Montravel wrote of
their 'original vices . . . extreme insouciance, indomitable laziness
and an excessive fickleness which often leads them to leave one
dwelling in order to make another elsewhere and to abandon next
day the work of the one before' (Montravel to Ministre, 27 Apr.
1854, ANOM, Carton 40). Lambert bemoaned the tendency for
new Belep converts to abandon the mission village for what, to
him, were trifling reasons: 'some quarrel, some dispute, a moment
of boredom' (1855–75:41), thereby instancing what I elsewhere
interpreted, during a more essentialist phase, as a widespread
preference for withdrawal over confrontation, manifestion of an
enduring Kanak ethos of restraint (Douglas 1990).

Linnekin and Poyer differentiated indigenous conceptions of
identity from 'Western' in terms of 'an Oceanic *theory* of cultural
identity that privileges environment, behavior, and situational
flexibility over descent, innate characteristics, and unchanging
boundaries' (1990:6, my emphasis). Superficially, this could be an
apt summation of social patterns described in the major modern
ethnographies of New Caledonia, which variously stressed
movement and relation over structure and entity (Guiart 1953,
1963; Bensa 1981, 1993; Bensa and Rivierre 1982; Pillon 1992). The
premise of an essentialized cultural opposition between the West
and the rest (at least until the latter become Westernized by
modernity) seems, however, to rest on the assumption that how
indigenous people were seen to *act* was mirrored and endorsed
by a coherent, enduring, regionwide indigenous cultural theory.
How one might know any such theory in the early contact and
colonial periods was not addressed. Bensa's recent work on New
Caledonia's *cèmuhî* and *paicî* language zones, which argued for
the operation of a dynamic, creative tension between ideology and

action, suggests the need for a more subtle, contextualized, dialectic conception of that relationship. On the one hand, he maintained, formal social models, usually phrased in the homogenizing idiom of consanguinity, stressed permanence, equilibrium and hierarchy, and fitted human groups to known spaces and places. On the other, at basic segmentary levels there were constant flux and competition for access to high-ranking names and longest-established house mounds, which made most groups very diverse in actual composition and meant that the 'territories' with which they were identified were in practice finely and ambiguously differentiated:

> the antiquity at the heart of the system of house mound-lineages which forms the clan is ... contained and manifested by the single name of the house mound-lineage inscribed in a formalized and hierarchized whole. This grid ... is, for the period covered by the society's actual memory, about a century and a half, without noteworthy change, the names of ancient house mounds retaining their quality beyond the historical vicissitudes those who bore it might have known. This nominal rigidity ... can in no case be identified with the practical working of the society; it contrasts with the extraordinary movement of persons, their capacity to circulate from one name to the other and, consequently, from one rank to another (Bensa 1993:4).

Linnekin and Poyer's case for a timeless categorical opposition of Western and non-Western theories of identity and personhood seems to rest on a comparison of the incommensurate: of the dominant political *ideology* of rampant nineteenth-century Western imperialism with piecemeal, albeit ubiquitous, indigenous political *practices*, assumed to enact a shared, regionwide cultural theory. In contrast, I argued above, from a historically, ethnographically and textually differentiated perspective, that formal nineteenth-century European images of New Caledonian politics might have reinscribed structured aspects of chiefly Kanak ideological representations, just as more casual moments in European texts registered something of the flux and contestation of indigenous social and political actions.

Colonial Nomenclature: Naming Places and People

Kanak nationalists and anthropologists concur on the overriding importance of place in Kanak identities (and in Melanesian, if not Austronesian identities generally (Linnekin and Poyer 1990:8)). According to Bensa and Rivierre:

> The genealogical integration of [*cémuhî*] kinship units is replaced by a spatial integration which uses itineraries as lines of descent, and points in space (house mounds) as ancestors to define an ensemble of house mound-lineages (*pwomwaiu*) maintaining between themselves, on the model of patrilineal descent ... , kinship relationships through space (1982:63).

Douarre's 1843–53 mission journal, the most detailed and circumstantial of the early texts, was liberally sprinkled with place and personal names, but remarkably sparing in descriptive labels: 'tribe', 'village', 'inhabitants', 'neighbours', 'friends', 'allies', 'strangers', 'enemies', plus a handful of French kinship terms – 'father', 'son', 'brother', 'sister', 'uncle', 'wife', 'husband' – and the odd 'concubine', were about all. This is no bad thing for ethnographic historians, who prefer action descriptions to the rehashed second thoughts of more formal contemporary texts. Consider Douarre's pedantic description of a 'property' laboriously acquired by the mission in a frustrating and intricate series of transactions with crowds of sometimes competing rightholders: 'we have now as limits, to the West, the Baïao stream, to the east a torrent; to the south a Ouangui [*waagi* in *yâlayu*, a streamer of bark cloth signalling a taboo] and the valley containing coconut palms and breadfruit trees; to the north, the sea with Tchope's banana plantations' (Journal, 16 Apr. 1844). Though the bishop no doubt construed the transactions in different ways from Kanak, his recourse to a variety of spatial markers hinted at the latter's multilayered engagement with elements in a landscape and at some of the constraints which this imposed on the transactions themselves. Compare the conventional, stilted, feudal model of 'land tenure' and social status with which Leconte prefaced his remarks on Douarre's land acquisitions:

> New Caledonians each own as much land as they can cultivate, and the chief of the village disposes of the rest ... The reputation of a

man of noble race is by reason of the extent of the cultivated lands that he owns, and he who has many pieces of land in cultivation and owns large coconut plantations is designated a great chief (1847:827).

None the less, despite the experiential vividness of Douarre's journal, the contemporary referents of names cited, especially place names, are generally obscure. 'Balade' itself was for Europeans a multivocal term. For Cook it was 'the Name of the district we were at' (1961:544). According to Laferrière, who transported the missionaries to New Caledonia, it was the name of that local chief's 'village' mentioned in an earlier citation (1845:69), located on a low point of land called Mahamate, opposite Cook's anchorage. Leconte, though, remarked that 'the village called [Balade] . . . by the natives is not very close [to Mahamate]' (1847:811), a position endorsed by a later military administrator, who maintained that 'Balade' was a 'curious name which has prevailed . . . [It] is a very small hamlet situated 2 leagues from the execrable roadstead of Balade which should be called Mahamate anchorage' (Testard to Ministre, 23 Apr. 1858, ANOM, Carton 42). Montravel suggested that the name henceforth applied to the port of Balade had been borrowed by Cook from a cluster of long-vanished huts (Montravel to Ministre, 25 Dec. 1854, ANOM, Carton 40).

'Balade' was commonly used by Europeans to designate loosely a district extending along the coastal plain north-west of 'Pouébo', an equally vague place name. The haphazard ways in which Europeans assigned and conflated names of places, 'districts' and 'tribes' were remarked (as was the mission's well-honed eye for a prime site) by Mallet, an experienced and ethnographically astute lay brother who worked for the mission from the early 1850s:

> It is Europeans who called the vicinity of the Mission by the name Poëbo. But the true name of the entire tribe is Mouélébet, the different districts and quarters have particular names, and the principal places particular chiefs . . . There is a village bearing this name ['Pouébo'] situated in the mountains an hour from the mission, and there was also a house of the high chief who reigned in 1846 (about) and which together with its surroundings was called Poébo [i.e. 'Pouébo' = the habitat of the *Tea Mwelebeng*]. It is the place occupied naturally by the Church ([1868]).

Montravel specified that 'the little territory of Balade occupies almost the centre' of the 'Pouma tribe' (Montravel to Ministre, 25

Dec. 1854, ANOM, Carton 40). Douarre generally used more precise local place names, but he regularly referred to the 'Balade tribe', which included the residents of Tiari, further to the northwest, and 'Koko', on the lower Diahot, on the far side of the coastal range of hills. Such names served Europeans as encompassing labels applied to a 'district' and by extension its residents, conceived as a 'tribe'. Only at Balade and to a lesser extent Pouébo did the early texts regularly identify places within the undifferentiated territory of a 'district' which a 'tribe' was seen to inhabit; for Douarre, his colleagues and their naval associates, 'Baïao', 'Mahamate', 'Bouélate', 'Ouenbane', were evidently names of Balade 'villages', presumed to encompass the cultivated lands amongst which their households were scattered, and conceived as territorial subgroups of the 'tribe' (Rougeyron to Sécrétaire-Général, 3 Sep. 1846, APM, 418.1; Douarre, Journal, 29 Apr. 1852; Lambert 1855–75:24).

If the geographical awareness of these early European residents emerges indistinctly from the texts, the vestiges therein inscribed of ways in which Kanak named and differentiated space are still more opaque, though Mallet perceptively implied a starting-point in local specificity rather than hierarchical encompassment: 'the true name of the entire tribe is Mouélébet, the different districts and quarters have particular names, and the principal places particular chiefs' ([1868]). Equally ambiguous were the many names attributed to persons, mostly 'chiefs' and almost all men: their local status as personal names, terms of relation, titles or clan names is quite unclear from the texts themselves.[15] At first Douarre used place names to differentiate people: 'the king of Coco', 'the chief of Bondé', 'the chief of Belep', 'the chief of Balade', 'the chief of Pouébo'. Only with the outbreak of fighting after April 1845 did the need for some political discrimination lead him to adopt the term 'tribe', implying an autonomous political unit, though he continued to use the phrase 'people/inhabitants of [a 'district' or 'village']' and to refer to 'the tribe of [a 'district']' (Journal, 1, 27 May, 15 July 1845). It was not until the end of 1845 that he mentioned 'the two tribes, the Pouma, where we find ourselves, and the Mouélébé [of Pouébo]' (Journal, 3 Dec. 1845), thereby registering, probably unwittingly, an indigenous tendency to extend the name of a high chiefly clan to all who acknowledged its authority (Leenhardt 1930:105),[16] and to conceive political ties in terms of fluctuating localized patterns of relationship between people and groups, rather than fixed territorial entities. Of the contemporary commentators I have read, only Mallet seems to have grasped this quality: 'What demarcates tribes is fairly vague[,] a river, a chain of mountains, externally; it is especially the honour and allegiance which are accorded the first chief, and especially at the time of convocation to war' ([1868], cancelled in original).

So far as I can tell from contemporary texts and the works of later linguists and ethnographers, there were no direct parallels in Kanak languages for the concept of 'tribe', in the sense of a permanent, autonomous, territorially defined sociopolitical unit. There was no neat mesh between spatial, kinship and political units, though toponymy and itineraries were key elements in naming and linking social groups.[17] The significant human inscriptions on the landscape of house mound, house and habitat served metonymically to classify various levels of indigenous sociopolitical integration, and metaphorically to denominate wider domains encountered with colonialism.[18] Local political geography provided a shifting variety of candidates for the colonial term 'tribe', depending on context and the relative fragmentation or hierarchical encompassment of local groups in particular places: they could be quasi-independent, rival residential clusters within a 'country', called *mwo-daame* in *cèmuhî* and *wârâ-ukai* in *paicî*;[19] they could be autonomous clan chiefdoms roughly coterminous with a 'country', such as the Pwèi of the upper Thiem (Pwèi) valley (Bensa and Rivierre 1982:119–24); they could be complex chiefdoms encompassing heterogeneous hierarchies of smaller chieftaincies and local groups under the name of the high-chiefly clan, such as at Hienghène, Canala, on the Isle of Pines and in the Loyalty Islands.[20]

Transcending the Local

Less congruent still with atomistic European models of New Caledonian government, and the primitivist scientific and religious discourses which helped shape them, were insistent implications in contemporary texts that Kanak had regularized translocal interests and relationships, corollaries of flux and domestic insecurity. The mission journal is studded with incidental references to small-scale 'intertribal' visiting and resident strangers, while the operation of regionwide patterns of alliance and enmity was implied by its authors' apparently casual attributions of the terms 'friends', 'allies', 'strangers', 'enemies': careful scrutiny of their particular deployment reveals the imprint of a web of enduring relationships in which the Puma of Balade were enmeshed, spanning the entire northern region and beyond, and fostering escalation of quarrels beyond a local arena. No contemporary mission text I have seen discussed the matter explicitly, but Mary Wallis – who credited much of her ethnographic information to 'the gentlemen of the mission' – did so, putting names to the relationship and hinting at an affinal dimension:

> The inhabitants of the islands are divided into two classes, one is called the *whawhap* and the other the *ot*. The towns of these two classes are intermixed. Although they live on friendly terms at times, they never have much confidence in each other. If difficulties arise, those who have married into the different tribe are often killed (Journal, 21 Oct. 1852 – Wallis 1994:146).

The naval surgeons Vieillard and Deplanche discerned a formal diplomatic/military institution, and qualified their image of tribal 'independence', cited above, by acknowledging that 'these tribes':

> form between themselves offensive and defensive alliances, the gathering of which gives rise to a confederation designated by a particular name; such, for example, are the confederation of the tribes of Ienghen, Balade, Arama, Kumac, designated under the collective name of *Wape*, and those of Bondé, Puebo, Belep, etc., known under the denomination of *Hot*. These sorts of alliances often result in a very wide span of country becoming engaged in a war of long duration over a simple quarrel, the cause of which is usually [a matter] of indifference to the majority of the allies (1863:21).

A century later, a field enquiry led Guiart to describe local groups in the northern quarter of mainland New Caledonia as distributed, patchwork fashion, between two mutually hostile, ritually opposed, often intermarrying, geographically defined groupings called Hoot and Waap. He detailed particular identifications where he could, confirming and extending those just cited. He interpreted Hoot and Waap as 'political and ceremonial phratries', instancing a New Caledonia-wide tendency for regional 'networks of solidarity' and 'identification' to transcend the 'atomism' of local allegiances based on kinship and coresidence (1963:630, 639, 647).[21] He thought that conquest of territory was not a feature of Hoot/Waap opposition, which, though often significant in alliance formation, implied mainly symbolic and ritual prestige.

Predictably, early French officials had remarked only military implications of supralocal patterns of relationship in the north. The first governor of the colony gave a name, but limited significance to the relationship: 'the diverse tribes are all independent; they are only grouped into two confederations known under the names *Ot* and *Uanap*; but the relations of tribes of the same confederation are limited to an alliance in time of war'.[22] Oblivious to the potential thus provided for far-flung alliances against the French, he anticipated easy pickings from a colonial 'divide-and-rule' policy (du Bouzet to Ministre, 14 February, 20 June 1855; see also Montravel to Ministre, 27 April, 25 December 1854, ANOM, Carton 40). It would, however, take more than sixty years to complete the French military conquest of New Caledonia, and Leenhardt opined that 'in all the struggles and rebellions of colonial history [in the north], one finds alliances or enmities between Oote and Waap' (1930:105).

Frequent references in the early mission texts to mutual visiting – as between Balade and Hienghène, Arama and Koumac, Arama and Balade, for ceremonies or for supplies during times of shortage – had long before put the lie to the blinkered military perspective and anticipated Leenhardt's later insight: 'these names [Hoot/ Waap] have a wider significance [than the purely military] . . . Any traveller able to lay claim to one or other [name] . . . is welcomed in regions corresponding to one or other of these divisions' (1930:105). In one journal entry Douarre used the cryptic phrase *'quelques étrangers de ses amis'*, which I take to mean 'friendly strangers' or 'allies' (Journal, 27 July 1851); its import was clarified by his subsequent differentiation of the guests attending a ceremony at Balade into 'strangers' (enemies) and 'strangers[,] friends of the [Puma] tribe' (allies) (Journal, 16 May 1852). This resonates with Guiart's comment that in ritual contexts, especially mortuary ceremonies, participants split into opposed groups of Hoot and Waap (1966:51).

It is important neither to exaggerate the coherence nor to oversimplify the complexity of Hoot/Waap identifications in northern New Caledonia. The chequerboard pattern of alliance and enmity implied in contemporary texts was framed by a Balade/Pouébo textual focus and the European propensity to divide the political landscape into permanent, juxtaposed 'tribes' – the region's chiefdoms – directly mapped on to contiguous 'territories'. Histories of movements of actual groups and persons between nodal points (house mounds) on itineraries, however, produced multiple, overlapping, more or less sustainable claims to names, roles, statuses, places and resources. To Europeans seeking to convert, control and exploit Melanesians, the mobility, competition and ambiguous allegiances of smaller groups throughout New Caledonia were easily dismissed or ignored: Europeans of all persuasions did their best to immobilize Kanak. In the 1950s Guiart sought to systematize hints provided by Leenhardt on the Hoot/Waap opposition, but was frustrated by lack of precision in information received. He decided that 'it was not a question of an ordered institution the mechanism of which informants can describe with a great wealth of details' (1966:49) and later concluded: 'it did not involve a dualism regulating traditional enmities, but a structure organizing ritual comple-mentarity and congealing territorial limits in such a way that war cannot end in conquest of the lands of others' (1985b:91). The modern Marist ethnographer Dubois also noted that Hoot/Waap identification was 'tied to territory rather than to genetic origin': he cited the case of members of a clan of Belep origin who, by changing residence and becoming 'subjects' of the Waap *Tea Ovaac* of Arama, had exposed themselves to attack by their Hoot Belep kinsmen (1985:43). The relative geographical permanence and regional balance of Hoot and Waap look, therefore, like an instance of Bensa's principle that ideologies stressing stability and equilibrium served both to contain and camouflage the constant flux and competition of Kanak political practice.

Hoot/Waap identifications delineated a loosely defined, by no means exclusive zone of regular ritual and political interactions and oppositions. The far north region of Kanaky is today known as Hoot ma Waap, a 'customary' name denoting unity rather than the complementary opposition of earlier indigenous relation-ships.[23] Residue of much older emphases in exchanges, marriage, political interaction and conflict, Hoot ma Waap is also a Kanak invention, a creative intertexture of old and new strands woven for deployment in a modern anticolonial struggle for independent identity and political autonomy.

Constructing *la Coutume*

Like other colonial roles and entities eventually systematized into the formal colonial domain of customary law (*le droit coutumier*), those of tribe and tribal chief were naturalized, managed and exploited in local experience and politics, usually in ways remote from the colonizers' intentions.[24] These days, from the perspective of Nouméa, Balade is a remote, lower-order segment in a still colonial hierarchy: a 'district' (an administrative unit headed by a *grand chef*, 'high chief') of the commune of Pouébo in the Northern Province, it comprises four *tribus* (nucleated villages, headed by a *chef*, 'chief', and occupying a 'reserve'), called Saint Denis (or *Pwiyiwe*), Saint Gabriel, Sainte Marie and Saint Paul. In 1989 there were 413 'tribal' members residing in the district (Institut Territorial de la Statistique et des Etudes Economiques 1989:211). From the even more lofty perspective of Paris they are no doubt an all but invisible handful of yokels. Yet these people are engaged, mostly as pro-independence activists, in very complex, ambiguous, multifaceted politics of identity. They practise, negotiate and contest *la coutume*, the fluid, varied 'custom' which Kanak characterize as an ancestral inheritance, while acknowledging its overlap, interpolation and at times deliberate confrontation with indigenized innovations, notably Christianity and the aforementioned colonial entities and roles. Thus both *le clan* ('authentically' indigenous) and *la tribu* (the colonial village and its reserve, at once an outcome of and a refuge from colonial dispossession) serve variously as sites for the construction and experience of modern Kanak customary identities; similarly, while Kanak often disparagingly differentiate 'administrative chiefs' from 'customary', they are by no means unanimous about attributing the labels.

The people of Balade, like Kanak everywhere, also objectify *la coutume* as a political and moral ideology through which they seek to engage creatively in modernization, political parties and the Western hierarchies of commune, province, territory, [nation, and ultimately Europe]. It is this mobilization of objectified custom to an anticolonial nationalist cause by a still colonized indigenous minority which presumably led Linnekin to charge Kanak activists with having transformed flexible, contingent indigenous identities into an exclusive, Western-style, oppositional ethnic identity, of seeking 'to polarize the population into Kanak/non-Kanak segments' (1990:170–1). Yet Kanak leaders do not notably advocate a present politics of ethnic exclusivity, though their European and Polynesian opponents accuse them of it, and do so themselves. Whether for 'cultural' or strategic reasons – or both, inextricably entwined – Kanak leaders during the serially tense 1980s often allowed for an inclusive conception of Kanak identity in a future independent Kanaky. The most persuasive proponent of this view was the late Jean-Marie Tjibaou, who stressed a Kanak 'tradition' of welcoming and incorporating the respectful stranger, and sometimes envisaged its extension to those he whimsically labelled '*Kanak blanc*', '"white Kanak"' (Tjibaou 1996:129 [1982], 168 [1984], 225–6 [1986]; Tjibaou and Shineberg 1982:35).

Conclusion

Why bother anyway? If the past is always a present construction, what is the point or propriety of narratives purporting to be 'about' the past? Are theories of native agency and indigenization of the exotic anything more than ethnocentric universalizing of a particular, present libertarian political stance, with the feel-good hidden agenda of dissociating 'us' from the sins of colonizing ancestors and displacing to the victims some of the blame for colonial oppression, 'Westernization' and their 'fatal impact'? Can textual relics of colonial incursions be regarded as anything other than impossibly biased, politically unacceptable, stereotypical evidence for the blanket iniquities of colonialism? Isn't 'understanding' them in discursive context another term for whitewashing?

Obviously, my responses to my own rhetorical questions will validate the epistemological politics already sketched and implemented. Claims to know the past are vital present resources in just about every area of human endeavour, formal and informal, not least for indigenous people demanding justice, compensation and reconciliation, as well as for their rivals and opponents. Conviction of absolute truth-value is affirmed in quotidian uses of the past, rather than the claim to even-handed objectivity of most conventional history, or to pluralism of antipositivist varieties. Reflexive, ironic perspectives on the past, however, serve to relativize, contextualize and de-essentialize present – as well as past – actions, values, relationships and seemingly inevitable outcomes. For example, by dislodging the tropes of monolithic colonialism, Westernization and nationalism, such perspectives can reveal the workings, the limits and the vulnerability of power. Discourse analysis provides an important tool for radical critique of obnoxious regimes, making better sense of their demise, as well as their seeming inevitability and irresistibility. A culturally, contextually sensitive conception of agency as both enabling and constrained can denaturalize the homogeneity and ineluctability of colonialism, as well as humanize and animate representations of the colonized. Appropriation/indigenization, as variously deliberate strategy and cultural/contextual reflex, I take as inarguable. De-universalizing the present permits less ethnocentric and anachronistic images and evaluations of the past and contributes to the construction of identities informed by past contextual values, mirroring present concerns knowingly rather than unthinkingly. I endorse White's endorsement of the classic nineteenth-century conception of the historical imagination as 'providing . . . a ground for the celebration of man's [*sic*] responsibility for his own fate': by 'inducing in men an awareness that their present condition was always in part a product of specifically human choices, which could therefore be changed or altered by further human action[,] . . . history . . . sensitized men to the *dynamic* elements in every achieved present' (1978:48–9, emphasis in original).

Notes

1. The Comaroffs argued similarly with respect to the Tswana of southern Africa (1991:225, 246). Bensa put a strong, if essentialist, case for Kanak receptiveness to innovation as an enduring element of the pragmatic interplay of ideas, rituals, horticultural techniques and politics – a 'dialectic of the archaic and the new' (1990:130).
2. A 'text' is any medium for representation: written or spoken words, memories, gestures, dress, objects, buildings, landscapes, and visual media like paintings, sculptures, photographs and films. My texts are mainly written.

3. 'Colonial texts', generically, include all kinds of texts produced about indigenous people by Europeans and their affiliates after initial contacts; in practice I discriminate finely between eras, genres and media.

4. 'All our endeavours to get the name of the whole Island proved enefectual, probably, it is too large for them to know by one name; when ever we made this enquiry they allways gave us the Name of some district or place which we pointed to' (Cook 1961:544); 'For them, their island is the whole world: so they give it no name' (Leconte 1847:823). I have translated all French quotations into English.

5. I use the conventional translation 'chief' for the *yâlayu* (Balade) term *têâma* and cognates in other Kanak languages, despite inappropriate connotations of acknowledged authority to rule and command, given multiple possibilities for diffusion of authority between 'chiefs' and those 'subjects' who controlled the land and important rituals (Bensa and Rivierre 1982:108– 11; Bensa 1986; Guiart 1992:12–13; Douglas 1994, 1995:60–6).

6. These 'villages' were Leenhardt's 'habitat' (*maciri* in *ajië*; 1930:24–5), Haudricourt's 'residence' (*kavebu* in *kumak*; 1963:52), Bensa and Rivierre's 'domestic space' (*pómwó* in *cèmuhî*; 1982:34). In 1856, in a detailed household census conducted on the Belep island of Art, the missionary Lambert counted a total populace of 479 distributed between 11 'villages', ranging from 13 to 94 residents and averaging 44 (1855–75:25–6).

7. Similar episodes mentioned in the official mission journal were – in accord with missionaries' and some chiefs' authoritarian designs – usually construed as infringements of established political norms (Douarre, Journal, 29 Apr., 18 Jul., 28 Nov. 1852). A Protestant and a democrat, Wallis's more libertarian bent inclined her to see legitimate sanctions against chiefly abuse – a position I find more congenial. Her journal is an important departure from the heavily male, missionary and French bias of colonial texts on New Caledonia.

8. For a succinct overview of the typical Kanak habitat in the 1950s see Guiart (1956:37–43).

9. Bensa remarked a similar tendency for modern *cèmuhî* villages to reproduce and telescope older contexts of spatial integration: 'the *pómwó* ['domestic space'] is a house . . . generally occupied by a nuclear family; the *mwo-daame* ['group of residences'] has become a quarter of the village . . . and the *amú* ['country'] can

be identified with the village and its land (sometimes with the 'reserve')' (Bensa and Rivierre 1982:49).

10. Montravel to Ministre de la Marine et des Colonies (hereinafter Ministre), 25 Dec. 1854, Archives nationales, section Outremer (hereinafter ANOM), Carton 40.

11. 'Code pénal de la tribe de Pouma [Balade]', 9 Feb. 1854; 'Code pénal de la tribu de Muélébé [Pouébo]', 15 Feb. 1854, ANOM, Carton 67; 'Décision du Gouverneur portant division administrative, en trois districts, de l'île d'Ouvéa (Loyalty)', 25 June 1865, *Bulletin officiel*, 1865:123–4; 'Arrêté du Gouverneur constituant le territoire [et la tribu] de Houagape et en nommant le Chef', 14 July 1866, *Moniteur*, 22 July 1866; 'Arrêté du Gouverneur déclarant, par voie d'interprétation des actes législatifs antérieurs, l'existence légale de la tribu indigène dans l'organisation coloniale de la Nouvelle-Calédonie', 24 Dec. 1867, *Moniteur*, 29 Dec. 1867; see also Ministre to Guillain (draft), 22 May 1868, ANOM, Carton 59.

12. Guillain, 'De la mission catholique en Calédonie . . .', 6 Apr. 1865 (APM), 'Démêlés avec le Gouverneur Guillain, 1863–9'; La Hautière 1869:70.

13. As a case in point, Bérard commented that the Hienghène 'tribe' in 1850 comprised 'an infinity of elements', including groups from elsewhere on the main island and the Loyalties (1854:97).

14. Leenhardt described the customary abandonment of a habitat following the death of its owner and the prohibition on its reoccupation by his descendants for a period thereafter (1930:24).

15. See Leenhardt (1930:99–105) on naming.

16. The *Tea Puma* or *Pumadaan* were in regular competition with another clan for the *Tea Bweoon* title at Balade; *Tea Mwelebeng* was the high-chiefly title at Pouébo (Guiart 1974:96; 1985a:81; Guiart and Bensa 1981). Apart from 'Pouma' and 'Mouélébé', which he used regularly, Douarre also occasionally referred to the 'Arama tribe' as 'Théaobaïte' or 'Téaubat'; to the 'Bondé tribe' as the 'Péac' or 'Paéak'; to the 'Téadianu' or 'Tiandianou', who lived mainly at Ouébia, near the headwaters of the River Ouaième; to the 'Téagomène' of Gomen. These names correspond to *Tea Ovaac, Paak, Tea Janu, Tea Gomen*.

17. E.g. a *cèmuhî* clan (*mwà*, 'house') might be named for the site of the original house mound built by its mythical apical

ancestor, and was identified with an *amú*, 'country', designated by the clan name, though in the 1970s the groups actually occupying an *amú* were usually of diverse clan origins and clans were more or less widely dispersed; each of the groups of residences (*mwo-daame*, 'container of chiefs') comprising a clan or occupying an *amú* bore the name of the house mound occupied by its chief (Bensa and Rivierre 1982:32–3, 49, 65, 79).

18. E.g. in *cèmuhî*, the name of the highest house mound was identified with the whole habitat, *pómwó*, 'domestic space', and with its occupants, conceived as a localized kinship unit, *pwomwaiu*, 'house mound-lineage', so that house mound, *bidaa-mwà*, and *pwomwaiu* virtually overlapped conceptually (Bensa and Rivierre 1982:45, 55; Leenhardt 1946:282, 283, 445). In *paicî*, the 'house mound-lineage' was called either *mûrûwâ*, 'house mound', or *wââo*, 'great house'; the latter term could also be extended further to mean 'clan', though another metonym for 'clan' was *wâ*, a generic Austronesian word for house, cognate of *cèmuhî mwà*, 'house', 'clan' (Bensa 1992:1; 1993:4). The term for 'container' was often extended to 'house' and thence to 'clan' or 'country': in *ajië*, *mwa*, 'container', 'house', became *mwaro*, 'great house', 'clan' (Leenhardt 1935:185–6; 1946:284, 289, 445, 513); in *kumak*, *mwa*, 'nest', 'shell', 'house', became *phwamwaaguk*, 'great house' and *phwaamwa*, 'country' (Leenhardt 1946:284, 289, 304, 513; Haudricourt 1963:60, 71); in *fwâi*, *nga*, 'container', house', became *hwan-nga*, 'habitat', home' (*chez soi*, *ensemble familial*), and *nga men thau*, 'peaceful abode', by metaphoric extension 'kingdom', 'whole tribe' (*ensemble de tribu*) (Leenhardt 1946:282, 284, 513; Haudricourt and Ozanne-Rivierre 1982:101, 146). As in the latter example, the term for 'habitat' often encompassed wider and altered social domains: in *ajië*, *maciri*, 'habitat', 'peaceful abode', meant metonymically 'group of villages dependent on a particular clan chief', and metaphorically 'territory under the jurisdication of an administrative chief', 'government', 'empire', 'kingdom [e.g. of God]' (Leenhardt 1930:24–5; 1935:173–4; 1946:282); in *kumak*, *kavebu*, 'habitat', 'residence', became also 'kingdom' (Leenhardt 1946:282; Haudricourt 1963:32).

19. Bensa and Rivierre (1982:47–50, 69–105); Bensa (1992:4). In 1866 colonial legislation 'reconstituting' the 'territory of Houagape' (roughly the 'country' identified with the Waka

clan) appointed the 'chief of the tribe of Houagape', referred
to 'the chiefs' of its 'several villages', and was justified on the
basis that 'the territory . . . has, for several years, been cut up
into small independent chiefdoms' ('Arrêté du Gouverneur
constituant le territoire de Houagape et en nommant le Chef',
14 July 1866, *Moniteur*, 22 July 1866).

20. 'Very important *moaro* ['clan'], like Buarate at Hienghène,
    Baxerea at Canala, end up absorbing in their name all the
    groups . . . of a region, and they become the symbolic name of
    a whole tribe. These names are also symbols of power'
    (Leenhardt 1930:105).

21. Guiart (1957:21–7; 1963:629–52; 1966:49–53); Guiart and Bensa
    (1981); cf. Bensa and Rivierre (1982:108, fn. 1; 1984:102–3).

22. The missionary Lambert's ethnography also stressed military
    aspects of the Hoot/Waap relationship: he began a chapter
    'On War' by explaining: 'When war breaks out between two
    tribes, the Ouaouaps must take up the cudgels for each
    Ouaouap tribe, and the Ots for the Ot peoples' (1900:173–4).

23. Bensa and Rivierre described an analogous transformation in
    the Poinda region of north-western New Caledonia, with the
    emergence of an encompassing political ensemble, Nädù bau
    Görötü, out of the complementary opposition of the Nädù and
    Görötü clans, partners in a preferential marriage alliance
    (1988).

24. Indigenous manipulations or evasions of the authority of
    officially sanctioned chiefs were described in ethnographies
    by the naval doctors Patouillet (1872:130–1), Legrand
    (1893:101–2) and Vincent (1895:22), and the ethnographers
    Sarasin (1917:77) and Leenhardt (1930:43).

References

Anderson, B. 1983. *Imagined Communities: Reflections on the Origin
and Spread of Nationalism*. London: Verso.

Archives nationales, section Outre-mer (ANOM), série Nouvelle-
Calédonie, Aix-en-Provence.

Archivio dei Padri Maristi (APM), section Oceania, Nova Caledonia,
Rome.

Babadzan, A. (1988). Kastom and Nation-Building in the South
Pacific. In: R. Guidieri, F. Pellizzi and S. J. Tambiah (eds),

Ethnicities and Nations: Processes of Interethnic Relations in Latin America, Southeast Asia, and the Pacific, pp. 199–228. Houston: Rothko Chapel.

Barthes, R. (1970). Historical Discourse. In: M. Lane (ed.), *Structuralism: a Reader*, pp. 145–55. London: Jonathan Cape.

Bensa, A. (1981). Références spatiales et organisation spatiale dans le centre-nord de la Grande Terre. In: *Atlas de la Nouvelle-Calédonie et dépendances*, plate 18. Paris: ORSTOM.

—— (1986). L'emprise comme institution: un cas d'organisation politique canaque (Nouvelle Calédonie). *Bulletin de Psychologie* 39:253–7.

—— (1990). Des ancêtres et des hommes: Introduction aux théories kanak de la nature, de l'action et de l'histoire. In: Roger Boulay (ed.), *De jade et de nacre: patrimoine artistique kanak*, pp. 130–60. Paris: Réunion des Musées Nationaux.

—— (1992). L'autosacrifice du chef: la question du corps dans les institutions socio-politiques kanak des aires paicî et cèmuhî (Nouvelle-Calédonie). TS, in author's possession.

—— (1993). Un cas de renouvellement de la chefferie kanak (Nouvelle-Calédonie ancienne): l'auto-sacrifice du chef. TS, in author's possession.

Bensa, A. and Rivierre, J.-C. (1982). *Les Chemins de l'alliance: l'organisation social et ses représentations en Nouvelle-Calédonie (région de Touho – aire linguistique cèmuhî)*. Paris: SELAF.

—— (1984). Jean Guiart et l'ethnologie. *L'Homme* 24:101–5.

—— (1988). De l'histoire des mythes: narrations et polémiques autour du rocher Até (Nouvelle-Calédonie). *L'Homme* 28: 263–95.

Bérard, L.-T. (1854). Campagne de la corvette l'Alcmène en Océanie pendant les années 1850 et 1851. *Nouvelles Annales de la Marine et des Colonies* 12:5–151, 153–79.

Bulletin officiel de la Nouvelle-Calédonie. Nouméa.

Carrier, J.G. (ed.) (1992). *History and Tradition in Melanesian Anthropology*. Berkeley: University of California Press.

Collingwood, R.G. (1961). *The Idea of History*. Oxford: Oxford University Press.

Comaroff, J. and Comaroff, J. (1991). *Of Revelation and Revolution: Christianity, Colonialism, and Consciousness in South Africa*, vol. 1. Chicago: University of Chicago Press.

Cook, J. (1961). *The Voyage of the 'Resolution' and 'Adventure' 1772–1775*, J.C. Beaglehole (ed.). Cambridge: Hakluyt Society.

Douarre, G. (1843–53). Journal, 21 December 1843 – 20 April 1853. MS copy. Nouméa: Archives de l'Archevêché.

Douglas, B. (1982). 'Written on the Ground': Spatial Symbolism, Cultural Categories and Historical Process in New Caledonia. *Journal of the Polynesian Society* 91:383–415.

—— (1985). Ritual and Politics in the Inaugural Meeting of High Chiefs from New Caledonia and the Loyalty Islands. *Social Analysis* 18:60–84.

—— (1990). 'Almost Constantly at War'? An Ethnographic Perspective on Fighting in New Caledonia. *Journal of Pacific History* 25:22–46.

—— (1994). Hierarchy and Reciprocity in New Caledonia: an Historical Ethnography. In: M. Mosko and M. Jolly (eds), *Transformations of Hierarchy: Structure, History and Horizon in the Austronesian World*, pp. 169–93. Special issue, *History and Anthropology* 7.

—— (1995). Power, Discourse and the Appropriation of God: Christianity and Subversion in a Melanesian Context. *History and Anthropology* 9:57–92.

Dubois, M.J. (1985). *Histoire résumée de Belep (Nouvelle-Calédonie)*. Nouméa: Imprimerie Graphoprint.

France, P. (1969). *The Charter of the Land: Custom and Colonization in Fiji*. Melbourne: Oxford University Press.

Guiart, J. (1953). Nouvelle-Calédonie et îles Loyalty: carte du dynamisme de la société indigène à l'arrivée des Européens. *Journal de la Société des Océanistes* 9:93–7.

—— (1956). L'organisation sociale et coutumière de la population autochtone. In: J. Barrau, *L'Agriculture vivrière autochtone de la Nouvelle-Calédonie*, pp. 15–43. Nouméa: Commission du Pacifique Sud.

—— (1957). Les modalités de l'organisation dualiste et le système matrimonial en Nouvelle-Calédonie. *Cahiers Internationaux de Sociologie* 22:21–39.

—— (1963). *Structure de la chefferie en Mélanésie du sud*. Paris: Institut d'Ethnologie.

—— (1966). *Mythologie du masque en Nouvelle-Calédonie*. Paris: Musée de l'Homme.

—— (1974). A Reply to Bronwen Douglas. *Journal of the Polynesian Society* 83:94–102.

—— (1985a). *Do Kamo*, de Maurice Leenhardt, relu en 1986. *Journal de la Société des Océanistes* 80:57–85.

—— (1985b). Ethnologie de la Mélanésie. Critiques et auto-critiques. *L'Homme* 25:73–95.

—— (1992). Progress and Regress in New Caledonia. *Journal of Pacific History* 27:3–28.

—— (n.d). Clans nord de la N. Calédonie: Balade-Pouébo. TS, in author's possession.

Guiart, J. and Bensa, A. (1981). Clans autochtones: situation pré-coloniale. In: *Atlas de la Nouvelle-Calédonie et dépendances,* plate 18. Paris: ORSTOM.

Haudricourt, A.-G. (1963). *La Langue des Nénémas et des Nigoumak (dialectes de Poum et de Koumac, Nouvelle-Calédonie).* Auckland: Linguistic Society of New Zealand.

Haudricourt, A.-G.and Ozanne-Rivierre, F. (1982). *Dictionnaire thématique des langues de la région de Hienghène (Nouvelle-Calédonie).* Paris: SELAF.

Hobsbawm, E. and Ranger, T. (eds) (1983). *The Invention of Tradition.* Cambridge: Cambridge University Press.

Institut Territorial de la Statistique et des Etudes Economiques (1989). *Recensement de la population 1989: Inventaire Tribal, Province Nord.* Nouméa: Graphoprint.

Jackson, M. (1989). *Paths Toward a Clearing: Radical Empiricism and Ethnographic Enquiry.* Bloomington and Indianapolis: Indiana University Press.

Jolly, M. (1992). Specters of Inauthenticity. *Contemporary Pacific* 4:49–72.

Keesing, R.M. (1989). Creating the Past: Custom and Identity in the Contemporary Pacific. *Contemporary Pacific* 1:19–42.

—— (1993). Kastom Re-examined. In: L. Lindstrom and G.M. White (eds), *Custom Today,* pp. 587–96. Special issue, *Anthropological Forum* 6.

Keesing, R.M. and Tonkinson, R. (eds) (1982). *Reinventing Traditional Culture: the Politics of Kastom in Island Melanesia.* Special issue, *Mankind* 13:4.

Laferrière, J. (1845). *Voyage aux îles Tonga-tabou, Wallis et Foutouna, à la Nouvelle-Calédonie et à la Nouvelle-Zélande, exécuté du 1ᵉʳ novembre 1843 au 1ᵉʳ avril 1844.* Paris: Imprimerie Royale.

La Hautière, U. de (1869). *Souvenirs de la Nouvelle Calédonie: voyage sur la côte orientale; un coup de main chez les kanacks; pilou-pilou à Naniouni.* Paris: Challamel Ainé.

Lambert, P. (1855–75). Petit journal, 1855–1875. TS copy of Petit journal de France à Belep, 1855–59; Petit journal de 1860–1875.

Nouméa: Archives de l'Archevêché.

——— (1900). *Moeurs et superstitions des Néo-Calédoniens*. Nouméa: Nouvelle Imprimerie Nouméenne.

Leconte, F. (1847). Notice sur la Nouvelle-Calédonie, les moeurs et les usages de ses habitants, par F. Leconte, capitaine de vaisseau. *Annales Maritimes et Coloniales* 32e année, 3e série, 2:811–69.

Leenhardt, M. (1930). *Notes d'ethnologie Néo-Calédonienne*. Paris: Institut d'Ethnologie.

——— (1935). *Vocabulaire et grammaire de la langue Houaïlou*. Paris: Institut d'Ethnologie.

——— (1946). *Langues et dialectes de l'Austro-Mélanésie*. Paris: Institut d'Ethnologie.

Legrand, M.-A. (1893). *Au pays des canaques: la Nouvelle-Calédonie et ses habitants en 1890*. Paris: Librairie militaire de L. Baudoin.

Linnekin, J. (1990). The Politics of Culture in the Pacific. In: J. Linnekin and L. Poyer (eds), *Cultural Identity and Ethnicity in the Pacific*, pp. 149–73. Honolulu: University of Hawaii Press.

——— (1992). On the Theory and Politics of Cultural Construction in the Pacific. In: M. Jolly and N. Thomas (eds), *The Politics of Tradition in the Pacific*, pp. 249–63. Special issue, *Oceania* 62.

Linnekin, J. and Poyer, L. (1990). Introduction. In: J. Linnekin and L. Poyer (eds), *Cultural Identity and Ethnicity in the Pacific*, pp. 1–16. Honolulu: University of Hawaii Press.

[Mallet, A. 1868]. [Commentaires sur] Moniteur de n[elle]. Calédonie[,] n°. 431. MS draft. Nouméa: Archives de l'Archevêché.

Moniteur de la Nouvelle-Calédonie. Journal officiel de la colonie. Noumea.

Patouillet, J. (1872). *Voyage autour du monde: trois ans en Nouvelle-Calédonie*. Paris: E. Dentu.

Philipp, J. (1983). Traditional Historical Narrative and Action-Oriented (or Ethnographic) History. *Historical Studies* 20:339–52.

Pillon, P. (1992). Listes déclamatoires (*viva*) et principes d'organisation sociale dans la vallée de la Kouaoua (Nouvelle-Calédonie). *Journal de la Société des Océanistes* 94:81–101.

Rochas, V. de (1862). *La Nouvelle-Calédonie et ses habitants: productions, moeurs, cannibalisme*. Paris: F. Sartorius.

Sarasin, F. (1917). *La Nouvelle-Calédonie et les îles Loyalty: souvenirs de voyage d'un naturaliste*, tr. Jean Roux. Bâle: Georg.

Saussol, A. (1979). *L'Héritage: essai sur le problème foncier mélanésien en Nouvelle-Calédonie.* Paris: Musée de l'Homme.

Segal, D.A. (1988). Nationalism, Comparatively Speaking. *Journal of Historical Sociology* 1:301–21.

Stivers, C. (1993). Reflections on the Role of Personal Narrative in Social Science. *Signs* 18:408–25.

Thomas, N. (1992). The Inversion of Tradition. *American Ethnologist* 19:213–32.

Tjibaou, J.-M. (1996). *La Présence kanak,* A. Bensa and E. Wittersheim (eds). Paris: Editions Odile Jacob.

Tjibaou, J.-M. and Shineberg, B. (1982). Jean-Marie Tjibaou on New Caledonia's Goals. *Pacific Islands Monthly* 53(4):35–7.

Trask, H.-K. (1991). Natives and Anthropologists: the Colonial Struggle. *Contemporary Pacific* 3:159–67.

Vieillard, E. and Deplanche, E. (1863). *Essais sur la Nouvelle-Calédonie.* Paris: Librairie Challamel Ainé.

Vincent, J.-B.M. (1895). *Les Canaques de la Nouvelle-Calédonie: esquisse ethnographique.* Paris: A. Challamel.

Wallis, M. (1994). *The Fiji and New Caledonia Journals of Mary Wallis, 1851–1853,* D. Routledge (ed.). Suva, Fiji: Institute of Pacific Studies and Salem, Mass.: Peabody Essex Museum.

White, H. (1978). *Tropics of Discourse: Essays in Cultural Criticism.* Baltimore: Johns Hopkins University Press.

—— (1987). *The Content of the Form: Narrative Discourse and Historical Representation.* Baltimore: Johns Hopkins University Press.

Chapter 3

Writing Local History in Solomon Islands

Ben Burt

The history and culture of the Pacific islands is seldom written by the people it most concerns, the islanders themselves, and this has long been recognized as a problem. From some foreign researchers, the principal authors of published Pacific ethnography and history, there have been calls for a voice for islanders who may be deprived of their own local history by their Western education, exploring the implications of translating from the oral tradition and making the results more accessible to them (see, for example, Howard 1993). For their part, islanders who have gained such a voice sometimes claim ownership of Pacific history in terms which challenge the validity of foreign scholarship, raising important questions about the political agenda of Pacific historians on both sides of the debate between 'insiders' and 'outsiders' (see, for example, Munro 1994). But these disputes over who Pacific history is written *by* can obscure some equally difficult questions about who it is written *for*. How far does this sometimes acrimonious debate echo the historical concerns of most ordinary islanders, when so many are disqualified by their lack of Western education even from hearing the echoes of their own voices in the published literature?

Cultural research by First Worlders in a Third World region like the Pacific is always susceptible to accusations of exploitation or paternalism, and likely to be regarded as parasitic on the oral tradition which supplies so much of its data. Its reputation is not improved by publications which pursue academic agenda more or less unintelligible to most ordinary islanders, sold at prices they cannot afford to pay, and these are poor defence against charges of profiting from their culture by rural people, or of academic imperialism by their educated compatriots. During the 1970s such objections were voiced in debates around the impending political independence of the new countries of Melanesia, which were taken up by many of the foreign researchers themselves, especially those based in academic institutions in the region such as the University of Papua New Guinea (UPNG) and the University of the South Pacific (USP) in Fiji. At a conference in 1975, published in *Research in Melanesia*, anthropologists defended the relevance and utility of foreign research through critiques of conventional academic agenda which recognized the obligations and responsibilities of researchers to their host communities and countries (see Strathern, Keesing, Frazer, Young, all 1975; also Horne 1975; Crocombe and Macdonald 1980). Such issues were high on the agenda of the first generation of indigenous scholars, including their own students, and were impressed upon future researchers like myself by the national research policies developed to safeguard local and national Melanesian interests through institutional control of foreign research and repatriation of its findings.

But, twenty years on, many of the issues raised in this debate are still unresolved. Neither national independence and research regulations nor the development of indigenous scholarship has prevented Pacific societies from exchanging their cultural autonomy for the cultural hegemony of 'the West', the ubiquitous culture of global capitalism, introduced through colonization but now increasingly mediated by indigenous educated élites. The oral traditions of the region, inherited as the local, often private, knowledge of families, clans and cults and renewed with the life experience of succeeding generations, continue to be marginalized and discredited by Western education, which has privileged the authority of published history ever since the first islanders learnt to read from the Bible. Oral tradition is being incorporated into the published indigenous literature required by increasingly integrated Pacific societies seeking new national and regional cultural identities, but how far this serves the interests of the local communities from which this oral tradition derives is another question. As islanders try to come to terms with Western culture and with the social dislocation entailed in the models of 'development' which it promotes, they have more reason than ever to retain the cultural autonomy which may enable them to learn from local experience of their past, as distinct from the historical and cultural perspectives which colour their formal education. As they struggle with opposing values of tradition and modernity, how might their work to reconstruct their cultures and identities be advanced by a history which develops from the oral tradition which it may eventually supersede? This is the question I want to explore[1] by looking at history in Solomon Islands.

Writing Solomon Islands History

When Michael Young commented in the *Research in Melanesia* debate that 'Melanesians must look primarily to each other – to artists, writers, historians, as well as anthropologists – in their quest for new identities' (1975:51), this was already beginning to happen in Solomon Islands. In the 1970s, historical and cultural studies by islanders of their own communities, islands or country were contributing to the development of an indigenous Pacific literature, paralleling that of the academically more developed centres of Papua New Guinea and Fiji. Joseph Waleanisia traces the florescence of Solomon Islands literature to the first generation of Islanders returning with overseas tertiary education, who began contributing to the *Kakamora Reporter* newsletter in 1970, as a medium for critical intellectual discussion in anticipation of the self-government and independence conferred in 1978 (Waleanisia 1989:38). During the same period the Solomon Islands Museum (later Cultural) Association was formed and in 1972 it began to publish a *Journal* with articles on local history and culture, not all by Solomon Islands authors, but intending 'to promote and preserve our unique heritage and cultural background', as the editor put it (Vol. 3, 1975:7). It also published booklets such as *Custom Stories* (Keevil 1972). As these initiatives faltered, new projects developed during the 1980s, with the crucial role of publisher taken mainly by the Institute of Pacific Studies of USP, through the USP Centre in Honiara. A Writers and Artists Association was formed in 1984 and a Historical Association in 1985, Islanders prominent in the colonial service wrote auto-biographies (Zoleveke 1980; Osifelo 1985) and others wrote works of fiction with autobiographical overtones (e.g. Orotaloa 1985), all providing commentaries on social change as experienced by the emerging educated élite. The Institute of Pacific Studies published important collections of articles, mainly by Islanders, on subjects of concern to Solomon Islands as a whole, such as land tenure

(1979), rural development (1981) and politics (1983). *'O'o*, an occasional *Journal of Solomon Islands Studies* published papers by Islanders, including *Oral Accounts from Solomon Islanders* on the Second World War (No. 4 1988), among its mostly academic, sometimes very specialized, papers. In the 1980s, writing on local history and culture as well as contemporary issues was promoted in secondary schools by the National Curriculum Centre, which published essays by secondary school students in magazines such as *Solomon Voices* (1982) and a schools newspaper *Kirio*, while newspapers such as *Solomon Star* and magazines such as *Link* from the Solomon Islands Development Trust gave increasing professional opportunities to Solomon Islands writers.

This indigenous literature, much of it historical, has been an important medium for Islanders to develop their own perspectives on their new country and its past. But the authors belong mainly to the small urban élite concerned with the administration and public policy of the Solomon Islands state. Their historical agenda has a special focus on the construction of cultural identities for the emerging political entities of islands, provinces, the nation or even the Melanesian or Pacific regions, furthering a project inherited from their colonial predecessors. This is spelt out quite explicitly in a particularly important contribution from the Institute of Pacific Studies, *Ples Blong Iumi* (1989), a collection of essays on Solomon Islands history, which is prefaced as follows by its (foreign) editor, the historian Hugh Laracy: 'this book has been designed as more than just an exercise in recording and commenting on the past. It is also an expression of nationalism ... an attempt to present an indigenous view of the Solomons' past. Indigenous, that is, in so far as the indigeneity it reflects is that of young, Western-educated, urban employed people of the 1980s' (Institute of Pacific Studies 1989:xi).

But how far is this indigenous view and its political agenda shared with the majority of less educated rural Solomon Islanders? In a critique of Pacific islanders own representations of their past, Roger Keesing (1989) points out that historical accounts are and have always been informed by political interests, but warns of the continuing hegemony of Western culture shaping islanders' views of their own history, even in political reaction against Western domination. As he suggests, the Western education of island authors may predispose them to objectify and essentialize the culture of the past under the influence of Western academic discourse. In the process they may also adopt representations of history and culture which are contradicted by rural people, at least according to more recent academic research. The example Keesing gives of islanders adopting anthropological misinterpretations, the representation of *mana* as spiritual power, is aptly illustrated in the contribution on religion in *Ples Blong Iumi*, written by an Anglican priest from the island of Malaita where Keesing researched his contradictory evidence for the indigenous concept (Fugui 1989). The kind of indigenous history represented by *Ples Blong Iumi* may be both necessary and inevitable to the process of political and cultural integration among a group of islands of about eighty different ethnic groups, originally united as Solomon Islands only by colonization. But many Solomon Islands authors are inevitably separated from the oral tradition of their ancestors by schooling away from home, and their work does not necessarily reflect the culture of the rural majority, or the agenda of a history they would read or write for themselves.

This divergence between the historical agenda of rural people and of educated élites can be a difficult issue for academic researchers, especially foreigners, who are likely to have a foot in both camps while belonging to neither. As Andrew Strathern pointed out in *Research in Melanesia*, as 'outsiders looking in' to rural communities, who take the position of 'insiders looking out', anthropologists should be able to communicate their research to both these indigenous parties (1975:24). However, their work is more often addressed to one another, and this is the common focus of more recent reflections on the subjective and cultural bias which anthropologists have brought to their representations of other people's realities. Such is the illuminating critique of these epistemological issues introducing Gewertz and Errington's *Twisted Histories* of the Chambri of Papua New Guinea, with which they legitimate their own commitment to the autonomy of their subjects in defence against 'Western hegemony' (1991:16–18). Their self-conscious attempt to communicate the experiences and aspirations of the Chambri is addressed to 'a relatively broad Western audience', in recognition that this may include some whose role in global economic relations will affect the lives of the Chambri themselves (1991:20).

For Solomon Islands, the strengths and weaknesses of this kind of academic agenda are well illustrated by the work of Roger Keesing, a strong advocate of researchers' responsibilities in the

Research in Melanesia debate, whose consciousness of Western cultural hegemony developed from his own research among the Kwaio of Malaita island. Keesing's response was to present oral testimony as an essential record of Kwaio perspectives on their own history and culture, quoting lengthy texts from his Kwaio informants as well as publishing extensive autobiographies of historical and anthropological interest (Keesing 1978; Fifi'i and Keesing 1989). While Gewertz and Errington direct their defence of Chambri autonomy against transnational forces of capitalist development such as tourism, Keesing also identifies threats to Kwaio autonomy within the national politics of their own country. He used Kwaio voices to address some difficult issues on behalf of a particularly disadvantaged and controversial Solomon Islands local community, at the expense of involving himself in some unpleasant local and national political rows.

But Keesing's accounts *of* the Kwaio (summarized, with his own research history, in Keesing 1992) do not seriously attempt to be *for* them since, like most Pacific histories, they are presented as scholarly discourse in expensive books, in a foreign language which inevitably distorts local concepts even for competent bilingual readers (of whom there are very few among his Kwaio informants). Despite the achievements of this kind of research in eliciting island voices and documenting and disseminating them around the world, it has not actually done very much to make these voices better heard within or between their own local communities, and this prompts certain questions on their behalf. Is there not another Pacific history to be written in which rural people might participate as both readers and writers? Might such a history help to empower their efforts to shape the development of their own societies, allowing them to represent themselves, to communicate with one another and with those intent on directing their futures for them? What might the content of this history be, and what could, or should, foreign researchers contribute to it?

In fact Keesing's contribution to Kwaio cultural autonomy, the focus of so much of his writing, also included practical measures which suggest some answers to these questions. He helped initiate a project, the Kwaio Cultural Centre, which did actually produce a body of literature not only about the Kwaio, but for them and also by them, as reading materials for the first local schools in the area. As described by David Akin (1995), one of the anthropologists responsible for this programme as foreign workers at the Centre, booklets derived from transcriptions of local oral history and stories were welcomed enthusiastically as a means of putting Western education to the service of indigenous knowledge in the cause of this cultural autonomy. This project illustrates well not only the distance between the kind of history rural islanders may be interested in reading and writing about and the agenda of academic research, but also the potential benefits of bringing the two together.

A range of similar practical responses are outlined in a study of *Oral Testimony and Development* (Slim and Thompson 1993), which pursues the principle of researchers 'applying what is heard in partnership with those who voice it' to give ordinary people 'a voice in the development debate', allowing them to challenge the autonomous power of the 'development establishment' (1993: 2–3). But this debate needs to begin among the local people themselves, while they are still unsure of the nature of the challenge posed by this 'development establishment'. It may not be simple for people to decide exactly what messages they want to voice, or to predict the implications of putting their oral traditions or political agenda into writing. They may find, like Gewertz and Errington's Chambri friends, that they cannot agree among themselves on what to write (1991:19, 147–68) or conclude, as both Keesing (1992:14) and Akin (1993:540) did for the Kwaio, that, even when they agree on what to publish, it cannot actually be written.

Solomon Islands History: A Local Agenda

I raised the question of what the agenda of a rural people's history might be with a man from another part of Malaita, Abraham Baeanisia, director of the Solomon Islands Development Trust and the chair of the Pacific Islands Association of Non-government Organizations (NGOs). He replied with a practical example of an exercise he had initiated himself, gathering members of his home community to check and compare their ancestry and kinship with one another in order to establish their relationships to their land, the principles by which they had inherited their various claims to it, and the practice of sharing and managing its use. This was not an academic exercise and it has not been published, but it is a useful illustration of the current historical concerns of Malaitans, which are very different from most published history of their island. It points to the contribution which members of the educated élite such as Baeanisia, and perhaps also foreign researchers, can make to local efforts at historical research by addressing issues such as land claims, which affect the people most immediately.

The significance people attribute to received tradition depends on the purposes it serves in interpreting the past to inform the present and predict the future. To explore this theme in more depth, and to anticipate some of the debates which might be raised by the writing of such local history, we should look into the oral tradition itself and what Islanders expect from it, before going on to consider what it might become if transformed into written history. I want to use the example of one small body of very local oral tradition from my own research on Malaita among the Kwara'ae people, neighbours of Keesing's Kwaio, to explore these questions and consider the implications of publishing what until now has been an almost entirely oral tradition. Having already published an academic history which draws upon some of this material and sets it in a broader context (Burt 1994a), I now want to consider what the oral tradition might contribute to the attempts at cultural reconstruction through which the Kwara'ae are seeking to direct their own futures, if it were published to communicate to them.

During the 1980s, while the Institute of Pacific Studies was publishing the works of educated Solomon Islanders, a learned but illiterate Kwara'ae elder called Samuel Alasa'a recorded several cassettes of stories for his sons, to pass on the knowledge he had gained during a lifetime of about a hundred years, from his own experience and from the stories of their ancestors since they first came to the island of Malaita. The result was a set of narratives in the Kwara'ae language, combining the history of these ancestors with the events of his own life; a kind of auto-biography of his family and clan, with comments on its significance for his descendants today. If read chronologically (which is not always how they were told) Alasa'a's stories begin with the origin of the Kwara'ae people, the establishment of their culture and the settlement of their lands, leading on to the migrations and feuds which shaped the local community of his own life and times. Much of this history is recounted with the explicit purpose of justifying important local political interests, in particular the identity, status and inheritance of Alasa'a's own ancestors, his family and clan, as well as the Kwara'ae people as a whole. The stories continue with the changes witnessed by his fathers and himself during the colonial period, from nineteenth-century labour migration to the arrival of Christianity in the 1900s, subjugation by the government in the late 1910s and his own experience of working on an overseas plantation and being tried by a colonial court in the 1910s. He contrasts his early years with the times of his own children and grandchildren, shaped by the economic development of Solomon Islands since the Second World War, with familiar warnings about the morality of the present generation.

For the present purpose, what is interesting about these stories is that they represent what a conservative and non-literate old man decided, and his literate but not highly educated sons accepted, were the most important experiences of his own life and of their ancestors which he had to pass on. He may not have expected them to be transcribed, let alone published (although he agreed to this in recording a last cassette for me shortly before his death) but they stand as a useful example of the kinds of oral tradition which Kwara'ae people wish to see documented and preserved. The story is full of important information on the culture of Alasa'a's life and times, usually implicit and often quite cryptic. This information may be intelligible, though unfamiliar, to his sons, rather less intelligible to his grandchildren, and quite mystifying to most people beyond Kwara'ae. However, there is hardly an incident in his stories which someone might not regard as more or less contentious. For local people, including Alasa'a's sons, for whom he recorded it, much of his account would be taken first of all as a series of claims and legitimations, sometimes in opposition to his own relatives and neighbours, sometimes with implications for broader debates in Malaita and Solomon Islands. A look at some of the themes of his stories will illustrate the kind of issues which would be raised by making Alasa'a's voice heard in Kwara'ae and beyond.

Alasa'a's Stories

Identity and Land

Chronologically, the story begins with an account of how the first ancestors of Kwara'ae came from Asia to settle the island of

Malaita, on the instructions of a Biblical god through the angel Gabriel. Versions of this story have been used by Kwara'ae activists since at least the 1940s to create a Kwara'ae ethnic identity and political solidarity, as a strategy for securing an otherwise fragmented tribal society against colonial and statist forces which seemed to threaten their own control of political, religious and economic development. As he tells it, the story proclaims Kwara'ae claims to their land as first settlers, their solidarity as descendants of common ancestors, and the Biblical origins and powerful taboos of the traditional religion of the ancestral ghosts which continue to inform their culture and identity as Christians.

As a symbolic statement of Kwara'ae political ambitions, there might be several implications to publishing this story, as I have already done several times, having been repeatedly presented with it for such a purpose (see, for example, Burt 1994a:22). On the one hand, Kwara'ae claims for local identity and autonomy, first made against the British colonial government, could be divisive and subversive to the solidarity of the new Solomon Islands state. During the 1980s there were indeed secessionist calls for a separate Kwara'ae 'province' (the status enjoyed by the island of Malaita as a whole). Given the somewhat problematic role of Malaitans as a political force within Solomon Islands, such claims might conceivably be used to support the kind of political campaigns fuelled by emerging class interests but disguised by the manipulation of ethnic tensions. On the other hand, despite the misgivings of successive governments, colonial and independent, such local pressures have already contributed to the development of a devolved system of provincial and local government in Solomon Islands. This, it could be argued, may provide some safeguard against the continuing exploitation of Solomon Islands by the kind of economic interests which operate by manipulating centralized political institutions through a co-opted governing élite. In either case, or other cases, the story has implications which go far beyond the discussions of Kwara'ae identity and political symbolism which I have used it for in academic publications.

But Alasa'a's main concerns are much more local, for the Kwara'ae origin story is a prelude to the history of his own family and clan and the birthright which he and his descendants inherit in the things established by these ancestors. For Alasa'a, as for all Malaitans, oral tradition concerns first of all the experiences of their own ancestors, who may be attributed a central role in events affecting their language group or island, while representing much more local interests and identities. The members of Alasa'a's clan, from Tolinga in the central bush, now live in various places west and east of the island, as well as in Honiara and other parts of the Solomons. Tolinga itself is but part of the larger dispersed Siale clan, named for the shrine said to have been founded by the first ancestors of Kwara'ae about thirty generations ago, where its members used to join for great sacrificial festivals in Alasa'a's younger days. In Alasa'a's account, it is the Siale or Tolinga ancestors who are credited with instituting the traditional religious and social order, as the early settlers dispersed throughout Kwara'ae but continued to send pigs back for sacrifice to their ancestral ghosts in the Siale shrine. This parochial view of Kwara'ae history is itself a reminder of the factionalism which Kwara'ae leaders have sought to overcome by using the story of Siale to emphasize their common ancestry, and as such it is likely to be contested by those whose own descent inclines them to believe other versions of events.

But for Alasa'a and his sons the real focus of this family history, the knowledge of their past which they regard as most important for their lives in the present, is the evidence it provides for the inheritance of their land. Much of this history is recounted as genealogies of one man begetting another, for the Kwara'ae inherit their strongest claims on both land and people through their ancestors in the male line. Men usually live with their fathers, brothers and sons, forming the core of a local clan whose mothers and wives come from other clans, as they give their sisters and daughters to marry elsewhere. These clans are named for the lands they inherit, including places they left generations ago as their ancestors migrated away, usually to live with relatives of other clans. Much of Alasa'a's historical knowledge is cited to demonstrate his family's claims to particular places by offering proof of occupation by their ancestors. As such it also demonstrates the important purpose of Kwara'ae oral tradition in explaining crucial relationships between people and land.

Tracing descent through the male line, Alasa'a describes how his ancestor came from Siale to settle Tolinga nine generations after the first ancestors arrived and fourteen generations before his own time, making Tolinga, in Kwara'ae terms, Alasa'a's original home. But his story mainly concerns that part of the Tolinga clan which moved, now seven or eight generations ago, to the land of Fairū in the district where Alasa'a spent most of his own life, near the east coast. Alasa'a explains how the first settlers of Fairū and the neighbouring lands also originated from Siale, sharing a common ancestor with the founder of Tolinga more than twenty generations ago, and moving down over several generations from the central bush to settle at various places nearer the coasts. Alasa'a would have some claim to these lands as a distant clan brother of the first Fairū settlers, born of the same ancestors through the male line. But closer and stronger are his claims through his mother, his father's mother and his father's father's mother, all daughters of Fairū, who linked their clan by marriage to Tolinga men. These were the ties which enabled his Tolinga ancestors to live and garden in Fairū and, until Alasa'a's own youth, to sacrifice to Fairū ancestors for the spiritual support and protection which affirmed their Fairū inheritance. Since Alasa'a's mother had no clan brothers, he was eventually able to claim control of Fairū land through his female ancestors and take on the priesthood for the Fairū ghosts.

The details of this story, actually a great deal more complex than indicated here, may not be of great interest to anyone who does not have a personal interest in Fairū land, beyond demonstrating how long and complex Kwara'ae history can be. But the story also raises issues which have a far broader significance for Kwara'ae and beyond, and the most obvious of these concerns current debates over the future of traditional land tenure systems in Malaita and Solomon Islands. Despite the emphasis which Kwara'ae place on inheritance in the male line, giving men 'seniority' and 'leadership' for the land of their fathers and clan, Alasa'a's claim to Fairū demonstrates the even more important principle that everyone inherits the right to live and garden on the land of both their parents and all their previous ancestors. This contradicts arguments within Kwara'ae and beyond for converting a flexible communal system of land tenure into more exclusive patrilineal patterns of inheritance, more compatible with Western models of rural economic development but not necessarily with the best interests of rural communities. Taking this kind of evidence into full account would certainly complicate some currently rather simplistic legislative proposals for a programme of land registration based heavily on 'primary rights' inherited in the male line.

Whether or not land is to be registered, publishing land claims such as Alasa'a's also raises the vexed question of the effect of fixing an oral tradition in more or less immutable written form. Anthropology has long recognized the flexibility of oral tradition in adjusting to the circumstances it is used to legitimate, particularly to land claims which are constantly modified according to demographic and political change. Until now this flexibility has probably played an important part in the equitable distribution of people over available land which is characteristic of Melanesian land tenure systems. Kwara'ae, on the other hand, constantly proclaim their genealogical charters to land as timeless and unchanging, confidently refuting evidence to the contrary when it comes in the form of contradictory genealogies. They have a special faith in documentation as a means of resolving such contradictions by legitimating genealogical history, preferably after it has been properly researched and agreed by everyone who has a vested interest in it, as in Baeanisia's experiment already mentioned. The most successful Kwara'ae efforts to write their own history have been programmes to record genealogies and landmarks, currently the focus of pan-Kwara'ae efforts to organize themselves politically through a 'Kwara'ae Traditional Culture and Environment Conservation Foundation' and to raise funds for land registration programmes. The organizers look to the nineteenth-century land registration programme in Fiji, undeterred by, or perhaps unaware of, the way this may actually modify their land tenure system, particularly by undermining the rights of those 'born of women' (see Burt 1994b for more detailed discussion of these land issues). Anthropologists may not be thanked for warning that fixing such histories in print could eventually cause new conflicts as the relationships they legitimate between people and land continue to change from generation to generation.

As Kwara'ae becomes an increasingly literate society, more people will seek to create such written charters for their land, both to secure their hope for a stake in the capitalist economy through some kind of 'development', and to guarantee their independence from this economy through subsistence farming. Such charters will be contested from the start if they are published unilaterally as the oral traditions of a particular family or clan rather than through the kind of consultation involved in land registration. Much of Alasa'a's history of Fairū and neighbouring lands and clans is of this kind, presented in defence of competing claims by his relatives and neighbours, often with rather vehement denunciations of them. In fact Alasa'a often speaks as if he were engaged in one of the land disputes which have plagued Kwara'ae in recent generations, where the parties quarrel in court over their ancestors' origins, their places of residence and their leadership for the land:

> Listen Rara, I deny Gwaunafau to you [the place where Rara lives]. Where is your [ancestor's] house site? Where is the men's house site where you [your ancestors] lived? How is it my landmarks are in you place and you're challenging me? You just go to 'Aenakwata [Rara's 'original home']. You were born of Ra'ena, you were born of Gwaulumu, you didn't live at Tolinga . . . [and so on]

But, given the nature of Kwara'ae oral tradition and its concern for the origins of local people and places, it would be difficult to publish a local history which did not have this potential for fuelling land disputes.

Old Grievances and New Disputes

To complicate matters further, in tracing his ties with neighbouring clans, Alasa'a relates incidents, characteristic of Kwara'ae local history, involving ancient quarrels, fights and killings which displaced and relocated families and clans. These events give important insights into the politics of the precolonial period, particularly the exchanges of death and wealth between groups of proud and vengeful men defending the honour and security of their local clans. But these too may reverberate in the present, fuelling antagonisms and possibly even stimulating new demands for restitution or retribution. Kwara'ae have long memories and some might consider such things better forgotten than revived and preserved by publication.

These considerations can become more immediate as oral traditions approach the present, in the kind of personal recollections which form the most recent section of Alasa'a's story. Earlier periods, between the arrival of the first ancestors and the arrival of the Europeans, have the undifferentiated and repetitive quality of genealogies, as one generation of tribal farmers succeeds the next. In contrast, later episodes illustrate the transformation of Kwara'ae society during the colonial period, for Alasa'a witnessed and recalled with remarkable clarity some crucial incidents leading to the Christian conversion and colonial subjugation of Kwara'ae.

Where there are contemporary written records such as missionary letters and government patrol reports, he corroborates them in unusual detail, with additional information on events such as the internal feuding which continued beyond the reach of colonial witnesses until about 1920. Unlike the ancient genealogical stories, this more recent past no longer even appears to repeat itself. The experiences of Alasa'a's early life are of a society facing the unprecedented and irrevocable change created by the colonial intrusion, first through labour migration and then by the arrival of mission and government. His recollections are of particular importance in explaining Kwara'ae society today, as the undifferentiated past of precolonial times becomes yearly more distant and exotic to younger generations caught up in processes of chronic social change.

Kwara'ae colonial history has until now been documented mainly in colonial records and academic histories, and Alasa'a's stories have an obvious interest in providing local perspectives to corroborate or contradict these accounts. He describes the effects of imported metal tools and crops in his father's time, marvelling at the contrast with the plentiful foods and iron-roofed timber houses of his old age; he recalls the blood-feuding of his youth and the taste of human flesh, and then describes the political and religious developments which abolished this institutional violence. Alasa'a was related both to the pioneers who returned from work on the plantations of Queensland to establish the first Christian settlements on the Kwara'ae coast in the 1900s, and to their persecutors who harassed them as a threat to the traditional religious and political order. He was a distant son to the man who assisted the government in subduing the local warriors and became the first government headman of the district, and he married the daughter of one of its most notorious warriors. His stories confirm the active roles of named Kwara'ae people on both sides of the colonial struggle, from a perspective their descendants may never read in Western accounts of these events, recounting a history which indeed belongs to local people, and not simply to their colonizers. Alasa'a acknowledges the role of government law in subduing the warriors of East Kwara'ae and seems to accept it, without either the resentment sometimes voiced by the most militant anticolonial resistance, or the triumphalism of the most enthusiastic Christians. As he puts it, 'I've upheld tradition, later on I went to law, and I belong to church today. . . . The law is mine and the government holds on to me, but my tradition will go on and the government watches over me.'

But such equanimity may not allow the Kwara'ae to escape the echoes of a violent past reverberating down the generations in communities which still inherit from their ancestors their loyalties and grievances, as they do their land. An illustration is provided by Alasa'a's account of how the famous District Officer William Bell finally subdued East Kwara'ae by killing four people in an attack on a village in 1919. As Alasa'a puts it, 'That's how the law came and spread over our country and prevented killing . . . He subdued the land of Malaita and they were afraid to kill anyone.' I first investigated this story in 1983, at a time when publicity around a book by Keesing on Bell's own death at the hands of the Kwaio in 1927 and the retaliatory police massacres (Keesing and Corris 1980) was reopening old wounds on Malaita (see Keesing 1992, ch. 18, on this controversy). Kwara'ae elders were reluctant to disclose details of the 1919 deaths for fear of renewing grievances of the kind still pursued by the Kwaio, more than fifty years on, as massive compensation claims from the government. Alasa'a's account gives graphic detail of how and where each of the Kwara'ae victims were shot; he helped to bury their remains. When such old grievances are revived they may fuel new disputes among the descendants of protagonists long dead, who included local people among Bell's supporters and avengers as well as his enemies.

Like the documentation of land claims, publication of such old stories will make it more difficult for local people to conceal, forget or amend their history to avoid or resolve conflicts of interest in the present. In fact it is likely to provoke new controversies as people become aware, sometimes perhaps for the first time, of other versions of local events which contradict their own family histories. Even an English-language publication available only in Honiara can provoke indignation among people in the rural area when relayed by readers who object to it for their own reasons, as with Keesing's history of Bell. Foreign researchers are of course easy targets for people wishing to make political capital from accusations of historical and cultural misrepresentation, but local authors, or in Alasa'a's case his sons, are also vulnerable to accusations of manipulating history for their own ends.

Towards History for Local People

Perhaps such controversy is the inevitable or necessary price to be paid for developing a written history from an oral tradition. To take up another comment from Abraham Baeanisia, as a Malaitan with special experience of cultural development issues in his island and country, only when such contested histories are published will people be able to address the issues raised by doing so, to decide what the agenda of a local history is to be. Only then will they begin to decide in their own terms the issues of research methodology, epistemology and representation which already concern academics, and recognize perhaps that written history may have to be negotiated in ways that oral tradition does not.

One of the questions they will need to deal with is the language of publication, given the widespread recognition of the inadequacy of English or Pijin to convey the subtleties of local culture. Considering that Pijin is the lingua franca of Solomon Islands, the fact that most local publications are still in the colonial language is only partly explained by the linguistic diversity of the country. English, the language of secondary education and the official language of the adminstration, has the additional advantage of communicating beyond Solomon Islands or Melanesia, but the difficulty which most Islanders have in reading it, let alone writing it with confidence and fluency, seriously diminishes the value of English publications for local histories. There have been a few attempts to develop Pijin as an alternative, more accessible, language for publication, notably *The Big Death* (Institute of Pacific Studies 1988), a book growing out of academic historical research but composed entirely of verbatim accounts from Solomon Islands veterans of the Second World War, with English translations. Other more modest Pijin publications include *Link Komik* cartoon books from the Solomon Islands Development Trust and occasional booklets (e.g. Ereba'ea 1982). But Pijin has yet to be generally accepted as the written language it has become in Papua New Guinea. It is more often treated as a variant of English and written accordingly, probably with much semantic confusion (as a glance at earlier Solomon Islands versions of the Jehovah's Witness *Watchtower* magazine will show).

But more to the point, although Pijin may reach a broader less educated readership than English, it is still a medium for a

Solomon Islands culture rather than for a history true to local cultural traditions, which requires first of all the use of local languages. In the *Research in Melanesia* debate, another researcher on Malaita, Ian Frazer, recommended that anthropologists 'involve people in our research much more as collaborators or equal partners,' and suggested writing 'straight history' in local languages (1975:48). Twenty years later, most local-language publications in Solomon Islands are still Christian texts, but a few histories have been published, including the Kwaio Cultural Centre booklets dictated by local people for local readers (e.g. Fifi'i 1993; Ma'aanamae 1993; Sulafanamae 1993), as well as various collections of so-called 'custom stories', often with English translations (Stubbs 1989; *Falafala Kwara'ae ki* (Institute of Pacific Studies 1990); Davis 1991; Makini 1991). The most ambitious of these is Rolf Kuschel's comprehensive oral history of Bellona island (1988), published as part of an academic project. Significantly, it includes English translations, to the benefit not only of academic readers but also of Solomon Islanders of other languages, who may thereby compare other local traditions for the better understanding of their own.

As for the agenda of such history, as Young pointed out in *Research in Melanesia* twenty years ago (1975:58–9), Melanesians are less likely to be interested in anthropology as a comparative study than in documentation of their own local cultures and oral history, a project in which local people can participate on their own account. Educated Islanders, like foreign researchers, may employ the insights of anthropology when they edit and word-process texts like Alasa'a's stories, or co-author accounts of local culture with local people (e.g. Burt and Kwa'ioloa 1993). If and when rural people are able to publish for themselves, they may produce oral history texts like the Kwaio, but they are as likely to concentrate on legitimating political and economic interests and cultural practices, from ethnic identities and land rights to traditional law and Christian ritual. They may well seek to support local oral tradition with the exotic literary sources which seem most accessible and relevant to their situation, but these may not be the relatively inaccessible academic histories and ethnographies. Biblical texts, especially from the Old Testament, originating as they do from rather similar oral traditions, have much more resonance with people like the Kwara'ae, and even non-literate religious sceptics like Alasa'a legitimate their historical origins in

Biblical rather than secular Western history. It is likely that some of the resulting histories will have more in common with the 'Chambri Bible' described by Gewertz and Errington, synthesized from often contradictory oral traditions and Biblical texts (1991:154), than with academic Pacific histories.

Academics whose own agenda requires them to cross-examine and deconstruct the symbolism of such literature may risk upsetting local historians, as islanders' objections to concepts such as the 'invention of tradition' have shown (see Linnekin 1992). But the academics might well pause to consider that they themselves are engaged in symbolic disputes in pursuit of political or ideological agenda which are equally questionable to islanders, and that looking askance at islanders' attempts to write their own history in their own terms will be regarded as patronizing and colonial. If anthropologists in particular are able to acquiesce and participate in local beliefs and practices they have no personal commitment to in the cause of their research, they can hardly decline to assist the development of Pacific local history merely because it contravenes the epistemological conventions and academic standards of their own discipline. If they are prepared to become involved in local publication programmes themselves, an offer of academic skills and resources will be no more than fair recompense for the research data they obtain in the process. The more important consideration would seem to be how we should evaluate the agenda of these histories in terms of their contribution to the ongoing transformation of the societies from which they emerge. This is a difficult task, full of contradictions and pitfalls, as the example of one small body of Kwara'ae history demonstrates. But the issues are those which anthropology claims to elucidate, so perhaps the constitution of local Pacific histories should be among its tasks.

Notes

1. I would like to thank Michael Kwa'ioloa for transcribing and making available the stories recorded by his late father Samuel Alasa'a and Abraham Baeanisia for sharing his own insights

into some of the issues I have raised. For helpful comments on
earlier drafts of the chapter I am grateful to Michael O'Hanlon,
David Akin and Andrew Strathern. None of these people are
responsible for the way I have interpreted their contributions.

References

Akin, D. (1993). Negotiating Culture in East Kwaio, Solomon
Islands. PhD Dissertation, University of Hawaii.
—— (1995). Cultural Education at the Kwaio Cultural Centre. In:
L. Lindstrom and G. White (eds), *Culture, Kastom, Tradition:
Developing Cultural Policy in Melanesia*, pp. 161–72. Suva:
University of the South Pacific, Institute of Pacific Studies.
Burt, B. (1994a). *Tradition and Christianity: The Colonial Trans-
formation of a Solomon Islands Society*. New York: Harwood
Academic Publishers.
—— (1994b). Land in Kwara'ae and Development in Solomon
Islands. *Oceania* 64:317–35.
Burt, B. and Kwa'ioloa, M. (1993). *Falafala ana Ano 'i Kwara'ae: The
Tradition of Land in Kwara'ae*. Suva: University of the South
Pacific, Institute of Pacific Studies.
Crocombe, R. and Macdonald, B. (1980) The Academic Imperialism
Problem. Correspondence in *Pacific Viewpoint* 21:71–2.
Davis, K. (1991). *Vivinei Ruruhu pa Hoava: Custom Stories from Hoava*.
Gizo: Western Province Government.
Ereba'ea, S. (1982). *Stori Abaotem Pita Abu'ofa*. [n.p.]: Solomon
Islands Christian Association.
Fifi'i, J. (1993). *Rua Siisifonga ala Jonathon Fifi'i*, D. Akin and
K. Gillogly (eds). Malaita: Kwaio Cultural Centre.
Fifi'i, J. and Keesing, R.M. (1989). *From Pig Theft to Parliament: My
Life Between Two Worlds*. Honiara: Solomon Islands College of
Higher Education; Suva: University of the South Pacific.
Frazer, I. (1975). What's in it for Us? *Research in Melanesia* 1:40–1.
Fugui, L. (1989). Religion. In: *Ples Blong Iumi: Solomon Islands, the
Past Four Thousand Years*, pp. 73–93. Suva: University of the
South Pacific, Institute of Pacific Studies.
Gewertz, D. and Errington, F. (1991). *Twisted Histories, Altered
Contexts: Representing the Chambri in a World System*. Cambridge:
Cambridge University Press.

Horne, J. (1975). Research No Practical Use? Correspondence in *Research in Melanesia* 1:1.

Howard, A. (1993). Reflections on History in Polynesia. In: T. Otto (ed.), *Pacific Islands Trajectories: Five Personal Views*, pp. 83–97. Canberra: Australian National University, Research School of Pacific and Asian Studies; Nijmegen: University of Nijmegen, Centre for Pacific Studies.

Institute of Pacific Studies, University of the South Pacific, Suva. (Authorship of these books is credited jointly to the contributors.)

—— (1979). *Land in Solomon Islands*.

—— (1981). *The Road Out: Rural Development in Solomon Islands*.

—— (1983). *Solomon Islands Politics*.

—— (1988). *The Big Death: Solomon Islanders Remember World War II*.

—— (1989). *Ples Blong Iumi: Solomon Islands, the Past Four Thousand Years*.

—— (1990). *Falafala 'i Kwara'ae ki: Kwara'ae Traditions*.

Journal of the Solomon Islands Museum Association (1975), vol. 3. Honiara.

Keesing, R.M. (1975). Anthropology in Melanesia: Retrospect and Prospect. *Research in Melanesia* 1:32–9.

—— (1978). *Elota's Story: The Life and Times of a Solomon Islands Big Man*. Santa Lucia: University of Queensland Press.

—— (1989). Creating the Past: Custom and Identity in the Contemporary Pacific. *The Contemporary Pacific* 1:19–42.

—— (1992). *Custom and Confrontation: the Kwaio Struggle for Cultural Autonomy*. Chicago and London: University of Chicago Press.

Keesing, R.M. and Corris, P. (1980). *Lightning Meets the West Wind*. Melbourne: Oxford University Press.

Keevil, D. (1972). *Custom Stories*. Honiara: Solomon Islands Museum Association.

Kuschel, R. (1988). *Vengeance is Their Reply. Language and Culture of Rennell and Bellona Islands*. Copenhagen: Dansk Psykologisk Forlag (Language and Culture of Renell and Bellona Islands, vol. 7, part 2).

Linnekin, J. (1992). On the Theory and Politics of Cultural Construction in the Pacific. *Oceania* 64:249–63.

Ma'aanamae (1993). *Mae Suria Waawane*, D. Akin and J. Laete'esafi (eds). Malaita: Kwaio Cultural Centre.

Makini, J. (1991). *Na Buka Vivinei Malivi pa Zinama Roviana: Roviana Custom Stories Book.* Gizo: Western Province Government.

Munro, D. (1994). Who 'Owns' Pacific History? Reflections on the Insider/Outsider Dichotomy. *Journal of Pacific History* 29:232–7.

Orotaloa, R.T. (1985). *Two Times Resurrection.* Honiara: University of the South Pacific Solomon Islands Centre.

Osifelo, F. (1985). *Kanaka Boy.* Suva: University of the South Pacific, Institute of Pacific Studies.

Slim, H. and Thompson, P. (1993). *Listening for a Change: Oral Testimony and Development.* London: Panos Publications.

Solomon Voices (1982). A Collection of Writing by Solomon Islands Secondary School Students. Honiara: Curriculum Development Centre.

Strathern, A. (1975). The Future for Research in Melanesia. *Research in Melanesia* 1:23–31.

Stubbs, L. (1989). *Manoga Maka Vavakato pa Ganoqa: Eleven Stories from Ranongga.* Gizo: Western Province Government.

Sulafanamae. (1993). *Mae na Si'isi'inga*, D. Akin (ed.). Malaita: Kwaio Cultural Centre. (First published in 1982.)

Waleanisia, J. (1989). Writing I. In: *Ples Blong Iumi: Solomon Islands, the Past Four Thousand Years*, pp. 31–40. Suva: University of the South Pacific, Institute of Pacific Studies.

Young, M. (1975). History or Nothing? *Research in Melanesia* 1:50–60.

Zoleveke, G. (1980). *Zoleveke: A Man from Choiseul.* Suva: University of Suva, Institute of Pacific Studies.

Chapter 4

'Noble Savages' and the 'Islands of Love': Trobriand Islanders in 'Popular Publications'

Gunter Senft[1]

Ist einmal . . . eine recht handgreifliche Abgeschmacktheit zu Papier gebracht, so rollt selbige unablässig von Buch zu Buch, und es ist das erste, wonach die Büchermacher greifen (Adalbert von Chamisso).[2]

The 'Savage' and the 'Civilized'

A closer look at the history and quality of the contact between European and non-European cultures overseas from the early days of colonialism in the fifteenth and sixteenth century till now reveals that this contact has been characterized from the very beginning by the conviction of dominant superiority of the Europeans with respect to the representatives of the overseas cultures.[3] This conviction manifests itself in between two extremes: overseas cultures experience(d) either intolerant damnation or pitiful recognition of their forms of civilization as being inferior with respect to European standards. The claim of European cultural supremacy was based on the military superiority of European weapons and warfare. However, it was also the ideological justification for turning the contacted cultures into colonies to be exploited commercially by the respective European power. Finally, this European position also justified activities to 'civilize' these inferior cultures.[4]

It is evident that this conviction of European superiority made any attempts to understand some of the characteristics of the contacted cultures extremely difficult. It is interesting, however, to note that with the very first ethnographic reports on overseas cultures we find the picture of the 'good savage' emerging, a picture that was revitalized and made permanent for the discussion of representatives of overseas cultures by Bougainville's 1772 description of the 'noble savages' of Tahiti (Bougainville 1985; see also Kohl 1986:19). The 'civilized' European was thus not forced any more to deal with the 'savage' only: there was the 'noble savage' as well; and this other, new 'ethnocentric' construction by overseas peoples' representatives made Europeans feel somewhat uncomfortable within their own culture about projecting their ideals, longings and hopes onto these 'noble savages' and their 'exotic' cultures, which were assumed to be 'unspoilt' by all negative aspects of European civilization, its rules, repressions and moral standards.

It seems that these 'discontents' of civilization had been strongest with respect to European standards of sexual morals and behaviour – if we keep in mind how Cook's, Forster's and especially Bougainville's travelogues, with their descriptions of how the Tahitians enjoyed their sexuality in their South Seas paradise of 'La Nouvelle Cythère', were received by the contempories of these explorers and scientists in Europe. With the myth of the 'noble savage' Europeans combined a utopian construction of the ideal exotic person living a natural life in a society imagined to be completely free from any kind of repression. However, 'noble savages' were also imagined to have no problems in adapting to European standards of civilized behaviour when being transferred from their 'exotic paradises' to Europe.

We are easily tempted to look at the 'noble savage' myth as being a mere historical fact. However, I will show that this is not the case. On the contrary, it seems that we are far from having outgrown this 'noble savage Utopia'. We still seem to misunderstand certain patterns of public behaviour and self-presentation, especially if these behaviour patterns are perceived as being erotic or sexually arousing – as Cook and his crew and other first visitors to the South Seas did – disregarding the fact that a closer look at these patterns would reveal important differences between underlying rules or regulations and the perceived form of the respective behaviour. Marshall Sahlins (1985; see also Rensch 1991) has convincingly summarized such cultural misunderstandings. It seems that in the South Seas bare-breasted women in short grass skirts, or athletic men wearing their loincloths, joking with Western tourists, still invoke in these foreigners the image of a sexual paradise – although we should know better by now. In what follows I will use the Trobriand case to illustrate these points.[5]

Malinowski's *Sexual Life of Savages* and Reich's *Invasion of Compulsory Sex Morality*

In 1929 Bronislaw Malinowski published his monograph *The Sexual Life of Savages in Northwestern Melanesia*. In this book the master of Trobriand ethnography describes comprehensively aspects of the Trobriand Islanders' sexuality, covering topics like sexual behaviour in children, adolescents and adults, sexual innuendoes in games and verbal interaction, sexual taboos, rules for marriage and married adults, sexual aberrations (from the Trobrianders' point of view), forms of, and variation in, sexual intercourse, and so on. Although many parts of this book present a rather dry sociological account of strict rules that regulate societal life on the Trobriands, those paragraphs that emphasize the sexual freedom and the general promiscuity of young unmarried Trobrianders immediately got a reception that distinctly reached beyond the circle of anthropologists. First, this reception remained within academic and literary circles: psychologists and literati[6] referred either in detail or just in passing to Malinowski's research. However, these references were soon picked up by the more popular media, especially by newspapers and periodicals, and up till now the Trobriand Islands are usually referred to in these media with the *epitheton ornans* 'the Islands of Love'. What is most striking is the fact that most writers referring to Malinowski's monograph or to the Trobrianders' sexuality seem to have not read Malinowski at all or to have read him with such a biased point of view that they completely misrepresent his insights into this part of the Trobrianders' life.[7]

One of the first, probably most influential, persons referring to Malinowski's research on the Trobrianders' sexuality was Wilhelm Reich. In his monograph *The Invasion of Compulsory Sex Morality*[8] Reich connects his research with Malinowski's book and claims to have used the facts the anthropologist presented to 'round up' his own research. However, it is actually the first 84 pages of Reich's book (of 202 pages) that topicalize the Trobrianders' sexuality. Although in his 1951 preface Reich expresses his hope not to have made any bad mistakes in reporting on Malinowski's research (Reich 1972:25), the very first page of the first chapter proves that this hope was in vain. I will illustrate this with a few examples:

Although many chapters of Malinowski's monograph deal with regulations that govern the Trobrianders' sexuality, Reich denies the existence of any of these rules, to which he refers as 'moral norms'. Thus, Reich (1972:30) denies that there is voyeurism on the Trobriands – with special reference to voyeurism in childhood. I have not only experienced voyeurism in Trobriand children and adults, I also collected four terms that refer to the act of 'peeping' (Senft 1986:539); the expressions *totadoyai* and *natadoyai* explicitly refer to male or female 'peeping Toms' – regardless of their age.

Although Malinowski (1929:433–51) describes the most important taboo on the Trobriands, the 'brother–sister taboo', emphasizing that siblings must not know anything about each other's love affairs, Reich states that children are sexually instructed by their elder siblings and that their parents discuss their children's sexual affairs (Reich 1972:31ff.). Even nowadays this sounds horrendous to any Trobriander – and there is no proof for this statement in Malinowski's monograph.

Reich denies any cases of suicides in puberty on the Trobriands because of sexual frustration; however, in Malinowski's days even an adolescent having had a sexual affair with a married person was forced to commit suicide once this fact became publicly known. This obligation was a strong moral norm supporting the ideal of the monogamous life of married Trobrianders (Malinowski 1929:97ff.). Although the verbal expression that refers to this form of suicide (*-lou-*) is still known on the Trobriands, the norm is no longer valid these days. However, extramarital affairs that become public knowledge are still regarded as something shameful and are looked at as really scandalous.[9]

Reich (1972:42) states that Trobrianders are direct in their courting behaviour. This is sheer nonsense (if we understand that courting behaviour results in seduction). Trobrianders are quite indirect in courting – which should not be mixed up with light-hearted, direct flirting. In verbal flirting and banter Trobrianders can always recede from what they have said by labelling it as *sopa*, as something they did not really mean to say, as a joke in a not serious relationship (Senft 1991:237ff.). As to courting behaviour, Trobrianders use the assistance of a go-between for arranging first dates. The basic motive behind this is to keep face if their proposition is turned down by the desired person. The better adolescents court (on the Trobriands and elsewhere), the better are their chances to have dates with desired partners. The most direct way to get a sexual partner is still the use of love magic; however, to get this love magic (usually transported in a betel-nut) to the desired person asks for much discretion and cleverness.

Reich (1972:52) also states that there is no homosexuality on the Trobriands. This is not true. Malinowski (1929:395, 397–8) refers to cases of homosexuality, and his observation that this form of sexuality is discriminated against and marked as aberrant by the Islanders still holds.

Finally, Reich (1972:56) postulates that the Trobrianders' erotic fantasies are 'relatively slothful'; this is just ridiculous. A look at the data my wife and I have been gathering on songs, play accompanying verses, jokes, lullabies, stories, fairy tales, etc., show that the Trobrianders' erotic fantasies are far from being under-developed; they may be rather blunt sometimes, but they can also be extremely sophisticated (Eibl-Eibesfeldt and Senft 1986, 1992; Senft and Senft 1986).

I will stop quoting Reich's misreadings of Malinowski here; his mistakes are too obvious for anyone familiar with the Trobrianders' culture. However, I want to point out that Reich has to be blamed for being one of the first writers who took the Trobrianders as proof for his ideals with respect to a human sexuality completely free from any neurotic aspects. Reich projected his ideals into the 'Savages of Northwestern Melanesia' – thus reviving the 'noble savage' myth and the imaginary ethnography of the nineteenth century (Kramer 1981). I assume that Reich's references to the Trobrianders had at least the same results for the Trobrianders as Mead's *Coming of Age in Samoa* (1928) had for the Samoans: Reich's references to the Trobrianders seem to have not been recognized as pieces of fiction but have been mistaken as fact – and, unfortunately, these 'facts' have been perpetuated by many others, as we shall see now.

The 'Islands of Love' – Fact and Popular Fiction

Ever since I started my research on the Trobriands in 1982, friends have been sending me copies of articles they have found that refer to the Trobrianders – and I also keep this collection up to date. In what follows I will present a random selection[10] of this collection to illustrate what some authors have to say about the Trobrianders – who for their part have (so far) hardly any means to protest against some of this propagated 'news'.

It is to be expected that writers for the American *Playboy* company pick up rumours about the 'sex paradise' on the Trobriands for economic reasons – and Roger Baker has done so. In 1983 he published a book on 'Free Love' (in a German *Playboy* paperback series), where – in a chapter on the Trobrianders (Baker 1983:67–75) – he declares Malinowski's monograph as being 'the bible' for all supporters of the free-love movement. Baker refers to the *bukumatula* as the house of unmarried girls where the Trobriand adolescents celebrate 'wild sexual orgies'. In Malinowski's time the *bukumatula* was a house built by the male bachelors where they had dates with their girlfriends. It was not too long after Malinowski's stay on the Trobriands that these *bukumatula* were abolished – under the influence of the Australian patrol officers and because of strong pressure from Lutheran United Church missionaries. When I first came to the Trobriands in 1982, the *bukumatula* was already history. As soon as a young man thinks himself to be old enough these days, he just builds his own small bachelor house – generally in the vicinity of his family's house. Baker also refers to kissing, but does not mention that the Trobrianders – at least at the time when Baker's book was published – did not kiss as Europeans do. They then had a form of sniff-kissing. Although Malinowski pointed out that monogamy was (and is) the ideal form of married life on the Trobriands, Baker does not hesitate to proclaim general promiscuity and exchange of sex partners between married couples. According to Baker, the change of sex partners by the hour is not uncommon for Trobriand adolescents. He denounces the Islanders not only as exhibitionists, but even worse as egotists who have no feeling of any kind of responsibility for their partners. Fantasizing like this he gives his readers the impression that his 'statements' were based on Malinowski's research. To sell this book in a country like America, however, where sexual explicitness is still tempered by Puritan ideas, Baker has to express – at the end of his 'essay' – his 'disgust' with respect to the described 'sensational' sexual practices, and to file his caveat with respect to possible demands to take over these 'savage' forms of sexuality in America or Europe. Thus, the author is completely aware of the double moral standards in his own culture – but does not care at all whether or not his writings about another ethnic group may insult members of this society.[11]

The publications by Reich and Baker were written by authors who never set foot on the Trobriands. However, people who visit the Islands and then write in the popular media about their impressions rather rarely surpass the 'quality' of accounts like those quoted above.

In 1985 Marianne Oertl reports on a visit of the Trobriand Islands in a German semi-scientific magazine under the heading 'The Trobrianders' natural eroticism: What will become of the "Islands of Love"' – and here we hit upon this *epitheton ornans* which is to be found as a part of the title of many articles on the Trobriand Islands in the popular press (therefore, I also used it in the title of this chapter). Oertl not only gets some of the basic facts about canoes, kinship and status wrong, she also perpetuates the myth of the Trobrianders' being unaware of the role of the father as 'genitor' and states that the famous *kula* exchange is endangered. Some of the things she reports must be based on hearsay only – like her reference to the *Melanesian Explorer* – a tourist ship that visited the Trobriands regularly on its cruises in Milne Bay Province. This ship, like the *Melanesian Discoverer* replacing it in 1989, could not carry more than 32 tourists; Oertl reports that, whenever the *Explorer* dropped anchor, hundreds of tourists were invading the Trobriand villages. She gives the impression that this kind of tourism is as responsible for destroying and perverting basic characteristics of Trobriand culture as the sex tourism of the worst kind that we also find there. However, the owners of these ships, Jane and Peter Barter, have been extremely careful not to disturb the villages and the people they visit with tourist groups in Papua New Guinea. I think the Barters have established an exemplary way to run a tourist business in a developing country.[12] What upsets the reader is Oertl's patronizing attitude with which she looks down on the Trobrianders from an arrogant and a presumed superior European point of view. In her article she speaks of some features of a minority complex she observed in some Trobrianders (a feature that neither Annette Weiner nor I – not to speak of Malinowski (1967) – have ever had the opportunity to observe with the Massim), and tries to protect the Trobrianders from civilization – opting for careful European support for the Islanders on their 'long and winding road' to civilization. Oertl's weird attitude culminates in the unwittingly revealing statement 'But the Trobrianders are human beings'! A few paragraphs before this statement, Oertl had no problem with denouncing some of the Trobriand women as prostitutes who could not resist the temptations of the white men's money and who – with their bare breasts, sexy grass skirts, and free attitude with respect to sexuality – are themselves responsible for attracting sex tourism. It does not seem to occur to Oertl – in a kind of European naïvety? – to ask who has been establishing, housing and fostering prostitution on Kiriwina Island. Moreover, it does not seem to occur to her, either, that it is exactly publications like her own article – with glossy pictures of Trobriand girls, innuendoes about the 'Sexual Life of Savages', and with headings like 'Why Tourists Call the Trobriands the Islands of Love' or 'Trobriand: a Market even for Love' – that help unscrupulous tourist agents to foster a tourism that promises the experience of the 'Sexual Life of Savages' on the 'Islands of Love'.[13]

That this image of the Trobriand Islands is indeed something tourist magazines use for their clientele is documented by Harald Ludwig's contribution to the German *abenteuer & reisen – Das Erlebnis Magazin* in 1987. The title of Ludwig's article together with the label 'South Seas' is also mentioned on the cover of the magazine – and by now we may not be too surprised to learn that it runs: 'The Trobriands – Islands of Free Love'. The author urges the interested tourist to rush as soon as possible to this paradise before it is lost. The article is full of mistakes: Ludwig gives Denis de Trobriand, D'Entrecasteaux's second officer who had the honour to have his commander give his name to the group, the credit for the discovery of the islands. Ludwig turns 'good old Malinowski' (as he refers to the ethnographer) into a German, states that there are no betel-nuts on the islands, and ignores, apart from Malinowski's 'standard publication' with the title 'Sex Life of Savages', the existence of any other literature on the Trobriands. Ludwig celebrates the Islands as presenting tourists with all the romantic feelings that they may have dreamed of ever since they had read *Robinson Crusoe* and *The Bounty Mutiny*, and praises the Trobriand girls as having 'the most beautiful breasts in the world'. According to him Trobriand girls 'seek to sleep with as many men as possible' and (therefore?) most often walk around topless without wearing anything below their mini grass skirts. The group this article aims at is not difficult to define: whoever dreams of some wild sexual romance on a South Sea island – with beautiful young half-naked women taking over the active part in these hoped-for affairs – will try to follow Ludwig's advice and visit these islands as soon as possible (and it is here that one may be thankful for the fact that this trip is extremely expensive).

If we may hope to find a different portrait of the Trobriands and their inhabitants in more serious publications than those mentioned so far, we are often disappointed. In 1989 Jean-Michel Cousteau and Mose Richards published the book *Cousteau's Papua New Guinea Journey*, in which we find a chapter on the Trobriands. Although the style in which this book is written cannot be compared at all with publications mentioned above, it is frustrating to stumble over many misnomers, clichés and mistakes. I list some of them. The authors cannot refrain from quoting the 'Islands of Love' cliché (Cousteau and Richards 1989:65) and they mention 'stories of sexual permissiveness' where girls 'scheme together, waylaying certain men and gang-raping them'. The authors allude to the *yausa* habit (Malinowski 1929:231ff.) to be found in a few inland villages at the time when the yams are harvested and brought from the gardens into the villages. For the majority of the Trobrianders this habit is abhorrent and abominable. What Cousteau and Richards refer to as 'gang-raping' are actually some horrible forms of sexual abuse. As Malinowski (1929:231ff.) had already reported, during the *yausa* a band of women may assault their victim, undress him, defecate and micturate all over his body, try to masturbate him and, if he fails to have an erection, torture his genitals. One of my consultants on Kiriwina Island told me about a case where women had one of their victims bound naked to a pole, with strings around his testicles and penis. They carried him into their village like a pig to be slaughtered for a festival. All the time they threatened to castrate him, wildly tearing at the strings strung around his genitals. It is no wonder, I assume, that this kind of sexual abuse hardly results in the women actually having sexual intercourse with their victim (if he is not a masochist, of course). However, this habit is something extremely exotic – even for the majority of the Trobrianders, but especially for some men, I presume – and thus, it seems, it has to be reported as a form of 'gang-raping', even in an overall serious publication like Cousteau and Richard's book.

After this excursus we now return to the popular press again, and this time we deal with an article published in a journal that claims to support feminism: in 1990 Ursula Pittroff and Regine Körner published their article 'Eine Insel für die Liebe' in the German edition of the *Cosmopolitan* magazine. A brief summary of this contribution offers especially the female reader information about 'secret sex cults'. The article has its first culmination in stating that 'this island is completely oversexed'. The authors claim that during the yams festival all Trobriand women indulge in free love and general promiscuity. By now it should be clear that the Trobrianders grant this sexual freedom – which seems to fascinate all these male and female European authors – to unmarried (or divorced and single) men and women only, but not to married persons – not even during the period of the harvest festivals (Senft 1996). Pittroff and Körner also refer to the *yausa*, presenting Malinowski as their source. Unfortunately, they must have read Malinowski extremely superficially – they spell his name 'Malinowsky', have him live on the Trobriands during the First World War as a banned German anthropologist who was 'bookkeeping' the Islanders' sexual practices. The *Cosmopolitan* authors also make Malinowski responsible for the fact that the Trobriands are called 'the Islands of Love' these days. They finish their 'adventure report' with the somewhat cryptic remark that the Trobriands represented for them a 'dream' with permanent shades of 'nightmares'. They are probably alluding to the briefly touched-on danger of acquired immune deficiency syndrome (AIDS) in this rather promiscuous society of adolescents. This may be at least something to praise the authors for, if their allusion results in keeping sex tourists away from the islands.

That even novelists publish a lot of nonsense about the Trobrianders is sadly documented by the American Paul Theroux. In 1992 he published the article 'Under the Spell of the Trobriand Islands' in the highly respectable *National Geographic* magazine – probably as an advertisement for his book *The Happy Isles of Oceania*, which he published the same year and which contains two chapters on, and many references to, the Trobriands (Theroux 1992a, b).

In his *National Geographic* article the American author states: 'the islands were little changed . . . Not even missionaries . . . have altered the Trobrianders' view that their islands are a paradise, full of magic and sensuality . . . Most islanders claim to be Protestant or Catholic, but Christian theology does not impinge very much on their traditional beliefs . . .' (Theroux 1992a:119f.).

In the same article Theroux also states that the Trobrianders eat yams only at feasts (p. 123), that the birth rate on the islands is low (p. 123) and that during the yams festival spouses are given licence for sexual adventures (p. 128). All these statements are absolutely unfounded. For the last 12 years I have been observing the tremendous changes that are affecting Trobriand culture and society (Weiner 1976, 1988; Senft 1992, 1994). Theroux's mistakes with respect to what he reports about Trobriand sexuality should be evident by now. And the birth rate has exploded in the last years – certainly also because of the (Catholic) missionaries' opposition to (almost) all forms of birth control.

In his article Theroux does not use the phrase 'the Islands of Love' – but we hit upon it in the first paragraph in the first chapter on the Trobriands in his book, together with the reference to Malinowski's 1929 monograph. Malinowski and the Trobriands are first referrred to on page 9 of this book, and then Theroux mentions them – like leitmotifs – over and over again (Theroux 1992b:13, 43, 48, 98, 129–95, 197, 221, 255, 277, 330, 337, 346, 350, 352–3, 402, 404, 573, 585, 631, 672). Given this observation one might infer that the author was positively impressed by the Trobriands; however, this is far from being the case. On the Trobriands Theroux feels threatened by the islanders' jokes about him. It is evident that the writer does not like the Trobrianders[14] and that he does not care to learn anything about them, either. His book presents many mistakes; I list just a few of them:

1 Theroux states that every Trobriander speaks English and he lets them speak Tok Pisin (pp. 182–4).
2 He mixes up the *kosi* (Theroux writes *khosa*) – the evil spirits that survive a deceased if s/he is not bewailed properly – with the *baloma*, the actual 'spirit of the dead' (Malinowski 1948; Senft 1985).
3 He introduces the Polynesian concept of *mana* to the Trobriands (p. 156).
4 He refers to the severest insults to be found in Kilivila as 'jokes' (p. 173).
5 He describes a meeting with the paramount chief Pulayasa (pp. 188ff.), although the description of the person Theroux is talking about does not match at all with this impressive and powerful Trobriand chief.

Moreover, Theroux refers to the 'Yam Festival' (p. 140). He reports that during this time some tug-of-war games between boys and girls end up in public mass 'fornication' (p. 151); but this is nothing special for the Trobrianders – at least according to Theroux.

Given all these mistakes, rumours and blunt lies, I cannot but agree with Theroux's statement that at the end of his stay – which lasted for a few days only – he could 'see the utter impossibility of [his] ever understanding the place'. It would have been better for him, for the Trobrianders and for Theroux's readers if he had not visited the islands at all.

The author also published a shortened, but not corrected, version of his *National Geographic* article in the German magazine *GEO* (Theroux 1993). With this article we find a brief contribution of an author whom we already mentioned above: Oertl (1993) comments in her article 'Von den Trobriandern lernen' on the Trobrianders and gives a rather idiosyncratic evaluation of Malinowski.[15] She also mentions that Tomalala, one of the inhabitants of the village Tauwema on Kaile'una Island, where I myself am doing my field research, lived for three months in Andechs in Bavaria. Invited by the Research Unit for Human Ethology within the Max Planck Society,[16] Tomalala helped his host Wulf Schiefenhövel to translate film-accompanying soundtracks. He did this by translating Kilivila into Motu, a lingua franca of Papua New Guinea with which his host, who does not speak Kilivila, is familiar. Then the human ethologist translated these Motu versions of the Kilivila utterances into German. Tomalala's visit to Germany and his cooperation with Schiefenhövel are praised by Oertl as 'another culmination of participant observation'. In what follows I will discuss this visit and some reports about it in the press.

Aotourou, Omai, Tomalala – Islanders from the South Seas Visiting Europe

Ever since Europeans had been in contact with so-called 'savages', we observe in them a rather strange urge to bring some of the representatives of these newly 'discovered' cultures back to their own European cultures. Thus, in 1441, the first ten Africans were brought to Portugal as a special present for Henry the Seafarer (Bitterli 1991:97); and Hans Plischke (1960:94) observes that ever since then some unfortunate human beings have been kidnapped to serve the Europeans as 'specimens' in a gradually growing 'collection' of foreign and 'exotic' races! However, it was the first visits of islanders from the South Seas that got 'the real publicity'. After his visit to Tahiti in 1768 Bougainville took with him – on a voluntary basis – one of the islanders, whom the French called 'Aotourou'. Aotourou stayed in Paris for eleven months, but died on his way back to Tahiti in 1770. The commander of the second ship in James Cook's second expedition to the South Seas, Captain Furneaux, succeeded in bringing the Tahitian 'commoner' Omai back home in 1775. After two years in England Omai returned to Tahiti, where he died three years later without getting any kind of special acknowledgement from his fellow countrymen for his sojourn in Britain. Aotuorou and Omai, however, were both extremely interesting objects for scientists in France and in England, and it was also partly because of their visits that a new scientific discipline called 'anthropology' was born (see Plischke 1960:100f., 103).

However, the visits of Omai and Aotourou also stimulated a lot of criticism in intellectual circles (see Bitterli 1991:186ff). It is interesting to realize that this criticism is not too different from the criticism I express myself in the final section of this chapter and with which I have been confronted (as a researcher who incidentally happens to do his field research in the same village as Tomalala's host) by critical intellectuals in connection with Tomalala's visit to Bavaria. But before I come up with this criticism, I will briefly outline how German newspapers reported Tomalala's visit.

In October 1992 Sabine Bader reports in the *Süddeutsche Zeitung* on Tomalala's 'excursion in a land without sun and moon'. This romantic title is explained by the fact that Tomalala's 'Stammes-brüder' warned him that if he accompanied Schiefenhövel to Germany he would come to such a country. This is a really nice bit of fiction. On my first visit to the Trobriands in 1982 I had a number of books on Germany with me to give to the Islanders, showing them something about the country I came from; ever since then, I have had many discussions with my friends and consultants about life, climate, agriculture, etc. in Germany. But back to Bader's article. After a brief outline of Schiefenhövel's research on the Trobriands, Tomalala's visit is explained in this newspaper article as a necessary further step in the cooperation between

Schiefenhövel and his 'logical partner'. Tomalala is said to be the only person in his village who speaks Motu, and, because Schiefenhövel is familiar with this language, but does not speak the 'island language', his research depends on Tomalala: he is the only person Schiefenhövel can communicate with in this Papua New Guinean lingua franca.[17] Tomalala is claimed to have developed into a researcher himself during his work as translator of film accompanying soundtracks at the Human Ethology Research Unit. I do not want to comment on some blunt mistakes reported in this article about Tomalala and aspects of Trobriand culture. What I want to point out here is the fact that Bader emphasizes that it is not too difficult for a South Sea islander said to be a farmer (not a yams gardener) and fisherman to become a scientific researcher who enjoys his new role during his visit in Germany.

In April 1993, Tomalala's story is taken up by another Munich newspaper. Gerhard Merk comments in the *Abendzeitung* on 'Tom in High-Tech-Land' and emphasizes that the 'Naturkind' – a man of 50 years of age – astonished scientists. It is emphasized in this article that Tomalala was not very impressed by the German way of life. The article also points out that according to Schiefenhövel Tomalala's visit was not at all problematic for visitor and host – with the exception, however, that the host had to keep an eye on Tomalala's love of beer.

Tom's story then spreads further north-east. In June 1993, the former official paper of the German Democratic Republic, the *Neues Deutschland*, published an article by Dieter Hannes on 'The Fisherman from the Trobriand Islands'. Tomalala, the 'guest from a different age', is introduced as his host's research partner who did not experience a 'culture shock' in Germany. The article sheds some strange light on the quality of archaeologists: Tomalala, visiting some excavations, is reported to have been the only one to identify a presumed stone axe as a whetstone. Thus, as the article phrases it, he helped these archaeologists with his 'prehistoric' knowledge and expertise.

These examples should suffice for the purposes pursued here. They illustrate that Tomalala's visit is met and reported with a certain form of arrogance with which representatives of a presumed superior culture look down on members of a so-called 'prehistoric' or 'primitive' culture. Although all articles mention that Tomalala astonished even the researchers who acted as his hosts, it is always implied that the encounter between 'the visitor from a different age' and the Europeans is clearly dominated by the latter because of cultural, and not out of economic, reasons (the hosts paid for their guest's expenses and provided him with a fellowship). Moreover, a critical reader easily gets the impression that the reported astonishment is only feigned. Do not readers as well as reporters of such a visit – and even the hosts of the visitor themselves – tacitly assume that a 'native' will have no problems in acquiring European skills and forms of behaviour during his stay away from home, and is it not exactly this process that is keenly documented in minute notes on how fast the visitor makes progress in his process of cultural adaptation? That such a visit and the reports about it also provoke a discussion about the ethics of field researchers is to be expected. In the final section of my chapter I want to discuss such questions.

The Savage and the Civilized – and Field Researchers' Ethics

One of the first and probably most important questions that have to be asked in connection with a visit like that of Tomalala's is what kind of consequences it may have for the visitor in his host country and back home. I will stick to the Trobriand example and briefly outline what I think one has to take into consideration when one invites a Trobriand consultant to Europe. First of all it is well known that the Trobriand society is highly hierarchically stratified. Thus, the first factor one has to consider is whether an invitation either clashes with the social status of the invited person or upsets, or causes feelings of envy in other persons with a higher social standing than that of the invited. In the Trobriand society a person who has more goods than someone else is forced to generously distribute this surplus to maintain status and to keep face as a good member of the community. Thus, before someone is invited, the host-to-be has to check whether he can ensure that the guest – after returning from his journey to the scientist's country – can fulfil these obligations. It goes without saying that such an invitation asks for extremely good relations between host and guest. Researchers who plan to invite consultants for a visit in their countries should always act on the basis of the general principle of professional responsibility that asks them to 'clarify the potential conflicts between doing science, and protecting and promoting the physical, social, and emotional safety and welfare of the people with whom [they] work' (Skomal 1994:4). I would not dare to invite one of my consultants to visit me in Nijmegen, because I think my yearly one- to two-month visits would not suffice to guarantee his/her 'physical, social, and emotional safety and welfare' after returning to Tauwema.[18] Moreover, I would have difficulties to justify such an invitation, because I cannot see the difference in kind and quality between the information I could get from my consultants in Nijmegen and the information I can get by organizing and doing my field research properly on the Trobriand Islands. However, this is of course a decision every researcher has to come up with on the basis of his or her own field site, field research experience and personal principles of ethics.

Another question field researchers have to ask themselves is what kind of influence they have on reports in the media like those referred to in this chapter, namely reports that deal with the people with whom they do their field research. One should always keep in mind that one may never know what will happen if newspapers get hold of what some journalists may think to be a good story. To attempt to correct at least some of the worst misrepresentations in the media sometimes resembles Sisyphus' task. However, I think we all have to try to see our field sites and the people we do our research with not wrongly represented there. Thus, I am afraid we have to continue to write letters to the editors or papers like the present one in the hope that we can change at least something by pointing out the problems and by creating a forum for discussing them. I believe this to be part of our responsibility for our field sites and the people whose language, culture and behaviour we research. To act and try to do something if we see that the image of the people we are studying and working with is tarnished by tabloid treatment and that they are defamed, slandered and libelled are part of our professional ethics.

Notes

1. This chapter is an abridged and updated version of my contribution to Bert Voorhoeve's Festschrift (Baak *et al.* 1995:480–510). I would like to thank the editors for their kind

permission to reprint this version here. The chapter is based on 25 months of field research on the Trobriand Islands in 1982, 1983, 1989, 1992, 1993, 1994, 1995 and 1996. I thank John Haviland, Ingjerd Hoëm, Steve Levinson, Barbara Senft and Wolfgang Wickler for comments and critical remarks. I thank the National and Provincial Governments of Papua New Guinea (PNG) and Milne Bay Province for their assistance with, and permission for, my research projects. I also thank the Institute for Papua New Guinea Studies and the Council of Chiefs of the Trobriand Islands for their support of my research. My deepest gratitude goes to the people of the Trobriand Islands, especially the inhabitants of Tauwema, for their hospitality, friendship and patient cooperation.

2. Chamisso is quoted according to Kramer (1981:74).
3. For detailed information see Bitterli (1991), Kohl (1986) and Kramer (1981).
4. It goes without saying that all attempts to 'civilize' the 'savages' involved Christian missionaries (Senft 1992, 1994).
5. For discussions of the 'noble savage' myth see Stein (1984a–c), Theye (1984) and Borsboom (1988).
6. Aldous Huxley refers to the Trobriand Islands in his novel *Brave New World* (1972:41). This novel was first published in 1932. Like many before and after him, Huxley quotes one of the few mistakes of Malinowski's. The field researcher mistook myth for fact, reporting that the Trobriand Islanders are ignorant of a man's role of 'pater' as 'genitor' (Malinowski 1929:3, 69, 148ff.); the fact that Trobriand women have been using traditional contraceptives – some of which they just use(d) before having sexual intercourse, being completely aware of why and for what biological ends they did, and still do, this – proves Malinowski wrong. For another reference to the Trobrianders see also Gore Vidal's (1969:7) novel *Myra Breckenridge*.
7. One could discuss the question whether Malinowski was not playing the same game as all the recipients of his monograph and that he actually 'started the whole thing'. One could ask whether Malinowski used 'science' as an excuse for talking openly about sex. This was not taken for granted in those days. A year before Malinowski's monograph D.H. Lawrence's novel *Lady Chatterley's Lover* was published (in a limited edition in Florence). It was immediately banned as obscene in several countries; it was first published in Great Britain in an

expurgated version in 1932, and the full text was only published as late as 1959 in New York. If one wants to argue like this, then Malinowski could be made responsible for having started a discussion that, once it took off, could not be stopped any more.

8. This German version, published 1932, saw a first revision in 1935; in 1951 Reich published a second enlarged version with a completely new preface in English with Farrar, Straus and Giroux. All references here refer to the German edition of this 1951 version.

9. This norm also holds for white married persons on the Trobriands.

10. There seems to be hardly any topic where you do not find hints as to the Trobrianders' sexuality. Even a well-researched sexual history, first published in 1974, of Christianity refers to some such 'facts' (Deschner 1984:386). I want to note that the label 'Islands of Love' is used in articles published within PNG, too – with the aim to attract tourists (see, for example, Croft 1978; Halstead 1978; Stocks 1984; Anonymous 1988, 1989).

11. Baker's book was published before discussions about 'political correctness' started in the USA.

12. The Barters cannot be made responsible for ideas their customers may utter about Melanesia in general and PNG in particular; such ideas are very ironically documented in Dennis O'Rourke's film *Cannibal Tours* (1987).

13. It is depressing to state that this *epitheton ornans* has only negative effects for the Trobrianders, who are completely aware of these negative aspects of tourism (Senft 1987:192).

14. Theroux's book documents that he generally does not like the people of the Pacific – with one exception: he feels at home and happy with his fellow Americans on the islands of Hawaii.

15. Among other things Oertl accuses Malinowski of not being a sociobiologist (one wonders how he could have been one, given the fact that sociobiology is a rather recent subdiscipline of biology) and of having had no feminist approach (again, Malinowski certainly did not live at a time when feminism was in vogue).

16. I feel forced to note that at the time of Tomalala's visit in Andechs I was no longer affiliated with the Human Ethology Research Unit. I was actually consulted about my views with

respect to a possible visit of a Trobriander in Bavaria. I argued strongly against the realization of such an idea. Given that in the last years I have been facing a number of situations where people asked me whether I was responsible for what they had heard of, and/or read about, Tomalala's visit in Germany, I am glad to be able to deny any kind of responsibility for, and involvement in, this visit.

17. I just want to note that I know many persons in Tauwema that know the lingua franca 'Hiri Motu' (or 'Police Motu'); this lingua franca should not be mixed up with the language 'Motu' spoken by the Motu people in the vicinity of Port Moresby (see Dutton and Voorhoeve 1974). For a grammatical description of Kilivila and a Kilivila/English dictionary see Senft (1986).

18. To come back to Tomalala: Tomalala always had a rather peculiar status in Tauwema (Senft 1987). Ever since coming back from his trip to Germany at the end of 1992 he has been having even more problems to (re)integrate himself into his own community and culture in Tauwema. In 1995 Tomalala divorced his wife and married a young woman from Kaduwaga. In May 1996 I learned that in 1995 the inhabitants of Tauwema exiled Tomalala together with his young wife and their newborn child. Moreover, they destroyed the couple's house as well as Schiefenhövel's house. For the social impact of such a ban (*yoba*) see Malinowski (1929:11ff.). Tomalala, *persona non grata* in Tauwema, is now living in Kaduwaga, the village of his second wife.

References

Anonymous (1988). Welcome to the Islands of Love. *South Pacific Magazine* 1(3):53–7.

Anonymous (1989). Getting into Full Swing for the Yam Festival in Trobriands. *Niugini Nius* 27, 10 July: 1, 7.

Baak, C., Bakker, M. and van der Meij, D. (eds) (1995). *Tales from a Concave World. Liber Amicorum Bert Voorhoeve.* Leiden: Projects Division, Department of Languages and Cultures of South-East Asia and Oceania, Leiden University.

Bader, S. (1992). Exkursion in ein Land ohne Sonne und Mond. *Süddeutsche Zeitung*, 19 October.

Baker, R. (1983). *Freie Liebe.* Rastatt: Möwig (Playboy Taschenbuch).
Bitterli, U. (1991). *Die 'Wilden' und die 'Zivilisierten'. Grundzüge einer Geistes- und Kulturgeschichte der europäisch-überseeischen Begegnung.* München: Beck.
Borsboom, A. (1988). The Savage in European Social Thought: A Prelude to the Conceptualization of the Divergent Peoples and Cultures of Australia and Oceania. *Bijdragen tot de Taal-, Land-en Volkenkunde* 144: 419–32.
Bougainville, L.-A. de (1985). *Reise um die Welt.* Berlin: Rixdorfer Verlagsanstalt (First published in 1772.)
Cousteau, J.M. and Richards, M. (1989). *Cousteau's Papua New Guinea Journey.* New York: Harry N. Abrams.
Croft, P. (1978). King Cam of Kitava. In: G. Dick (ed.), *Best of Paradise,* pp. 50–3. Hongkong: Air Niugini.
Deschner, K. (1984). *Das Kreuz mit der Kirche. Eine Sexualgeschichte des Christentums.* München: Wilhelm Heyne. (First published in 1974.)
Dutton, T.E. and Voorhoeve, C.L. (1974). *Beginning Hiri Motu.* Canberra: Research School of Pacific Studies, Australian National University (Pacific Linguistics Series D-24).
Eibl-Eibesfeldt, I. and Senft, G. (1986). *Trobriander (Ost-Neuguinea, Trobriand Inseln, Kaile'una) Fadenspiele 'ninikula'.* Göttingen: Institut für den Wissenschaftlichen Film (Film-No.: E 2958).
—— (1992). *Trobriander (Papua-Neuguinea, Trobriand Inseln, Kaile'una) Tänze zur Einleitung des Erntefeier Rituals Film E 3129. Trobriander (Papua-Neuguinea, Trobriand-Inseln, Kiriwina). Ausschnitte aus einem Erntefesttanz Film E 3130. Publikationen zu Wissenschaftlichen Filmen, Sektion Ethnologie 17.* Göttingen: Institut für den Wissenschaftlichen Film.
Halstead, B. (1978). Islands of Love. In: G. Dick (ed.), *Best of Paradise,* pp. 130–2. Hongkong: Air Niugini.
Hannes, D. (1993). Der Fischer von den Trobriand-Inseln. *Neues Deutschland,* 12 June.
Huxley, A. (1972). *Brave New World.* Harmondsworth: Penguin. (First published in 1932.)
Kohl, K.-H. (1986). *Entzauberter Blick Das Bild vom Guten Wilden.* Frankfurt a.M.: Suhrkamp.
Kramer, F. (1981). *Verkehrte Welten: Zur imaginären Ethnographie des 19. Jahrhunderts.* Frankfurt a.M.: Syndikat.
Ludwig, H. (1987). Inseln der freien Liebe. *abenteuer & reisen – Das Erlebnis Magazin,* 1/87, 59–64.

Malinowski, B. (1929). *The Sexual Life of Savages in Northwestern Melanesia.* London: Routledge and Kegan Paul (1987, Boston: Beacon Press).

—— (1948). *Magic, Science and Religion and Other Essays.* Glencoe, Ill.: Free Press.

—— (1967). *A Diary in the Strict Sense of the Term.* London: Athlone Press.

Mead, M. (1928). *Coming of Age in Samoa: A Psychological Study of Primitve Youth for Western Civilization.* New York: Morrow.

Merk, G. (1993). Tom im High-Tech-Land: Nur Steak vom Hai mochte er nicht. *Abendzeitung München,* 2 April.

Oertl, M. (1985). Die natürliche Erotik der Trobriander: Was soll aus den Inseln der Liebe werden? *Peter Moosleitners interessantes Magazin,* 18 October, 11:114–20, 122, 125.

—— (1993). Von den Trobriandern lernen. *GEO* 11:48–9.

O'Rourke, D. (1987). *Cannibal Tours.* Canberra, Port Moresby: O'Rourke & Associates, produced in association with the Institute of Papua New Guinea Studies.

Pittroff, U. and Körner, R. (1990). Eine Insel für die Liebe. *Cosmopolitan* 6: 212–14, 218–222.

Plischke, H. (1960). Insulaner aus der Südsee in Europa am Ende des 18. Jahrhunderts. *Ethnologica,* NF 2:94–104.

Reich, W. (1972). *Der Einbruch der sexuellen Zwangsmoral. Zur Geschichte der sexuellen Ökonomie.* Köln: Kiepenheuer & Witsch. (First published in 1932.)

Rensch, K. (1991). The Language of the Noble Savage: Early Perceptions of Tahitian. Paper presented at the 6th International Conference on Austronesian Linguistics, Honolulu, Hawaii.

Sahlins, M. (1985). *Islands of History.* Chicago: University of Chicago Press.

Senft, B. and Senft, G. (1986). Ninikula – Fadenspiele auf den Trobriand Inseln, Papua Neuguinea. *Baessler Archiv – Beiträge zur Völkerkunde,* NF 34:93–235.

Senft, G. (1985). Trauer auf Trobriand – eine ethnologisch/ linguistische Fallstudie. *Anthropos* 80:471–92.

—— (1986). *Kilivila – The Language of the Trobriand Islanders.* Berlin: Mouton de Gruyter.

—— (1987). Nanam'sa Bwena – Gutes Denken. Eine ethno- linguistische Fallstudie über eine Dorfversammlung auf den Trobriand Inseln. *Zeitschrift für Ethnologie* 112:181–222.

—— (1991). Prolegomena to the Pragmatics of Situational-

Intentional Varieties in Kilivila Language. In: J. Verschueren (ed.), *Levels of Linguistic Adaptation. Selected Papers of the International Pragmatics Conference, Antwerp, August 17–22, 1987,* Vol. II, pp. 235–48. Amsterdam: Benjamins.

—— (1992). As Time Goes By . . . Changes Observed in the Trobrianders' Culture and Language, Milne Bay Province, Papua New Guinea. In: T.E. Dutton (ed.), *Culture Change, Language Change: Case Studies from Melanesia,* pp. 67–89. Canberra: Research School of Pacific Studies, Australian National University (Pacific Linguistics Series C-120).

—— (1994). Darum gehet hin und lehret alle Völker . . . Mission, Kultur- und Sprachwandel am Beispiel der Trobriand-Insulaner von Papua-Neuguinea. In: P. Stüben (ed.), *Seelenfischer – Mission, Stammesvölker und Ökologie,* pp. 71–91. Gießen: Focus.

—— (1996) Past is Present, Present is Past. Time and the Harvest Ritual on the Trobriand Islands. *Anthropos* 91:381–9.

Skomal, S.N. (1994). Lessons for the Field – Ethics in Fieldwork. *Anthropology Newsletter* 35: 1, 4.

Stein, G. (ed.). (1984a). *Die edlen Wilden.* Frankfurt a.M.: Fischer.

—— (1984b). *Exoten durchschauen Europa.* Frankfurt a.M.: Fischer.

—— (1984c). *Europamüdigkeit und Verwilderungswünsche.* Frankfurt a.M.: Fischer.

Stocks, I. (1984). In Search of Malinowski. *Paradise – Air Niugini Inflight Magazine,* 46, May, pp. 20–4.

Theroux, P. (1992a). Under the Spell of the Trobriand Islands. *National Geographic* 182, 1 July, pp. 117–36.

—— (1992b). *The Happy Isles of Oceania.* Harmondsworth: Penguin.

—— (1993). Trobriand-Inseln: Das gerettete Eden. *GEO* 11:32–48, 50–8.

Theye, T. (ed.). (1984). *Wir und die Wilden.* Reinbek: Rowohlt.

Vidal, G. (1969). *Myra Breckenridge.* London: Panther.

Weiner, A.B. (1976). *Women of Value, Men of Renown. New Perspectives in Trobriand Exchange.* Austin: University of Texas Press.

—— (1988). *The Trobrianders of Papua New Guinea.* New York: Holt, Rinehart and Winston.

Part II

Ways of Constructing Identities

Chapter 5

Contrasting Transcripts: Constructing Images and Identities in Mediations among the Wam People of Papua New Guinea

Nigel A. Stephenson

Introduction

At the centre of this chapter stands a dispute, an episode of conflict talk, which takes place within the framework of a mediation among the Wam people of the East Sepik Province (ESP) of Papua New Guinea (PNG).

Broadly defined, a mediation is an act of bringing about peace between two opposing parties (cf. also Caplan 1995). Greenhouse (1985:90) gives the following definition: 'Mediation . . . is a triadic mode of dispute settlement, entailing the intervention of a neutral third party at the invitation of the disputants, the outcome of which is a bilateral agreement between the disputants . . . Mediators, as opposed to arbitrators and adjudicators, have no authoritative sanctions at their disposal (such as threats of imprisonment and fines).' As Gulliver (1977:16), who quotes A.S. Meyer, maintains, 'mediation and arbitration have conceptually nothing in common. The one involves helping people to decide for themselves; the other involves helping people by deciding for them. However, the two processes have a way of shading into each other.'

The topic of this specific mediation are accusations of sorcery, more specifically they are accusations concerning the spreading of rumours about sorcery. The rumours circle around a number of deaths that have occurred within the last year leading up to the mediation in Warengeme, the largest village in the Wam area. The deaths constitute important aspects of the narrated events but they are only part of the story. More important than the actual deaths themselves is to find out who is responsible for the rumours – who the authors of the rumours are. I call the rumours hidden transcripts. They relate to factual events of the past but they do not necessarily represent the objective facts as they happened. They are only possible versions of the way things happened. The 'hidden' is a reference to the form they are articulated in and the mode they are communicated by, i.e. along informal if not even secret channels, spreading from a central source spatially and socially.

Rumours are in themselves a type of theory or hypothesis that makes alternative propositions concerning the course of an event and/or the responsibility of participant actors (cf. Paine 1967). Rumours spread around the village and over the whole area very quickly, and, just as rumours proliferate spatially and socially, they tend to snowball in terms of content as well. There is little if any feedback or discourse between the different levels a rumour traverses; there is, therefore, also very little validation or repudiation as the rumour gradually proliferates. Also, since rumours pass through a multitude of nodes in the course of proliferation, and their messages are often extended, manipulated or distorted in the process, it becomes extremely difficult to allocate responsibility, and to reconstruct who exactly told whom, what and when.

In the context of the mediation these hidden transcripts are hauled to the front, on to the stage so to speak, and in front of an audience. Through this shift they are transformed into public transcripts and then they are dissected, discussed and, in our specific case, repudiated. Other, equally hypothetical versions of what happened in the past are held against them and from these contrastive transcripts an accountable version of the recent past is constructed. Since this all happens in a situation of conflict the elements of discursive ability and power come in and it becomes a question of who can make his account count.

In the course of disentangling the different transcripts many more aspects of the recent past in the village are dealt with than just the deaths and the rumours they trigger off, and the dispute actually takes on the aspect of a full-scale state-of-the-village debate in which not only an accountable version of the recent past is constructed, but also the effective relations of power in the nominally egalitarian polity are reified and made explicit, and the village's position on the road to development and change is discussed.

Such mediations as I discuss below are recurring events in Warengeme. Their occurrence is unpredictable but experience shows that they come about every six to eight months. In view of the plasticity of social formation and the transience and volatility of political allegiances – even more pronounced under the impact of a reorientation towards a broader and more encompassing politicocultural system – these mediations constitute significant discourse occasions in which the village defines itself and construes an accountable image of itself. As Watson-Gegeo and White (1990:3) postulate, in such encounters 'people not only pose and counterpose interpretations of events, they may also negotiate the premises upon which they act. Disentangling discourse is thus a critical focus for understanding the processes – conceptual, communicative, and institutional – through which the people continually create and transform the reality in which they live.'

The Setting

Before I come to the actual speech event I offer a short outline of the ethnographic background of the Wam and briefly address some of the keys issues in the context of which village discourse takes place. These include the notions of *kastom* and *komuniti* and the nature of political factionalism in Warengeme.

Ethnographic Background

The Wam form an ethnic and linguistic group in the southern foothills of the Torricelli Mountains in the ESP of PNG (Stephenson in press). The Wam territory is located a few miles north of the Sepik Highway between Maprik and Dreikikir. They are horticulturalists, growing, and subsisting on, a variety of tubers (yam, taro, sweet potato), sago, and diverse vegetables and fruits which they collect in the surrounding bush. Trade-store foods (e.g. tinned meat, tinned fish, rice) today supplement their diet and are used in ritual contexts as well (e.g. for funeral feasts).

The Wam number approximately 2,800 people and populate eight villages of different size. They break into two dialect groups, which are designated as Wam 1 and Wam 2, the former populating four villages to the north, in more elevated country, the latter in the other four villages in the southern part of the territory. Warengeme, which belongs to Wam 2, is the largest village with around 650 inhabitants.[1] Warengeme, like all the other villages too, displays a dispersed settlement pattern, with a total of fifty-two hamlets spread over an area of roughly 4 square kilometres. The present villages do not represent the traditional form of territorial and political organization. They are a product of colonial administration. The traditional focus was on the ward, *aniher sululepeni* or *kastom ples* (custom place) as they are called in Tok Pisin, which was made up of a number of hamlets orientated towards a ceremonial ground, on which stood a ceremonial house during the long ritual cycles.

Although no longer ritually significant the *kastom ples* still are important in terms of political and social orientation and allegiance. In Warengeme there are four such wards: Talkeneme, Wolhete, Warengeme (which gave the village as a whole its name) and Wohimbil. Due to its size, Warengeme was divided into Warengeme 1 (consisting of Warengeme and Wohimbil) and Warengeme 2 (Talkeneme and Wolhete) by the colonial administration. The two parts are approximately equal in size, and the boundary between the two is not discernible by naked eye. But in sociopolitical and historical terms there is a division, which becomes marked in times of tension (as in the case described below), in the sense that the people of Warengeme 2 describe themselves as the original inhabitants of the area, whilst the lineages making up Warengeme 1 are said to be immigrant lines.

Nominally, the Wam could be described as having a patrilineal, lineage-based social system. Named lineages, *alamel piressi* (lit. yam family), do exist but only as social categories and not as social groups, i.e. they form reference units and not action groups. More significant for the pattern of the social order are the two central principles or modes of exchange, which I would define as 'informal sharing' and 'formal exchange', which underly the social process (cf. Weiner 1982).

Equality, namely equality between men, is a fiercely contested and key issue among the Wam. One could describe the Wam as being an egalitarian society but equality is a relationship quality that is not readily and easily granted to each other, but a matter men have to compete for and defend instead. The practice of the social order is to be seen as an ongoing contest between the principle of hierarchy and equality (cf. Lutkehaus 1990:181). The main arena for this contest in earlier days was the men's cult called *sulu*, or *tamberan* in Tok Pisin. During initiation cycles to the three grades of the secret male cult and especially within the context of the exchange feasts, which were central events in such a cycle, men competed for status, power and influence through the exchange of ceremonial yam, pigs and other valuables. The *tamberan* was the forum where bigmen were made but also where established bigmen were challenged and lost influence. In the game of bigmanship, sorcery was seen to play a central role. It was the means by which established bigmen were threatened and disposed of, but also, and more commonly, bigmen were seen as using sorcery to extend their influence or curb unwelcome rivals. Not that they themselves commanded the art of sorcery, but they commanded the necessary resources to hire sorcery specialists. In the *longue durée*, equality prevailed because there were checks and balances built into the system that prevented individuals from establishing enduring hierarchy.

The experience of colonialism and postcolonialism over the last roughly seventy years has changed the way of life among the Wam in many significant ways. Labour migration, the coming of the Christian missions, the imposition of colonial administration and law, cash cropping, formal education, the building of the road and independence with its novel institutions are all forces of change which have led to a reorientation in their outlook on the world and on the mode of organizing social and cultural processes. One of the most far-reaching effects this reorientation has had has been the relinquishment of formal exchange as a key element in social formation. This not only refers to the cessation of the *tamberan* and the exchange feasts but also to other pivotal nodes in the social process such as marriage, adoption and death ceremonies, which were all based on the principle of balanced, formal exchange. The ethos of equality and its counterpart hierarchy, however, are still valid, and the struggle for status and influence is still going on but the allocative and authoritative resources men draw upon in this contest have shifted, away from growing yam, raising pigs and knowing the secrets of the ritual complex, to commanding access to monetary resources, holding leading positions in 'new' village organizations (e.g. business groups, youth groups, churches) or being part of the modern, encapsulating political order. Of course, this is an oversimplified and abridged description of the complexities of change in the village, and in practice the process bears many more 'twisted elements' than I have posited here but it reflects more or less the view people take on their situation at present.

Kastom and *Komuniti*

The village discourse on change is coined today by two key terms. These are *kastom* and *komuniti* (custom and community). The two terms are antithetical and exclude each other. *Kastom* stands for the traditional Wam culture (in its widest sense) and the past. Unlike in many other Melanesian communities (cf. Keesing and Tonkinson 1982; Linnekin 1992), where the concept stands for the validity and the value of the traditional way of life in the face of the dominant 'world system', the term among the Wam is (at present at least) negatively connoted. The term stands for ignorance, competition, jealousy, backwardness, superstition and strife, and as long as a *kastom* habitus prevails, the people feel, tangible change and real development will not reach the village. This does not mean that the Wam do not basically hold their *kastom* in esteem – they view themselves as having been the actual source of all culture in the area – but they only value it as a concept of the past. *Kastom* and modernity to them are absolutely incompatible. At the other end of the scale stands *komuniti*. The concept is associated with prosperity, progress, true equality, peace, harmony and unity. It denotes a future state of being, a communal form of life which the villagers are, or at least should be, aiming at and striving for.

No one in the village today would subscribe to the *kastom* option any more. The ideals of *komuniti* are not doubted nor are they contested. Everyone agrees on the direction the village should be heading for, but there are very different views on how this future form of existence is to be attained. The village is seriously divided on this issue and breaks into various rival factions which tend to quarrel bitterly over the possession of the right way to attain *komuniti* (thus in itself contradicting the ideals of the postulated aim). There are those who believe that economic development, education, trust in the law and the elected authorities, as dictated by the modern state, and also Christian belief will eventually effect an inner change in the people and make them righteous and contented (call them the pragmatists), and there are those who postulate the necessity of an immediate and complete moral conversion of the people which then will, in the very near future, lead to a state of prosperity, harmony and bliss (call these the utopians).

A closer look at the factional boundaries shows that they reflect very much deeper and older conflicts between different segments of the village, which have their roots elsewhere. Moreover, it becomes evident that the two catchwords *kastom* and *komuniti* are far from being clear-cut concepts but are used as rhetorical ploys by the factional leaders and political competitors. All actors in village disputes like the one described below accuse each other of (mis)using the notion of *komuniti* as a cover-up in order to gain power and influence and create hierarchy in the village, aims which, of course, are identified with the old *kastom* habitus. The fact that the majority of people still die of various forms of sorcery, especially *arukwineme* sorcery (*sanguma* in Tok Pisin), is evidence enough that the village is still deeply entangled in the meshes of *kastom*, or, the other way round, that *kastom* is still in the people.

When speaking of the factional configuration in Warengeme we are speaking of pervasive factionalism, i.e. there are a large number of interest groups which tend to form alliances at times for special purposes. These alliances can be quite durable; usually, however, they break up again when the issue at hand has been settled. Moreover, factions tend to turn on each other when the surrounding conditions change. Fluidity, volatility and the flexibility of factional boundaries are hallmarks of pervasive factionalism. Also, superficial amiable relations tend to mask bitter rivalry at times. The way people act and talk in the presence of others, i.e. on stage, is not necessarily, or to a marked degree, what they think and say about them in their absence, i.e. backstage (cf. Goffman 1959). The mutual awareness of the double-facedness of social relations and the fact that the lineages do not represent havens of security – siblingship antagonism and agnatic conflict in general are widespread – help to explain the reticence and wariness people display when interacting with each other. It is in this field of ambiguity that rumours flourish and proliferate.

Warengeme Factions

Taking the complexity and volatility of factional relations into account, I can only give a very basic outline of pattern of conflict here, as it pertains to the event I am going to describe. The baseline, so to speak, of conflict in the village is the split between Warengeme 2 and Warengeme 1, the people of Warengeme 2 claiming precedence over their counterparts on the basis of their status as original inhabitants of the area. Over the last decades, however, it has been men of Warengeme 1 who have held positions of authority that are associated with and seen as representing the encapsulating outside (i.e. the colonial and postcolonial establishment), such as the councillor, the village magistrate, the local Member of Parliament (MP), a director on the board of the Sepik Producers Coffee Association (one of the main cooperative societies in the province) and a number of church leaders, all positions the villagers have expected development and advancement to come from. I call this group and their supporters the 'E-faction' (E = established), for the sake of argument. Although Warengeme 2 is torn by bitter enmities as well, it usually unites against Warengeme 1 when necessity calls for it. Over the last few years, Warengeme 2 has rallied and created an organizational structure (in the form of a Youth Group and Business Group) under the leadership of a small group of younger, educated men, as a counterforce to the dominance of the E-faction in the village. This Warengeme 2 faction I shall call the 'O-Faction' (O = opposition).

Whereas the inhabitants of Warengeme 2 predominantly are followers of the Catholic Church, Warengeme 1 is split along denominational lines. Beside those who belong to the Catholic Church (to which the majority of the E-faction belongs) there is a new and very strong religious movement which gathers under the New Apostolic Church (NAC). Behind its official church appearance, the NAC is a millenarian movement (cf. Camp 1983; Gesch 1985; Stephenson 1994). It recruits its members nearly exclusively from Warengeme 1, mainly from the ward of Wohimbil, the youngest ward of the village. The members of the NAC, and especially its leading figures, are the most bitter opponents of the men of the E-faction, whom they see as representatives of the encapsulating system (in its negative sense) in the village and whom they make primarily responsible for keeping the village 'down' (according to their millenarian outlook). I call this group the 'I-Faction' (I = irritant). It is not only bitterly antagonistic towards the E-faction, it also faces opposition from the O-faction, which sees in the NAC (in its millenarian form) a completely outmoded and irrational option. Thus we have a triangle of conflict as the basic pattern. The three factions face each other in opposition. Notably, however, and typical of pervasive factionalism, this conflict pattern does not rule out that there exist amiable, personal relations between single individuals of the opposed factions.

Before coming to the actual mediation I must briefly recount the development of events leading up to that point. As hinted at above, the local MP for the Wam-Urat constituency was a man from Warengeme, more specifically a man from the E-faction, called Kulau.[2] He had held that position ever since the provincial parliament system had been introduced in 1978. During the last parliamentary term leading up to the 1987 elections he had been the Speaker of Parliament. In 1984 a man from Warengeme 2 called Akis returned to the village after a number of years working as a teacher in different provinces. He was to become the leading figure of the O-faction. Over the next two to three years he built up various development-orientated organizations in Warengeme 2, thus establishing a power basis for himself in the village. He never made a secret of the fact that, eventually, he was aiming at a political career. In PNG, 1987 was election year, first the national elections and a few months later the elections for the provincial parliament in the ESP. Akis registered as a candidate for the Melanesian Alliance (MA) Party. The MA Party, it must be noted, plays a prominent role in the millenarian ideology of the NAC movement (according to their view, the instalment of an MA Prime Minister in PNG will coincide with the return of Jesus Christ and the beginning of the millennium). In the course of the election campaign Akis became Kulau's most serious rival, capitalizing on the reputation he had made for himself as a prominent man in the Youth Movement of the area. Also a very significant factor was the fact that Akis received the backing of the various NAC congregations in the area, notably also from the I-faction in Warengeme, previously his opponents in the village, who recognized the chance of toppling Kulau from power, and thus weakening the entire E-faction decisively, and also moving a step closer to the expected millennium. Although he in no way shared their millenarian convictions, Akis, naturally, embraced the support he received from the NAC people for tactical reasons.

The campaign was fought bitterly in the village. On one occasion it even came to blows between members of the rival groups. Moreover, in the hottest phase of the campaign rumours began spreading in the village that Kulau and his supporters were responsible for a number of recent deaths in Warengeme. These rumours are the *Leitfaden* of the mediation below. In the end Akis and his factional alliance won the elections by a safe margin; moreover, Akis's party joined a coalition and formed the government, and Akis became a provincial minister. This victory not only meant that the party power relations in the province were changed, it also meant a major reallocation of status and power in the village. Specifically, it meant a serious loss of standing for the, until then, prominent E-faction but it also meant that, for once, the I-faction found itself on the winning side, which gave the NAC as such, and its leaders especially, a tremendous boost.

This completely new configuration of power in the village, which had grown out of and, at the same time, produced an unusual pattern of alliances, begged an explanation, and needed to be moulded into an accountable and comprehensible form by, and through, the body politic of the village. Specifically, an accountable version of how this constellation had come about was needed, not least as a basis for understanding and reasoning in respect to the future development of relations in Warengeme. Such an official, accountable version of the recent past did not exist. The village had passed through a specific phase of time (or had time passed through the village?); what remained were numerous experiences and a variety of views of the past, coined by those experiences. What it needed now was *one* accountable version which had to be produced in discourse from the various transcripts in existence. Since this speech event took place in a conflict situation, in a dispute form, the issue of power comes in, in the sense of who can make his version of events count, and accountable.

The Mediation

The dispute took place in a legal framework, the mediation. Officially, the mediation had been called in order to bring light into a number of charges dealing with sorcery. As mentioned above, sorcery accusations had been raised in rumour form during the election campaign against the sitting member in parliament, Kulau of the E-faction, claiming that he was responsible for a recent death in the village. Although he took action against this at the time, the rumours did not subside, even after the elections were over. On the contrary, they snowballed, drawing other members of the E-faction into the plot in the process. At the time, the source or sources of the rumours had not been established but, as it became evident when the mediation was called, the prime suspects were located among the I-faction. It was the E-faction that demanded to have a mediation to clear up this matter, approximately six weeks after the elections. Thus, we have the following situation at the outset: allegedly the I-faction had accused members of the E-faction of sorcery killings. In the mediation itself the roles of accusers and suspects are changed around: now the E-faction accuses three members of the I-faction of slander, i.e. spreading the rumour that they (E-faction) were responsible for the deaths.

The mediation was held on two days in November 1987 on the central meeting ground in Warengeme, next to the *haus kiap* (government rest-house) and the court-house. The cast of this social drama is extensive and there is no space here to give a detailed account of who's who in the event. Suffice it to say, therefore, that there are four groups in the cast with different roles. First of all we have the four accusers or plaintiffs from the E-faction: Kulau the deposed MP, Ganja the councillor of Warengeme, Moli a leading *bisnis* man in the village (these three men are half-brothers, having the same father but different mothers), and Emul, a prayer leader of the Catholic Church, who himself is not accused in the rumours but creates his own involvement, officially on behalf of his sister's husband, who is one of the alleged sorcery victims. On the other side are the three suspects or accused of the I-faction. Pondo, a head priest of the NAC, and the two men Tete and Balif, who have no official function in the church but rank as important ideologists of the movement. Thirdly, we have the mediators. On the first day this role is taken over by the village magistrate Hausa (who is known to be a close friend of the E-faction), on the second day, when Hausa raises his own accusations against the I-faction, two mediators from neighbouring villages are brought in. Fourthly, there is the audience, the villagers of Warengeme, recruited from both factions but, notably also, men and women from Warengeme 2, i.e. supporters of the O-faction. The role of the public was that of a silent jury. Most significantly, Akis, the newly elected member and provincial minister, was there too during the whole event. On the agenda of the mediation were six recent deaths in the village; a seventh death was woven into the dispute on the second day. Although emotionally highly charged at times, the event was very informal in structural terms. There was no fixed seating or speaking order, and the event developed its own order as matters proceeded.

The Transformation of Disputes

In the context of a different writing project (my PhD thesis (Stephenson in press)) I transcribed and translated the entire speech event from tapes and attempted an analysis of it (significantly the whole mediation was held in Tok Pisin and not in the Wam language). As my analytical framework I used the concept of the 'transformation of disputes'. The term originally comes from the sociology of law. It is a heuristic device and it is useful in order to show 'how law and other normative frameworks are articulated, imposed, circumvented, and created as people negotiate social order in their transactions with each other' (Mather and Yngvesson 1981:775).

For Mather and Yngvesson the transformation of a dispute means 'a change in its form or content as a result of the interaction and involvement of other participants in the dispute process' (Mather and Yngvesson 1981:777). These other participants include the mediators, the witnesses that are summoned during the course of the mediation, and, last but not least, the audience, the men and women from Warengeme that came to witness and to participate in the dispute. In the end it is this audience conceptualized as a body representing the village's moral conscience which the actors are playing to and for.

There are three processes in the transformation of a dispute: rephrasing, narrowing and expansion. The three terms refer to three distinct processes, but they do not necessarily represent three consecutive steps the dispute passes through. Moreover, they refer to different directions and intentions the dispute is given in the course of the process. These different processes alternate.

The concept of rephrasing refers to reformulating the dispute into public discourse (Mather and Yngvesson 1981:777), i.e. the hidden transcripts in the form of rumours into public transcripts, public statements witnessed by the audience. In part, this actually is already effected in the act of calling in and staging the mediation in the first place.

The second process is that of narrowing. Mather and Yngvesson (1981:778) define it as follows: 'Narrowing is the process through which established categories for classifying events and relationships are imposed on an event or series of events, defining the subject matter of a dispute in ways which make it amenable to conventional management procedures.' They go on to specify more closely that 'narrowing ... means fixing or circumscribing a framework in which the dispute is defined, rather than simply reducing or limiting the number of issues' (1981:778).

Acquittal of the accusations of sorcery contained in the rumours is one of the primary aims of the plaintiffs, who, at the same time, are the initiators and the driving force behind the mediation. But the dispute addresses many more issues than merely these specific charges of sorcery. And it is here that we encounter the next process in dispute handling, that of expansion.

Expansion is the process by which new topics or aspects are introduced and woven into the dispute by altering or shifting the viewpoint or perspective of the discourse.

Expansion ... refers to a rephrasing in terms of a framework not previously accepted by the third party. Expansion challenges established categories for classifying events and relationships by linking subjects or issues that are typically separated, thus 'stretching' or changing accepted frameworks for organizing reality. Expansion does not necessarily imply the increase or magnification of issues in a dispute (although this may occur); it refers to change or development in the normative framework used to interpret the dispute (Mather and Yngvesson 1981:778).

The Dispute Process

The mediation starts with strongly voiced accusations on the side of the plaintiffs, maintaining that the three suspects of the I-faction were responsible for the spread of the rumours (at the same making it quite clear that there was no truth in them). The dispute gets bogged down very quickly and threatens to lose its direction. It is here that the process of narrowing sets in visibly. This process is effected not primarily by the mediator but by the plaintiffs themselves, making it quite clear who is in command of the show. The dispute is narrowed by moulding and articulating the broad and opaque accusations contained in the rumours into a clear structure based on three central issues, or *stori* as they are called in Tok Pisin. These central issues are three of the total of six deaths the mediation sets out to clear up. The remaining deaths are woven into the structure as the mediation moves along. Each of the three main deaths is allotted to one of the plaintiffs in turn: the death of Loto is linked to Ganja, the death of Ieti to Kulau, and Uhuru's death is allocated to Moli, in accordance with the rumours which portray each of these three men as responsible for one of the deaths. Thus we have neat couples consisting of victim and the person responsible for the death: Ganja–Loto, Kulau–Ieti, Moli–Uhuru. Accordingly, in the mediation the issues are addressed as Ganja's or Loto's *stori*, Kulau's or Ieti's *stori*, or Moli's or Uhuru's *stori*. The mediation digresses and talks about many other issues during the two days but it always returns to these central *stori*, thus giving the event a structure. The deaths, however, not only structure the meeting itself, they also structure the recent past in chronological (and sometimes causal) terms, i.e. Tete died before Ieti, Ieti died before Uhuru. The other deaths are then also included in this chronology. Into this temporal reference frame other events in the village are then inserted: so-and-so left the village before Tete died, or Kulau was in Wewak when Ieti died, that meeting was held two days before Uhuru died, etc. In this way the recent past is mapped, and secured as safe ground to move upon (at least for the plaintiffs).

The process of rephrasing refers to the changing of the transcriptual form of statements, i.e. of rumours that had, until then, travelled along hidden paths, shrouded in 'secrecy', which are now dragged out into the open and made public. Significantly it is not the suspected rumour mongers who do this, but the plaintiffs, i.e. the men of the E-faction. They rephrase the rumours they have heard in hypothetical self-accusations and present them to the meeting, in form like 'it is said that I collected money from *x* and *y* and gave it to some *sanguma* in the bush so that they kill Uhuru. Who knows anything about this?' or else 'we have heard people saying that Ganja killed Tete. Who knows anything about this?' Naturally, in the early phases of the mediation nobody ventures any suggestions concerning the authorship of the rumours, for fear of incriminating himself or herself. But in the course of the event the plaintiffs manage by a variety of strategies (the details of which I cannot go into here) to move the suspects into their focus and to hook the rumours on to them. What is sought in the process is the actual source of the rumours, the authorship. Under the pressure of the inquiry the suspects reluctantly admit having knowledge of them (but then the majority of the audience had known the contents of the rumours too) but deny having started them. In all cases responsibility is passed on to people who are not present at the meeting, either because they are in other villages, have migrated to one of the towns in PNG, or are dead. In due course, however, the plaintiffs succeed in twisting and turning the suspects' words – with the generous help of the suspects themselves, who, after a while, start contradicting themselves and incriminating each other – so they are able to 'construct' the necessary evidence to prove that it was the three suspects themselves that had started the rumours. Notably, this process is ongoing and goes up to the final stages of the mediation. The strategy is successful mainly because the plaintiffs succeed in expanding the dispute.

As described above, expansion does not mean merely adding new aspects to the dispute, but shifting or altering the viewpoint or perspective of the entire discourse instead. This, again, the plaintiffs accomplish in two ways. First, they succeed in changing the 'interpretative scheme' (Giddens 1979:83) of the encounter – in the narrower way, in the sense that they create a new, reverse scenario which shows that it was not they who had killed, or were trying to kill, their co-villagers but the other way round: the suspects, i.e. the three men of the I-faction, were responsible for some of the deaths and, more important, they were trying to have them, the plaintiffs, removed. They do this by picking up shreds of rumours that had caught their ear, chance statements that a suspect had made on an earlier occasion (but in quite different, neutral contexts), and by describing the suspects' habitual behaviour in the village, and then weaving together this new scenario.

Secondly, they expand the discourse by contextualizing the narrated events (the rumours and the deaths) and placing them in a much broader debate on the state of the village, within the framework of the metaphors of *kastom* and *komuniti* and with clear identities within this context. Here the creation of images plays a central role, images of self and images of others. The suspects too try to create images of themselves as righteous, law-abiding villagers that live up to their social and moral obligations but they are overwhelmed by the rhetorical competence of the plaintiffs.

The accusers' strategy has a number of prongs. First of all, they exploit the symbolism of mediations, i.e. what mediations stand for in their broader meaning. Although conflict resolution through talking also belonged to the traditional means of managing tensions in Wam culture, mediations in their present form are a modern institution and are associated strongly with the concept of *komuniti*. Theoretically, mediations are a means to put aside quarrels by talking with each other, by achieving a consensus over a disputed issue, in order that harmony and unity can prevail again in the community (practice belies theory here). Some of the main characteristics of a mediation should be transparency, openness and honesty on the part of the parties to the encounter, in line with the way the people believe modern society functions. This part is played in masterly fashion by the plaintiffs. In the course of the dispute they at times reveal knowledge that would have the quality of well-guarded secrets in traditional Wam society, such as the status of specific names (i.e. whether they are classified as ancestral, and thus significant names because different rights are attached to them), or the ownership rights to specific tracts of land, or for instance whether a man is a true member of a lineage or only adopted. Significantly, they display openness especially in reference to their own person and even when it could, under different circumstances, mean a loss of face. For example, at one stage in the mediation, talk turns to a disputed patch of sago the ancestral rights over which had been an issue in the rumours and a possible motive for the sorcery killings. Ganja is able to invalidate the allegations by confessing that, contrary to what people thought, his family had no claim to this land by force of ancestral names. Below, the names Hepi, Selim and Salio refer to three deceased lineage 'fathers' of Ganja:

> Alright, listen to this, all of you. This name Selim that John was given, and this name Hepi that Peter was given, there is nothing attached to these names, they are empty names [i.e. they are not ancestral names]. Salio too, Hepi and Salio, these are both empty names. . . . There is nothing attached [i.e. no land] to this name Hepi, nothing at all. You cannot bring in this talk about the sago in Turmo! This sago doesn't

belong to Selim, this sago doesn't belong to Hepi, nor to Salio! It belongs to somebody completely else. Do you hear me! These are empty names! . . . There is no land that goes with these names, none at all. And all the land that Salio used, it didn't belong to him, it belongs to some men of Selni [a neighbouring village].

This type of confession creates the impression that the plaintiffs are speaking the truth, not only on this specific point but all along the way, thus enhancing the credibility of their charges. They are thus complying with the stated ideals of *komuniti*.

Even though the charges become quite vicious in the course of the event and the three suspects are demoted and ridiculed, the *appearance* of a mediation is upheld right up to the end. Although the suspects are made to pay compensation in the end, it is made explicit that this is not to be regarded as a form of punishment but merely as a sign of reconciliation. The three men are even asked whether they agree with this measure. They do. Thus, the meeting ends on a fabricated note of consensus, and on the fiction of true equality, which is a central feature of the idea of *komuniti*. However, from a strategic point of view, retaining this appearance of a mediation gives the plaintiffs space to manoeuvre and bring over quite different messages to the meeting which have little to do with real social equality.

Churches are an important issue in the expansion of the dispute, mainly the status of the NAC in the village, under the wings of which enmity towards the E-faction was strongest. Whereas the suspects, above all Pondo, who is a so-called head priest in the NAC, profess their loyalty to the Christian faith and a righteous life by reference to their habit of belonging to the NAC and regularly attending service, the plaintiffs address the issue of faith and religiosity on a much broader scale. They do not refer to any single church organization but resort to a higher level of authority to lay claim to their righteousness, namely the Bible and God himself. Here especially Emul excels, the prayer leader in the ranks of the plaintiffs. Time after time he makes it quite clear to the meeting that he is acting not out of self-interst but that his innermost conviction drives him to 'bring these things out', i.e. make these charges against the suspects. At one point, early on in the mediation Emul raises charges against Pondo and the other suspects about spreading sorcery rumours in the village:

Pondo is just the right man to start such a thing. Their [i.e. the suspects'] way of life is not good, they look at their elder brothers and think of them as bad men [meaning *sanguma*]. And they spoil their good names. And also, they are plotting to kill them, they are out to kill them. . . . I cannot leave it hidden away, I cannot keep this hidden away inside me. We are all people of the church, when you talk, tell the truth. I speak all thoughts that I have inside me. What I hear with my ears and then goes down inside me, I must speak about. . . . I cannot hide this inside me, I'm telling you, I must say all these things. I thought about these matters and then I filed this complaint, because, in my opinion, on the part of the church, you are breaking the law of the church! God said it is forbidden to kill another man! God forbid this! Section number five [the fifth commandment]! It's the law of God, you're breaking this law about killing people, ruining a man's life, a life God made. You cannot kill others, that's bad, it isn't God's way, no, that's the way of Satan. This is what I thought, so I must put this out in public.

The other accusers, although not exactly famed for their religiosity, follow in his footsteps. In this way the plaintiffs succeed in creating the impression that they are the real representatives of the moral order in the village and that they are acting not out of self-interest but merely for the good of the community (which is of course only partly true).

As a sign of their unending faith and trust in God they point out that they are not afraid of *sanguma* sorcery, in fact they don't even believe that such a thing exists. Ganja underlines this claim with the fact that for many years he has been sleeping outside his house and not once has he heard or seen any evidence of sorcerers. In stark contrast, they then depict the suspects as weak and hysterical cowards who see sorcerers behind every tree. Ganja makes this point when he states:

I'm fed up with you weaklings, do you hear me! If you see a *sanguma* why don't you shoot him? Where I sleep in Eimuteneme, I don't lock myself in, I don't sleep in my house, not in the last 30 or 40 years. My hair is white now, I'm going bald, all my children are grown up now, but I've never seen a *sanguma*. But you, all the time you are seeing *sanguma*, *sanguma*, *sanguma*, and now I'm fed up of hearing what you see all the time, and fed up of talking about it.

In a next step in the line of this strategy they sketch (in words) a kind of 'sorcery map' of the village, showing in which areas and hamlets incidents of sorcery sightings and fear of sorcery are prevalent. Naturally the hamlet areas of the three suspects figure most prominently on this map. Further, they show the suspects not only to be hysterical cowards but, through describing their habitual behaviour, also as being secretive, furtive and reticent (e.g. staying away from the games of soccer, from parties, not coming to council meetings, etc.), thereby gradually fabricating an image of the suspects as exemplary figures that deal in sorcery. The picture is then rounded off with references to their role in the NAC, claiming that the suspects use their professed allegiance to the NAC as a cover-up for their sorcery activities.

This is one of the ways the NAC as a millenarian movement is brought into play, placed in the dock and reflected on in the framework of *kastom* and *komuniti*. They portray the NAC not as being modern, open and striving towards the ideal of *komuniti*, as it claims to be doing itself, but as deeply enmeshed in *kastom*. Furtiveness, reticence, superstition, sorcery, jealousy and rivalry (as the driving forces behind sorcery) are hallmarks of a *kastom* habitus. In combination with additional metaphors of past and future, tradition and modernity, light and darkness, dirt and purity, the plaintiffs are able to depict the three suspects, the NAC and, by associative extension, the entire I-faction as the epitome of *kastom*, thus laying the entire blame for the poor state Warengeme is in at their feet.

Images of Self

Whilst the I-faction is identified with and actually shown to be the epitome of *kastom*, the plaintiffs portray themselves as the paradigms of *komuniti*: open, forward-looking, modern, law-respecting and with true faith. They create images of themselves as responsible, valiant and outstanding leaders of the community, who are cabable of transcending the narrow confines of the village universe. For them Warengeme is no longer a self-contained entity but a part in a wider, more encompassing sociopolitical (and cultural) system. It is through men like them, their message goes, Warengeme will progress and play a formative role in the extended body politic of the ESP and PNG. In the fabrication of this image they apply a variety of rhetorical means. Thus, for instance, they emphasize their 'cosmopolitan' habitus showing themselves to be at home both in the village and the modern environment of Wewak (the capital of the ESP). They make frequent reference to figures of national or provincial significance (such as Bernard Narakobi) in a manner that suggests that they are well acquainted with them; they use terms and concepts which are not familiar in the village setting (such as the term lawyer); or else they exaggerate in their terminology such as when Ganja warns the suspects that if they don't cooperate now they will be taken to court 'under the correct section of the Village Court Act of Papua New Guinea inside the law of the Provincial Government and the National Government together!', making it look as if they have the full institutional force of the state behind them.

Another strategy they apply is the use of formality. The sudden switch to a highly formalized style of speech in a setting which is otherwise marked by informality not only boosts the speaker and the person addressed but also intensifies the impact of the message made. This type of formality is characterized by 'the invocation of positional and public identities rather than personal identities, an emphasis on social distance over intimacy, a showing of respect for the established social order . . . and general tone of seriousness' (Watson-Gegeo and White 1990:25–6). Thus, the plaintiffs frequently address, or refer to, each other not by their names but by their official positions: Kulau is 'honourable member and former Speaker of Parliament', or Ganja is addressed as Councillor or Master Councillor, or else they become instead of simply Ganja, Kulau or Moli, Mister Ganja, Mister Kulau, Mister Moli.

Apart from this indirect mode of making status claims evident, they occasionally, but very effectively, apply the direct mode, but not before the ground has been rhetorically prepared. By this I mean that they openly assert their identity as bigmen, thus quasi 'talking their status into existence'. At the end of one of his longer statements on the second day, Kulau wraps it all up when he exclaims:

> We the sons of this family [meaning himself and his two brothers Ganja and Moli] we've brought good things to the village, like the talk of the law, so that we can have peace in the village, and so that we can change our way of life. But no, you haven't changed, you're still the same as before. This concerns all the families here [i.e. the entire village], whatever ideas you have, whatever ways [to development] you have, I hold the key to it. If I remain a *kanaka* [a

backward, ignorant person], you too will remain a *kanaka*. I'm telling you here, if I remain a *kanaka* then you will stay *kanakas* as well. Or can *you* build modern houses with corrugated iron? No, you can't! I'm telling you.

In statements like this, and others, they make it quite clear to the meeting that, whilst their opponents are miserly, backward-looking rubbish-men, they themselves are true bigmen, not in the old sense necessarily, but modern leaders who are able to lead the village to development, but who all the same command the same degree of status and power as the former bigmen of the *tamberan*.

The creation of images, and thereby of identities, is both means to an end, and an end in itself. The immediate aim the plaintiffs are following in the mediation is of course the refutation of the rumours in the village which show them to be power-hungry evildoers who hire sorcerers to have people killed. The creation of powerful and contrastive images (themselves as responsible community leaders, the opponents as vile dabblers in sorcery) produces the necessary interpretative background to make the rumours look absolutely preposterous and, therefore, unfounded. This they achieve, of course. The second, and actually more substantial, aim they are following is the reordering of the power and status relations in the village and imprinting the order on the village's conscience in a public and accountable form, in other words, making it quite clear to the villagers who are the 'leaders' and who are the 'led'. As I mentioned earlier on, these power relations had become reversed, temporarily at least, through the elections and the fact that the NAC movement had gained a victory over the E-faction through supporting the newly elected MP, Akis. This pattern the plaintiffs set out to correct.

Naturally, the plaintiffs, especially the deseated MP Kulau, have to acknowledge that Akis has become the pre-eminent figure in the political order of the village, at least at present. There is no way of getting around this fact. They do it not ungrudgingly, but in style. One of the first things they have to do is to deliver a cogent explanation why Kulau, and with him the E-faction, lost the elections in the first place. Kulau was not re-elected, they argue, not because the people were dissatisfied with him – he had not failed to live up to the standards expected of him – but because of the insidious rumours that claimed him to be dealing in sorcery. Kulau himself brings this point over quite clearly when he states at one stage: 'I know that I lost this election because the word spread to all the areas that I was a *sanguma* man. I couldn't win any more then. I would lose.' The plaintiffs accept this fact and even endorse the new MP calling upon the villagers to support him in his work (thus at same time providing evidence that they are not power hungry). They do this, however, not without weaving a few little pinpricks into the statements. Thus, for instance, Kulau and Ganja frequently refer to Akis as their son ('my son beat me in the elections'), which, in terms of kinship, is correct but of course belies the present configuration of authority. At the end of one of his longer statements Kulau says to the audience: 'So, I release you people into his hands, and you stand by me and together we will support him, for he is our new member.' He makes it look as if Akis's ascent to power needed his consent and, in addition, he calls on the people to stand by *him*, faintly implying that he still had influence over the new MP's doings.

Akis himself had been an attentive listener to the dispute over the last two days. At the end of the mediation he was given the platform to address the meeting. Since the election campaign a few months earlier, he had not been on speaking terms with anyone of the E-faction, and the audience was eager to hear his opinion on the whole matter. Actually his speech attained the quality of an unofficial verdict, or at least result, of the contest, and a final assessment of the 'state of things' in the village, and the state of the village as such. In the course of his speech he clearly sides with the plaintiffs, his former opponents, and confirms their view of the situation. He uses the same tropes of formality as the plaintiffs did during the mediation, such as addressing Kulau as the 'Honourable Former Speaker of Parliament' and Ganja as 'Honourable Councillor'. The bigmen confirm each other in their status positions. At the same time, he condemns the suspects, his former allies, blaming them, as the plaintiffs had done before, for all the unrest and problems in the village, thus making it quite clear that, not only is he dissolving the factional alliance that had helped to bring him to power, but that he is placing them distinctly below himself and his former-opponents-become-allies. He lifts the latter up to nearly (but not quite) the same status level as his own and draws a clear line between those in the village who can claim bigman status and the other, 'normal' villagers. For a brief moment they are making hierarchy explicit. In the final phase of the dispute the preparations for having a communal meal, which all the disputants are called to contribute to likewise, are discussed. Thus the clear statements about the factual inequality in the body politic are absorbed quickly again and covered with the fictitious fabric of harmony and equality.

Conclusion

In the foregoing passages I have tried to describe how a mediation among the Wam people shifts its basis and its focus in the course of the event and develops a different form and quality of dispute.

Sorcery, deaths and rumours remain the *Leitfaden* of the event and structure it, but, through the processes of narrowing and expansion, more central and encompassing issues are woven into the discourse, which relate to the village as a whole.

One such issue is the effective order of the body politic and the ideological postulate of social equality. Like a picture captured on a photograph, the mediation briefly discloses the effective reality of unequal social relations, or, more precisely, the vexing interplay between the two principles equality and hierarchy become evident. For a passing instant identities of self and others are constructed in images, and differences in standing are made transparent and accountable. The reigning bigmen curb their competition and animosities towards each other for a brief moment in order to reify their joint interests and make hierarchy explicit, but, at the same time, the postulated differences between them and the remaining polity acquire relativity through the circumstance that it all takes place within a framework which is identified with equality, namely the mediation. Here I see certain parallels with the traditional culture in the sense that a similar pattern is discernible in the context of the *tamberan*, where the exchange feasts, which were staged at the end of an initiation cylce, provided the opportunity for bigmen not only to establish and prove themselves but also to briefly make status differences visible and accountable in a social order otherwise characterized by an egalitarian ethos.

Images of individual identities are important in this face-to-face society, but they are not the only images that are designed in the meeting. The village as a whole talks about itself, how it has fared in the recent past and where it stands in relation to the dominant, encapsulating modern world around it. The evaluation of the polity that has been constructed from the contrasting transcripts in the course of the event, acquires the quality of being the only, and the official, view of matters, at least until in a future mediation the present findings are possibly challenged, invalidated and replaced with a novel version which is congruent with the new setting. Not all those present were necessarily in agreement with the conclusions the meeting had reached but, given the reified power relations and the saliency of the accounts rendered, there was little leverage to challenge them and propagate an alternative transcript of the past and the reigning political order.

In order to grasp the deeper significance of the dispute one has to place it into a wider context of meaning. Although Warengeme faces numerous internal difficulties these, today, are always perceived and interpreted in the light of the higher aim the village has set itself: full participation and integration in the modern world. *Komuniti* is the envisaged state of existence but, in spite of the fact that the instrumental means for achieving *komuniti* are basically at hand (cash crops, road, school, churches, law, even a minister in the government), real *komuniti* is proving highly evasive. Moreover, the few fragments of *komuniti* that have been attained are constantly being threatened by the persistence of *kastom*, which lies hidden away but is evidentially ever present. Reaffirming the values of *komuniti* and expressing these in discourse are a vital process in this respect because they lend them a different texture. They are no longer merely the properties of ideational constructs which the villagers hear about in church or read about in the Bible. They become the properties of social practice, things members of their social universe did or, exactly the opposite, failed to do. On a deeper textual level one finds that the dispute develops a whole catalogue of contrasting values which defines the framework of morality in the village universe. Thus, for instance, public talk is set against rumours, openness against secrecy, the truth against lies, belief is held against superstition, clean is contrasted with dirty, generosity with selfishness, togetherness is opposed to singleness, law and order stand against anarchy, reconciliation against vengefulness, the new against the old society, the present and future versus the past, progress versus standstill, in short: *komuniti* versus *kastom*.

Notes

1. I conducted fieldwork in Warengeme in 1984/85 and again in 1987/88 for a total of eighteen months. The research was supported by a grant from the Swiss National Science Foundation.
2. In reference to people of Warengeme I have used pseudonyms.

References

Camp, Ch. (1983). The Peli Association and the New Apostolic Church. In: W. Flannery (ed.), *Religious Movements in Melanesia Today*, Vol. 1, pp. 78–93. Goroka: The Melanesian Institute (Point Series No. 2).

Caplan, P. (ed.). (1995). *Understanding Disputes: The Politics of Argument*. Oxford: Berg.

Gesch, P. (1985). *Initiative and Initiation: A Cargo Cult-Type Movement in the Sepik against its Background in Traditional Village Religion*. St. Augustin: Anthropos Institut (Studia Instituti Anthropos 33).

Giddens, A. (1979). *Central Problems in Social Theory: Action, Structure and Contradiction in Social Analysis*. Berkeley: University of California Press.

Goffman, E. (1959). *The Presentation of Self in Everyday Life*. New York: Doubleday.

Greenhouse, C. (1985). Mediation: A Comparative Approach. *Man* 20:90–114.

Gulliver, P. (1977). On Mediations. In: I. Hamnett (ed.), *Social Anthropology and Law*, pp. 15–52. London: Academic Press (ASA Monograph 14).

Keesing, R.M. and Tonkinson, R. (eds) (1982). *Reinventing Traditional Culture: The Politics of Kastom in Island Melanesia. Mankind* (special issue) 13(4).

Linnekin, J. (1992). On the Theory and Politics of Cultural Construction in the Pacific. *Oceania* 62:249–63.

Lutkehaus, N. (1990). Hierarchy and 'Heroic Society': Manam Variations in Sepik Social Structure. *Oceania* 60:179–97.

Mather, L. and Yngvesson, B. (1981). Language, Audience, and the Transformation of Disputes. *Law and Society Review* 15(3–4):775–821.

Paine, R. (1967). What is Gossip About? An Alternative Hypothesis. *Man* (n.s.) 2:278–85.

Stephenson, N. (in press). *From Kastom to Komuniti. A Study of Equality and Inequality in a Changing Society: the Wam of the East Sepik Province (Papua New Guinea)*. Basel: Wepf (Basler Betiräge zur Ethnologie 39).

—— (1994). Gais Nein zu Apels Appell. Eine millenarische Mythe als Kulturkritik bei den Wam (East Sepik Province, Papua-Neuguinea). In: B. Hauser-Schäublin (ed.), *Geschichte und mündliche Überlieferung in Ozeanien*, pp. 73–90. Basel: Wepf (Basler Beiträge zur Ethnologie 27).

Watson-Gegeo, K.A. and White, G.M. (1990). Disentangling Discourse. In: K.A. Watson-Gegeo and G.M. White (eds), *Disentangling: Conflict Discourse in Pacific Societies*, pp. 3–49. Stanford: Stanford University Press.

Weiner, J. (1982). Substance, Siblingship and Exchange: Aspects of Social Structure in New Guinea. *Social Analysis* 11:3–34.

Chapter 6

The Identity Construction of Ethnic and Social Groups in Contemporary Papua New Guinea

Berit Gustafsson

Introduction

Here we shall be concerned with the construction and maintenance of group identity in modern society in Papua New Guinea, and the occasions during which boundaries that distinguish one group from others would be defined.

The notion of identity would not be problematic for anthropologists only, but for people in Melanesia also, where concepts belonging to the indigenous culture are constantly challenged by extremely rapid and often radical social and political changes. Today there is also a steady increase in migration, from all parts of the nation, to the urban centres and to the provincial towns. Here individuals who are not related through kinship, nor are members of the same ethnic group, and who might not even speak the same language, are expected to associate regularly through work as well as in their spare time. In the urban centres, therefore, one could expect to find several new groups, consisting of colleagues, school mates and fellow members of, for example, sports teams. Although it would be most interesting to study the identity construction in urban centres, the focus of this study will be mainly on one 'ethnic' group, the Titan in Manus Province, where people still live a more 'traditional' life, and close to their kin.

Parkinson (1911) divided the people living in Manus Province into three ethnic groups, the Titan, the Matankor and the Usiai. Characteristic for the three groups was that they occupied different ecological niches, which was due to differences in their subsistence economy. Manus people would not, however, speak about themselves in those terms, and the ethnic group would never constitute a political or social unit, but, as is common in many Melanesian societies, the clans and villages constituted the largest cooperating units (Schwartz 1982). People certainly were aware of social, cultural and linguistic differences already then, only these referred to villages and neighbouring groups rather than to ethnic groups.

The Titan shared the same language, and for them belonging would be equal to the *wantok* system.[1] The Usiai and the Matankor, on the other hand, spoke different languages even among themselves, and were spread over several islands. It seems unlikely therefore that these geographically dispersed groups would have felt as if they were members of a larger ethnic group.

Even nowadays it is the Titan mainly who speak about themselves as a group, and the Usiai to a certain extent, while the Matankor would refer first of all to their village or language group. The notion of ethnic belonging is used, it seems, mainly when talking about others in a negative sense, to describe 'bad' customs among others, in contradiction to the 'good' customs of one's own group. When an individual identifies himself with a larger group, and not his descent group or clan, therefore primarily it would be with his *wantoks*. It is through your *wantoks* that you might get a job, a seat on the plane, and so on. The ethnic group thus never was a bounded unit and if it is important today this seems to be the result of modernization rather than of traditionalism. Thus it would be through school education, work and increased mobility mainly that people have become aware of the existence of ethnic differences.

I shall not continue to discuss ethnic groups here, partly because the subject is too big, and, as mentioned above, I doubt that the people (in Manus Province) have always identified themselves with an ethnic group, or have been aware of its existence even. What remains, then, is the second notion mentioned in the title – the construction of social groups. In society there would be a number of groups that all could be referred to as social; here, however, it will be used to describe one particular form of social unit only, a village.

The Notion of Group in Melanesian Society

The notion of group in Melanesian society is problematic, since as a rule 'the basic structures of these societies are not groups, but *relations of groups*' (Harrison 1993:14).

In Manus Province an individual, for example, primarily would identify himself with his descent group, and cooperation is mainly between members of this group. Secondly, it would be with his *tali* (the Titan word for clan), consisting of a number of descent groups who all trace origin from a common ancestor. Every village in the province is inhabited by several *talis*, each represented by its own leader, a *lapan*; yet these are no permanent cooperating units and are activated only occasionally, as in relation to life cycle rituals, when there is to be a distribution of wealth between affinal kin and when cooperation is demanded for a large-scale project of some kind. And only thirdly would an individual identify himself with the village, which would also be the same as his *wantoks*.

A village could be considered a relatively homogeneous unit, but from what has been said above it is obvious that it is not, and would consist instead of a number of more or less independent descent groups each constituting a political and social unit. A village therefore would not constitute a permanent unit with clearly defined boundaries towards the outside world. The descent groups are not autonomous, however, and each would have its own network of relations, established mainly through marriage and trade, extending outside the village. One easily could get the impression therefore that the villages are completely diversified. There are certain occasions, however, during which the dividing lines between the descent groups of the village would not be emphasized, and they would all identify themselves as a single unit.

In the traditional society this happened mainly in relation to warfare and trade. In Manus Province almost every village was specialized in the production of artefacts and food, and through a very elaborated sea-trade system the food and goods were distributed throughout the province. This trade was controlled mainly by the Titan, who lived along the south coast and on the smaller islands, and by the Matankor on the north coast. In trade each man was responsible for collecting the food and valuables that he would exchange later with his personal partner, belonging to a different village. A man did not travel alone, however, but several canoes from the same village, each occupied by members of the same *tali*, would travel in a convoy. The convoy was led by a man who, apart from being leader of his own *tali*, was authorized to lead the expeditions (Gustafsson 1992:84).

The other occasion when a village would be constructed as a unit was in relation to warfare. In Manus Province there were two kinds of warfare. The descent groups each might have their personal enemies, in the same village even, and fights broke out frequently. These fights never led to the involvement of other descent groups, and were between the two parties only.

The second kind of warfare happened between villages, and here all men in the village would fight together as a group. In this warfare, as in trade, there was only one of the *tali* leaders – who inherited his skill to lead raiding parties, from his father – who was authorized to lead the expeditions. Should another man, although he was also in a leadership position, take over, the expedition would be expected to fail.

As yet I have not studied Manus warfare in any detail; still, from earlier ethnographies we learn that raids were performed as part of the ritual system, and were undertaken especially in relation to initiation of young men, and when there was death in the village (Mead 1937:233–349). War raids usually were planned against neighbouring groups with whom one already had established relations through trade or marriage, and rarely against more distant villages. The Usiai were said to capture bodies in war while the Titan were headhunters, and the goal was to kill an enemy and to take a trophy. The heads were brought back to the village where they were placed in the men's house (Nevermann 1934:364).

According to custom, when a man who had been the head of his house died, his skull was kept in the house, to protect and prosper his living relatives. Skulls from enemies killed in war were, on the other hand, kept in the men's house, to which all men in the village had entrance. The skull belonging to a dead relative protected and prospered the individual descent group only and, as I have argued elsewhere (Gustafsson 1992), symbolized the unity of the smaller group. A reasonable conclusion therefore would be that the skull of a stranger, which was brought inside and after being transformed by the men, had power that prospered the community. Skulls captured in war would thus symbolize the social and political unity of the community.

Warfare and trade were special occasions in more than one way. To start with, the village would then function as a unit *vis-à-vis* other units constructed in the same way. Secondly, there was one man only who had authority to lead the expeditions, consisting of members from all *talis* in the village. The single leadership, I shall argue here, was a further expression of the unity of the village.

Simon Harrison, who made studies on warfare among the Avatip, in the Sepik area, describes a political system similar to that found in Manus Province. The Avatip villages, he says, are no actual political units, but the political units are the dozen or so local descent groups that compose each village (1993:133). The only time when the (Avatip) village is formed as a single interlocking whole is in relation to the men's cult and the headhunting raids that are (or were) part of the cult (1993:76). In the men's cult the village is portrayed as a sharply bounded and unified social universe, and the men are thereby trying to transform a conception of themselves as simply a co-resident collectivity of kin and neighbours interacting in various ways with each other and with outsiders, into a conception of a specifically political entity independent of others (1993:150).

Both in the middle Sepik area and in Manus Province, although the reasons might have been different, it was only in relation to war, and (on Manus) trade, that villages would separate themselves out from each other and identify themselves as distinct groups. Boundaries between villages, then, were not permanent, they did not exist in everyday life, and repeatedly these had to be reconstructed, and, as pointed out by Simon Harrison, '[in Melanesia] it is not so much groups that make war, but war that makes groups' (1993:18).

Processes of Modernization

The problem discussed here, how groups are constructed and defined in contemporary society, automatically would lead to questions such as what do we mean when talking about modernization? Modernization as a concept has been used in many senses: as an attribute of history, to describe a specific transitional process, and as development policy in Third World countries. Furthermore it has been viewed as a universal process, characteristic of human societies rather than a concrete historical process taking place in specific societies during specific periods, or modernization has been related to economic growth, and equated with Westernization (Hettne 1990:62).

Although modernization theories have been much criticized they still constitute the popular image, and Western thinking is even nowadays predominant also in many developing nations. It has been deemed necessary therefore for the 'new nations' of the decolonized world to imitate the Western model. As part of this process people have become subject to definitions of themselves held by remote others (such as a centralized administration), to the needs, aspirations and values of people they do not know, and they become dependent upon, and vulnerable to, institutions and resources outside and beyond their control or understanding (Berreman 1978:53). Further, it has led to the adoption of new institutions which are assimilating, in the sense that they unite people from different social and ethnic groups. People are now expected to associate with colleagues, to look upon each other as Christians, wage workers, carpenters, school teachers, and to associate on a friendship basis in various leisure activities such as soccer, netball and hockey.

These assimilating processes have not, however, led to a complete integration between the Titan, the Matankor and the Usiai in Manus Province, but instead to a growing concern with cultural identity (which is shown also through other recent studies, such as those by Carrier and Carrier (1989) and Otto (1991)). The modernization of Manus society has not, therefore, at least not so far, led to that people abandoning their distinctiveness, but in fact they work actively to maintain, or create even, separate cultural and linguistic identities. People living in the same village thus would not define themselves as a group, and the descent groups are still the basic cooperating units, each with its own network of relations. Permanent relations, then, are still based on the same criteria as in the old days, such as, kinship, marriage or the *wantok* system.

We can therefore expect individuals to continue to deploy customary ways for the creation of groups also, and for the construction of boundaries towards others. Warfare and the more elaborated trade have long since been officially discouraged, and the only kind of activities that one would find today that would be performed on a more regular basis and involve several villages are sports, especially soccer and hockey, and to a certain extent gambling. Occasions of sports and gambling, therefore, I shall argue here, are modelled upon warfare and the more elaborated trade systems, and have replaced the latter two as a framework for communication between groups.

Earlier Studies on Sports and Gambling

Sport and leisure activities have been studied mainly by sociologists such as Norbert Elias and Eric Dunning (Elias and Dunning 1986; Dunning and Rojek 1992), both departing from a theory referred to as 'process sociology', and by Desmond Morris (1981). Morris is concerned with football as a transformation of hunting, and the sport to kill in Roman arenas. He speaks about the team in a football game as a tribe, and the game which involves two tribes is a symbolic combat, where the team try to pass by the other tribe in order to perform a symbolic killing. According to Morris's own interpretation the football is the weapon and the goal is the victim which is symbolically killed by the ball (Morris 1981:15). Every football season, then, is a formalized combat performed either to improve the status of the tribe or to defend it.

In 'process sociology', development is seen as a process of evolution, leading from a more primitive and violent society towards one which has more control over people. According to Elias and Dunning (1986:41), then, the popularity of sport is related to developments in (English) society, and the increasing need to control strong feelings of antipathies towards people, of anger, wild hatred and so forth. Under such circumstances people would develop some countermeasures against the stress tensions that thereby are generated, and sport as a form of physical combat of a relatively non-violent type has become a means through which these feelings can be expressed (Elias and Dunning 1986:26, 41, 165). In the case of societies at a relatively late level of civilization one could therefore observe a considerable variety of leisure activities with that function.

Dunning and Rojek (1986:4), finally, do not say directly that sport is performed like a war raid, only that the two spheres are interconnected; both involve forms of conflict that are subtly interwoven with forms of interdependence, cooperation, and 'we-group' and 'they-group' formation. Today most people would agree that there is a connection between war and sports, that the meanings associated with warfare often have been transformed into occasions of sport. What Dunning says is interesting; yet he fails to develop the discussion to include other aspects of society, and more importantly, which is opposite to what is maintained here, he takes for granted the existence of groups and that the matches would serve to defend already defined boundaries.

Anthropologists have as yet not devoted themselves to any extensive studies on the meaning of sports in society. Harrison, for example, mentions sports only, and says that the Avatip's attitudes towards war are still evident nowadays in football matches and other sports contests which villages arrange with each other (1993:81–6). Football matches have become something of a modern substitute for headhunting raids, and many of the ritual preparations that were performed before a war raid are performed also before the games. As described earlier it was only in relation to the men's cult and the headhunting raids that the village was portrayed as a bounded social and political entity. If we accept that Avatip football matches are transformations of headhunting raids, then these would be the occasions in modern society during which the village would be constructed as a single bounded unit.

Peter Lawrence (1966) observed already in the 1950s that the Garia in the Madang District played football as if it was a war raid. Football was played between teams from different security circles, and the aim was to shame the other team, the 'enemy', by scoring quickly and then running off with the ball, or to play on to a draw if the players wanted to settle their dispute. The Trobriand cricket games are a further example of how people have adopted a game from outside, and have transformed a traditional notion, i.e. warfare into a modern context.

It is unfortunate that anthropologists have not devoted themselves to studies on sports, and have only included their observations in their reports, especially since we could expect that the meanings associated with these kinds of activities in Melanesia, for example, would be quite different from those associated with sports and games in a Western society. Although certain kinds of sports and gambling have gained popularity all over the world and almost everywhere the same rules are applied to the games, this does not give us reason to conclude that they are performed for the same reasons everywhere.

Sports and gambling, then, I am arguing here, are not merely leisure activities, nor do they serve as outlets for feelings no longer accepted by society, but represent aspects of the culture in which they are performed. A game or sport could be seen as a collective ritual, when dividing lines between people living in the same village disappear for a moment and they all become members of a single bounded unit. Using Turner's phrasing, the occasions could be seen as liminal periods during which people need not be concerned about status relationships with one another or with one's roles in ongoing daily life (Turner 1983:123–64). The atomism of the different descent groups thus would lose its divisiveness in the presence of the game, and through the game they become a social unit in relation to other groups.

One can be almost certain that, especially when members from several villages participate, there exist some tension. Rituals of sports and games that make visible a collective connection with some common symbol or activity can, however, minimize for a moment their disconnections and conflicts in a crowd, even while depicting them (Moore and Myerhoff 1977:5). Rituals of sports and games thus may do much more than mirror existing social arrangements and may help even to create and to define them.

Sports meets, I said, are collective rituals and are occasions during which individuals would identify themselves primarily as members of a larger group, such as a team or a village. The notion of identity therefore would be intimately bound up with the social context. A person does not have just one single identity, however, but he carries simultaneously a range of identities, just as each individual occupies a number of statuses and plays a variety of roles (Epstein 1978:100). Goodenough (1965:2) referred to statuses and roles as social identities. The social identity thus would be an aspect of self and would differ depending on the occasion, whether the person is acting as a colleague, a relative or a friend. An individual when he plays soccer with the village team would thus identify himself as a villager, while in everyday life he might work together with men of the same descent group, in his role as a relative. The social identity thus is not permanent but, as I said above, depends on the occasion.

The identity of a social group could be described in a similar way, only its identity would be affected by its status *vis-à-vis* other groups, and not individuals. Leach (1967:34) referred to ethnicity as a matter of classification: '*I* identify myself with a collective *we* which is then contrasted with some other . . . What *we* are, or what the other is will depend upon context.' What Leach says implies that we are who we are by virtue of some common attribute or property we see ourselves as sharing, as against those who are perceived not to possess it.

Although Leach is talking about identity of ethnic groups, what he says, I shall argue here, could well be applied to social groups also. Social identity could thus be seen as a two-way process (Epstein 1978:14); in differentiating others one is also defining oneself. The sense of group identity appears, therefore, as a function of the interplay of external and internal perceptions and responses.

The Introduction of Sports and Gambling in Papua New Guinea

Many of the sports and games, which today are played all over the world, in a more or less identical manner, originated in England. They spread from there to other countries mainly in the second half of the nineteenth and first half of the twentieth centuries (Elias and Dunning 1986:126). Sports, and cricket and soccer especially, were introduced in Papua and New Guinea by the colonial administrations and the missions. This was done to present an alternative to the cultural practices they had outlawed, and also it was an attempt to make former enemies associate on a friendly basis (Matane 1972:68–72). The Papuan Government Anthropologist F.E. Williams felt 'tempted' even to suggest 'Less Christ and more Cricket' as the solution (Wolfers 1971:45). Both soccer and cricket were assimilated almost spontaneously into the activities and institutions of traditional society, and officially encouraged by the colonial administrations as a substitute for warfare, as a means of releasing pent-up energy.

In Manus Province gambling was first introduced by Chinese tradesmen who early established themselves in the area. The Chinese did not, however, arouse the local people's interest in card games, and it was not until the arrival of American soldiers, who were stationed in Manus Province during the Pacific War, that gambling became popular in the villages. Gambling, however, was soon made illegal by the administration. It is uncertain exactly when soccer and other games were introduced; however, it seems most likely that it was done by missionaries who arrived in Manus Province at the beginning of this century. The Paliau Movement[2] also contributed to the popularity of sports, and its leader Paliau Maloat encouraged villages to play against each other.

Sports in Manus Province

When visiting villages in the province today, one is struck by the enthusiasm people show when they talk about sports and gambling. In villages on the south coast especially, there is a lot of gambling, with cards and bingo, and in the province there are also several sports tournaments. The eastern part of the province, inhabited mainly by the Matankor, for example, has its own sports tournament, Rabatona Cup, and the Titan have their own Titan Cup. The tournaments are restricted, however, in the sense that the winning teams would never meet to play against each other, and the Titan therefore would never constitute a single group that would play against the Matankor or the Usiai. The tournaments, as mentioned above, consist mainly of people belonging to the same 'ethnic' group. This, however, is not due to strong feelings of solidarity; rather, they have become 'ethnic' since people with the same subsistence economy tend to live in the same areas.

The Bismarck League Hockey Games

The following example derives from M'buke Island, which is situated on the south coast of Manus, where I conducted my fieldwork. The majority on M'buke would say that they are interested in sports, and yet very few actually practise any kind of sport on a regular basis. People would gamble with cards, and every night there would be bingo, but there are no permanent sports teams. There are, however, two tournaments: the Titan Cup and the Bismarck Hockey League, the latter being confined to M'buke only. The hockey teams consist of men and women who have migrated to the urban centres, Port Moresby, Wewak, Madang, Lae, Rabaul, Lorengau, and then there are M'buke teams. Each group would have teams both for men and for women.

The Bismarck League is held every second year only, and in 1994 there was special excitement in the village since they were to celebrate its tenth anniversary. The teams started their training about five or six months before Christmas. While there had been no sport activities prior to this, suddenly almost every young man and woman would be engaged in hockey. M'buke has a youth club which is responsible for arranging youth activities; yet it was only after some of the village leaders had decided that it was time to start making preparations for the Christmas activities, i.e. the League, that the games were being organized. The initiative thereby came from the older men, who also sent a message to those who have migrated from M'buke and now live in the urban centres, that they also should start their training.

The hockey matches on M'buke that henceforth were played every afternoon were, as far as I could see, rather loosely organized. The players followed the rules of the game, but the composition of the teams varied, depending upon who had the time and desire to play, and the number of players on each side was not always even. And, seemingly, there was no emphasis upon winning, and no competition between the local teams, maybe because in the end they were all to play for M'buke.

The teams usually would play in the afternoon, on a field in the centre of the village and close to the community house, after they had finished work, and before the evening meal. Although there was much talk about the game and about the forthcoming activities, the audience that was present each afternoon did not take much notice of what was taking place on the field. Rather, this seemed to be an occasion for both men and women to sit down, to chew betel-nuts, to relax and to chat a little. Thus it was not the actual game that was interesting, but, I shall argue here, rather it was an occasion to join in a mutual activity, and those who did not play could make an excuse to get away from the house and from work, for as long as the training lasted.

The Finals

On M'buke there is a large field outside the schoolhouse, on the edge of the village, and this is where the Christmas hockey games would be held. At one end of the field a podium would be erected for the occasion, for sponsors, organizers and functionaries; otherwise it is just a large grass field where the audience would squat along the sides. Above I said that the games involve M'buke

Titan only, and yet the players are divided and the teams are constructed according to where people live. The teams certainly are playing to win, and they would all have their supporters, in those who are not playing but live in the same urban centre, or on M'buke. Thus the challenge and competition is there, and yet the games are friendly and arguments or fights would rarely, if ever, occur. The purpose of this contribution is to describe the construction of groups, and since the games strictly follow international rules, and nothing spectacular would happen during the matches, these will not be described here.

When the games are over, after three or four days, the chairman of the occasion, who this year was the leading *lapan*, would distribute the prizes. Usually there are two trophies in the village, one for the winning male team and one for the female. Each trophy would be used for a certain number of years only, and the team who win the games of the last year, would keep the trophy. Otherwise it is up to the winning teams to decide whether the trophy should remain on M'buke, if the players live elsewhere, or they should take it with them, only to bring it back for the next league. In 1994 there were no trophies, however, and instead the winning male and female teams received fifty kina each.

The trophy is not the only reward, but the efforts of individual players, such as the best kicker and the best goal maker, would be noticed and rewarded. All players, and especially those who are working and come home for their holidays, are asked to buy goods, such as torches, thermoses, pots and pans, or whatever would be of some use in everyday life, and which could be used as prizes. The chairman would first give the trophies to the winning teams, and then the minor prizes to individual players.

Finally, when the games are over and the prizes have been distributed there would be a big party at night. The women prepare the food, which then would be displayed on a long table erected on the field. The table is for the food only and the guests, after they have taken their food, therefore would have to find a different place to eat, sometimes not even close to the table.[3] This is the only communal meal in relation to the games and it is not for the players, the audience and functionaries only, but for all people on M'buke. The meal marks the end of the games.

After the games there might be some further celebrations among the teams themselves. In this case, the teams from Port Moresby organized their own picnic on a nearby island. Other villagers who wanted to join them were refused and were told that this party was for those who came from Port Moresby only, and who had helped in sponsoring their teams.

Above I said that the players are divided in teams, depending upon where they live now. This division does not extend outside the field, however, and the individual players primarily are members of and live with their families. Players from different teams therefore might live in the same house and eat together even while the games last. Earlier I said that an individual has several social identities. During the games not only one identity would be emphasized, but an individual would be both a villager, or a migrant, in relation to the games, and a relative, outside the field.

It is obvious that the goal in the Hockey League is not to create boundaries between *talis*, since each team would consist of members from different *talis*. Neither do the games create boundaries between locals and migrants, since outside the field both groups would associate and sleep in the same houses. Further, the games are friendly and individual efforts are recognized. A reasonable conclusion thus would be that the games are what Turner would call liminal periods (1983:123) during which status relationships and rules of respect and avoidances are not emphasized. What is emphasized rather is the unity of the village, not towards others – there are no outsiders present – but between themselves. We shall return to this discussion but first let us continue with a description of soccer games between villages.

The Titan Cup

The Titan Cup, unlike the Bismarck League, involves people from several villages. The name indicates that it is for the Titan only; yet Usiai people who live nearby would be welcome to watch, and even join, if they can present a team. Both the Titan and the Usiai, should they participate, come from villages that once used to establish relations through marriage, trade and war. The tournaments therefore would consist mainly of former friends and enemies.

The soccer tournaments are not set especially for Christmas, but could be performed at any holiday, such as Easter or the (British) Queen's birthday. There are no M'buke soccer teams in the urban centres, and those who happen to be at home during the holidays would therefore join the local teams. Certainly migrants are encouraged to support the village teams, but due to short holidays and expensive transport few would come home apart from during Christmas.

The teams that participate in the Titan Cup all come from the south coast of Manus, and come from places such as Timbunai, Baluan, M'buke and Pere. Some time before the games are due to start, it is decided where to play. If, for example, Pere is chosen, the villagers would have to make certain preparations. Apart from having to prepare the field, they also have to make sure there are houses available for all teams. The teams would not stay together, and thus there would be one house for each village, i.e. one for M'buke, one for Timbunai and so on. Before and during the games there is no communal eating, but each village, consisting of teams and supporters, has to bring its own food and to prepare it on its own fires. Which means that already before the teams depart from their home villages, not only do they have to prepare themselves for the games, but also they would have to collect food. The games usually last three or four days, and during this time all the teams and their supporters would stay together in the same place. In a village with a population of a few hundred there might therefore be thousands of people.

These sports meets are bigger and last longer than any other kind of get-together outside the village. Each occasion would therefore have to be sponsored, planned for and organized a long time ahead. Organizers and sponsors thereby might improve their reputation and gain prestige, but more importantly it is the prestige of the community that is at stake. The prestige that comes with winning the cup, and having the trophy, as we shall see, is for the village as a unit and not for the organizer, or for the teams.

When soccer was first introduced in the province the rules of the game were interpreted rather differently. As yet I have not been able to get information on how these earlier matches were performed; today, however, as in hockey, the teams would follow international rules. The games will not therefore be described here, but instead I shall be concerned with how the teams relate to each other.

Supporters would join the teams and their 'job' is to challenge the players before they go to the field. The aim is to make the players fierce and aggressive, since then they are expected to play better. To win is the ultimate goal. In the old days, before a war raid, and even before a trade expedition, the men would gather in the men's house to eat and to dance on a special dancing-beam called *tjinal*, in order to get prepared for the coming raid or expedition. Dances were also performed on the *tjinal* in relation to distributions of wealth, where the side who was giving wealth insulted and challenged the other side to accept the goods and make a return payment later (Mead 1930:68–9). The performance by supporters before the match, it seems reasonable to conclude, then, is like the preparations before a war raid in the old days, and a challenge to make the players ready for battle.

The heated atmosphere thus achieved would have effects on the game and, in contrast to the hockey games, in soccer conflicts and fights often would emerge while they are still playing. The aggression is not directed towards other players only, but disagreements with the referees could be a reason to start a fight. Furthermore it is not unusual to have fights after a match, and these usually would be initiated by teams who have lost their games.

That it is not only among the Titan that matches could lead to a fight I found out through some very disappointed younger men, who had been prevented from playing in the Rabatona tournament, for the same reason. The games had already started, when a woman was insulted by a man from a different village. The two villages were enemies by tradition, and immediately the young men from the woman's village got hold of spears and bush-knives and hunted their 'enemies' into the bush. The older men then decided that those who had been fighting would not be allowed to participate in the game.

It is obvious that tensions exist between villages, and, although the match might minimize for a moment their disconnections and conflicts, little is needed to disrupt the order. Old feelings of hostility are not forgotten. The tendency, especially among the younger men, to fight has led to the older men on M'buke temporarily stopping the games, and no one is willing to sponsor the teams. Thus for the M'buke right now there are only the hockey matches.

After three or four days, when the games are over, the chairman or organizer would hand over the trophies to the winning teams, one male and one female. As in the Bismarck League, a trophy would be used a limited number of years only, and each year the names of the players of the winning team are engraved on it. Here there is no doubt where the trophy should be placed; however, the winning teams always would take it to their village. When the M'buke won the trophy it was placed in the community house, and was shown to visitors with pride.

In the Titan Cup there are no prizes for the individual players, however; here it is only the teams that are recognized and rewarded.

When the games are over, if further arrangements have not been postponed because of fights, then for the first time there would be a large communal meal, to mark the ending of the games. Larger gatherings, whether they consist of members from the same village or come from different villages, would end in the same way, with a communal meal. It is worth mentioning that peace ceremonies, in the old days, always would end with the sharing of betel-nuts and a meal. It was only after this that the peace was confirmed.

Conclusion

The aim here has been to discuss the identity construction of villages in modern society, how they define and maintain their boundaries towards others, and the occasions during which this would happen. Warfare and the more elaborate trade with personal partners, which were the occasions when villages would function as social groups in the old days, have disappeared and, as I have been arguing here, have been replaced with sports, and in Manus Province especially with the tournaments. The tournaments thus, I said, are transformations of warfare and (among the Titan) the more elaborated sea-trade expeditions.

War never was made primarily to achieve more land, but raids were performed as part of the ritual system and the aim was to transform power from outside, through the capture of a skull (among the Titan) or a body (among the Usiai). The skull, the trophy, was then kept in the men's house as a symbol for the social and political unity of the village, which was never manifest in everyday life, where the basic cooperating units were the descent groups.

Sports teams are also ad hoc alliances and are not based on the normal network of kinship relations, but are composed of members of all *talis* in the village. Earlier we said that an individual has several social identities, sometimes as a colleague, as a relative or as a villager. In the tournament it is obvious that only one of the identities is emphasized, that of the villager, and there is only one communal goal – to win the tournament and to capture the Cup trophy. Winning therefore always is spoken of in terms of the village, and not in terms of the teams, and the trophy, typically, never would be kept in a private house, but in the community house, to which all villagers have entrance. The Cup trophy then could be seen as a transformation of the skull belonging to an enemy killed in war, which is brought into the village, where, after being transformed, it would symbolize the unity of the village collective.

One important goal with the tournaments, then, is to define the social and political boundaries of the village, to create and maintain a group identity. During the tournaments the lines that in everyday life divide the descent groups of the village would lose their divisiveness, and the players and the supporters (who accompany the teams) would look upon themselves primarily as members of their village. Thus, even today the village is not a permanent social and political unit, but repeatedly has to be reconstructed, and in conclusion one could say that, if it was war that made groups in the old days, today it is soccer that makes groups.

Although the Bismarck League is organized in a similar way to the Titan Cup, the construction of the teams is based on residence, as if they came from different villages, and the challenge, the goal to win the trophy, is there. Still, there are differences. First of all, in the League the teams would not constitute a single group with defined boundaries towards the other teams. The dividing lines between different descent groups do not cease to exist entirely, and when the games are over for the day, the individual players would identify themselves mainly as relatives and would eat and sleep with their families. The goal with the Bismarck Hockey matches, thus, is not to create a single unit, to define boundaries towards the outside. Yet it is the village that is emphasized and not the *talis*, since each team would consist of members from all *talis*. Thus, although divided, the division of the teams does not follow the boundaries between descent groups and *talis* that exist in everyday life.

A reasonable conclusion therefore would be that, while the tournament is an occasion during which boundaries are created, in a rather aggressive way, towards outsiders, the League is an occasion when the villagers confirm, in a more peaceful way, the unity of the village, not towards the outside, but among themselves. Thus the normal organization of the village would not be denied entirely, and individual efforts also would be recognized.

Earlier I said that in sociological studies violence would be seen as something negative and undesired, something which might destroy society and thus has to be suppressed and controlled. Sports therefore would be seen as a substitute, as a means through which 'undesired' feelings could be expressed. The violence associated with Manus warfare was never negative, however; it would not destroy society – there were no permanently bounded units to defend – and instead war served to create groups and to help identify the boundaries between them. As mentioned earlier, the tournaments involve groups of people who as a rule already have established peaceful relations through marriage or trade. Violence that might occur during a game therefore is not necessarily negative; the aim is not to destroy, and violence rather is a social activity symbolizing a certain kind of relation – that between villages as wholes. The meaning of sports in Manus society would therefore be rather different from that associated with sports in European society, at least as it is interpreted by Elias and Dunning. Rather the violence in sports is part of the ritual system, where violence is 'used' to capture the trophy, symbolizing the strength and unity of the village.

It has not been possible to discuss gambling here; in the early 1950s, however, the Titan had developed a system with gambling with cards where every man had his personal partner in another village, and large sums of money changed hands every week. Special gambling rules and ethics were developed, and the games were referred to in the same way as warfare had been spoken of in pre-Christian days (Mead 1956:253). This system was not, however, given a chance to develop fully; gambling was forbidden by the Government, and nowadays takes place within the village only.

In village gambling individuals that normally would have to avoid each other, due to kinship regulations, would sit down and play in the same room, sometimes beside each other even. Individuals would play against each other, and the winners are expected to distribute their gain amongst members of their own descent group only. The players therefore, although they are involved in a shared activity, do not cooperate for a single communal goal; there are no teams, but individuals challenge each other. The prestige a successful gambler might achieve would therefore fall to himself only and his descent group, never the village. Gambling, then, shares more similarities with trade, where, although it was a collective activity, each man had his own partner.

Notes

1. *Wantok* is Tok Pisin and refers to people who all share the same indigenous language.
2. A political and religious movement that was established in the province in 1945, and which is still active now under the name *Win Neisen*.
3. This is nothing extraordinary, however, and as yet I have not seen people sit down at the same table.

References

Berreman, G.D. (1978). Scale and Social Relations: Thoughts and Three Examples. In: Fredrik Barth (ed.), *Scale and Social Organization*, pp. 41–77. Oslo: Universitetsförlaget.

Carrier, A. and Carrier, J.G. (1989). *Wage, Trade, and Exchange in Melanesia: A Manus Society in the Modern State*. Berkeley: University of California Press.

Dunning, E. and Rojek, C. (1992). Introduction: Sociological Approaches to the Study of Sport and Leisure. In: E. Dunning and C. Rojek (eds), *Sport and Leisure in the Civilizing Process: Critique and Counter-Critique*, pp. xi–xix. London: Macmillan.

Elias, N. and Dunning, E. (1986). *Quest for Excitement: Sport and Leisure in the Civilizing Process*. Oxford: Basil Blackwell.

Epstein, A.L. (1978). *Ethos and Identity. Three Studies in Ethnicity*. London: Tavistock.

Goodenough, W.H. (1965). Rethinking 'Status' and 'Role'. Toward a General Model of the Cultural Organization of Social Relationships. In: M. Banton (ed.), *The Relevance of Models for Social Anthropology*, pp. 1–24. London: Tavistock (ASA Monographs 1).

Gustafsson, B. (1992). *Houses and Ancestors. Continuities and Discontinuities in Leadership among the Manus.* Gothenburg: Institute for Advanced Studies in Social Anthropology (IASSA).

Harrison, S. (1993). *The Mask of War. Violence, Ritual and the Self in Melanesia.* Manchester and New York: Manchester University Press.

Hettne, B. (1990). *Development Theory and the Three Worlds.* Harlow: Longman; New York: Wiley.

Lawrence, P. (1966). The Garia of the Madang District. *Anthropological Forum* 2(3–4):387.

Leach, E. (1967). *A Runaway World.* London: Oxford University Press.

Matane, P. (1972). *My Childhood in New Guinea.* Oxford: Oxford University Press.

Mead, M. (1930). *Growing up in New Guinea. A Comparative Study of Primitive Education.* New York: William Morrow and Company.

—— (1937). *Cooperation and Competition Among Primitive Peoples.* New York and London: McGraw-Hill Book Company.

—— (1956). *New Lives for Old: Cultural Transformation – Manus 1928–1953.* New York: William Morrow and Company.

Moore, S.F. and Myerhoff, B.G. (1977). Introduction: Secular Ritual: Form and Meaning. In: S.F. Moore and B.G. Myerhoff (eds), *Secular Ritual,* pp. 3–24. Assen, Amsterdam: Van Gorcum.

Morris, D. (1981). *Fotbollsfolket.* Stockholm: Nordstedts Förlag.

Nevermann, H. (1934). Admiralitäts-Inseln. In: G. Thilenius (ed.), *Ergebnisse der Südsee-Expedition 1908–1910 II. Ethnographie: A. Melanesien Band 3.* Hamburg: Friederichsen, De Gruyter & Co.

Otto, T. (1991). *The Politics of Tradition in Baluan. Social Change and the Construction of the Past in a Manus Society.* Canberra: Australian National University; Nijmegen: Centre for Pacific Studies.

Parkinson, R. (1911). *Dreissig Jahre in der Südsee: Land und Leute, Sitten und Gebräuche im Bismarckarchipel und auf den Deutschen Salomoninseln.* Stuttgart: Strecker and Schröder.

Schwartz, T. (1982). Cultural Totemism: Ethnic Identity Primitive and Modern. In: G. DeVos and L. Romanucci-Ross (eds), *Ethnic Identity: Cultural Continuities and Change,* pp. 106–31. Chicago: University of Chicago Press. (First published in 1975.)

Turner, V. (1983). Liminal to Liminoid in Play, Flow, and Ritual: An Essay in Comparative Symbology. In: J. Harris and R. Park

(eds), *Play, Games and Sports in Cultural Contexts*, pp. 123–64.
Champaign, Ill.: Human Kinetics Publishers.
Wolfers, E.P. (1971). Games People Flay. Whose Ethnohistory? *New Guinea and Australia, the Pacific and South-East Asia* 6(1):43–55.

Chapter 7

Reinventing Identities: Redefining Cultural Concepts in the Struggle between Villagers in Munda, Roviana Lagoon, New Georgia Island, Solomon Islands, for the Control of Land

Gerhard Schneider

Introduction

This chapter is concerned with how cultural concepts of the past are modified in the present to validate claims of land ownership. In this process social identities are reinvented in order to exclude related people from the control of land and as a consequence of the distribution of royalties from logging operations.

I begin by introducing the issues of land disputes and the related identity reinvention. Then I will look at traditional culture, which ceased to exist with the end of headhunting, the establishment of the British Solomon Islands Protectorate (BSIP) and the Methodist missionaries at the beginning of the twentieth century. I briefly discuss terms such as 'traditional culture', 'reinvention', 'objectification'. Afterwards I will consider a landmark court case of 1971 to illuminate both the development of arguments about traditional culture and the ensuing land disputes and related court cases in Munda. Then I review the various arguments about traditional cultural concepts which are made by people of Dunde village of the Munda area to further their respective land claims. In the end I provide a summary of the relationship between reinvention of identity, international capitalist exploitation of natural resources and the redefining of traditional cultural concepts.

Today Munda is the scene of bitter disputes concerning land ownership fought out between villagers of the area. Munda is situated at the western end of the Roviana Lagoon on the south-western tip of New Georgia island in the Western Province of the Solomon Islands and has a population of about 2,000.

The tribe occupying the Munda area is called Kazukuru. Munda is divided into the following politically autonomous villages – from west to east – each headed by a chief, though political office and role are disputed: Kindu, Kekehe, Dunde, Kokorapa, the latter which lies on Nusa (island) Roviana in the Roviana Lagoon opposite Dunde. Two areas of Munda are alienated land: Kokeqolo (east of Kindu), which belongs to the United Church (formerly Methodist Mission), and Lambete (between Kekehe and Dunde), which belongs to the Solomon Islands Government (SIG). The Munda airstrip – the second largest runway in the Solomon Islands – which runs in a south-westerly direction from the western end of Dunde through Kekehe and Kokeqolo, is also owned by the SIG.

Tribal members of the Munda villages are recruited by male/female links from founding ancestors of three major descent categories. They are called Turana (m), Vivisi (m) and Vakorige (f), who are brothers and sister to each other (see Figure 7.1).

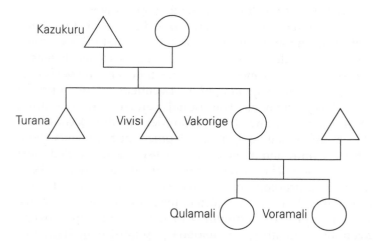

Figure 7.1 Some focal ancestors of major cognatic descent categories of the Kazukuru tribe.

The Kazukuru people who speak Roviana – an Austronesian language – are also referred to as Roviana people. West of the Kazukuru/Munda political entity are the Kalikoqu and Saikile polities – headed by chiefs – whose people are closely related to Kazukuru tribal members and speak Roviana as well.

Until the turn of the nineteenth century the Munda people were famous for their headhunting raids, which they extended as far as Guadalcanal. Heads and human sacrifices were considered vital for the establishment of political authority and the maintenance of the social order. Politico-economic and religious spheres were closely associated in the organization of headhunting and it was from activities of those realms that people gained their social identity and solidarity. To stage successful raids required the cooperation of leaders active in those spheres and the mobilization of members of social groups recruited by a cognatic descent principle.

The Roviana people have now become famous for their land disputes. I am mainly concerned with a land dispute in Dunde village (population 800), but not without referring back to earlier land disputes in Munda from which the current one in Dunde stems. The long-standing disputes have so far prevented the actual operation of logging companies. In this process tradition is objectified not as a unifying symbol, but in order to validate contesting claims over vast ares of forest land. Formal court procedures assess the validity of such claims. Cultural concepts like *banara* (chief), an office which still exists today, *hiama* (priest) and indigenous concepts of rights to land are all modified in the interests of furthering some people's claims. By disputing the genealogy, claimants try to turn closely related people into people of separate social origins. This process entails the negation of former common social identities predicated on traditional cultural concepts and results in a reinvention of social identities that reflect economic concerns of people. A division of land – achieved only through the courts – into the so-called Kazukuru Left Hand Land (KLHL) and Kazukuru Right Hand Land (KRHL) (the English terms are always used), which are concepts that did not exist traditionally, has led to a division of people.

There are three main factions in Dunde who lay different claims on land ownership, but within factions people are further divided by separate interests. Faction 1 claims to be the sole land owner of the Dunde village portion of Kazukuru land (Map 7.1, Dunde/

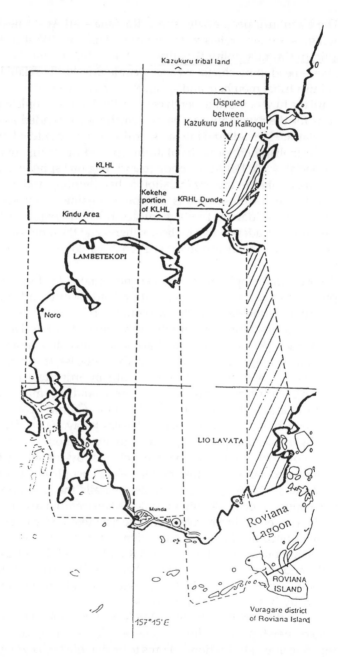

Map 7.1 Munda land divisions drawn in the early 1970s.

Kazukuru land). They argue that the village is divided into a 'group of land owners' and a 'group of chiefs'. The latter are said to be of different tribal origin to the former. Faction 1 says that the 'group of chiefs' possess inferior land rights – so-called 'secondary rights' (for which there is no Roviana word) – and have to ask the 'group of land owners' – who they argue hold primary rights – if they intend to develop a piece of land for garden and residential purposes. Faction 1 opposes logging by a certain company which faction 3 is negotiating with. Faction 1 receives royalties from logging operations in North New Georgia through genealogical links to ancestors of that area. Faction 1 maintains that they are the only descendants of the ancestor Voramali, a daughter of Vakorige (see Figure 7.1), who is said to own the KRHL, thus creating a new social category – the 'Voramali tribe'. The KLHL – corresponding to the Kekehe and Kindu portions of Kazukuru land (see Map 7.1) – is supposedly owned by the descendants of Qulamali, a sister of Voramali. Faction 1 argues that Vakorige had divided the Kazukuru land into KLHL and KRHL for her two daughters Qulamali and Voramali, respectively.

The 1971 landmark High Court case was the first to decide upon a hierarchy of land rights distributed to different groups of people. It also tried to establish land boundaries concerning Kazukuru land at a time when economic policies promoted the diversification of the export structure of the Solomon Islands, in which timber and fish came to play the dominant role. The new concepts of KLHL and KRHL had not appeared as such in this court case.

Members of faction 2 discard the notion of the 'Voramali tribe' as the land-owning group of KRHL. Rather, they uphold the new concept of a 'land guardian' as defined in the 1971 High Court case. They argue very strongly for a matrilineal descent principle conferring superior land rights. The person who was awarded 'land guardianship' is the mother's brother of members of faction 2, the latter wishing to succeed to this position in order to establish themselves as the sole land owners in opposition to factions 1 and 3. While faction 1 regards a former priest – who was responsible for soil fertility and healthy growth of the plants for the whole Kazukuru tribe – as a 'land owner' and its members as descending from a 'land owning' lineage, faction 2 regards itself as succeeding to the office of 'land guardian', who is a descendant of Qulamali. The latter asserts that the traditional priest was always a 'land guardian' vested with superior land rights. Members of faction 2 can show an unbroken chain of female ancestors to Vakorige. But, if one takes the Kazukuru genealogy as a whole, it is a cognatic descent principle that assigns people to descent categories from which they may claim equal land rights.

Faction 3 regards all people of Dunde as 'land owners'. They negate a division of the Kazukuru land and the existence of a hierarchy of land rights. Though they are united in opposition to factions 1 and 2, they are internally divided as some of them claim that the chief has always been chosen by the people. The current chiefly office holder – though he does not exercise this function – who was nominated by the preceding chief, is thus disputed by members of all three factions.

Traditional Culture

I refer to traditional culture here as a social formation in which social relations have not become commoditized in the capitalist sense, that is, production is not geared towards exchange value. I follow Otto's (1993:8) definition of the concept of tradition as the passing on of 'the customs of society', in which sense tradition becomes interchangeable with culture. But traditions are not static, they are 'always in flux . . . [and] adapt . . . or change by internal process of cultural invention' (Otto 1993:9). I use the terms 'reinvention' and 'objectification' to denote an internal process of sociocultural change in relation to outside influences – colonial and postcolonial – of a different economic and political order. Otto (1993:10) writes about the objectification of culture, which fits the Munda case of furthering land claims: 'tradition has always come to denote a conscious objectification of culture. Selected parts of a culture are constructed as "traditional" in order to imbue them with greater authoritative force.' Referring to the use of 'tradition' as 'cognate to construction', Otto (1993:11) writes:

> This usage may be traced back to Wagner's powerful book, *The invention of culture* (1981) in which he argues that 'culture' and also 'a particular cultural description' are inventions of the ethnographer. This kind of invention is in fact a universal process of cultural construction which does not create cultural meanings de novo but is grounded in conventional and negotiated values. In this sense

traditions are always invented whether they are 'lived in' or 'objectified', and the discussion about authenticity assumes the character of a red herring . . .

I use the term 'reinvention' and 'objectification' of culture in contrast to 'invention' as defined above. In the Roviana instance, these two terms refer to the *de novo* creation of cultural meanings and the 'discussion about authenticity' becomes important and necessary. I agree with Tonkinson (1993:598) that 're-readings of the past in all cultures are undertaken from the perspective embedded in the context of present needs, orientations', but the Roviana 're-readings of the past' include 'conscious fabrication' and 'manipulation'. I reconstructed traditional culture, but I did not reinvent it,[1] as it was operative in the era of headhunting, which ended at the turn of the nineteenth century. Heads had to be taken for the aggrandizement of prestige of the chief and for ritual purposes to stabilize internal relations of the social group. Members of the localized cognatic descent group called *butubutu* were drawn from a wider cognatic descent category.[2] All the Kazukuru people trace descent from three apical ancestors of major descent categories called Turana (m), Vivisi (m) and Vakorige (f). A localized cognatic descent group comprising a village served as one level of effective *butubutu* organization headed by a chief. The village is subdivided into hamlets led by an elder called *palabatu*.

The Kazukuru people lived on the island (*nusa*) of Roviana, where they had built a fortress-like stronghold situated on a hill, to which they retreated when attacked from groups from outside. The Kazukuru political entity on Nusa Roviana is called Kokorapa. The chiefly lineage is recruited from the ancestor Turana. Succession to chieftainship is cognatic. Hocart confirms this succession rule. After naming all the chiefs of Munda and their successors Hocart (n.d. MS 22:11) writes: 'The conclusion we draw from all these instances is that succession is both patrilineal & matrilineal.' Hocart's collected genealogies (n.d. MS 14; MS 43; MS 50), which span seven generations at most – within this span his and my genealogical records coincide – show the tracing of descent via male/female links.

Kindu was the only Kazukuru village established on mainland Munda before the first hamlets of today's villages of Kekehe and Dunde were founded by Kazukuru people living on Nusa Roviana.

Kazukuru members of Kindu trace descent from Vivisi.

Hocart confirms my findings that the Kazukuru people of Kokorapa had their gardens on mainland Munda (Hocart n.d. MS 22:3–4): 'The Kokorapans also own the mainland opposite their home; they use it as planting ground, but now have a few permanent hamlets there . . . Sasambeti [chief of Kokorapa], Riambule [the last priest before conversion to Christianity] & others were constantly going backwards and forwards between the island [Nusa Roviana] & the mainland and seemed to live equally in both.'

Feasts and shell valuables – the general name for the latter is *poata* – had to be given to attract labour and followers in order to stage successful raids. Named garden plots, called *emata*, whose produce was vital for the provision of feasts, were developed from virgin forest, called *muqe*, through the exchange of shell rings presented by the *hiama* (main priest) to the spiritual world.

A leadership trio of the Munda Roviana polity was made up of *banara* (chief), *hiama* (priest) and *varane* (warrior), whereby a chief could also be a warrior.

Banara and *hiama*, who worked together closely, were closely genealogically related. The chief administered entitlements to land while the priest handed over a new piece of land to the entitled person by performing certain rituals. Their role and function complemented each other as they were both responsible for the physical survival of their fellow group members in overlapping activities of sacrifices, feast-giving and headhunting raids. The chiefs exercised jurisdiction over their own villages. They would join forces when going out for raids. But where one's physical boundary ended had not been defined at that time. Each village estate consisted of dwelling and garden areas and an undefined realm of virgin forest, in which spirits were located and where bush materials were collected and animals hunted. The chief's authority was symbolized by the most valuable shell ring, called *bakiha zinara*, which exhibit a larger yellow stain than the *bakiha*. A *bakiha* was made of the fossilized giant clam shell found in the bush areas of the interior of the island of New Georgia. The chief was responsible for the organization of headhunting raids. These necessitated the building of *tomoko* (war canoes), *paele* (canoe houses) and *zelepade* (ceremonial structures) in which heads taken back from raids were strung. *Mata zona* (craft specialists) produced *tomoko*, *paele* and *zelepade*, as well as the various kinds of shell valuables. A *mata zoņa* possessed the ability to spot those clam shells in the bush.

Munda was the centre of production of the shell rings, which were distributed over the Western Solomons in exchange for food, services and craft items. Traditionally the various kinds of shell valuables had their specified social spheres of circulation. Only with the intensification of trade with Europeans were an internal exchange value and monetary value (see Hocart n.d. MS 6:5) assigned to the shell valuables in order to facilitate the flow of European goods and the trade in copra. German trader Ribbe (1903:294) mentions that the European traders attributed an exchange and monetary value to the shell valuables. In this way Munda was able to amass many European goods, as Bennett (1987:84) notes: 'To obtain their copra and tortoiseshell the traders often had to provide these rings along with articles of Western manufacture, thus guaranteeing an abundance of goods for the Roviana people', who were thus able to intensify the shell valuable production, leading to an 'inflationary' process in which the control of production and circulation was lost, which in part contributed to the end of headhunting.

The chief also practised sacrificial rites at a head shrine to appease the spirits who were regarded as having caused sickness and misfortunes within the *butubutu* after rules of conduct had been broken.

The *hiama* (priest) practised rituals for soil fertility and healthy growth of the plants for all garden plots of Kazukuru tribal members at a main shrine called *hope maņini*, which is situated (I saw its remains) on the Munda mainland. A shell valuable called *upahae* was the insignia of the *hiama*. It is a rough manufactured clam shell ring (made of the fossilized giant clam) displaying the sinuous edges of the giant clam. Minor priests restored the healthy growth of the plants at a local *hope maņini* (fertility shrine) belonging to a segment of a localized descent group by putting a plain, white clam shell ring, called *poata*, over tree stumps, called *reqe*, as a 'gift' presented to the spirits. The insignia of the minor priests was the *bareke*, which looks similar in shape to that of the *upahae*. Hocart (1922:284–9) describes similar rites for soil fertility and crop productivity practised by priests on Simbo island.

A named garden plot is called *emata*, which refers to both one under cultivation and one that lies fallow. The general Roviana term for garden is *inuma*. Someone who wanted to develop a new *emata* from virgin forest handed over a *poata* to the *hiama*, who put it over the *reqe* at the main *hope maṇini*. This transaction is called *sosope la pa reqe* (*poata* is put over the tree stumps). Through this exchange of a shell ring a 'great spirit', called *tamasa*, is asked to hand over the control of a piece of land to its cultivator. A different person attempting to dispute this *emata* would have feared punishment from *tamasa*. The cultivator takes possession of the *emata* by using it – cutting down the virgin forest and planting the area. But one could not control or take possession of a piece of land without using it and one could not use it without having received the control over it from the spiritual world through the exchange of a shell ring. Vast areas of virgin forest full of tropical timber were not owned by anyone. Individual garden plots are demarcated from each other by planting shrubs around it, but no boundaries were ever drawn over extensive areas of virgin forest. It was visited for hunting purposes and to collect bush materials, fish from the rivers and fresh water. These areas were known by topographic features. It was perilous to leave those known areas and proceed too far into the bush, because one would have run the risk of being abducted by a forest spirit.

Members of a localized lineage segment (hamlet) have direct access to its pool of *emata* which had been developed over time by its ancestors. Some *emata* reverted back to bush, but they remained within this pool for future use. Certain named *emata* then always stay within a certain lineage segment. The lineage (hamlet) elder, called *palabatu*, controls its pool of *emata*, but does not own it. He gives out *emata* for use to members of his hamlet. This transaction, which still occurs today, did not involve an exchange of *poata* as the segment's ancestors had already exchanged *poata* with the spirit. Regarding this function the Roviana *palabatu* would resemble the Kwara'ae 'leader for the land' (Burt 1994:319).

But a Malaitan model of a categorical distinction of people into 'bush' and 'saltwater' (see Keesing 1982:4; Burt 1994:319, 325) does not exist in this part of the New Georgia lowlands. People who lived on the island of Roviana had their gardens on the mainland, where the shrine for land productivity is situated. Kazukuru people produced the shell valuables at the coast whose material they found in the bush. Some Kazukuru people – in times of land disputes – try to establish this kind of categorization and try to turn the priest into a 'land owner'.

A Landmark Court Case and the Development of Further Court Cases about Land

High Court of the Western Pacific. Native Land Appeal (NLA) Case No. 9 of 1971

Appellants: 2a and 2b (he was later recognized as co-appellant)

Witnesses for Appellants: 1a and 1b, Y

Respondent: X

This 1971 High Court (HC) case can be regarded as executing the priority formulated by the 'Sixth Development Plan', which put stress on assisting 'customary land owners to establish claims to ownership and determine boundaries as a necessary prelude to effective land utilisation' (BSIP 1971:38). It can be termed a landmark court case in the sense that it ratified new cultural concepts and that its decision given by a 'Western' judge was wrong. The redefined traditional cultural concepts officially acknowledged here were the establishment of boundaries over vast areas of Kazukuru land, which later led to the official recognition of the division of the Kazukuru land into KLHL and KRHL. A hierarchy of land rights was established through the introduction of new concepts of 'primary' and 'secondary' land rights. Cognatic descent was replaced by 'matrilineal descent' as conferring 'primary' land rights. A new office was created, that of a 'land owner' and later 'land guardian', or 'leader of the land', who is regarded as exercising 'primary rights' of 'ownership'. The 'land owner' or 'land guardian' attributed with an overall control of extensive areas of land was said to be able to withdraw permission to use land given to so-called holders of 'secondary rights'. The chief's authority had become disconnected from land issues, resulting in later attempts to assign separate identities to people, that of a 'group of land owners' (of mainland Munda) and of a 'group of chiefs' (from Nusa Roviana in the lagoon).

The chief justice overturned the decision of the Roviana local court of 1970 – which had awarded X just an *emata* – on points of custom. He granted control over a large area of land (including virgin forest), which came to be regarded as KLHL, to 2a and 2b on the following grounds (High Court of the Western Pacific 1971:3): 'I find that the appellant . . . [2a] is right when he claims primary interests in the Kazukuru land by reason of his direct

matrilineal descent from Vakorige, and I find correspondingly that
. . . [X]'s claims are secondary for he is basing his claims upon
descent from Turana, who was but Vakorige's brother and could
not pass interests in Kazukuru land to his sons.' It is important to
note that Turana and Vakorige are here regarded as brother and
sister by the disputants. 2a and 2b can show an unbroken chain of
female ancestors to Vakorige. X claimed to be patrilineally
descended from Turana and can show an almost unbroken chain
of male ancestors to Turana. His only female link is his father's
father's mother.

I cannot review here on which grounds all the introduced
concepts were based, but it will be interesting enough to see that
the conclusion about the predominance of 'matrilineal descent' in
Kazukuru was ultimately arrived at by referring back to River's
The History of the Melanesian Society (1914).

First, the chief justice cites an article by Waterhouse (1931), who
was a missionary teacher at Kokeqolo in the 1920s, published in
Man, for which I found evidence that 2b was the informant of
Waterhouse.[3] The decisive passage reads (Waterhouse 1931:124):
'The Kazukuru people speak of a man who came from . . . who
married a prominent chieftainess Vakorige from whom . . . [L]
and . . . [M] 2 sisters claim descent.' L is the mother of 2a and M
the mother of 2b, but Vakorige was never a 'chieftainess'.

The chief justice had to find more evidence for 'matrilineal
descent'. This he thought to have found in the report by the Special
Lands Commission conducted by Colin Allan in the 1950s. Here
one finds the following passage (Allan 1957:89): 'The exception to
the unilateral principle is the New Georgia group. Irrespective of
the position now, every indication exists that in pre-protection
times the matrilineal rule applied. This was the conclusion come
to by the first Lands Commissioner, Mr. Phillips.'

The second Lands Commission was aimed at recommending a
policy for future land developments. In this respect Allan regarded
cognatic descent systems, which he found existing in Roviana, as
an obstacle to development. He writes (Allan 1957:90) that
'Disputes will become prevalent, and the multiplication of interests
will . . . be restrictive to economic development.' He advises 'to
adopt either a patrilineal or matrilineal principle' or that legislation
should 'restrict descent to the ambilateral principle'. Allan, who
lived during his investigations in Munda at 2b's house, complained
about the latter's constant attempts to influence him to further

2b's land claims. Allan (1989:42) writes: 'at that time, September 1953, I was one of the few who was well aware of the vast virgin timber forests which existed in north-west New Georgia, some of which lay within the dramatic claims of . . . [2b] and the Kazukuru people'. Allan had based his contention about the prevalence of 'matrilineal descent' on the report of the first Lands Commissioner Phillips. Phillips (1925:49–50) concludes: 'That a matriarchal system of descent and land inheritance was once dominant and general in the Western Solomons, I feel convinced, because it still prevails practically untouched in the Island of Vella La Vella.' Thus for Phillips Vella La Vella is the 'surviving element'. He seems to have received his theoretical formulations from Rivers (Phillips 1925:49): 'In Sydney, recently, I was able to refer to the late Dr. Rivers' *History of Melanesian Society.*'

Phillips, while reading Rivers, must have come across the following passage (Rivers 1914:102–3):

> The inquiry . . . has led to the conclusion that matrilineal descent is a feature of Melanesian society which now possesses far less social significance than in the past. In some places it is perhaps the last relic of a condition of mother-right which once governed the whole social life of the people; which regulated marriage, directed the transmission of property, and, where chieftainship existed at all determined its mode of succession . . .

When a lands officer tried to negotiate timber rights in Munda in the early 1970s, including X, it was 2a, 2b and 1a and 1b who claimed to be the 'land owners' of the whole Kazukuru land, arguing for the first time that Vakorige had no siblings and that X was not a Kazukuru man at all. In 1976, 2a and 2b took Y to court trying to exclude him from the then established KLHL and arguing that 2a and 2b would be the owners of the KRHL. In the early 1980s, Y, who descends from Vivisi, was awarded 'primary rights' over the Kindu portion of KLHL. 2b's descendant went to court in 1979 to 'strategically' oppose 1a and 1b, in order to have them recognized as the owner of KRHL and 2a and 2b as owners of KLHL. 2b's descendant claimed an *emata* within Dunde area. This was awarded to 1a and 1b, but not the whole KRHL, as they claim until today. The ownership of the Dunde portion of Kazukuru land had never been decided upon. In 1984, a Customary Land Appeal Court (CLAC) awarded members of faction 3 together with faction

1 to stand as trustees in order to grant timber rights to a logging company. This was decided under the 'Forest and Timber Amendment Act of 1977'. According to this Act a social group, on whose land the timber is to be extracted, is represented by a number of trustees, who are entitled to grant timber rights to a logging company in return for royalty payments. Finally, a logging licence was granted to cut timber on Dunde/Kazukuru land. Faction 1 took faction 3 to High Court under the 'Forest Resources and Timber Utilization Act of 1992', which specifies the procedures for obtaining a logging licence, but does not deal with land ownership. Faction 1 succeeded because the logging company did not get its licence in a fully correct legal way. Faction 1 regards this decision as supporting their claim for sole land ownership of KRHL.

Arguments about Traditional Culture

I add a few more arguments as they explicate contradictory statements and the reinvention of social identities.

Faction 1 claims that Vakorige as the only founding ancestor of the Kazukuru tribe 'had come out of the ground' and had neither parents nor siblings. She had gone to the Munda coast, 'turned around and divided the land into Kazukuru Left Hand Land and Kazukuru Right Hand Land' (the English terms are used in conversation and in court cases), which she had given to her two daughters Qulamali and Voramali, respectively. The 'group of land owners' and the 'group of chiefs' created by faction 1 are said to have their own, separate genealogy, place of origin and settlement. Faction 1 argues that the 'group of land owners', who had come from the bush, and the 'group of chiefs', who had come from Nusa Roviana, are of different tribal origin. The logical contradiction in their argument lies in the fact that they have to argue that some of the descendants of Qulamali had gone to live on the island of Roviana (the Voramali descendants are claimed to have always stayed on the Munda mainland) as they cannot deny the 'group of chiefs' connection to Qulamali – who in fact also trace descent from Voramali.

This reinvention of cultural concepts runs counter to Hocart's research and my reconstruction of traditional culture. As mentioned above, Hocart (n.d. MS 22:3–4) notes that the people of Nusa

Roviana 'also own the mainland opposite their home'. Faction 1 cuts out sub-branches of the Voramali tribal segment to deny its relations to members of faction 3. These genealogical connections – referred to by faction 1 as 'inventions' – are depicted in Hocart's genealogical tables,[4] but he does not link them to Voramali. These recordings correspond to my genealogical records. Members of Faction 1 regard the last priest for the Kazukuru tribe Riabule, whose existence is affirmed by every faction, as a 'land owner' and try to include him into their genealogy. But they do not succeed, as Hocart (n.d. MS 22:3–4) – in accordance with my findings – indicates that Riabule is of the island of Roviana and descends through a sub-branch of Voramali which faction 1 denies to exist (see also Hocart n.d. MS 43: table 46). This, together with Hocart's recordings of the residence of ancestors of members of faction 1 at Nusa Roviana before they moved to the mainland (see Hocart n.d. MS 43: tables 67 and 138) totally invalidates faction 1's claims as sole land owners of Dunde/Kazukuru land.

2e, a member of faction 2, regards the descendants of Vakorige and Turana as members 'of the same tribe' in contrast to faction 1, but in accordance with faction 1 regards the lineage of Vakorige as the one that deals with the land while the lineage of Turana deals with politics. In contrast to faction 1, 2e claims the 'Voramali group' to have been responsible for soil fertility traditionally, while Qulamali, from which 2e can show an unbroken chain of female ancestors, confers 'land ownership' of Dunde/Kazukuru land. 2e is in the line of succession to 2a as 'land guardian' and consequently argues that the last priest Riabule was a 'land guardian'. 2e exhibits two conflicting identities: his father's father was adopted by Riabule and his mother's brother was awarded the title of 'land guardian'. 2e's conflicting identities are reflected in a contradictory argument. He describes the ceremonial function of the priest in presenting a shell valuable to the spiritual world in the process of developing a new garden plot from virgin forest. Conversely he regards the 'land guardian' as having absolute control over vast areas of unused virgin forest, which no single person could appropriate by giving away shell valuables.

Some members of faction 3 possess a detailed knowledge of traditional culture, though faction 3 does not stand as a unified group in relation to certain aspects of arguments. Some members try to enhance their own position by disputing the current chief's nomination. 3e, who is said to be in the possession of the *upahae* (the insignia of the last priest), claims that the priest was a 'land owner'. 3f, whose father is the brother of 3e, stated that the word *hiama* would not denote a priestly function, but reflects a concept of 'land guardianship'. The shell valuable *upahae*, he argues, signifies 'land ownership'.

Summary

Logging and fishing operations have become dominant in the economy of the Solomon Islands and these two economic activities engage people in disputes over the control of land and sea areas. Reef 'ownership' – bait-fishing royalties flow into the area – is disputed in Munda as well, which also is leading to the creation of new social identities. The place name of the reef areas that people were and are occupying is called Vuragare, which can be translated as 'where the sea breaks'. People who are living in those reef areas were part of the Munda polity and of the Kazukuru genealogy in times of headhunting. Today these 'Vuragare' people claim to be the only reef owners of the Munda area by creating their separate 'tribe' from the Munda people, who have become divided themselves by the reinvention of different social identities.

Since 1985 timber and fish account for up to 70% of total export earnings (Central Bank of Solomon Islands 1993:24). The forestry sector alone had a percentage share of 56.7% of total export value in 1993 (Duncan 1994:27). In 1992 Western Province of the Solomon Islands had a timber production quota of 597,000 m³ of total licensed production for log export of 1,122,400 m³ or 53% of the total, whereby New Georgia island had a production quota of 270,000 m³ or 45% of Western Province's total (Montgomery 1992:11). Timber prices were booming in 1993–94, due in part to the ban on log exports in Malaysia (Duncan 1994:XII). The logging companies operating in the Solomon Islands are foreign owned. Asian companies dominate the scene – the exploitation of timber and the appropriation of profits. The Solomon Islands (Government and 'land owners') are plundered of economic surplus, which should be rightfully theirs, through the mechanism of transfer pricing. This is the conclusion come to by Duncan (1994:22–3), who writes that 'there is very convincing evidence that serious price underreporting has been practised in the Solomon Islands', which resulted in economic surplus foregone to logging companies of an estimated value of SI$130.4 million (approx. £26 million). This amount lost by the Solomon Islands Government and villagers to foreign-owned companies equals 53% of government revenue (1994 budget). More than 1,000 health clinics and 7,000 classrooms could have been built with this amount of money (Duncan 1994:XVIII).

The Solomon Islands are trapped. 'Development' inhibits development on a large scale. Fierce fights between villagers in Munda about their share of economic development reflect the domination of the exploitation of their natural resources by international capitalism. The hunting for heads has been replaced by the hunting for commodities, in which land and sea areas have become the battlegrounds. The struggle between villagers about the internal control of their natural resources is not yet decided, but it has led to violent conflicts: the start and the end of my investigations were marked by such. At the beginning of my research, a group of people stopped a surveying group of a logging company by threatening them with bush-knives. At the end of my stay, somebody threw a hand grenade at a house whose occupants belong to an opposed group. Fortunately it did not explode.

The process of individualization of the 'ownership' of natural resources or the attempts of expropriation of assets shared by a community of people and vital for their physical survival are leading to an individualization of social relations, reflected in an amazing array of arguments in which the particularity of interests becomes apparent. Manifestations of communal support and undertakings like marriage feasts, funeral ceremonies and today's birthday parties are still important aspects of social life in the village, but they cannot reconcile social tensions or bring the contestants together, as there are no spirits any more to appease through sacrificial rites.

Past traditions are solely invoked today by a group of people in defence against an attack of usurpation of the means of production by a related group of people. The former group feels threatened by the denial of their identity by the latter group, but they cannot base their own identities on traditional cultural concepts any more, as social life has become very compartmentalized through the pursuit of cash earnings, which every single household in Dunde is engaged in. People are still attached to their land which they have used for many generations without attempts of alienations by others who have never used those

garden plots. This usurpation of vast areas of land by a few people
was first tried in the early 1970s. Even though a small group gained
control over a large area of land in the High Court of 1971, they
were not successful in exercising this control 'on the ground', for
instance to restrain people from cultivating their land which their
ancestors had developed long ago.

A Roviana answer to (Eastern) capitalist hegemony lies in the
attempt to establish an internal hegemony. An attempt is made to
achieve this by the reinvention of separate identities of closely
related people through the modification of traditional cultural
concepts. These reinventions are based on a Western model of
'owner' versus 'producer'; in Munda it is 'land owners' versus
'land users'. This process of the establishment of private property
over the means of production by turning people of the village into
strangers leads to the estrangement of people from each other (see
Marx 1975a:270–82). Common historical identities – related to
genealogy, politics, religion and economics – are renounced in
unidentical histories. 'Western' people (administrators, judges,
missionaries) have been used by Roviana people in this process
of reinvention of identity, as well as some concepts developed in
'Western' academic discourse, e.g. anthropology: 'primary-
secondary, bush–saltwater, left–right' dichotomies. A theory of
evolutionism had also found its way into the land dispute.

Shell valuables have long lost their social value, and the social
relations, which today are being based on a monetary value,
can be described by referring to a Western-derived concept of
commodity fetishism. Marx writes about 'the fetish character of
the commodity' (commodity and money) and, referring to the
actors engaged in the exchange of products, he notes that 'to them
their own social action takes the form of a movement of objects
under whose control the actors are instead of being in control of
them' (Marx 1975b:89, my translation into English).

Notes

1. I investigated as widely as possible traditional culture and the
   land disputes, with as many people as possible, with all factions
   involved and with people from the whole Roviana Lagoon.

Written sources complemented the data that I collected. Some of Hocart's unpublished manuscripts (he spent six weeks in Munda in 1908; see Hocart 1922:71) confirm my data about the traditional culture of Roviana. His genealogical records, which are more shallow than mine, correspond to my genealogical records. Special thanks go to Christine Dureau of the Division of Pacific and Asian History, Research School of Pacific and Asian Studies, Australian National University, Canberra for sending me copies of all Hocart's unpublished manuscripts.

2. I follow Scheffler's (1965) distinction between descent categories and descent groups. But the Roviana material does not provide any evidence for the existence of a hierarchy of land rights based on the categorical distinction between 'born of men' and 'born of women' (Scheffler 1965:46–7; Keesing 1987:439, 441) that would confer 'primary' and 'secondary' membership.

3. 2b launched another article in an anthropological journal which was published in the 1960s. It was never used in any court case, because the author explicitly mentioned 2b's name, though it is much more sophisticated in arguments concerning land ownership than the one by Waterhouse (1931). I cannot tell the name of the author or the name of the anthropological journal in order not to reveal the identity of 2b.

4 Hocart n.d. MS 14, tables 100, 102; MS 43, tables 46, 57, 67, 92, 100, 102, 138; MS 50, tables 8, 21.

References

Allan, C.H. (1957). *Customary Land Tenure in the British Solomon Islands Protectorate*. Report of the Special Lands Commission. Honiara: Western Pacific High Commission.

—— (1989). *Solomons Safari, 1953–1958*. Part I. Christchurch: Nag's Head Press.

Bennett, J. (1987). *Wealth of the Solomons. A History of a Pacific Archipelago. 1800–1978*. Honolulu: University of Hawaii Press.

British Solomon Islands Protectorate (BSIP) (1971). *Sixth Development Plan*. Honiara: Secretariat.

Burt, B. (1994). Land in Kwara'ae and Development in Solomon Islands. *Oceania* 64:317–35.

Central Bank of Solomon Islands. (1993). *Annual Report 1992*. Honiara: Government Printer.

Duncan, R.C. (1994). *Melanesian Forestry Sector Study*. Canberra: Australian International Development Assistance Bureau (International Development Issues 36).

High Court of the Western Pacific (1971). *Native Land Appeal Case No. 9 of 1971. Judgement and Decree on Appeal*. Honiara.

Hocart, A. (n. d.) Unpublished manuscripts. Originals held by the Alexander Turnbill Library, Wellington. On microfilm in Research School of Pacific and Asian Studies, Division of Pacific and Asian History. Canberra: Australian National University.

―― (n.d.). MS 6. Trade and Money.

―― (n.d.). MS 14. Kinship.

―― (n.d.). MS 22. Roviana. Topography, Districts, Chiefs.

―― (n.d.). MS 43. Genealogies. Solomon Islands; Lakemba; Fiji.

―― (n.d.). MS 50. Notebook containing jottings and genealogies.

―― (1922). The Cult of the Dead in Eddystone of the Solomons. *Journal of the Royal Anthropological Institute* 52:71–112, 259–305.

Keesing, R.M. (1982). *Kwaio Religion. The Living and the Dead in a Solomon Islands Society*. New York: Columbia University Press.

―― (1987). African Models in the Malaita Highlands. *Man* (n.s.) 22:431–52.

Marx, K. (1975a). Economic and Philosophic Manuscripts of 1844. Estranged Labour. In: K. Marx and F. Engels, *Collected Works*, vol. 3, pp. 270–82. London: Lawrence and Wishart. (First published in 1932.)

―― (1975b). *Das Kapital. Kritik der politischen Ökonomie Erster Band, Buch I: Der Produktionsprozess des Kapitals*. Berlin:Dietz. (First published in 1867.)

Montgomery, P.J. (1992) *Pricing and Marketing of Forest Product Exports from the Solomon Islands. Timber Control Unit Project. Solomon Islands. Project Report No. 8*. Canberra: Australian International Development Assistence Bureau.

Otto, T. (1993). Empty Tins for Lost Traditions? The West's Material and Intellectual Involvement in the Pacific. In: T. Otto (ed.), *Pacific Islands Trajectories. Five Personal Views*, pp. 1–18. Canberra: Australian National University; Nijmegen: University of Nijmegen, Centre for Pacific Studies.

Phillips, B. (1925). Lands Commission. British Solomon Islands Protectorate. Lands Commissioner Report. Native claims 30–37, 55, etc. (Levers Certificate of Occupation, etc.), 21. 4. 1925. Honiara: National Archives, BSIP 18/I/26 (items 19–28).

Ribbe, C. (1903). *Zwei Jahre unter den Kannibalen der Salomo-Inseln*. Dresden: Elbgau-Buchdruckerei, Hermann Beyer.

Rivers, W.H.R. (1914). *The History of Melanesian Society*, vol. II. Cambridge: Cambridge University Press.

Scheffler, H.W. (1965). *Choiseul Island Social Structure*. Berkeley and Los Angeles: University of California Press.

Tonkinson, R. (1993). Understanding 'Tradition' – Ten Years on. In: G.M. White and L. Lindstrom (eds), *Custom Today*, pp. 597–606, *Anthropological Forum* special issue 6(4).

Waterhouse, J.H.L. (1931). The Kazukuru Language of New Georgia, Communicated with Notes by S.H. Ray. *Man* 31: 123–6.

Chapter 8

'Alas! And On We Go'

Philippe Peltier[1]

It was ten or so years ago, on our first trip on the Sepik. To give our journey an aim, we had decided, Mondher Kilani – as much a beginner as I – and Milan Stanek, our mentor, to ask about the Second World War. Whenever we stayed in a village for enough time, we would ask the 'elders' to come and tell us their memories of the war. When night had fallen, a few men would gather in the house we were using and tell their stories. We had high expectations of these accounts. But they quickly turned out to be disappointing: in village after village we heard the same stereotyped story. The 'elders' would relate events whose interest we found hard to understand. For those talking to us, telling their combat stories – or minor events – was probably an effective way of not revealing what they thought about the relations of power or the social changes spawned by the war. We had been too quick to forget that, even though we were not Australian and, even though we had unconsciously designated a common enemy (the Japanese), in their eyes we belonged to the white man's world. To mention the war was to raise a subject that was more painful than we had thought, relations of domination. We were forced to admit that we had not found the right method.

In 1987 I returned to the region of Porapora.[2] Immediately Arese, one of the men of the village where I was staying, brought out his old war stories again. For him it was a foregone conclusion that I was still interested in these events. Made cautious by the earlier fiasco and my mind on other matters, I listened politely, without turning on my recorder. But we fell into a routine and, as the months passed, Arese brought up his memories more and more often. Sometimes I would take down passages I found interesting. But it was only on my third trip, in 1991–2, that I slowly grew aware of how rich his memories were. For gradually he was caught up in the game of remembering. His testimony became something out of the ordinary. Indeed, he now talked at greater length and in greater detail. At last I began asking questions to clear up obscure passages or to pin down the sequence of important events. From rambling conversations, we had imperceptibly drifted into methodical investigation, without ever saying as much. Arese always talked when he felt like it, and the hours spent were like a time-out from the more directive work of the ethnographic study, a sort of breathing-space entirely up to him. I must admit that he found this more interesting than the long and sometimes fastidious interviews on warfare, initiations or men's houses. Nor was this interest probably free of ulterior motives: several times Arese remarked that, all in all, telling one's life was a good way to go down in history.

And so, as the months went by, bits and pieces of life piled up in no logical order. Arese's account did not follow a chronological or thematic thread. He would skip from one episode to another with no thought for making these fragments particularly consistent. When I returned to France, after transcribing the tapes I tried to establish a chronological order and to synthesize the different variations of given episodes. The excerpts given here are therefore an arrangement. I have added a few comments and attempted brief analyses in order to recreate the context. It may be objected that this way of going about things presents several risks, that to the autobiographical fiction I have now added a narrative fiction far removed from what was originally said. This criticism has often been levelled at reconstructed biographies; it lies at the heart of a vast debate that I will not go into here. Let me say simply that a certain amount of fiction seems indispensable if the reader is to follow what is often a confused account marked by repetitions and afterthoughts. It also introduces the distance that should be fundamental to all work in anthropology: a critical distance which is not totally lacking in Arese's account, but which often follows idiosyncratic laws. Arese usually sticks to the facts. He relates an event just as men tell about their exploits when they return from a hunt. Exceptionally he might slip in a critical remark or a moral judgement. But as a rule, if I wanted judgements, I had to ask questions. Arese would not reply immediately. He preferred to think them over. Some days later, with no warning, he would repeat a story, adding a passage, or would relate another episode that would shed a new light on the events. In this he was following traditional practice, in which, for instance, one myth would be illuminated by another, one story by another story. But this second part was never offered up on the spot. And so the account grew to look like splinters of story which had to be glued back together – an operation left to the industry of the listener – in order to acquire, if not its *full* meaning, at least *some* meaning. An autobiographical account is an open-ended work, a fiction that is illuminated at different points each time the pieces are rearranged. And it is in this way that Arese literally constructed his autobiography.

And yet, in Arese's tale, there are certain episodes that do not follow this rule, those that touch on the history of the community. These incidents have to do with the earliest times. The versions of these stories that I was given presented few variants. Whoever the storyteller, they came out as a block, all following the same story-line, emphasizing, down to the very words used, the same events. These stories furnish an authoritative version of the facts, then. Their authority is born of consensus. Here we are witnessing – and I will return to this – the birth of historical accounts, which may or may not still be part of autobiography. Yet I have included them for at least two reasons: the first is that Arese was often an eyewitness; the second is that he is often regarded as someone who knows, and who is in possession of the authoritative version.

The reader may be surprised that the account breaks off so soon. Arese told me very little about his life after the early 1950s, a date that corresponds to his return from the plantations. He had nothing to say about his life in the village or the changes he saw taking place in society, a gap that is all the more singular as Arese was born in the early 1920s and thus belongs to the generation which, having undergone their initiations in the 1930s, was adult at the end of the Second World War. His life coincides exactly with that period in which society changed courses in an attempt to adapt to the conditions imposed by the colonial powers. Now, as his account amply demonstrates, Arese's strength lay in having been quick to grasp that the world was changing and that it was better to be one of the actors than a passive victim. And so he struck out to explore the opening world. He must have harboured the secret and probably obscure hope of understanding how it worked, of benefiting from it and of using what he learned to serve his community. And these hopes were realized in part, because for a few years he exercised the functions of *doktoboi*. But many of the white practices and customs surprised him. Worse yet, he understood neither the mechanisms of business nor the logic of work. Telling the story of his life, and that to someone from a society of which he had perceived only the froth, was a new means of reflecting and trying to draw away the veil masking the mysteries of a world that had no place for exchange. Was I not a good witness? Someone who was supposed to know? I might as well confess right away: I was most often incapable of providing answers to the questions Arese asked me. And this was probably the reason for a sort of disenchantment that can be glimpsed here and there.

First Contacts

Apart from his war stories, the first thing Arese spoke about was pacification. This account no doubt has an emblematic value; it opens on a new page in the story.

A man from the Adjirab village of Pinam, Matot, was among the first to leave for the plantations. But he rushed back when the news reached him that his wife had been seduced. Now it turned out that the seducer was none other than the newly appointed *luluai*[3] of a recently pacified neighbouring village. When he got home, Matot bided his time, waiting for an opportunity to kill the culprit. One day the opportunity made the thief. The *luluai* paid a visit to the village of Pinam, accompanied by some young boys. Matot welcomed them and offered them the hospitality of his men's house. That night, he slipped into the house, armed with an axe brought back from the plantations and, with the help of two kinsmen, killed the *luluai*. Only one of the visitors survived the massacre.

> And here is how this story began, how a big affair started. For when the *luluai* of the region learned of the matter, they set out for Marienberg.[4] They made a formal complaint to the Australian government. All the *luluai* and the *tultul* of the region went to Marienberg to ask for justice.

They obviously had the support of the Australians, who, in revenge for the flouting of their authority, mounted a police operation.

There is not room in this article to go into all the details of this fairly confused story, but the crack-down was used as a pretext to extend colonial power to all villages in the area. The repression was savage. Several men were killed, and the village of Pinam was destroyed by the police forces, who included many men from the neighbouring region of Aion. Matot resisted for a long time and then fled to the region of Ramu, where he was finally captured. He was tried at Madang and pardoned. Nevertheless, when he was brought back to his own village,

> two big men demanded his hanging to pay the blood price. The *kiap* didn't want to hang him. The people of Aion had destroyed the men's house that belonged to Matot's clan and all the houses in Pinam. The *agur* clan's *tambaran* had gone up in smoke . . . The people of Pinam were demanding revenge for these destructions.

And so Matot was hung. Arese thought that the whites didn't understand a lot about Matot's case. To be sure, they had grasped that, in killing the *luluai*, Matot had been within his rights because he had not been attacking the representative of the new order but his wife's seducer. That is why they had pardoned him. But Arese had two other explanations for Matot's hanging. Matot was not well liked. He had come back from the plantations 'with white hair', probably after the fashion of the islands, which seemed highly suspicious, and he no longer took much part in village life. In sum, he had become a foreign body that had to be eliminated. His act fell into a long history of headhunting between villages, and the big men, fearing an endless series of revenge, felt it would be opportune to bring hostilities to an end by hanging the culprit. By executing Matot in response to the demands of the local big men, the *kiap* had become involved in a game they did not fully understand. The confusion was carefully maintained by the big men, who judged that it was not useful to tell everything. The relations contracted by the two parties therefore rested on a number of unspoken assumptions. An ambiguous struggle ensued. While the new law was accepted without too much resistance, the Papuans turned the whites' intervention to their own ends. They concealed a number of revenge killings, but, above all, they used the police intervention to put an end to the most oppressive situation – endemic warfare – while shifting the responsibility of Matot's death to the foreign forces. Arese still thought that, by complying with the big men's requests, the whites had accepted that enforcement of the law was to be shared.

During a discussion, André Iteanu mentioned that he had already heard a similar story elsewhere. This was disturbing: how could the same story appear in different places? Can such a coincidence be explained by an identical process of pacification alone? Whatever the case, the status of these twin accounts raises a question: are they meant to explain historical events or should they instead be regarded as variants of a contemporary legend founding the modern world? In other words, is the main function of these accounts, above and beyond simply relating historical facts, to create a common identity with regard to the outside world? If this is the case, where and in what circumstances did these accounts undergo their alterations and refinements? In the present state of our knowledge, I'm afraid we must leave these questions open. But I hope that similar accounts will be published and regret the destruction of the colonial archives, as they were the only sources that could have provided us with even a partial understanding of the process of their transformation.

Over several months the events at Pinam were represented to me as being the first contacts with the white world. Upon asking a few questions, however, it turned out that the following events were even older. For in earlier times some recruiters had suddenly turned up one day:

> When they arrived we hid in the swamps and the forest. We were afraid they'd kill us. The village was empty. They came looking for us. We stayed hidden in the swamp grass, we would dive under the water when a canoe came by. We stayed there for several days. There wasn't anything to eat and it was raining. Our bark belts started to fall apart. We lived naked, like savages. The whites finally caught a man named Awang. They tied him up and took him away. . . . The people went back to the village. . . . Awang's parents came home and found an axe, *laplaps*,[5] shellrings like we'd never seen before, matches, tobacco . . . That was his purchase price. Awang's parents took all these objects, wrapped them up carefully in a piece of bark and hung them from the rafters of the house. They never touched the bundle again. They wept for their son and began the first mourning rites.

Other recruiters came and other men left. Some time later, a man returned to the village. Having fallen ill, he had been dismissed from the plantation where he worked. He claimed that Awang was indeed alive and he described the new world he had seen, explained the work on the plantations and in the mines, taught the young people a few words of Pidgin. Then more men returned. They came home with four huge crates that the boys went to bring back from a Banaro village in Keram. When they arrived in the village, they were the centre of everyone's admiration and curiosity:

> Once they were brought back to the village, their owners were in no hurry to open them. They went hunting, they smoked some meat, then they asked the flutes to come and play in the men's house. Only then did they open them up. They were full of bush knives and axes. They called all the clans and began distributing the axes and bush knives. Each house received something. The men had worked in the gold mines. They had been paid with the old money, money that was worth something. Gold money.

At last what had begun as a tragedy ended in triumph. The Adjirab now had direct access to powerful and efficient tools, and no longer just old fragments of blades obtained dearly from traditional exchange partners in the coastal villages. But this was not the end of the wonders. The men told stories that showed there was indeed, out there, not so far away, an astonishing world where people spoke a different language, obeyed different laws, knew other kinds of wealth.

The pride of place given the events at Pinam in the narrative order shows that the two contact periods were perceived differently. The first contacts were a one-off event and did not entail any fundamental change in the society other than an influx of new goods and a redistribution of social positions as a result of the prestige accruing to any returning traveller. As Arese remarked one day, the passage of the recruiters fitted in with a familiar logic – that of headhunting or warfare. The form was slightly different, reflecting the new actor-partners. The story of Pinam, on the other hand, was really the beginning of a new world. The repression was savage; it was marked by an unthinkable act – Matot's hanging – and ended with a ban on war and headhunting. So began a new era.

Yet rapidly, under the pressure of events, the course of things was again to change.

The War

The Japanese were welcomed with open arms. Not only did they cost the Australians their prestige, they also announced a bright tomorrow. They were seen as the awaited people, the people the Australians kept from coming.

> With the Japanese we earned a lot of money. The Japanese coins were rectangular pieces of metal. The Japanese told us: 'Be careful, don't lose them! When we win the war you will be able to buy lots of things . . . Brick houses. When the war is over, to pay you back for the hard work you did for us, you will be able to build real houses, set up shops and buy lots of goods all for yourselves.'

The Japanese enjoyed an aura of prestige, favoured by their situation: their survival depended on being supplied by the villagers. They paid for these supplies with pieces of metal endowed with future magic powers. And the people dreamed. They dreamed of the promises: opening their own shops, building their own Australian-style houses, in short, obtaining those much coveted goods. The women, with the help of the men, worked big gardens, raised pigs, provided sago, supplied the occupying army.

A number of young boys, among them Arese, travelled down the Sepik to Marienberg, where the first river mission had been established, then the government station. There they received training – something that remains a mystery for me since Arese does not remember anything about it – and learned a smattering of Japanese.

> I've forgotten everything I learned with the Japanese. All I remember is how to count. They would tell us: 'Go back to your village, stay two weeks and teach the men and women Japanese. Call them together every morning and start teaching.' But when we got back to the village we didn't really have the time. We were always coming and going. At that time the stretch of river between Ombos and here was blocked by aquatic weeds. Upstream from Ombos it was overrun with grass . . . You had to pole the canoes along to reach the mouth. The trip took a long time. In the village all I did was teach a little Japanese to my mother and my sister. I had just got married and had to filter sago for my young wife. At that time my wife was a tiny little thing.

In the beginning all went well. Then, as the war wore on, tensions grew. The Japanese forces, cut off from their supply lines, drew more and more on the countryside. There were cases of extortion, heads were cut off. The situation turned, and people began to realize that the Japanese were not the chosen people.

Arese recounted the slow death of some Japanese in the swamps. The Papuans watched the soldiers die. They helped them, but only out of obligation, resenting it deeply. One day Arese gave vent to his bitterness. Bitterness at having been deceived, cheated. All those promises hadn't come true, all that work by the women that hadn't been paid back.

> When the war was over, the Japanese went home . . . They lied to us. The wealth never came. When the Australians came back they warned us: 'This is Japanese money, it won't buy anything in our shops.' We filled up big sacks full . . . A man from Kambranba came to collect the sacks . . . Some maintained that the Japanese were coming back, and they kept their money. We made fun of them. How many sago palms, pigs, sweet potatoes did we bring them? . . . We worked hard for them. When we brought them sago they paid us and gave us clothes, but only to the men . . . The poor women didn't get anything, not one piece of clothing. They worked hard for nothing. We didn't spend any of this money. The Japanese didn't have any shops. They told us: 'Just wait, when we win the war, we'll build lots of shops and you'll be able to buy everything you want.' Only it was the Australians who came back. They told us: 'This money won't work in our shops. If you try to pay with this money, you'll find yourselves in jail!' And so we threw whole sacks away. Big sacks . . . We threw them into the swamp. We said to ourselves: 'Too bad!' That money wasn't worth anything any more, not like the Australians' money.

Resentment against the new order was all the greater as, with the war, something had again changed irrevocably. This something can be understood from an episode in Binda's life as told by Arese. Binda was a villager who was working on the plantations when the Japanese invaded New Guinea. He ran away with the Australian forces, and then was inducted into the American Army. He is often presented as a frightening devil of a man, a killer of Japanese. But his glory as a headhunter is enhanced by one unimaginable act. One day he quarrelled violently with an American officer in defence of one of his friends. He was thrown into jail, tried and apparently acquitted. In Arese's opinion, he owes this acquittal to the defence he presented at the court martial:

> 'Do you want to hang me? Be quiet! Listen to me! I'm a black man, a New Guinea man, and I won the war. The Australians couldn't win the war. The Japanese made soup of you. When the Japanese arrived, they hunted you down like game. They ate you up!' They listened to him and they set him free. He returned home two months after the others because he had done two months in jail.

In other words: you are nothing without us. You were beaten by the Japanese and your rewon power you owe to us. You can't be more straightforward.

And in line with the logic of shared victory, the Papuans hoped to see different relations emerge. For them it made little difference whether the Australians or the Japanese were in power as long as they got what they wanted. And what they wanted had not changed: relations between equals, laws that stemmed from dialogue, and wealth that was at last shared.

This is obviously not what happened. The colonial system returned. The brotherly relations between men (and not between armies as the heroic wartime imagery sometimes suggested) born of the war were short-lived. Even worse, the region of Porapora was abandoned immediately after the war. The *kiap* felt little inclination to patrol a region that was remote and particularly mosquito-ridden.

Nothing had changed. Life picked up where it had left off.

Doktoboi and the Plantations

Nothing had changed; or almost nothing, since for Arese a third phase was beginning.

This was a complex period, marked by two antithetical experiences: the acquisition of knowledge that had previously been the preserve of whites (*doktoboi*) and the plantation experience. The young man who set out for the plantations had nothing in common with the one who had watched Matot's hanging. Something happened at Angoram, where Arese was training to be a *doktoboi*, which will help one understand this.

One day the *kiap* returned from their far-flung expeditions with some 'savages' they had just captured in a region that Arese locates in the upper Sepik valley. The whole village turned out to gape at this spectacle, which was as rare as it was fascinating:

> The biggest were really very big. They were taller than any of us. Their spears were completely different from ours. They were made out of a piece of palm tree with no bamboo point. The arrows were different, too; they were very short, just like their bows. They had wide armbands with shells, like the ones we used to wear. They also had necklaces made from dogs' teeth or pig tusks cut in half. They had beards that came down to their chest and long hair. And breech-cloths made from bat-skins that showed their balls hanging down and their bare butts. They were like wild men. When they arrived we all went to see them, but the *kiap* told us to keep our distance. We stayed well back. We stared at them. The *kiap* shaved them. They stripped off their ornaments, worthless things, they threw their bat-skins in the river and gave them clothes.

'We stared.' 'We stayed well back.' In a few terrible words, Arese showed that he had indeed stepped through the looking-glass, to the other side.

Arese spent a few months in Angoram, long enough to complete his training as a future *doktoboi*. There he learned to read new signs, to recognize diseases and to use medications. But that was not the most important. The most important was that at last knowledge was being shared. When he put on the insignia of his new function – the *laplap* and the white-brimmed helmet – Arese changed worlds for good. The baby of the family had, by dint of hard work, achieved a new status.

But Arese remained discrete about his work as a *doktoboi*. It already affected his life in the village and seems to have rested on a precarious balance.

> If you keep your temper, if you know how to take care of people, if you give, then you have nothing to fear. You aren't afraid of magic spells. If you say anything that comes into your head, if you don't know your work, in that case.

He never elaborated.

At the other end of the spectrum and parallel to his new status of *doktoboi* stands Arese's plantation experience. Under the Australians, the job of *doktoboi* was a volunteer activity, unpaid.

To earn some money, Arese signed up in the early 1950s for a year on the Burns Philp plantation, on the island of Buka, in the Solomons. This was a particularly harsh experience. Once more the men fell under the colonial regime with its hierarchy. Whatever experience they may already have had or knowledge they had acquired, they worked under foremen who themselves answered to whites, who appeared as good or bad tutelary powers, depending on the circumstances.

Arese never admitted outright that this had been a time of regression. He simply spoke of a hard, repetitive and unrewarding job (picking up coconuts), which he tried to get through as fast as possible while trying to take advantage of every opportunity. In many respects, this work was less prestigious than that of the villagers who had gone to work in the gold mines before the war. Less profitable as well: the return home was humble, without glory. But this work again raised major questions. For months on end, the plantation workers would produce copra, which was first stored in big sheds, then shipped to some unknown destination. Who were these dried coconuts for? What were they going to be used for? To what wonderful, forbidden world were these rivers of copra flowing while only a trickle of goods came back to the workers? As usual, Arese did not put these questions directly. He merely alluded to them, metaphorically, by means of the story of a fleeting contact with a woman:

> There was a woman who worked on the plantation with the director. His name was Masta Fesse. He beat the people who worked for him. Whenever his wife took our side, he would get mad. So she sent a letter. An answer came back. It said: 'Very well, get rid of him!' He left. It was the government that gave the order to fire him. His wife was left alone. She was left alone to run the plantation and the shop. Lord, was she nice! She gave us the director's clothes. And on Saturday she would give us tobacco, cigarette paper and more clothes . . . shirts, pants, dresses for the women who lived on the plantation. She told us: 'All the time he was here the director wouldn't let me help you and give you things. Now that I'm alone, I can give you whatever you want.' That only lasted a short time. Then another director came. His name was Masta Gumich. He also hit the men working on the plantation. And the poor woman had to leave.

Another time, talking about another plantation, the same motif cropped up repeatedly:

> She was a very good woman. When the director had left, she came to see us, she gave us everything. She gave away lots of food, free. She also gave us shirts, pants and *laplaps*. She told us: 'Above all don't say anything. If I were the only one here, I'd give you lots of things. But, alas, the director won't let me.'

She even admits that, if it were only for her, she would have opened up the warehouse to them.

This episode, as it was told us, is in all likelihood a fantasy. And that is what is interesting. Two familiar themes of New Guinea mythology appear: the women's secret and the forbidden access to places bulging with goods. It is also, with its classic image of the mother, provider of food and protection, the condensation of the well-known 'cargo' problematic; and, with this image, the reappearance of a classic binary opposition: the world of women – ready and willing to give – and the authoritarian and violent world of men. The first make wealth tangible, while the second, by their insurmountable authority, continue to forbid access. Once again, then, Arese raises the nagging question of 'cargo' and its distribution.

I will come back to this problem in my conclusion, but I would like first to point out a side-effect of plantation life: the emergence of a new perception of identity. While the prewar Pax Australiana enabled the Adjirab of Arese's generation to travel, nothing forced them into long-term contact with the reality of a new world. Nor was there anything to challenge the founding principles of their society, always largely protected by the swamps that surrounded the villages. After the war, the massive exodus of young men to the plantations would upset this state of affairs. Those who left were forced to seek their place in a much wider world than the one they had formerly known. They had to redefine themselves and reorganize their world view. In doing this they used new landmarks, which they laid out in concentric circles according to the more or less familiar features they recognized in their discoveries.

The first circle took in the *wantok*, those who spoke the same language. Using a tried and true technique, recruiters would scour a region, systematically signing up all the young men. Thanks to this methodical procedure, recruits found themselves with kinsmen or other clansmen, but with whom, because of the distance separating the villages and endemic headhunting, they had until then had only sporadic contact. For swamp people, the inhabitants of Ramu, even though they spoke the same language and belonged to the same family, had been regarded as 'Johnny-come-latelies' and therefore already part of a different sphere. On the plantation, these men came to recognize not only that they shared the same language, but that they also had a common history and ancestors. On the plantation, they were housed in the same quarters and, on their now-familiar grounds, they held dances and a few rituals, but above all they carried on the exchanges traditional between kinsmen. And so they refashioned life 'like it was at home', thus announcing to other groups their attachment to shared values and a specific identity.

A second circle was comprised by the Sepik groups. There was everything to gain by associating with them. To their great surprise, Arese and his comrades realized that there was no basic difference between their customs, but above all that they might well share certain mythic heroes. And so a complex geography emerged, linking the various groups by a network of ancestral pathways. Familiarity played a part here, and a Sepik 'identity' grew up. While it is not easy to pinpoint the component features of this identity from what Arese has to say, it is easy to see how it worked: it was comprised of mutual assistance (which was not immune to conflicts and fights), exchanges of food, goods and money. Everything circulated, was redistributed according to complex laws in which friendship but also countergifts played a part: each Adjirab man chose a partner to whom he owed assistance and respect. The 'Sepiks' formed a bloc, then, they were proud of their way of life and their traditions, of which they boasted every time they had the occasion.

The inhabitants of Buka were excluded from these formal exchanges between Sepik groups. They formed the third circle. With them relations were at once more distant and more personal. More personal because every man on the plantation had a 'mother' in Buka whom he visited on weekends. He was supposed to give her presents – soap, tobacco, clothes or money – in exchange for food. More distant because, while they entertained civil relations with the men from the next village, they had very little in common with them. This distance was probably encouraged by the people of Buka themselves, who were obliged to protect themselves against repeated invasions of rowdy young plantation workers. It was in their interest to seize every means of controlling them. And to this end they had recourse to magic.

> In the villages there were meeting houses. Sundays everyone went there to relax and eat. These houses were very different from our men's houses. On each side there was a bench where you could sit and talk. The Buka men would warn you: 'Don't do anything foolish while you're here, otherwise you could die.' Buka magic is completely different. We were afraid of it. We didn't fight them. We behaved ourselves. In Buka people were calm. They didn't go looking for trouble. And then, they'd warned us: 'If you get mad at us, if you fight us, you'll die.'

Magic is a good barometer of the cultural distance. Another is approval of Buka songs and dances. Arese did not like them, to say the least. He found them boring and lacking in grace. And he was not alone. It seemed self-evident for the Sepik that one could not feel close to people with whom there was no possibility of competition or exchange. Indeed, the people of Buka were definitely from another world.

Lastly, there is the fourth circle, that of the whites. It is the most remote, both in outlook and behaviour. The plantation director and the emigrant personnel lived by themselves on a hillside overlooking the coconut groves. Contacts between the two groups were fleeting and distant. Sometimes they were marked by violence. Exchanges with this fourth group were one way only, reduced to requests for services and to goods for work. A new geography fell into place, then, from least to most distance, from most familiar to utterly other. But from this dynamic between groups was born, in Arese's mind, a wholly new organization of the world. It was no longer simply a patchwork of neighbouring groups, but a much wider world in which a nation was emerging. According to Arese, the idea of nation began taking shape for those who lived on the plantations.

Nevertheless, the key to the whole system still lay in the hands of the colonial power. A power that, according to Arese, carefully protected access to its world, allowing only a glimpse of small openings, giving rise to many, often disappointed, hopes. This probably explains why Arese never threw himself wholeheartedly into the white adventure. He handled it with extreme caution and, however fascinated he may have been, always maintained a distance. His disinclination to tell about his life in the village may well stem from this desire to preserve his independence. He was always careful to stay on the right side of a second looking-glass.

Nevertheless, we see one preoccupation running through the many episodes of Arese's life, like a thread or, better, a blind spot, for Arese never spoke of it: this was the question of access to wealth. Yet in the 1950s a cargo movement swept through Porapora. The police intervened, and the leaders were jailed. Despite my questions, however, neither Arese nor any other of the village men would talk about this period. If they are to be believed, no such movement ever existed. It has been thoroughly mystified, impossible to discuss. As though the disappointments and errors of judgement to which the intrusion of the white world had given rise could be explained by fragments of lives, but one of the central questions could not be uttered. As though this episode was the accursed share of our relations.

But just before I left, Arese and some other men of the village timidly put to me the major questions they were burning to ask: Why didn't the wealth come? Why were the Japanese driven out? What is so terrifying about the white world that it remains inaccessible? But that is another story . . .

Notes

1. Translation by Nora Scott.
2. This is the name of the marshy region that lies between the Ramu and Keram Rivers in the lower Sepik valley. The term does not convey the full reality, though, since the region is divided into at least two linguistic units: to the north the Aion villages and to the south those of the Adjirab.
3. Headman appointed by the Australian colonial government.
4. Administrative and missionary centre set up on the Sepik. Shortly before the war, the administration relocated at Angoram.
5. A skirt-like garment made of a strip of cloth tied around the hips.

Chapter 9

Resource Management in Lavongai and Tigak Islands: Changing Practices, Changing Identities

Ton Otto

Introduction

Customary ownership and management of natural resources has become a topical theme in Papua New Guinean anthropology, not least because of the rich mineral finds, which have led to fierce struggles over mining royalties and have engendered countless claims for compensation for environmental damages. Also the rapidly developing timber industry has intensified debates about the rights of 'traditional' owners. However, the issue of traditional rights to land and resources has a much longer history. In the early 1960s the colonial administration introduced legislation to facilitate the transition from customary tenure to Western-style individual ownership with the aim of encouraging modern economic development. While this legislation was initiated to transform indigenous forms of resource management, it also provided them with a legal base. The expansion of indigenous plantation agriculture and the possibility to register land titles has gradually put some pressure on traditional systems of resource management in many regions of Papua New Guinea (PNG), including New Ireland and New Hanover. Another development that has influenced conceptions of indigenous rights is the payment of royalties for fish caught by foreign fishing companies in coastal waters.

In this chapter I am particularly concerned with the relationship between cultural constructs of 'ownership' and changing practices of resource management. Cultural concepts of ownership involve much more than a definition of access to natural resources. Evidently they also define social relations and, as a consequence, imply conceptions of group and individual identities, which play a role in the regulation of resource use. It is probably a Western bias to consider conceptions of resource ownership as purely or primarily of economic relevance. In their article 'Profitless Property', Carrier and Carrier (1983) argue that on Ponam in Manus (PNG) rights in fishing techniques do not provide an economic advantage. Nevertheless, these rights are carefully maintained and transferred by patrilineal inheritance. The Carriers conclude that marine ownership rights on Ponam concern first and foremost the articulation of group identities.

> This indicates that the underpinnings of the system of marine ownership lie in social rather than in the purely economic aspects of Ponam life. Ownership of the means of production here is an expression of the segmentary lineage system and the central part it plays in the society, and is not simply a consequence of the desire and ability of certain groups to secure advantage over their fellows. In a very real sense, then, the system is not about who gets what, but about who is what, about which lineages there are and who belongs to them, a matter central to Ponam social existence (Carrier and Carrier 1983:149).

Concepts of ownership thus concern the definition of social identities as well as the regulation of access to natural resources. This suggests that historical changes in management practices may have an impact on the construction of identities. In this chapter I argue that this has been the case in Lavongai and Tigak in northern New Ireland. The data for the following description were collected in the last quarter of 1989 when I worked as a consultant to the Department of Fisheries and Marine Resources. My brief was to develop a feasible system for the distribution of royalties paid for baitfish caught in the coastal waters. This consultancy project was commissioned in anticipation of the re-emergence of a pole-and-line tuna fisheries in the region. In this chapter I will deal with the consequences of baitfish royalties for conceptions of marine ownership but I will also describe changing conceptions of land ownership, which involve some different principles.

Lavongai Island (also known as New Hanover) lies north-west of the mainland of New Ireland. Administratively it is part of New Ireland Province and consists of three census divisions, which also function as electoral constituencies, namely North Lavongai, West Lavongai and South Lavongai. My research focused on North and West Lavongai, where most of the baitfish was caught. I also visited some villages on the east coast of South Lavongai which participated in the distribution of the royalties. In between New Ireland mainland and Lavongai Island lie a great number of small islands called Tigak Islands. They belong, together with the northern tip of New Ireland, to the Tigak census division. The Tigak Islands and three villages on the west coast of New Ireland also received royalties for baitfish caught in the surrounding waters, particularly the Silver Sound. These villages were included in my research.

In the area two different languages are spoken, namely 'Lavongai' (or 'Tungak') on New Hanover and surrounding islands and 'Tigak' in the Tigak census division.[1] The two languages are closely related according to their vocabulary (the lexicostatistical relationship is 66 per cent) but grammatically they may be somewhat more diverse (Beaumont 1988:87). Dorothy Billings, who is one of the very few anthropologists to have worked in the area, constructs a sharp cultural division between Lavongai and Tikana (Billings 1991, 1992a, b). With the latter term she refers to the people living in northern New Ireland, who speak three different but related languages, namely Tigak, Kara and Nalik. My own data on land and water management do not support such a sharp distinction but rather point to many commonalities. It is possible that this difference in perspective is the result – at least partly – of work in different areas. Billings worked mainly in the village of Lavongai on South Lavongai and on the west coast of New Ireland, whereas my fieldwork concentrated on North and West Lavongai and the Tigak Islands. Especially in the latter region there is a great deal of intermarriage with Lavongai people, resulting in the presence of Lavongai clans in Tigak communities. In the following description I deal with the two cultural areas together but I mention differences where they are relevant.

Administratively, the four census divisions are subdivided into census units or communities. The resident population of a community ranges roughly from fifty to 400. West Lavongai consists of seventeen communities, North Lavongai has twenty-two, South Lavongai counts twenty-nine and Tigak comprises twenty-six communities and seventeen 'rural non-villages' (schools, plantations, etc.). Twelve Tigak communities are within the area where the bait royalty distribution took place. Normally a community consists of only one village, but sometimes more than one village or island combines to form one community. An example is the community which appears under the name Upuas in the Tigak census book. It consists of the inhabited islands of Kulinus, Utukul and Upuas and the settlement Patimaian on Salapiu island.

The residential structure of villages varies. There may be a clear centre with a concentration of houses, but a more spread-out structure is equally common. Normally a village is composed of several distinguishable hamlets, more or less concentrated, in which local clan groups reside with their spouses and sometimes some other relatives. Membership of a community and actual residence do not necessarily coincide. Sometimes people live in the area of a community different from the one in which they are registered. The reason for this may be recent settlement or long-time loyalty to the other community. Often the number of non-community-member residents is quite insignificant, but in some cases it is substantial. In Nonovaul, for example, twenty-seven residents were counted who belonged to a different community (excluding teachers and other temporary residents); and in Mamion 19 per cent of the people, who took part in a census conducted by the researcher, were members of the neighbouring community Tsoilik.

Descent and Marriage

Large matrilineal descent groups, which I will call clans, are an important feature of Lavongai and Tigak societies. The indigenous term for such a descent group in Lavongai is *mani* or *patmani* and in Tigak it is *manui* or *patmanui*. Both *mani* and *manui* mean 'bird'. At birth a child becomes a member of the clan of its mother and remains a member for life. Membership is inalienable; even if a child is adopted and raised by another woman, it still remains a member of the biological mother's clan. The assumption is that membership is transmitted through the blood of the mother. Ideally clans are exogamous groups. In practice, however, marriage within the same clan sometimes occurs.

According to Lavongai oral tradition, all the clans originally derive from one group which lived in central Lavongai. Conflict and migration led to the formation of twelve clans, which spread out to occupy the mainland of New Hanover and the surrounding islands. All the clans have bird names except for one which is named after the flying fox. The twelve clans of Lavongai are: Tien (small yellow bird), Siavun or Kikiu (kookaburra), Nguma (crow), Yanga (parrot), Kanai (seagull), Manilava (eagle), Valus (pigeon), Vengevenge (hornbill), Silau (kingfisher), Sui (related to kookaburra), Maligom (flying fox) and Valuskaup (grey pigeon). I found representatives of the first ten clans in the twenty-nine Lavongai villages I visited and an additional clan called Gila, which is said to be split off from Yanga.

Tigak oral history also has it that all the clans were originally one. From the place of origin, Lamusmus, on New Ireland mainland, the different clans broke away and moved eastward. Some groups crossed the water and settled on the islands between New Ireland and New Hanover. Six clans are present on these islands. They are (in parentheses is the name of the corresponding bird in the vernacular plus an English translation): Makantitien (*tutut*/small yellow and black bird), Makanaga (*gak*/parrot), Makon (eagle), Makanuk (*valus*/pigeon), Tivungau (*manga*/small parrot), Tivungur (*taula*/big black bird).

These matrilineal clans are large groups and members of the same clan live in different villages. The representatives of one clan in a single village may be called a local section of that clan. This is the relevant group as far as ownership of land is concerned. In Lavongai a village normally houses between four and nine local sections of clans. Some of these groups are really small and do not own land; they consist of people married to the big land owning local clan groups. The number of the land-owning sections of clans in a single village ranges from one to four. The figures for Tigak are a little bit different. In one village there may be two to five local sections of clans, of which one to three may be land-owning groups.

The picture has to be slightly complicated, because a local section of a clan is sometimes subdivided again into two or more named groups. Those groups appear in particular when there are opposing or different claims on land. For this reason there is sometimes resistance to identifying the subgroups, because villagers fear that this might divide the local clan group. The origin of these subgroups is explained as follows. When the clans migrated to occupy new territory, they sometimes split again into smaller groups, each under their own war leader. These subgroups, which I will call subclans, followed their own route and left groups of people behind in various places. Sometimes two subclans would meet again in the same village. Another obvious reason for the presence of more than one subclan of the same main clan within one village is marriage and the subsequent settlement of descendants.

In Lavongai a subclan is named after a place where the group once resided. It is called the eye (*mata*) of a clan (in North Lavongai) or the (female) breast (*tus*) of a clan (in South Lavongai) in that particular place. Some of the subclans of the very large Tien clan are for example 'Mata i Patituas', 'Mata i Malebang', 'Tus i Venge' and 'Tus i Pakai'. Patituas, Malebang, Venge and Pakai are the names of places. In Tigak the subclans have names of fish, birds, other animals and even shells. The clan Makantitien has amongst others the following subclans 'Manal' (gar fish), 'Makanpes' (parrot fish) and 'Mumbogo' (the line of the pig). Some of the subclans of Makanaga are 'Kuiei' (a small shell) and 'Kaukau-vualai' (green lizard).

The local section of a subclan might be divided into even smaller groups, which can be called matrilineages. Such groups consist of the descendants of a single grandmother or great-grandmother. These groups also play a role in management of land resources, but in most cases the local sections of (sub)clans are the most relevant units. Thus far I have identified five types of descent groups, or, to put it differently, five types of group identities based on the cultural assumption of the matrilineal blood line. In the order of their size, these groups are the clan, the subclan, the local section of a clan, the local section of subclan, and the matrilineage.

The criterion for membership in these groups is matrilineal descent but in the case of the local section of a clan or subclan a residential factor appears to be involved as well. This residential aspect is, however, not predominant. People remain members of the local clan group in which they were born and they remain co-owners of the properties of this local clan group even if they live in a different community. The descent groups have two main functions. In the first place the local sections of clans, subclans and matrilineages are the corporate groups who hold property rights in land (cf. Lomas (1979:57), who writes about Tigak mainland). Secondly, important social events like funerals, mortuary parties and marriages are organized by clan groups. Thus clan groups have social as well as economic functions.

The burden of day-to-day economic tasks, however, is carried by a different group. This is the household, which has to provide for the basic economic and social needs of the individual, such as shelter, food, clothing, schooling (fees), care in case of sickness, etc. A household normally consists of two parents and their unmarried children, though it is sometimes extended to include a grandparent and/or a married child with spouse. If a household needs help, it not only relies on the local clan group, but also on other relatives, such as paternal kin and affines. The general term for all these relatives is *antogon* in Lavongai language (in Tok Pisin the term *bisnis* is frequently used).

As already mentioned, the main rule for marriage is that one cannot marry a person of one's own clan. However, some informants in Tigak maintained that one may marry within the clan if the spouse is from a different subclan. There are indeed quite a few examples of this kind of marriage practice. Nevertheless, the majority follow the rule of exogamy and consider it shameful not to do so. When asked whether the wife moves to the place of the husband or vice versa, people will answer that the general rule is that the wife follows the man. This was confirmed by a small census carried out in three communities. In Mamion (North Lavongai) 83 per cent of the marriages were virilocal; the figure for Noipuas (West Lavongai) was 75 per cent virilocal, and in Salapiu (Tigak Islands) it was 62.5 per cent virilocal.

Because ownership of land is vested in local clan groups and membership of these groups is matrilineal, one would expect people to live on their mother's land (cf. Lomas 1979:57). Combined with the virilocality of the majority of marriages, this means that a man leaves his father's place and settles on his mother's clan ground when he marries and starts his own household. This picture is supported by the census results of Noipuas (70 per cent matrilocal) and of Salapiu (81 per cent matrilocal). Mamion, however, deviates from this pattern, because 55 per cent of the households live on the land of the father (in most cases the father of the husband). It may be that Mamion represents a trend, which was also observed in other communities. In the section about land management I will deal further with this question.

Types of Leadership: 'Traditional' and Modern

Before I discuss resource management in relation to group identities based on descent and residence, I give a short historical description of types of leadership. This provides some additional information on the political function and organization of the groups involved. Moreover, it shows that 'traditional' leadership as it is understood today greatly differs from such leadership in the past.

According to oral tradition, there were very clearly identified leaders of clan groups in precolonial times. One of their main functions was to lead their group in the wars against other clans. According to my informants the traditional Lavongai and Tigak societies were very belligerent and the men in their men's houses had to be always ready to fight. In Lavongai a clan and war leader was called *pasingan* and the men's house *rangama*. In Tigak the names were *bomleie* for leader and *garama* for men's house. Colonization brought the demise of traditional war leaders and the gradual disappearance of the men's houses.

At present the words *pasingan* and *bomleie* are in disuse. They are avoided because they have the connotation of warfare. A term that is sometimes used is *maimai*, which refers to a great orator and organizer of mortuary feasts (*malanggan* in Tigak and *matanangan* in Lavongai). This kind of leadership comes from New Ireland mainland and is not a part of the traditional Lavongai and Tigak Islands culture. People on the Tigak Islands told me that they would sometimes 'borrow' a *maimai* from the mainland to give prestige to their ceremonies. At present, a number of villages show a lively interest in tradition and in this kind of leadership. This trend towards the revival of *kastam* (as it is called in Tok Pisin) is part of a nationwide movement in which tradition is re-evaluated as source for local identities and political leadership (Otto 1991; Jolly and Thomas 1992).

In most villages people are able to name their clan leaders if asked to do so. They do not have, however, a vernacular word for them and use the English word 'clan leader' or the Tok Pisin term *mausman* instead. Only in two cases a vernacular word was produced (*iganinlava* in Lavongai and *aininoiai* in Tigak) but these words proved to be very unfamiliar. The common opinion is that this type of leadership is in fact a recent introduction, or, better, a modern form of 'traditional' leadership. It has been developed in the context of timber royalties and land disputes, when clans were asked to produce representatives or leaders. This view is supported by the fact that a number of villages who were never involved in timber royalties and who had no major land problems had some difficulties in determining their clan leaders.

The main functions of these clan leaders lie in representing their clan groups when there are land problems and when there are royalty moneys to be distributed. They are selected on the basis of their knowledge of the clan history and on their ability to speak in public. Although clan leaders have an important voice in land matters, they certainly do not have the right to make decisions on their own without consultation of the other clan members.

The history of the development of Western political structures probably started with the appointment of *luluais* and *tultuls* by the colonial government at the beginning of the century. A further major step in this development was the creation of 'Local Government Councils' from the 1950s onwards; these political bodies had some limited administrative authority and were led by democratically elected representatives from the indigenous population. The first council to be formed in New Ireland was the Tikana Council in 1957, which comprised the Tigak area. The Lavongai Council followed in 1961, but this council was to have a troubled history. The outbreak of the 'Johnson cult' (Billings 1969, 1991, 1992a, b; Miskaram 1985) took away much of the support for this council. Many of the cult followers became organized in the Tutukuwul Isokal Association, which is generally referred to as TIA. This association was originally set up as a cooperative society and as such it certainly achieved positive developments for its members. However, a strong cultist influence persisted and the TIA became more and more a political body opposed to the existing council. This led to the self-dissolution of the Lavongai Council in 1973 (by vote). In West Lavongai support for the TIA was not so strong and here a new small council was established under the name Matas Council.

The main development after independence was the introduction of the Provincial Government, which superseded the so-called Area Authority. New Hanover has three representatives in the provincial parliament and Tigak has one. Another recent change is the introduction of community government in two selected areas in New Ireland, one of which is West Lavongai.[2]

This brief sketch of political developments serves to explain the confusing variety of political leaders that can be found in Lavongai and Tigak. Where a council is in existence (Tigak), there will be councillors and their elected representatives in the villages (*komiti kansol*). At the time of my research West Lavongai was in transition and one could find (ex-)councillors next to community government members. A large area of New Hanover was neither incorporated in a council nor any longer involved in TIA. These villages had 'community leaders', who were mostly elected by the villagers in a more or less informal way (without fixed terms). In some villages there were both a TIA leader and a non-TIA community leader.

Thus in Lavongai and Tigak every community has a Western type of political leader of some sort and sometimes two. Clans do not have an official political role any more. The clan leaders' main competence lies in land matters and customary practices. Political leadership is vested in elected community leaders, making communities the main political units.

Management of Land Rights

The main land-owning groups are the local sections of clans and subclans. As these are matrilineal descent groups, title to land is inherited through the mother. The tendency of marriages to virilocality means that most children grow up in the place of their father. Most people have to leave this place later in their lives. Men leave when they want to settle on their rightful land with their mother's clan group. This may happen when they marry and start their own household, or they may wait until the death of their father. Women normally leave their father's hamlet when they marry and join their husband.

Although the majority of marriages are virilocal, a married couple is completely free to settle on the wife's land. In Salapiu village this happened in 37.5 per cent of the cases, in Noipuas the percentage was 25 per cent and in Mamion only 17 per cent. A reason for moving to the wife's place may be the availability of land. A clear disadvantage for the man is that his status is lower than it would be in his own clan group. For the children, however, the situation is favourable, because they are already living on their mother's land. Any improvements done on the land will be theirs.

If a man lives on the land of his wife's clan, he will never acquire ownership rights on this land. He may, however, obtain right of usage for himself and his relatives by presenting a gift of food, money and *mis* (traditional shell money). The name for this practice on Lavongai is *luvekme* and in Tigak it is *gumutngur*, which means 'to shut someone's mouth' (so that no complaints are heard about the use of the land and trees). Traditionally it was also expected that the wife would make a gift to the husband's family for the use of land and crops if she settled with them, and especially if she wanted to obtain use right for her visiting relatives as well.

The main principle of land ownership is that people hold rights to the land of their mother's local clan group by virtue of their membership of that clan group. There is, however, a traditional way to obtain rights to a piece of the land owned by the father's local clan group. The ceremony in which the rights are transferred is called *tatvauk* in Lavongai and *makate* in Tigak. It consists of the presentation of a gift of pig, taro, banana, sago, other food, *mis* and money. The gift is called *marum* or *katam*. It may be presented by a father to his own family on behalf of his child or children. It is also possible that the children themselves do the presentation, if, for example, the father has died. The traditional occasion for this ceremony is during a big mortuary feast, called *matanangan* in Lavongai and *malanggan* in the Tigak area.

The people on whose behalf the *katam* is given enjoy full usufructuary rights on the piece of land during their lifetime. It is, however, not clear if they also receive proprietary rights. Opinions are clearly divergent on this point. Discussions about it have a strong ideological component and are often emotional, because people have opposed interests. Many people maintain that the clan group of the father has the right to claim the land back after the user has died. The opposite opinion, that the transfer of rights is definitive, is also forcefully defended.

In the past this was apparently not so much a problem as it is today. The traditional solution for a man living on his father's land was to marry a woman from his father's clan group. This would ensure full proprietary rights for his children on the land of this clan group. This method is still practised, although most young people do not want their choice of a marriage partner to be restricted in this way.

In the last decades the problem of the permanence of the rights obtained through the father has become more acute for several reasons. In the first place more men marry women from distant places, even from other provinces. This often makes it difficult for their children 'to go back' to the place of their mother. Secondly, people tend to make more commercial use of their land. This also affects the attitude towards inheritance, as was explained to me in the following way. If a man has made a great effort to improve his land by planting cash crops, he would rather pass it on to his own children than to his sister's children, who are the customary heirs. Thirdly, more and more people make use of the possibility to register their land with the Land Titles Commission. This practice is especially widespread in the villages near Kavieng. According to my informants, official demarcation and registration imply that the registered owner of the land has the right to determine his successor.[3]

All these developments mean a clear shift in the practices concerning land use and land ownership. An illustration is afforded by Mamion village, in which I conducted a census. In this village the number of people living on their father's land actually exceeds the number of those living on their mother's clan land. This has led to the unusual situation that the biggest clan group is not a land-owning group. The original land owners in Mamion belong to the Tien and Kanai clans. Obviously a lot of Tien and Kanai men married Nguma women, mostly from the neighbouring village. They produced Nguma offspring, who are still living in Mamion village and now form the biggest clan group there. However, Nguma clan does not own land as a group, although the members hold individual titles to pieces of Tien and Kanai land through their fathers. A lot of these people have fulfilled the traditional obligation of presenting *katam* and some have registered their land. They will do their utmost to transfer their rights to their own children instead of seeing the land go back to their father's clan group. If they succeed (and there are examples of the second generation still occupying the land), it will represent an obvious subversion of the matrilineal local clan group as the customary basis for land ownership.

Apart from inheritance through mother or father there is a third way to acquire rights to land, namely from non-kin. In precolonial times warfare was, of course, a notorious way to obtain land. A group could actually seize land or they could assist another group to defend themselves, which would oblige this group to donate a piece of land. Sometimes land was also given as a gift in return for substantial help with mortuary feasts. This last way is still open although rarely practised. What happens more frequently nowadays is that people actually buy land from a non-related clan group which possesses more land than it needs. This purchase normally follows the same pattern as in the case of children securing a piece of their father's clan land, namely the presentation of a gift (*katam*). The quantities of food and amounts of money given seem to be comparable. Like the transfer of rights from father to children, the buying of land also encourages a trend from group ownership of land to individual ownership.

Boundaries between the territories of clan groups are not always clearly marked. This is especially so in villages which occupy a large area and which have not been involved in a timber rights purchase (TRP).[4] Within the territory of a clan group there are often pieces of land, usually with well-defined boundaries, which are owned by smaller groups (matrilineages) within the same clan group or by a different clan group. The claims to those pieces of land are frequently based on the story that an ancestor of the matrilineage was the first to clear that part of the common land for his or her own use. Work on a piece of land appears to establish proprietary rights. This is especially so if trees – fruit, sago, rubber, coconut or cocoa trees – are planted. The trees are individually owned by the person who plants them and at the same time this person establishes a lasting claim on the piece of land used for the plantation (provided that this person is a member of the clan group who owns that piece of land). Strict boundaries are enforced by population pressure and by commercial use of the land in the form of cash crops or timber harvesting. Official registration of land titles, of course, means fixation of the land boundaries.

In summary three trends in the pattern of land ownership in New Hanover and Tigak may be identified. Although matrilineal inheritance is still predominant, there is a pressure towards inheritance through the father. Secondly, there is a gradual shift from ownership by local sections of clans and subclans towards ownership by matrilineages and individuals. Thirdly, boundaries tend to become better defined and more fixed. The consequence of this is that a relatively flexible system, which provides for demographic fluctuations of clan groups, is gradually transformed into a more rigid system (cf. Lomas 1979:64–5). In addition, the existence of clan groups themselves is undermined by weakening one of their main functions, namely the corporate ownership of land.

Management of Marine Resources

In Lavongai and Tigak management of water resources differs from land management. Whereas the land of a community is divided up over small land-owning clan groups, this is not so in the case of the sea. In general the sea and beach adjoining a village are considered to be the communal property of the villagers. Clan groups within the village, including the land-owning groups, do not claim exclusive rights to the sea and the reef or parts thereof.

There is, however, one exception. The island Kullik lying east of Ungalabu Island in West Lavongai is owned by a local subclan of the Noipuas community, namely Tien Vukavuka. Four members of this subclan live more or less permanently on the island, together with their spouses and children. The clan group claims exclusive rights on the reef surrounding the island and requires that other people, including those of the Noipuas community, ask permission before using it. The claim of this group is generally considered to be an anomaly and contrary to Lavongai tradition. It is argued that at least the families of the spouses of the inhabitants should have the fullest right to use the reef on the basis of affinal obligations.

It is thus safe to assume that generally the unit which owns marine property is the village community. There is no differen- tiation of rights among the members of the community. As a rule the residents have equal access to the marine resources claimed by the village as a whole. It appears, then, that the principle on which co-ownership is based is residence rather than descent. This concurs with Walter *et al.*'s findings (1986). It should, however, be kept in mind that common residence is almost always the result of kinship ties and marriage. Moreover, in the views of the people the sharing of rights by residents is motivated through their kin relationships. Although resident outsiders, such as traders, may be allowed to fish for their own consumption, they do not automatically acquire rights to benefits, such as royalties.

There is one traditional exception to the rule that community members have free access to the reef of their village. In the past a person could put a temporary ban on the use of a particular part of the reef. He could do this when he was applying magic (*timiniem*) to that piece of reef to attract fish. This was often done to secure a big catch in preparation for a feast. The area would be marked by poles (*bale*). Nowadays this way to restrict access is not practised any more.

Although the inshore waters are held in common ownership by villagers, the means to catch fish are not. Nets, spears, traps and also magic are individually owned. A distinction has to be made between individual and collective fishing methods. If an individual fishing method, such as spear fishing, is used, the catch belongs to the person using the spear (generally the owner). In the case of collective fishing methods, the leader of the expedition, who is normally the owner of the equipment used (such as nets or weirs), has the obligation to share the catch with the people who participated. Traditionally there was also an obligation to share with the whole village in the case of very big catches, but this custom has been discontinued.

Because there is a connection between use of water resources and claims of ownership, I will first discuss traditional and modern fishing practices before dealing with modern claims on sea areas. In the precolonial past, fishing was restricted to the reefs and shallow waters close to the village. One reason for this was that it was too dangerous to venture far away from their own village because of the continual threat of ambush and warfare. In addition, people did not possess the techniques and equipment required for deep-water fishing. Thus they only fished in the shallow waters close to their own place.

People of Tigak and Lavongai had developed a wide range of fishing methods prior to the arrival of white people. It is beyond the scope of this chapter to describe in detail all the fishing techniques people could remember, but I will sum up the categories into which they can be put. In the first place, there are several methods which only need the human hand. Important are the various forms of magic to attract fish to the shore or to a certain place where a trap is built. There are two types of stone structures built in shallow waters of the sea. One is a weir or stone fence to trap the fish at low tide and the other is a heap of stones and coral blocks to attract the fish that are looking for shelter. There are various methods involving a dam or a weir built in rivers, estuaries or creeks. Fish poison was (and is) frequently used, often in combination with the methods mentioned above. An old method is a funnel-shaped trap made from cane with thorns, which was used in combination with bait. Nets of various sorts and sizes were used. The rope for the nets was made from the bark of a tree. Sometimes the fish were driven into a weir, a net or a hiding-place by a line of people making noise. Fish could also be driven by a leaf sweep made from coconut leaves tied around a rope; it is, however, possible that this last method is not originally from Lavongai and that it was imported in colonial times. Finally, there are a whole series of methods for using a fishing spear, such as standing in shallow water, walking, standing on a canoe, etc. Some informants maintained that the fishing spear was a recent invention or introduction and that formerly a stick was used to kill the fish. The fishing-line and hook are strikingly absent from the above list and we have to assume that they are recent introductions.

For all their variety, the fishing methods listed have one thing in common: they are all practised in shallow waters. Concerning the fishing techniques, a division of labour by gender was observed. Some methods were mainly practised by women (such as *herauk*, this is catching a fish under a stone with the hands). Others are exclusively for men, such as the use of nets.

Nowadays many of the fishing methods mentioned above have been replaced by modern techniques and materials. However, some of them are still practised, such as fish poison, driving the fish and building stone heaps. Of course, nets and spears are still of utmost importance as catching devices, but modern materials have taken the place of the traditional ones. In the order of frequency of use, the fishing-line with hook seems to be the most important modern method, followed by spearing the fish at night with the help of a pressure lamp. Also very popular is diving and shooting the fish with a spear gun (at night with the help of a torch). Nets are still in common use, but not everybody has them because they are quite expensive. Two methods which seem to be frequently practised but are also very controversial are the use of fish poison (*pun* in Tok Pisin) and of dynamite. These methods give the biggest yields and are easy applicable, although they are not without danger for the user (especially dynamite).[5]

Apart from fish, there is also other marine produce which is being harvested, predominantly for commercial purposes. The most important species are lobster, trochus shell, *bêche-de-mer* and green snail. Because these creatures are more confined to a certain area, their pecuniary value has intensified the discussion about the desirability of drawing marine boundaries.

To gain a good understanding of the present problems with marine boundaries, we have to adopt a historical perspective. In interviews with villagers, there often appeared to be a discrepancy between what they indicated as the fishing grounds of their ancestors and the area they lay claim to today. In some cases, the problem had obviously been solved by adapting the ancestral fishing grounds to present demands. It is clear, however, that in precolonial times people were quite restricted as to where they could catch their fish. As already mentioned, there are two main reasons for this. In the first place, the fishing equipment was only suitable for shallow waters and not for the deep sea. Secondly, it was too dangerous to fish far from one's own village because one would be an easy prey for wandering warriors looking for victims.

In colonial times, this situation changed drastically. Pacification put an end to tribal warfare and people could travel without the ubiquitous danger of being attacked. Moreover, contact with white people and other areas within Papua and New Guinea led to the introduction of new fishing techniques, including those for deeper waters. People started to fish further away from their own villages and islands. Often they ventured into areas which traditionally belonged to other villages. Normally this did not cause any problems, because people would follow lines of kinship and marriage relations. The whole system was relatively open and this was enforced by a government policy which was not supportive of territorial claims on the sea.

At present, more and more people call for the closure and protection of their marine territory. The main reason for this is without doubt the increasing commercialization of PNG society. People need cash for a variety of things and as far as islanders and coastal inhabitants are concerned the sea is one of the main sources of income.

The question of marine boundaries has to be specified by asking the additional questions of boundaries for what and for whom. Most people seem to agree that they have an exclusive right to harvest the sedentary species such as trochus and *bêche-de-mer* in the area claimed by their village. Outsiders always have to ask permission if they want to collect these things. Concerning fish, the situation is somewhat different. Fishing for one's own consumption is considered to be free and boundaries do not apply in this case. Some people, however, maintain that it is still better (and certainly more polite) for outsiders to ask for permission. Fishing for commercial purposes is again the exclusive right of the owners of the sea area and outsiders are always required to obtain prior permission. There is, however, a marked distinction between neighbours and more distant outsiders. The application of the rules mentioned above to neighbours seems to be less strict and permission is easily given, even after the actual fishing has taken place. The principle of reciprocity seems to play a more important role here: if you fish in my area, I may also fish in yours.

In Lavongai and Tigak, marine boundaries are not only a matter of discussion. Some villages have set charges for fishing in their waters. However, they complain that it is difficult to enforce the fees. Often kin relations are invoked to avoid the charges and in most cases villagers lack the means to pursue trespassers. Nevertheless, in a number of cases people have actually been chased away and their catches have been taken from them. Although the number of cases is still very small, they are probably indicative of a trend towards well-defined marine boundaries and well-defined marine property claims.

Baitfish Royalties

A development that had a strong impact on local conceptions of marine ownership and boundaries was the payment of royalties for baitfish used in tuna fishing. One of the methods for catching tuna is the pole-and-line technique. When a shoal of tuna is located, live baitfish is thrown into the water to attract the tuna close to the catcher boat and to bring them into a feeding frenzy. Subsequently individual fishermen can easily hook the tuna with short fishing rods and lines. For this fishing method, it is essential to have good baitfish, which are caught in shallow waters near the coast. In the 1970s, there were large-scale tuna-fishing operations near New Hanover, Manus, East and West New Britain. Because there had been some resistance to the presence of large numbers of foreign boats catching fish, the Minister for Natural Resources, B. Jephcott, decided in 1975 that royalties had to be paid to the 'traditional owners'.[6]

The main motivation for the decision appeared to be to 'keep the people happy who have traditionally harvested fish in the baiting areas'.[7] However, the new rule had some important consequences. It gave official recognition to customary ownership of marine resources, also in areas where this had not been an issue of great concern. In addition, it generated a considerable flow of money in the direction of local groups. As the original decision did not indicate how the money was to be divided, it was left to the provincial governments (at first the Area Authorities) to solve this problem. In New Ireland a rather complicated system gradually evolved, in which the money was divided over nine village groups. The major part of the money (65 per cent) was distributed over all village groups, and the rest was distributed only among those groups where actual baitfishing had taken place (in general, six of the nine groups). Of the latter sum, again one part (50 per cent) was distributed equally and the rest according to frequency of baitfishing. The division between the villages within a village group was based on population numbers. Thus the New Ireland system had incorporated the two criteria that finally, in 1978, were set as national guidelines, namely 'baiting frequencies' and 'population'. However, a substantial share of the money also went to areas without baitfishing. In addition 25 per cent of all the moneys was contributed to project funds which were to benefit the whole area.

Not surprisingly, the system of distribution was rather opaque to most villagers. However, as very large sums of money were pumped into the province, it was possible to 'keep the people happy' for a while. Later, discontent emerged about misappropriation, wastage and also about the principles of distribution. A new committee was instituted, which devised a slightly different system that did not work long since all tuna fishing in PNG stopped at the end of 1981. Another fishing company commenced pole-and-line tuna fishing again in 1984, but this lasted only until the end of 1985. Again the system of distribution was altered. A zone system was introduced in order to monitor baitfishing and to facilitate distribution. This time it was explicitly stated that money could only go to areas in which baitfishing had occurred. Villages within a village group where baitfish had been caught received their share according to population numbers. Within villages the money was further distributed among clan groups, or, more frequently, among all the adults of a village. Again there was dissatisfaction, which partly derived from faults in the zone system: people had seen baitfishing boats in 'their' waters but had been left out at distribution time.

After the second company had failed, the national Fisheries Department actively tried to get the tuna fisheries going again. In this context it was deemed necessary to develop special legislation to regulate the distribution of royalty moneys. To prepare for such legislation the Department commissioned a sociological study 'to try to ensure that distribution of revenue aspects of the legislation among resource owners is soundly and rationally based'. Two anthropologists were hired for the task, namely James Turner from the University of PNG and the author, then at the Australian National University.[8] We had to map the customary systems of land and sea tenure, develop an alternative method of distribution and identify agents who could act on behalf of an owning group. The Department obviously believed that knowledge of customary tenure (and leadership) would provide the key to the distribution of bait royalties. This was, however, not so straightforward.

One of the things I discovered in the case of Lavongai and Tigak was that baitfish were caught outside the areas that could be regarded as traditional fishing grounds. Baitfish are caught in the deeper parts of the passages between the islands in water that is at least 20 metres deep. Traditional fishing techniques did not cover this part of the sea. I argued, however, that, as a result of the introduction of new techniques, such as deep-water nets and fishing-lines, people now did use the baitfishing grounds for fishing. This usage provided a right in a customary sense, which had de facto been acknowledged by the Minister's decision in 1975. After having thus established a basis for the right to baitfish royalties, I devised a new system of distribution which comprised some of the tested elements of former systems, albeit with corrections (such as boundaries between zones and village groups).[9] Unfortunately, this new system has thus far not been put to the test because a PNG pole-and-line tuna fisheries has not emerged.[10] What is of relevance for the present discussion is the anthropologist's role as codifier of custom; the anthropologist was asked to describe traditional tenure in order to provide a basis for legislation. Thus I contributed to the formalization of an evolving system of practices and therefore to the invention of 'tradition'. Ownership of marine resources on the basis of residence has become strongly established in the minds of the villagers, it has been confirmed by government practice and may end up as law with the help of the anthropologists' investigations.

Conclusion

I began this chapter with postulating a relationship between practices of resource management and cultural constructs of identity. Before I summarize the main trends in the recent history of Lavongai and Tigak Islands, I ought to emphasize the complicated nature of cultural identities. Culturally constructed notions of identity play a role at all levels of social interaction. They define a person's position in a network of relations and constitute the person as an agent. Identities may overlap, encompass other identities, and may even conflict. In this chapter I am concerned only with those identities which relate to the management of natural resources. Also in this domain multiple principles can be found which are operative at the same time. In the trends I describe this multiplicity should be understood. What I describe are shifts in focus and emphasis.

In the domain of the management of marine resources, some clear developments can be discerned. In the precolonial past, ownership of the sea was not an issue of concern. Fishing grounds were restricted as a result of technology and the ubiquitous danger of being ambushed or raided. Colonial peace and the introduction of new techniques expanded the range of fishing activities enormously. A relatively open system developed in which there were few restrictions on the use of the sea. However, with the emergence of commercial fishing and, more importantly, the harvesting of sedentary marine products, concepts of boundaries and ownership gained more currency. The areas that were claimed were generally larger than the fishing grounds used in precolonial times. Access to sea resources was generally not divided between clan groups living in the same village, with the result that residence became a determining factor for property rights. The payment of baitfish royalties in the 1970s and 1980s strengthened the emerging trend towards the definition of sea boundaries. It provided government support for the principle of sea ownership, which in many places had not been an important issue at all. Moreover, the government distribution system acknowledged residence as the basis for marine property rights. Villages became the most relevant units for the division of the royalty moneys. Within villages, clans sometimes played a role, but mostly the money was divided among all adult individuals.

Also in the domain of land management a trend towards the definition and fixation of boundaries is observable. Originally clans and subclans were the relevant units in claiming and dividing the land. In recent times, smaller groups, such as matrilineages and even households, have gained in importance. A rather dramatic development is that more and more people try to escape from the principle of matrilineal inheritance. This is partly the result of new marriage practices, which make it sometimes difficult to return to the land of the mother, because of the distances involved. More important is the commercial use of the land: fathers prefer to pass on the fruits of their labour to their own children instead of their nephews. Also government legislation to facilitate the registration of personal titles has had an impact on notions of ownership.

The developments in resource management have influenced notions of identity in four major ways. In the first place, they have contributed to the gradual decline of the central importance of clan identities. The very basis of the matriclans has become a point of discussion. Membership is traditionally defined as deriving from the blood of the mother. However, the work of the father has become an issue of practical concern and people point to the advantages of patrilineal systems in this respect.

Secondly, residence has become a more important criterion for defining someone's identity. This trend was greatly enforced by the baitfish royalties but has a much longer history. Village communities have become the relevant political units in which elections take place and which participate in government development projects. Community leaders are better known and have a higher profile than clan leaders.

In the third place, there is a trend towards linking one's identity with better-defined and smaller areas of land. Clan identities are not so much tied to a place but to historical war leaders. Subclan identities refer to a historical route of migration and former places of residence. However, matrilineages and households as managing units become closely tied with the land which they have improved by planting cash crops or fruit trees.

Fourth, the distribution of baitfish royalties among individuals and the possibility to register individual titles have strengthened notions of individual identity and agency.

Thus a general shift can be described in ideal-typical terms: from the central importance of inalienable clan membership based on blood ties, with resource ownership and residence as secondary, derived aspects, towards a greater emphasis on individuals working their land in small groups and living in larger residential communities.

Notes

1. In one case political and cultural boundaries do not coincide. The three south-eastern Tsoi Islands are called Tsoi Lau-ung, which means 'Tsoi Tigak' in Lavongai language. These islands are part of the North Lavongai census division, but the population, concentrated in the villages Ungakum and Kavulikau, is predominantly Tigak-speaking.
2. Recently, in August 1995, a new organic law on Provincial and Local Governments was passed by the National Parliament. This law aims at reducing the power of Provincial Governments and at giving more financial means to local governments.
3. This was confirmed by N. Oliver of the Land Title Commission (oral communication), who explained that the Land Tenure Conversion Act (1963) makes it possible to transform customary land into freehold land.
4. The selling of rights to harvest timber involves an offical demarcation of clan territories.
5. In quite a number of villages, people expressed their concern about these methods, because they realized that the stock of fish was affected by their regular use. They suggested that the government should regulate the use of fish poison and tighten the control over the (illegal) use of dynamite.
6. This quote is from a letter from Mr Jephcott to the tuna fishing company dated 30/6/1975. The full sentence reads: 'But I am sure that you will agree with me that the time has now come whereby the traditional owners of the areas from which your company vessels harvest bait must receive some compensation from your company for the bait taken from their traditional areas.'
7. From a letter from P.R. Jones, who was the Special Projects Officer in charge of bait royalty payments in New Ireland.
8. James Turner in West and East New Britain, the author in New Ireland and Manus (see Otto, Turner, and Filer 1990).
9. See Otto (1989).
10. Tuna is now caught by foreign companies (under licence) with techniques such as purse-seining which do not require baitfish but involve much higher capital investments.

References

Beaumont, C.H. (ed.) (1988). _Lavongai Materials by Josef Stamm, Tamsin Donaldson, Clive H. Beaumont, M.J. Lloyd._ Canberra: Department of Linguistics, Research School of Pacific Studies, Australian National University (Pacific Linguistics Series D 82).

Billings, D.K. (1969). The Johnson Cult of New Hanover. _Oceania_ 40:13–16.

—— (1991). Social Organization and Knowledge. _The Australian Journal of Anthropology_ 2(1):109–25.

—— (1992a). The Theater of Politics: Contrasting Types of Performance in Melanesia. _Pacific Studies_ 15(4):211–33.

—— (1992b). Cultural Hegemony and Applied Anthropology. _Canberra Anthropology_ 15(1):35–57.

Carrier, J.G. and Carrier, A.H. (1983). Profitless Property: Marine Ownership and Access to Wealth on Ponam Island, Manus Province. _Ethnology_ 22:133–51.

Jolly, M. and Thomas N. (eds) (1992). The Politics of Tradition in the Pacific. _Oceania_ special issue 62(4).

Lomas, P.W. (1979). Malanggans and Manipulators: Land and Politics in Northern New Ireland. _Oceania_ 50(1):53–66.

Miskaram, N. (1985). Cargo Cultism on New Hanover: A Psychopathological Phenomenon or an Indication of Unequal Development? In: C. Loeliger and G. Trompf (eds), _New Religious Movements in Melanesia_, pp. 75–89. Suva: University of the South Pacific and Port Moresby: University of Papua New Guinea.

Otto, T. (1989). _A Sociological Study of the Baitfish Areas in New Ireland and Manus Provinces: Report Prepared for the Department of Fisheries and Marine Resources, Port Moresby._ Canberra: Department of Anthropology, Research School of Pacific Studies, Australian National University.

—— (1991). _The Politics of Tradition in Baluan: Social Change and the Construction of the Past in a Manus Society._ Canberra: Australian National University; Nijmegen: Centre for Pacific Studies.

Otto, T., Turner, J. and Filer, C. (1990). _The Sociology of Baitfish Royalties in Papua New Guinea._ Port Moresby: University of Papua New Guinea (Occasional Paper 6, Department of Anthropology and Sociology).

Walter, M.A, Sam, J. and Vonole, R. (1986). _A Sociological Investigation of Major Baitfish Areas in Papua New Guinea: Summary Report._ Boroko: IASER.

Chapter 10

Metaphors, Media and Social Change: Second-generation Cook Islanders in New Zealand

Thomas K. Fitzgerald

Media Discourses about Culture and Distorted Metaphors

Although we need to learn to recognize, appreciate and respect cultural differences where they genuinely exist, there are important social, psychological, structural and symbolic similarities and differences that also have to be considered. The real challenge is how to reach beyond culture. To quote Renato Rosaldo (1989:ix), in *Culture and Truth*: 'These days questions of culture seem to touch a nerve because they quite quickly become anguished questions of identity.'

In the past few years, my research has focused broadly on the interrelationships of culture, identity and communication. This focus has caused me to view groups differently from the ways I used to conceptualize them in the past.[1]

Certainly diversity is the raw material out of which we learn to create new elaborations and transformations in the communication process. This emphasis on diversity generally has been seen to be positive. But what are the characteristics of diversity in an emerging world culture? Are all 'cultures' equal? Do we want to preserve behavioural patterns demonstrated to be no longer functional in an information society? What are the complex – often contradictory – relationships between identity, culture and social change?

It is my thesis that more and more people of different social and cultural backgrounds share an overlapping culture influenced by mediated communication. At the same time, there is a strong tendency for certain groups to insist that they are at least symbolically distinct. Evidence suggests that, in today's information society, we are dealing less with *cultural revivalism* and more with assertions of *identity*.

This peculiarly modern tendency for certain groups to try and keep their traditions, by clinging to an identity, has created a huge gap between the rhetoric about culture and everyday realities of social change and adaptation. What is called for is a rethinking and clarification of the *culture* label, as well as questioning some of the underlying philosophical assumptions about change and adaptation.

In defiance of all anthropological common sense, one can witness serious metaphorical leaps in media abuses of the concept of culture: drug 'culture', deaf 'culture', black and white 'cultures', gay and straight 'cultures', women's 'culture', Catholic 'culture', corporate 'culture', 'culture of poverty' and even the bizarre-sounding 'culture of death' (an attack on those favouring abortion).[2] Even scholars have attempted to avoid the negative connotations of race by substituting the term 'ethnic group' and then the elastic term 'culture' for both ethnicity and race, thus ultimately confusing the constructs race, ethnicity and culture.

Virtually everything nowadays – at least, in the USA – is called a 'culture'. Such distorted metaphors leave us open, at the very least, to romantic sentimentality but, more seriously, to ideological manipulation. Furthermore, labels, slogans and self-naming have become, through media dialogues, important contemporary political goals, not to be confused with scholarship about cultures. Certain principles, then, would seem to be almost universally agreed upon today:

1 People should have a right to their own 'culture' without being at all sure what that culture is.
2 People have a right to maintain their own 'cultural' identity whether involving a separate culture or not.

In short, almost any more or less distinguishable group can claim the 'right' to both a separate identity and a matching 'culture' of its own choosing. This presumption rests on the dubious assumption that cultures can be discarded or created ('constructed' is the current image) as a matter of human will.

There is still a wide gap between everyday *social* realities and unsupported discourse about *culture*. Confusing culture and society, and subsequently culture and identity, is surely part of the difficulty, often rendering overly simplistic solutions to problems of change. Social change and culture change are not identical, and to confuse the two often leads to serious misinterpretations about communication.

Even more serious, however, is the confusion of culture and identity. Identity does not necessarily involve the maintenance of a separate culture, and social changes may not detract from self-conscious self-awareness; rather, such changes often enhance identifications. In other words, the loss of culture is often accompanied by an intensification of identities. Identity, in fact, may well have functions that transcend culture as such. Therefore, one must not fall into the trap of assuming that where you find identity assertions, you necessarily find a corresponding culture.

Cultural Relativism and Identities Without Matching Cultures

Ideological support for this philosophical position has been traced to a philosophy of 'vulgarized cultural relativism', according to Eugeen Roosens (1989:152). In its heyday, cultural relativity was a powerful doctrine of intellectual critique, a strong liberal challenge to the neglect of human diversity (Marcus and Fischer 1986:20).

This rather straightforward form of egalitarian humanism, however, has come to be interpreted as 'the equal validity of all value systems', thus making moral judgements virtually impossible (Marcus and Fischer 1986:32). Extreme forms of relativism can easily lead to positions without objective standards. Placed in the context of the so-called culture debates, part of the heated rhetoric (unsupported discourse) must be understood as deriving from this intellectual heritage of cultural relativism, a philosophical stance that John Edwards (1985) claims presents more problems than it solves. The result is often an unwholesome polarization where antirelativism is offered as antidote to the excesses of cultural relativity. Unfortunately, both scholars and the media participate in this brand of moral polarization, supported by simplistic metaphorical images of culture. There surely must be some middle ground in this debate.

Although we may wish that people determine the content of their own 'cultures' (lives) in an unrestrained manner, it may be an error to confuse culture with society or, by extension, culture change with social changes. Related to the elastic use of the culture concept is the increasingly widespread tendency today to treat culture and identity as essentially the same entity.

An ethnographic example from the South Pacific will illustrate how the media, as well as generational positioning, have contributed to changes both in culture and, to a lesser extent, identification, thus challenging the positive implications of so-called 'cultural' revivals. This research suggests that identity – in large part, due to mediated communication influences – loses its 'place-defined' quality and, in both form and function, begins to act independently of culture *per se*. In short, the functions of identity transcend culture as such.

Recognizing that the media are powerful shapers of culture and identity, Joshua Meyrowitz (1986), a communication scholar, has hypothesized that the electronic media – especially television – have led to radical restructuring of social life and social performance, undermining the traditional relationships between physical setting and social situation. Even the concepts we use to define ourselves today are influenced by media as symbolic place.

His argument, in brief, is that media restructure social life and performance by blurring the dividing line between private and public experience, the result being a diffusion of group identities, or what Meyrowitz (1986:71) calls a 'placeless culture'. Groups once physically isolated and socially ignored are no longer so segregated or denied 'voice'. The media have changed both social relationships and perceptions of self. Meyrowitz (1986:133) also makes this important point: sharing special experiences creates a *paradox* as far as minority consciousness is concerned. While many minorities today loudly proclaim special identities – often based on putative cultures – unconsciously they hope to shed at least part of their 'specialness' in becoming a part of a larger grouping.

The conclusion should be clear: people can be 'different' in various *social* ways while still sharing the same culture. This is essentially the theoretical message of Raymonde Carroll's (1987:145) *Cultural Misunderstandings;* the 'rhetoric of distinctive-ness' may change without the culture itself altering very much.

To confuse social change with cultural change, in short, is an error with serious implications for intergroup communication.

Cultural identity need not presume the existence of an 'objective' cultural continuity. Though seemingly a paradox, it is quite possible today to find examples of cultural identity without a corresponding culture. Cultural absence, however, does not preclude identity persistence. In many cases, change actually accelerates identity formation. The influence of the media (incidently, a much-neglected area of research in anthropology) on achieving such reconstructed ideologies is enormous! At the very least, the media have given instant exposure, hence more 'voice', to many of the historically deprived minorities (Gergen 1991). The media and other information channels also, from time to time, have perpetuated various misleading metaphors about identity and culture, so misleading in fact that they can begin to cause serious confusions about culture and race, culture and gender, and culture and class.

Culture, Identity and Social Change: Case Study of Second-generation Cook Islanders in New Zealand

Ethnic pluralism is a familiar characteristic of modern societies and New Zealand is no exception. However, under conditions of rapid social change, there is often intensification of ethnic identity at the same time that the traditional culture is clearly diminishing. My study attempted to raise some theoretical questions about identity and identity change as these are related to migration, generational positioning and media influence (Fitzgerald 1991, 1993).

The critical issue for second-generation, New Zealand-born Cook Islanders is how to maintain identity over the generations. Using a tripartite 'adaptive-growth' (performance) model, effective communication – whether involving cultural or social competencies – engages the individual in at least three separate adaptive dimensions of personality: motivation, knowledge and the ability to perform situationally appropriate roles. Interview questions were aimed, then, at measuring *actual* cultural participation – cultural performance, if you will. Identity, as the bridge between culture and communication, functions to assure a degree of 'communicative competence'.

Competence, in short, is both a reflection of social skills (knowledge) and social outcomes (performance), as well as – naturally – some degree of desire (motivation) on the part of individuals for acting out these skills. Henry Treuba (1990:123) gives an example of the educated Mexican-American, who – rather than choosing either Chicano *or* mainstream American culture – maintains flexibility by developing bicultural skills in 'code-switching' between the two contexts.

In communication language, good communication equals appropriate performance, which involves more than mere motivation if identity is to have outside validation, either by persons or media. There are, to be sure, some dangers in adhering too closely to a performance model of communication (Roloff and Kellermann 1984:215); human beings are often more complex than the research models used to describe them. With this warning in mind, the essential question in my research was to what degree was performance compromised by generational status, migration or media.

The present research documented a case where ethnic identity is still alive and well in a modern, urban setting (Wellington, New Zealand); but identity, in this study, did not necessarily involve the maintenance of a separate culture. In other words, whereas New Zealand-born Cook Islanders are becoming assimilated into their country of birth, this primary commitment to New Zealand does not result in total repudiation of all things Cook Island – namely, identity remains although the cultural environment has dramatically altered.

Returning to our tripartite model (motivation, knowledge and ability), the data (Fitzgerald 1991, 1993) suggested strong *motivation* to identify as some form of 'Cook Islander'. This motivation was, not, however, primarily culturally inspired. But *knowledge* of Cook Island culture or actual participation in Cook Island activities and events (cultural domains, such as language, foods, dress, naming, ceremonies, and so on) was, with this sample, statistically weak. Cultural erosion was well documented in this study. Eugeen Roosens's (1989) claim that the second generation, being a true 'cultural mutation', cannot return to a traditional culture that it never had in the first place was not challenged by this research. Motivation alone, then, could not assure the ability to perform appropriate role behaviours in a New Zealand context. Finally, *performance* (ability to perform role behaviours associated with Cook Island culture) was complicated by place being primarily, if not exclusively, New Zealand. Even when there was a fair knowledge of Cook Island heritage, there were few places in New Zealand to act out this knowledge (these were restricted contexts for cultural elaboration).

Ultimately, one has to ask what are the rewards for ethnic self-affirmation? For this generation especially, rewards were clearly New Zealand-based. A hypothesis offered by Anya Peterson Royce (1982) is that people identify today as 'ethnics' primarily because such groups offer stable extended-family functions in an age of declining family. Certainly, the essence of the Cook Island way (Cook Islanders rarely used the label 'culture') in the 1980s was first and foremost family, respect for the elders, a sense of community (albeit restricted) and a continuing link with an idealized island paradise (Fitzgerald 1993).

Certainly this generation of Cook Islanders was marked by the disappearance of many island symbols of distinctiveness. The New Zealand-born had only dim memories of the traditions their parents associated with the true homeland. An overemphasis on cultural identity, based on authentic culture, may be largely counterproductive for this group.

A good example would be language loyalties. What was the 'first' language for this generation? Language used in the home was predominantly (79 per cent) English; the 'mother tongue' for the majority of these Cook Island New Zealanders was clearly English. In New Zealand there were, in fact, special difficulties involving different dialects and a high rate of intermarriage. If the language (Cook Island Maori) were to be taught in the schools, which version of the language would be chosen?

Two media outlets for Cook Island news in New Zealand were, at that time, 'Pacific Island News' on radio and 'Tangata atu motu', a television programme. When these young people were asked if they listened to either regularly, only 10 per cent mentioned either news event and then only 'occasionally'. The vast majority (90 per cent) did not. A typical reply was 'No, can't understand it when in Maori language.' Ethnic consciousness, based on language loyalties, is a short-sighted strategy unless it is certain that the next generation will be motivated to follow.

In a rapidly changing world, Pacific islanders are concerned with who they are and where they are going. Increasingly, however, this generation of Cook Islanders have considered both the costs as well as the benefits of 'cultural exclusiveness', and a substantial number have chosen between ethnic identification and national identity and decided on the latter. In short, it is possible that Cook Islanders of this generation do not need any inflated Pacific island cultural ideology to establish their identities. Access to media technology, and its associated powers, also seems to have prevented any turning back to any real 'cultural' revival for this generation.

Identity, as exemplified by this model, seems to fulfil a kind of 'psychic shelter' function, a face-saving device in circumstances of stressful social change, which psychologically protects individuals until they are ready to proceed along the path to integration or accommodation. (American writers assiduously avoid the emotionally charged label 'assimilation'.)

Furthermore, it is my thesis that too much concern with culture, cultural revivalism and exclusive identity may actually have negative implications for these locally born children of immigrants in New Zealand. To insist on a cultural identity that only partly fits, as David Lowenthal (1985:318) has poignantly stated the case, can in fact be 'a kind of patronizing colonialism dressed up as liberal social science', even a kind of psychological compensation for economic inequalities. Rather than helping this generation solve its identity problems, it may well intensify such conflicts. Overemphasis on cultural identity based on authentic culture, then, may be largely counterproductive.

To repeat: identity may have important functions that transcend culture as such. With or without culture, though, identities often persist.

None the less, identity can be a powerful psychological reality, whether based on authentic culture or not. The argument here is that linguistic and cultural assertiveness need not imply more cultural diversity. Paradoxically, the compensatory need to assert distinctive identities – probably due to mediated communication influences – parallels the homogenization of cultures throughout the world. Strictly speaking, it is not always culture that is at issue, but identities with or without matching cultures.

Cultural differences – where these indeed exist – are, of course, important. Unfortunately, there is the tendency today to misinterpret and overinterpret such differences. Culture often helps to delineate identity groups, but identity groups do not always constitute separate cultures. To assume that each group, because it is different in some way, constitutes a separate culture may be a serious error. These so-called cultures are described in strokes so broad that *non*-cultural differences, e.g. communication styles and social behaviours, are not fully explained. This has been especially true with studies of black–white communication styles in the American context.[3]

Identity has become the critical focus around which many minorities in the 1990s have polarized, and thus remains a political force to be dealt with. Communication between diverse groups, social or cultural in origin, is no doubt essential for our global survival. What we seem to be witnessing today are dramatic exhibitions of identities based on ethnic/gender/ race/sexual orientation (among others), at the same time that we are clearly seeing more and more media-induced cultural homogenization, at least of Western societies.

Acceptance of different lifestyles, sexual minorities and ethnic interest groups – as well as authentically different cultures – none the less, will be the ultimate challenge of the identity of the future. In other words, we need to become more aware of the diversity of cultures *and* subgroups (whether strictly speaking 'culturally' distinct or not). We need to know why and how communication most effectively occurs, taking into account factors such as race, ethnicity, gender, age, sexual preference, physical disabilities, religion and culture itself.

In the multiethnic New Zealand context, the educational challenge will be to encourage a strong national identity while still recognizing a variety of different interest groups, ethnic styles and the persistent need for separate minority identities – albeit, identities which carry with them a degree of self-esteem, dignity and pride. This pattern of recognizing identities without separate cultures fits the official, though yet unrealized, goal of an emerging diversification of New Zealand society.

Contemporary Educational Debates and the Implications of the 'Multicultural' Movement

The debates over 'multiculturalism'[4] in contemporary discourse often represent examples of contradictory rhetoric supported by the media's attention to so-called 'balanced coverage'. In mass media reproductions, 'symbolic ethnicity' is today rampant.

Whether 'real' or not, however, these images can be powerful indeed. Compare the overromanticizing of American Indians of yesteryear in the nostalgic movie, *Dances with Wolves*. In such a rarefied, romantic atmosphere, a national culture and identity are too often viewed with suspicion.

Minorities no doubt need a feeling of 'closeness' that comes with group identity. When accused of falsely pretending to be 'culturally different', they will react as if this closeness were in jeopardy. The real issue, as George and Louise Spindler (1990) point out, may be one of social participation rather than cultural exclusiveness. Separating identity from culture, then, may be one way out of this dialectical dilemma.

Jean Jackson (1989:139) goes to the heart of the multicultural debates with this penetrating question: is there a way to talk about 'making culture' without 'making enemies'? She believes that what we need are more neutral terms – culture is not a politically value-free term these days – to describe minority resurgence that 'neither romanticizes not denigrates the process' – a process that she, unfortunately, calls 'inventing culture'. Certainly the complex relationships between culture and identity, as these ideas are played out in the cultural media, remain largely unexplored. No doubt, we need better models and metaphors to analyse, in non-derogatory language, the contemporary phenomenon of group assertiveness worldwide. A problem I see with Jackson's position, however, is precisely this tendency to equate culture and identity.

Although not as evident in New Zealand as in the USA, groups claiming to 'invent culture' are today mostly asserting identities *in the name of culture*. Current evidence favours identity. Unfortunately, debates which frame arguments either 'for' or 'against' are rarely adequate. Both sides of this polarized educational argument, from time to time, take on an excessively self-righteous tone. This is especially true when academic dialogues are articulated in a modern media context.

Acknowledging the widespread inclination today to confuse cultural issues with social ones may be the key to understanding the so-called culture debates. The present argument attempts to solve the dilemma of 'making culture' or 'making enemies' by separating culture and identity. Self-conscious group awareness for whatever positive reasons – economic, psychological or political – refers mainly to identification and its functions.

Identity – what I (Fitzgerald 1993) have defined as the academic metaphor for self-in-context – may be the crucial variable in explaining communicative competence. Culture, 'invented' or not, may have little to do with it. If culture is the logic by which we give order to our worlds, then something is seriously out of sync when groups use mainstream logic to bolster rhetoric about largely non-existent cultures.

Looking at education specifically, the irony in many countries is that the battle to preserve ethnic 'cultures' may ultimately doom certain minorities to academic failure (Foley 1991:66). Are well-meaning supporters of 'cultural' diversity preventing some minorities from effectively functioning in the mainstream culture? Arguing much the same point, Mosgrove (quoted in Edwards 1985:120) stressed that multiculturalism is, of course, valuable if it promotes sympathy for other groups, but schools must 'open windows onto wider worlds'. Translated not too loosely: education can open the way to employment opportunities. Continuing with this didactic metaphor, the 'culture' debates today would seem to threaten to close these metaphorical doors/windows.

It is still possible, however, to assume a national identity with common *public* goals, without necessarily implying wholesale destruction of *private* social and cultural behaviours that retain positive psychological meaning for individuals and/or groups.

Although these conclusions remain controversial, the dialogue itself suggests that increased tolerance for diversity has often gone hand in hand with increased social fragmentation. There are surely some poignant contradictions inherent in the debates over the role of the school in maintaining separate cultures as opposed to separate identities.

Overenthusiastic approaches to 'multiculturalism', I would argue, can have negative as well as positive effects. 'Militant multiculturalism' can actually be used to force people into positions of less, rather than more, awareness of cultural and social diversities (Edwards 1985:136). To narrowly emphasize cultural or personal identity, in effect, may be to work against effective interpersonal and intercultural communication.

In fact, 'culture' for many groups seeking social equality today is often viewed as a kind of shared 'property' (Fitzgerald 1993). Using this distorted metaphor, identity is confused with culture; and ethnic markers associated with a particular group come to be viewed as its own unique 'property'. Thus, outsiders wanting to share in the symbols that mark this property – say, dress, dance or language – may be resented, as if the outsider were attempting a form of 'cultural' theft. A pointed example from an educational context in the USA is the 'Check Me' dance, wherein black students in a racially mixed class ignored and rejected a white girl's attempts to participate because the dance had become the 'property' of the black students (Hanna 1994).

This is a case where good educational intentions can go astray, and a simple misunderstanding in everyday life can be inaccurately interpreted as 'racism'.[5] Certainly the assumption that giving children more self-esteem through the creation of putative cultures will result in more success in school is not proved. Attempts to improve student self-images through promoting ethnic heritage classes have often produced a new negativity instead (Hanna 1994).

In the name of 'community', particular groups today sometimes uncompromisingly defend their own turf while refusing to consider joining larger associations. Such groups use the romantic metaphor of community to enhance 'compulsive intolerance' of those who do not belong to their particular factions (the extremes of educational particularisms, or 'militant multiculturalism,' being a case in point). This is too exclusive a definition of community. The media, unfortunately, often encourage such group polarization.

Thus, we are all familiar with the narcissistic tendencies of our times: an unwholesome focus on self-gratification for individuals and the horrendous consequences of nationalism for groups. But, surely, from the individual's point of view, the positive side of identity is self-growth, self-actualization, through our relationships with others in the human family. Reaching beyond culture, the question is how do we maintain the positive aspects of human identity: the celebration of diversity and the reaffirmation of our common humanity, yet retaining a sense of being part of a larger community?

Notes

1. Much of the discussion that follows is drawn from my book, *Metaphors of Identity: A Culture–Communication Dialogue* (Fitzgerald 1993), which addresses not only the 'culture debates', but the influence of mediated communication on social

behaviour. For more fieldwork discussion, see Fitzgerald (1992).

2. Culture, for me, is basically an ecological idea, referring to learned collective, public knowledge and skills necessary for individuals/groups in order to successfully cope in specific environments. Emphasis is on public knowledge and environment. In addition, culture is something passed down from generation to generation. This important distinction helps to avoid metaphorical leaps into look-alike formats, such as speaking of 'drug cultures'. The distinction can also help us to consider what is and what is not merely a transient fad as opposed to a fundamental culture change.

3. The current movement by American blacks to have the term 'African American' adopted by the larger culture reflects a contemporary concern with ethnic identity as political force rather than cultural authenticity. Identity politics, then, is being expressed today as cultural rhetoric.

4. It is important to make a distinction between 'the study of many cultures' (multiculturalism as academic subject) and the 'multicultural movement,' whose primary goal has clearly been to increase 'curricular visibility' among certain underrepresented groups (in the USA, these *identity groups* are primarily women, blacks, gays and the handicapped). Cerroni-Long (1993:109) wisely asks: 'Does the American definition of multiculturalism involve any real interest in culture?' The present author is not at all opposed to giving more curricular visibility to underrepresented groups; but, for the sake of intellectual integrity, it would be wise not to call such identity groups 'culture' groups. The solutions to social problems involving primarily identity groups are vastly different from those involving true culture groups. Culture change models are simply not adequate to handle the psychology of identity and identity change.

5. While superficial stylistic markers like dress, hair, dance and food can be innocuous enough, there are areas of more serious concern when identity and culture are confused. Consider the recent attempt by middle-class black social workers in the USA to pass a law forbidding whites from adopting black children – in the name of preserving African-American 'culture'. This law would surely prove damaging to the children, since there simply are not enough black families willing or able to adopt these orphans.

References

Carroll, R. (1987). *Cultural Misunderstandings: The French–American Experience*. Chicago and London: University of Chicago Press.

Cerroni-Long, E.L. (1993). Teaching Ethnicity in the USA: an Anthropological Model. *Journal of Ethnodevelopment* 2(1): 106–12.

Edwards, J. (1985). *Language, Society and Identity*. New York: Basil Blackwell.

Fitzgerald, T.K. (1991). Media and Changing Metaphors of Ethnicity and Identity. *Media, Culture and Society* 13:193–214.

—— (1992). Media, Ethnicity and Identity. In: P. Scannell, P. Schlesinger and C. Sparks (eds), *Culture and Power*, pp. 112–33. London and Newbury Park: Sage.

—— (1993). *Metaphors of Identity: A Culture–Communication Dialogue*. Albany: State University of New York.

Foley, D.E. (1991). Reconsidering Anthropological Explanations of Ethnic School Failure. *Anthropology and Education Quarterly* 22(1):60–86.

Gergen, K.J. (1991). *The Saturated Self: Dilemmas of Identity in Contemporary Life*. New York: Basic Books.

Hanna, J.L. (1994). Issues in Supporting School Diversity: Academics, Social Relations, and the Arts. *Anthropology and Education Quarterly* 25(1):66–85.

Jackson, J. (1989). Is There a Way to Talk about Making Culture without Making Enemies? *Dialectical Anthropology* 14:127–43.

Lowenthal, D. (1985). Mobility and Identity in the Island Pacific. In: M. Chapman (ed.), *Mobility and Identity in the Island Pacific*, pp. 316–26. *Pacific Viewpoint* special issue 26(1).

Marcus, G.E. and Fischer, M.J. (1986). *Anthropology as Cultural Critique*. Chicago: University of Chicago.

Meyrowitz, J. (1986). *No Sense of Place: Impact of Electronic Media on Social Behavior*. New York and Oxford: Oxford University Press.

Roloff, M.E. and Kellermann, K. (1984). Judgments of Interpersonal Competency: How Do You Know, What You Know, and Who You Know. In: R.N. Bostrom (ed.), *Competence in Communication*. pp. 175–228. Beverly Hills and London: Sage.

Roosens, E.E. (1989). *Creating Ethnicity: The Process of Ethnogenesis*. Newbury Park: Sage.

Rosaldo, R. (1989). *Culture and Truth: The Remaking of Social Analysis*. Boston: Beacon Press.

Royce, A.P. (1982). *Ethnic Identity: Strategies of Diversity*. Bloomington: Indiana University Press.

Spindler, G. and Spindler, L. (1990). *The American Cultural Dialogue and its Transmission*. London and Philadelphia: Falmer Press.

Treuba, H. (1990). Mainstream and Minority Cultures: a Chicano Perspective. In: G. Spindler and L. Spindler (eds), *The American Cultural Dialogue and its Transmission*, pp. 122–43. London and Philadelphia: Falmer Press.

Chapter 11

Identity Construction as a Cooperative Project: Anthropological Film-making with the Vaiakau and Fenualoa Peoples, Reef Islands, Temotu Province, Solomon Islands

Jens Pinholt[1]

Introduction

> Almost always, we are doing our research to satisfy ourselves, emotionally and intellectually, and to build our careers, to make our own lives better. If people put up with us and cooperate in our research, it is because their curiosity and generosity work to our benefit. But our work remains marginal to their lives . . . (Salzman in Borofsky 1994:31).

> If anthropology has something to say about the Human Condition, it should have something interesting – perhaps even something hopeful – to say about what is happening to the futures of the Pacific Islanders whose lives we have been privileged to share (Keesing 1993:30–1).

For generations anthropologists have been descending on the Pacific Islands following the people closely to study their lives. After having enjoyed hospitality and generosity for a considerable time, we leave the field and the people who ostensibly are the main reason and subject for our research. Back in our home base our further attention and research work tend to focus on the national and international anthropological community. This is where the material resulting from our stay in the field can be transformed into symbolic capital for *our* purposes.

But what about the purposes of our former hosts and friends, those obliging people who made it all possible? What are their chances of reaping the fruits of the research? What are we doing to ensure their continued participation?

These, of course, are questions a growing number of Pacific anthropologists have to deal with nowadays, either because their own sense of ethics and responsibility urges them to do so or because the new political reality in the Pacific world forces them to do so. I consider this to be a great boon to our anthropological profession because it reminds us of what in my opinion are two necessary conditions to anthropological work: (1) Research should be based on sound ethnographic work as a sustained dialogue between people and researcher. (2) Anthropological research should aim to further the actual people's and our understanding of real-world problems and to give them strength and means to cope with them.

The anthropological film project dealt with in this chapter may be seen as an effort to work along these lines together with the Vaiakau and Fenualoa peoples in the Reef Islands.[2] The life of these people is firmly but marginally integrated into the modern world realities of global capitalism and the utterly dependent state, Solomon Islands. These facts seen in a local historical perspective are clearly of vital importance for an understanding of the recently growing cultural awareness and the wish to put into film certain of the distinctive social ceremonies and other aspects of the cultural tradition. These people hosted me and my family generously during fieldwork in 1973–5 and later on shorter visits. They are now eagerly waiting to start a cooperative project aiming to document on film their cultural traditions. They perceive this to be highly necessary and relevant to their own present and their children's future lives in a rapidly changing world.

Cultural Traditions on the Rise in an Economically Stagnant Pacific World

For quite a number of years we have witnessed in the Pacific an intensification of phenomena generally labelled 'cultural inheritance' and 'tradition'. In the south-western Pacific, which is the scene of the project discussed in this chapter, the local Pidgin term *kastom* has gained prominence. Certain cultural phenomena are singled out for special attention and usage on the regional, national and local level and they are thought and talked of as *kastom blong iumi*, significant symbols in the expression of group membership and loyalty and in strengthening the individual members' feeling of selfhood and belonging. Often the most powerful symbols do not seem to have a strong relationship to the present modernist reality of the people in question. Rather they refer to an earlier or alternative historical and cultural context shared by the indigenous people.

All this is happening at a time of stagnation and accumulating societal problems caused by the strong impacts and constraints of modern development. R. Keesing characterized the present state of 'development' in the Pacific in general:

> The Pacific countries where we work are increasingly trapped in the cycle of pauperization and dependency. They are being stripped of remaining resources – timber, minerals, marine life – at a frightening rate and with no possibility of renewal or sustainability; and the old economic mainstays of the tropics, copra and palm oil and other plantation crops, are vanishing from the industrialized world's shopping lists (Keesing 1993:30).

J. Friedman has argued that the growing interest in cultural matters and the use of these in creating identities, which can be observed in similar or alternative forms in many other parts of the world, somehow is connected with the dynamics of the global system (Friedman 1992). This certainly seems to be the point in the case of the marginal Temotu Province of the Solomon Islands, which is under consideration in this chapter.

The historical truthfulness and authenticity of such newly accentuated examples of cultural inheritance or traditions and their importance and meaning to Pacific people on different levels of the national and regional context have been widely debated among anthropologists (Babadzan 1988; Keesing 1989; Carrier 1992; Jolly 1992; Thomas 1992). N. Thomas reflects on the ongoing substantivization of practices which seems to result from the growing awareness of people concerning their cultural heritage and its importance to their present life. As he points out, there is an important difference between practices and ideas which are simply done or thought, or simply take place, and those set up as definite entities to be reflected upon and manipulated by the people in the situation under consideration. . . . A ceremony that is named, and thus can be conceived of us an entity separable from particular enactments, can become a vital element in the self-expression or regeneration of a group . . . It is of great importance whether a 'custom', 'code of behavior', or whatever is reified as such by those who do it and think it, or only by the anthropological analyst (Thomas 1992:64–5).

But, keeping in mind the importance of substantivization of practices to the process of identity construction among Pacific people in the present situation, it is also necessary to stress that the difference between 'practices and ideas simply done or thought' and 'substantivized cultural practices' does not warrant a dichotomy of, on the one hand, genuine and unchanging traditions, a heritage from the ancestors, and, on the other, invented or manipulated traditions. M. Jolly (1992) has reminded us that it is a common anthropological mistake to oppose the 'authentic' custom of innocent, harmonious village people with the 'inauthentic' custom of clever, educated politicians. But, as pointed out by T. Hylland Eriksen, criteria for authenticity in cultural matters are not prerogatives of the anthropologist.

Criteria for authentic ethnic identity are generated intraethnically as well as interethnically, and the dynamics of these criteria are themselves part of that social reality we study (Eriksen 1993:131).

However, this is not only an academic debate. The heated exchange between anthropologists and educated members of indigenous groups concerning the cultural traditions of these groups and their relation to historical 'reality' is proof of their importance to the present-day life of the people (see, for example, Keesing 1989, 1991; Trask 1991). It is also proof that anthropology and its practitioners are definite parts of real-world processes, even if any surviving 'neutral' researcher should try to deny this. To engage in anthropological research on the cultural ways of very much live Pacific islanders at the same time means to interfere with their world for better or for worse, to make oneself part of their life projects. As responsible researchers we must accept this fact, even if it tends to complicate and in some cases to render almost impossible anthropological work. The present attempt to combine cultural documentation with identity construction in a dialogical cooperative effort between Reef Islands people and an anthropological film team should be seen and judged in this light.

I venture to conclude that the whole debate about historical correctness, truthfulness and authenticity of cultural traditions is a rather futile exercise. It is doubtful that it can lead to further conclusive insights concerning the meaning or importance of this characteristic phenomenon in the social life of Pacific islanders. The recent growing interest among modern Pacific groups in their long-waning traditions and their symbolic significance as powerful tools for building self-esteem and pride should testify to their value and importance to the people who practise them. Surely this is a more pertinent measure of authenticity than any anthropological statement, however convincingly argued.

This also points to far more interesting and pertinent aspects concerning cultural traditions and their importance to modern Pacific peoples. What are the reasons for the recent growth of interest in traditional matters, at the very moment when many have weakened considerably or completely disappeared? What is the importance of the revival or construction of cultural traditions to modern people's lives? Though these questions cannot be answered here it is evident that a distinct growing cultural awareness has manifested itself with the Vaiakau and Fenualoa peoples of the Reef Islands as with many other Pacific peoples. It is also taken to be highly probable that this growing awareness could become of major importance to the people and their efforts to cope with modernization and development by strengthening their feeling of selfhood and cultural identity. These are considered to be indispensable preconditions for a successful and self-determined process of integration into the national and global realities of modern life.

From 'Sea of Islands' to 'Islands in the Far Sea'

In a recent article Epeli Hau'ofa has directed our attention to the fact that

> In Oceania, derogatory and belittling views of indigenous cultures are traceable to the early years of interactions with Europeans. The wholesale condemnation by Christian missionaries of Oceanic

cultures as savage, lascivious, and barbaric has had a lasting and negative effect on people's views of their histories and traditions (Hau'ofa 1994:149).

In a wider perspective Hau'ofa identifies two contrasting views of the Pacific. A common and popular way of viewing it is to stress the plight of small and remote 'islands in a far sea' as opposed to the far more positive view 'a sea of islands'. It is his point that, whereas indigenous Pacific peoples, who long ago had made the sea their home, traditionally entertained the 'sea of islands' view, outsiders, such as colonialists, social scientists and others, have favoured the first view, stressing the isolation and marginalization of the peoples.

The precolonial Pacific in reality was 'a sea of islands' and Pacific people's world-view was in accordance with this fact. Imperialism not only changed this real world. It also enforced the negative view which came to dominate thinking about the Pacific:

> Theirs was a large world in which peoples and cultures moved and mingled, unhindered by boundaries of the kind erected much later by imperial powers. From one island to another they sailed to trade and to marry, thereby expanding social networks for greater flows of wealth. . . . Melanesia is supposedly the most fragmented world of all: tiny communities isolated by terrain and at least one thousand languages. The truth is that large regions of Melanesia were integrated by trading and cultural exchange systems . . . Lingua francas and the fact that most Melanesians were and are multilingual . . . make utter nonsense of the notion that they were and still are babblers of Babel. It was in the interest of imperialism and is in the interest of neocolonialism, to promote this blatant misconception of Melanesia (Hau'ofa 1994:153–4).

The negative view dominates nearly all aspects of thinking concerning the Pacific today. The island world is seen as marginal and underdeveloped – even by many islanders – and from a realistic point of view this certainly would seem to fit the facts. However, Hau'ofa is worried about the damaging influence on Pacific people's images of themselves and their ability to cope with the global system that has engulfed them if this negative view is not countered with more constructive views. He touches on problems highly relevant for development in the Pacific in general.

In the project being considered here I venture to see present initiatives in the Temotu Province aiming to revalue cultural traditions as the people's effort to re-establish a more constructive view of themselves and their cultural reality. This, I would argue, is an important prerequisite in their struggle to cope with the challenges of the modern world.

Traditionally the Vaiakau people and their Fenualoa neighbours were active participants in a trading network encompassing all of the Reef Islands (including the Vaiakau and the Fenualoa peoples), the Taumako Islands and the northern part of Deni or Santa Cruz, the major island in the region.[3] Colonization and the marginal integration into the global system, however, made them into insignificant, far-away and little-known groups of people in the national and international world, which is today an extremely powerful reality in their life. To survive in this drastically changed world of theirs, a large and growing number of individuals are compelled to be away from the islands periodically or permanently in order to acquire land, education and work. Production for the outside market, which was introduced as a means to stimulate 'development' has meant neglect of traditional, locally or regionally orientated production. At the same time, unfavourable world-market developments[4] and defective communication and transport between islands in the district and with the outside world have hampered local development.

Socially this present-day situation of the Vaiakau and Fenualoa peoples is marked by increasing disruption of the networks based on regional, local and kinship connections which used to integrate life in most of the islands in Temotu. Thus, historically the social and cultural scene of today is mainly a result of the interchange between the local peoples and the expanding global system. This was accompanied by a complete destruction of the trading network which had been the major supporting pillar of the social and cultural life.

A Cultural Inheritance Without a Meaning

Even in the first half of the twentieth century the trading network was still functioning.[5] W. Davenport, doing fieldwork in the area in 1958–60, has been able to reconstruct fairly accurately significant aspects of life in this setting by interviewing people who had participated in the earlier form of life and who were still alive (Davenport 1968, 1969, 1972, 1975).

The network not only secured a flow of food and products vital for the participating local communities. By circulating marriageable young women and the precious red-feather rolls, it was of fundamental importance to the reproduction of the social order in each community. This also meant that the participating communities, even though representing historically different languages and cultural stocks, with the passage of time had acquired significant common traits.[6]

However, there were certain marked differences in the way local communities were integrated into the total network. The big fertile island of Deni was the powerful centre. The raised coral islands of the eastern Reefs, including Fenualoa, had comparatively fewer resources and so played a less dominant role, while the low coral islands in the western Reefs with their Polynesian population (Vaiakau) were definitely the most dependent participant. Here the trading network was absolutely necessary for social and cultural reproduction. The meagre land resources made it imperative that a constant supply of root crops, betel-nut and house-building materials were brought in from the more fertile islands. At the same time, a surplus of Polynesian women were married off or sent as whores to men's houses in the richer islands.

The two neighbouring populations of the Polynesian islands and Fenualoa were unequally integrated in the trading system. To the Vaiakau people, the *puki* trading canoes were the sole important means of production, the leading bigmen being in control of them. The Fenualoa people had more fertile land, even though they could not match their Papuan neighbours further towards the east in the Reefs, let alone the powerful rich people in Deni. The flow of women in the reproductive system was further proof of the unequal status of the groups. It ran from the poor Polynesian islands towards Fenualoa, the eastern Reefs in general and ultimately Deni. The red-feather rolls, supreme symbols of power and prestige and necessary means of social control and reproduction all over the trading system, had to be acquired in Deni, where they were made by specialists.

Locally, men's houses controlled by the leading bigmen were the dynamic hub of economic and ceremonial life. From here, all trading and other productive efforts were organized, and these again were the basis of the food distributions and exchanges that were an important part of life, together with the endless chain of ceremonies defining status of groups and individuals and strengthening sociocultural belonging and unity.

By 1973, when I did my first fieldwork in Fenualoa and the Polynesian island of Nifiloli, the trading system had definitively broken down. The *puki* trading canoes disappeared in the 1960s and in 1970 the last big Polynesian canoe-sailor and bigman, Basil Tavake, had gone out to sea in his small dugout canoe to disappear for ever with the way of life he has come to symbolize. But mature people could still reminisce about trading voyages in which they had participated; young schoolboys holidaying on the island played in the lagoon with *puki* model canoes. The men's house, which used to be the centre of economic and social life in every local community, had lost all functional meaning in the Polynesian islands.[7] In Fenualoa each village still had a functioning men's house and the traditional ceremonial life could be observed on a less reduced scale than in the Polynesian islands. Social ceremonies and cultural arts, such as customary dancing, maturation feasts and other ceremonies staging elaborate food exchanges as well as the use of the highly esteemed red-feather rolls, were still parts of life, although in a modified form.

Thus changes were less radical in Fenualoa than in Nifiloli and the rest of Vaiakau, where the whole way of life had been based one-sidedly on the *puki* trading canoe. But it was quite evident that the old social matrix had been undermined and its cultural paraphernalia were giving way as people were forced to reorientate in the radically altered economic and political environment.

British colonial rule and the effects of the world market had helped to destroy the old ways without introducing the necessary preconditions for a new way of life. But everywhere there was a clear focus on the imagined possibilities of modern development to be introduced from outside the islands. In this context, only minimal attention was paid to traditional culture, which had evidently lost it purpose.

A Cultural Inheritance with a New Meaning

Revisiting Deni and Reef Islands alone in 1992 and together with visual anthropologist Peter Crawford in 1994, I could observe that visible traditional aspects of cultural life had further weakened or totally disappeared from the social scene. Consequently, they are only vaguely known and understood by young people and children. Red-feather rolls have not been made in Deni since the 1970s and they have nearly disappeared altogether from social life in the Reefs.[8]

Independence from colonial rule in 1978 did not put an end to the marginal situation of the Reef Islands – on the contrary. Colonial power had controlled the relations between the many different ethnic groups in the Solomons and by and large left the people of the far away Temotu Province to themselves. Compared with other parts of the new Solomon Islands state, only scattered developmental initiatives have reached Temotu and today the local people characterize their part of the country as 'the last province in the Solomons'.

With the retreat of the colonial power, however, relations with other ethnic groups living in distant parts of the new country have intensified and the competition for the scarce advantages and resources of the state has become more open. At the same time, the Temotu people are becoming acutely aware of their disadvantage compared with more powerful and favoured groups in other parts of the country. This is one major reason why a growing interest in the disappearing cultural heritage is beginning to manifest itself. A Reef Islands Cultural Association has been formed by a number of educated people, with the explicit purpose of reviving traditional and cultural values and inheritance. But the interest is not confined to this exclusive association. With children and young people increasingly being educated in school and leaving the home islands for shorter or longer terms, associating with other ethnic groups on the regional and national levels of the new state, the importance of the cultural heritage, as it is still practised or was practised until recently, is becoming plain to most adult people. They feel the need to be able to face other groups and the representatives of the state from a visible, common cultural platform: a platform from where to identify and to be identified by others as a significant and legitimate member group of the national community.

Even though there is a growing interest and awareness concerning this cultural heritage from the indigenous ancestors, it must be recognized that Christianity, brought into society by Anglican missionaries, is firmly established and recognized as a fundamental value in life, overruling and modifying major parts of the earlier cultural traditions. This means that today's cultural heritage is the outcome of a continuous historical process rather than a timeless repetition of pre-Christian forms. Actually the missionaries took a very active part in changing or destroying much of the traditional cultural heritage which people now intend to revalue.

Visiting the Reef Islands in 1992, I brought with me several hundred colour slides and enlarged black and white photographs documenting life in the islands during the fieldwork period in 1973–5. This pictorial material was donated partly to the Solomon Islands National Museum and partly to the Vaiakau and Fenualoa people. I have no doubt that this material, which was enthusiastically received, helped in an important way to raise awareness locally of the power of pictures to preserve and document memories of deceased relatives and of the former ways of life.

This experience certainly stimulated the general wish to keep within memory of those present the traditional cultural heritage and thus led to the film project. The presence of the anthropologist, whom the people of Fenualoa and Vaiakau have known for years and whom they dare trust as a necessary partner in the complicated cooperative project, is what has made it feasible.

And Now on to Film-making[9]

The initial plan was to concentrate the film on Nifiloli and Malapu village on Fenualoa. From fieldwork I am most familiar with these two localities. However, talks with the Vaiakau and the Fenualoa Area Councils have made it clear that every village or island in the two administrative districts wants to actively participate. This indicates that the administrative bodies wish their cultural communities to be represented without any part being left out. Of course, one can interpret this as a sign of solidarity and unity, but it is also evidence of opposing interests and differences within and between local communities. No specific interest group is allowed beforehand to reap special advantages at the expense of others left out.

Without doubt, then, there are political and ideological aspects in this project. It is the anthropologist's responsibility not to avoid these but to expose them and to carry out the project accordingly as far as possible.

Each local community decides which of the ceremonies actually planned to take place in the normal course of social life during the scheduled time of filming it wants to include in the film.

The preparatory work is coordinated by local leading men. The selection of certain ceremonies or cultural elements from the existing inventory of cultural traditions to be focused on and to be preserved on film for future generations as true *kastom blong iumi*, together with the communal preparation and making of the film, is significant.[10] Without doubt, all this will stimulate local discussions about what are genuine and correct traditions and it will contribute to the general awareness of the people concerning their cultural heritage and its meaning to their present life.

The substantivization of cultural practices taking place in connection with the film project is an outcome of the dynamics of the conflict-ridden and contradictory colonial history and present of the participating people. Whether this is understood or accepted by the participants or not, it must be the responsibility of the anthropologist in the film project to expose it. The film in the end should attempt not to show cultural heritage as an eternal truth outside the context of history and social reality. Rather it should show the actual context and process whereby the participants, assisted by the anthropologist and the film team, substantivize their cultural traditions.

This again makes it necessary to visualize those processes which make the lives of the Vaiakau and Fenualoa peoples a paradox of modernity's global development and a cultural identity rooted in local history. An important step towards achieving this understanding is to follow the admonition given by J. Clifford concerning the controversial culture concept: 'we should attempt to think of cultures not as organically unified or traditionally continuous but rather as negotiated, present processes' (Clifford 1988:273).

In the cooperative work of making the film the whole process favours a kind of dialogical anthropology. F. Ginsburg has emphazised the dialogical perspective in a recent paper, in which she argues for 'a reconceptualization of "the native voice" as one that should be in more direct dialogue with anthropological interpretation' (Ginsburg 1994:9).

The ongoing exchange between people and anthropologist is intended to lead up to the final presentation of the film to the local people, followed by a common debate and evaluation. The end-product is to be kept for the future use of the local people.

To conclude, this film project, being a dialogical venture, aims to achieve several goals in the joint interest of the participating partners:

1 To document cultural forms and processes in the Reef Islands which are under constant and rapid change.
2 To support the efforts of the Vaiakau and Fenualoa peoples to mobilize a cultural identity based on their common history and traditional heritage. *Kastom* in the modern Melanesian world is a powerful resource of symbols which can strengthen people's self-image, as well as other people's image of them. As such, it is an important precondition for coping with the difficulties of the modern world.
3 To raise national and international awareness about these small and easily ignored groups by showing the film to wider publics. This could help to promote and solve some of the urgent local issues concerning the future life and welfare of the people, e.g. the acquisition of more and better land for subsistence, and the introduction of tourism with a cultural emphasis and on a carefully monitored level.

Anthropology after all might *not* remain marginal to people's lives and it might have something interesting – perhaps even something hopeful – to say about the futures of the Pacific islanders whose lives we have been privileged to share.

Notes

1. I wish to thank visual anthropologist Peter Ian Crawford, who is cooperating with me on this project, for stimulation and support. Also I thank the Danish Development Research Council and the Aarhus University Research Foundation for generous support during the preparatory phase of the project.
2. The total population of Polynesian speaking Vaiakau people in the 1970 British Solomon Islands Protectorate Census were enumerated at 462. However, the actual number could easily

be twice as big, as many Polynesians had already by then left their islands for shorter or longer periods. The scattered Polynesian islands are Nifiloli, Pileni, Matema, Nukapu and Nupani. Of these it is mainly Nifiloli that is dealt with here. The somewhat marginal Nupani will not be considered at all. The Papuan-speaking people of Fenualoa (Papuan name: Ngasinue) in 1970 numbered 777, comparatively fewer of these being away from their home island. They are settled in four main villages: Tuo, Mwalubu, Tange and Malapu.

3. Archaeological evidence supports the assumption that the trading system in an early time reached much further out.

4. Colonial and postcolonial planners and developers never gave much attention to these coral islands. But copra production was definitely encouraged. Today very few people, if any at all, would consider allocating time and work to this very poorly paid productive effort.

5. W. Davenport says about the number of outrigger trading canoes: 'In the 1920s and 1930s there were in the Northern Santa Cruz Islands perhaps as many as 200 *puki* ... In 1960 there were two *puki*, both built at Taumako, and these were the only ones that had been made there in the preceding decade' (1968:177).

6. In Davenport's words: 'Despite the separate and reciprocally recognized social identities of the small-island people, there is a shared set of cultural values from Deni to Taumako, so that one can speak of a northern Santa Cruz Group culture' (Davenport 1975:73).

7. The last men's house in Nifiloli had belonged to Basil Tavake, who died in 1970. It was demolished by a gale in December 1974 and was not rebuilt.

8. During my stay in Fenualoa in 1992, I was approached one night in privacy by a man who wanted my advice on what to do with his three last rolls. In 1994, Peter Crawford and I located some of the remaining rolls in Fenualoa. They were kept by Alfred Melotu, one of the few remaining traditional leaders, who agreed to have them video-filmed in his house.

9. Film work involving visual anthropologist, Peter Crawford, photographer, Gary Kildea, a representative of the Solomon Islands National Museum and the author will be carried out on location between June and September 1996.

10. Especially the Vaiakau people have embraced Christianity

wholeheartedly. At the same time, cultural traditions have weakened considerably more with them than with the Fenualoa people. It is significant that one Vaiakau local settlement has expressed the wish to contribute to the film about their traditions by having their church and some of their Christian worshipping and ceremonies included.

References

Babadzan, A. (1988). Kastom and Nation-Building in the South Pacific. In: R. Guidieri, F. Pellizzi and S.J. Tambiah (eds), *Ethnicities and Nations: Processes of Interethnic Relations in Latin America, Southeast Asia, and the Pacific*, pp. 199-228. Houston: Rothko Chapel and University of Texas Press.

Borofsky, R. (ed.) (1994). *Assessing Cultural Anthropology*. New York: McGraw-Hill.

Carrier, J.G. (ed.) (1992). *History and Tradition in Melanesian Anthropology*. Berkeley: University of California Press.

Clifford, J. (1988). *The Predicament of Culture*. Cambridge: Harvard University Press.

Davenport, W. (1968). Social Organization Notes on the Northern Santa Cruz Islands: The Duff Islands (Taumako). *Baessler-Archiv*, Neue Folge, XVI:137–205.

—— (1969). Social Organization Notes on the Northern Santa Cruz Islands: The Main Reef Islands. *Baessler-Archiv*, Neue Folge, XVII:151–243.

—— (1972). Social Organization Notes on the Northern Santa Cruz Islands: The Outer Reef Islands. *Baessler-Archiv*, Neue Folge, XX:11–95.

—— (1975). The Population of the Outer Reef Islands, British Solomon Islands Protectorate. In: V. Carroll (ed.), *Pacific Atoll Populations*, pp. 64–116. Honolulu: University of Hawaii Press (ASAO Monograph 3).

Eriksen, T H. (1993). *Ethnicity and Nationalism*. London: Pluto Press.

Friedman, J. (1992). Narcissism, Roots and Postmodernity: The Constitution of Selfhood in the Global Crisis. In: S. Lash and J. Friedman (eds), *Modernity and Identity*, pp. 331–66. Oxford: Basil Blackwell.

Ginsburg, F. (1994). Culture/Media. A (Mild) Polemic. *Anthropology Today* 10(2):5–15.

Hau'ofa, E. (1994). Our Sea of Islands. *The Contemporary Pacific* 6(1):148–61.

Jolly, M. (1992). Specters of Inauthenticity. *The Contemporary Pacific* 4(1):49–72.

Keesing, R.M. (1989). Creating the Past: Custom and Identity in the Contemporary Pacific. *The Contemporary Pacific* 1(1–2): 19–42.

—— (1991). Reply to Trask. *The Contemporary Pacific* 3(1):168–71.

—— (1993). A Tin With the Meat Taken Out: A Bleak Anthropological View of Unsustainable Development in the Pacific. In: T. Otto (ed.), *Pacific Islands Trajectories. Five Personal Views*, pp. 29–55. Canberra: Australian National University and Nijmegen: Centre for Pacific Studies.

Thomas, N. (1992). Substantivization and Anthropological Discourse. The Transformation of Practices into Institutions in Neotraditional Pacific Societies. In: J.G. Carrier (ed.), *History and Tradition in Melanesian Anthropology*, pp. 64–85. Berkeley: University of California Press.

Trask, H.-K. (1991). Natives and Anthropologists: The Colonial Struggle. *The Contemporary Pacific* 3(1):159–67.

Part III

Australia after Mabo

Chapter 12

National Identity: Australia after Mabo

Robert Tonkinson

Introduction

Recently, a debate of major national significance has erupted in Australia over possible constitutional reforms, aimed principally at creating an Australian republic but also at affirming the existence and rights of the country's indigenous minorities.[1] As never before in their history, the people of Australia are examining nationhood and the meaning of what it is to be an Australian. Two kinds of nation-building are occurring simultaneously: the first is that of Australia as a whole, and the second is that of Australia's indigenous minorities, as 'nations' within the nation-state, and their struggle to achieve greater self-determination.

Notable among the reasons for the first kind of nation-building are a national policy of multiculturalism, the realities of an increasingly diverse population, and economic and other pressures to increase Australia's influence in the Asia–Pacific region (Tonkinson and Tonkinson 1994:183). However, Australia's record of ill-treatment of its indigenous population leaves it vulnerable to criticism, especially when its leaders speak out on international human rights issues. Sensitive to international opinion, the Federal Government is attempting to respond to Aboriginal aspirations and to remedy past injustices. Although the indigenous population is a tiny minority (*c.* 1.5 per cent of the total population), it has become highly visible and increasingly vocal.[2] The Government is well aware that the condition of its indigenous minorities is a crucial aspect of any redefinition of Australia's nationhood. Accordingly, the Government has made reconciliation between indigenous people and other Australians a major goal.

Many Australians would like to see an end to the country's 200-year-old colonial attachment to Great Britain and the monarchy. By becoming a republic, and by writing Aboriginal people into the Constitution, the nation could lay claim to a much more ancient and impressive 40,000-year lineage. Only then could Australia proclaim for the first time a truly national unity.[3] The overlap between Aboriginal aspirations and Australia's attempt to present itself on the world stage as a mature, just and independent society is thus a central issue in understanding both sets of nation-building activities. In this context, the nation as a whole must reimagine itself via a myth-making process, in which the search for distinctively Australian national symbols may well include elements drawn from indigenous cultures (Morton 1996).

The Mabo decision of the High Court of Australia, which recognizes native title for the country's indigenous Aboriginal and Torres Strait Islander peoples, is undoubtedly an important moment in the history of their struggles for greater self-determination. A significant aspect of this decision is that 'native title' was deemed to be part of Australia's 'common law' heritage. Mabo (as the decision is now commonly termed) does not stand alone, however; it is, as Prime Minister Keating stated, one of a number of 'practical building blocks of change'.[4] Its importance thus needs to be assessed in the context of an ensemble of related developments.

My aims here are, first, to outline briefly the Mabo decision and reactions to it, and then to relate these reactions to historical and contemporary challenges to Aboriginal nation-building efforts. Such challenges are manifest in both Mabo itself, which paradoxically affirms British sovereignty even as it recognizes that the Aboriginal people occupied the continent and had ownership of it; and in reactions to the decision, which reveal limits on the effective political action of a tiny, marginalized and relatively powerless ethnic minority. Whether one views Aboriginality primarily as a cultural construction, an 'imagined community' (Anderson 1983; Beckett 1988a) or as a form of substate nationalism characterized by discourse grounded in concepts of culture and 'race' (Archer 1991:168), the encapsulated, 'Fourth World' status of Aboriginal people is fundamentally significant. Constructions of a pan-Aboriginal identity, whether by the state or by positive self-ascription, are contested by many members of the dominant society, who use different and, for most Aboriginal people, debilitating criteria in assigning Aboriginal identity.

Accusations of inauthenticity and the persistence of racial stereotyping negatively influence Aboriginal identity construction and undermine processes of reconciliation. This negativity contributes to the oppositional and reactive tone apparent in Aboriginal self-identification. Yet there are signs of positive change. The growing national visibility of, and interest in, Aboriginal achievements in writing, art, music, sport and dance suggest an increased willingness on the part of the wider Australian community to accept that Aboriginal people and the symbols of their distinctiveness are part of the nation. For many Australians, the 'real' Australia is one with country people, mateship, kangaroos, 'the outback' and Aborigines. Aboriginality is thus becoming a force not only for the cultural identity of Aboriginal people but also, potentially, as a symbolic resource for the nation itself. Not all Aboriginal people welcome this development, however; some see it as yet another act of appropriation that lessens their control over their own cultural symbols and perpetuates the cultural hegemony characteristic of past government policies of assimilation.

The pendulum of social change appears to be swinging away from Aboriginality defined and expressed emically in terms of a political rhetoric of resistance, towards a more culture-centred – and to non-Aboriginal Australians more easily accommodated – emphasis on Aboriginal commonalities, continuity and survival. There is a dialectical relationship between these two closely interwoven dimensions of Aboriginality, the 'political' and the 'cultural', and I suggest that Mabo provides an explicit and therefore powerful nexus between them.

The Mabo Decision

Prior to 3 June 1992, Australia was the only former British colony that had failed to recognize in law the prior land ownership of its indigenous inhabitants (Hocking 1993:184). On that day, in *Eddie Mabo and others* v. *the State of Queensland*, the High Court of Australia handed down an historic judgment that signalled an important legal as well as symbolic change in relations between the nation's two indigenous peoples and Australian society at large. For the first time, the Court accepted the argument that, under common law, the native title of Australia's indigenous inhabitants could be recognized. In so doing, the Court abandoned a 200-year-old legal fiction, which held that, at the time of the first British settlement, the continent was *terra nullius*, 'a land without owners'. Just how powerfully entrenched this notion has been in Australia is conveyed in the following quote, from a 1980 speech by the then Premier of Western Australia, Charles (now Sir Charles) Court:

> The land of Western Australia does not belong to the Aborigines. The idea that Aborigines, because of having lived in this land before the days of white settlement, have some prior title to land which gives them perpetual rights to demand tribute of all others who may inhabit it is not only inconsistent with any idea of fairness or common humanity, in fact it is as crudely selfish and racist a notion as one can imagine. Nor is it an idea which has even accorded with the law of this nation.[5]

The High Court found that, although native title had prevailed despite the assertion of British sovereignty, such sovereignty was not justifiable in an Australian court. However, some legal experts have found some 'sovereignty' implications in the decision (Nettheim 1993:109, 117). Also significant is the finding that grants of freehold and some leasehold titles by the Crown extinguish native title, either completely or to the extent of inconsistencies between the two. This extinguishment leaves most of southern and eastern Australia unclaimable. Also, most of Australia's quarter of a million Aboriginal people have been displaced from their ancestral lands and now live in urban areas and large country towns,[6] so Mabo offers the potential for some security of tenure to only 10–30 per cent of them.[7] Yet to focus solely on such statistics would be mistaken, because land rights carry a heavy symbolic load for Aboriginal people throughout Australia.

Mabo and its consequent enabling legislation (the Native Title Act 1993)[8] are problematic because, in both the content and scope of native title, important issues are left unclarified. For example, a claimant group, besides being an 'identifiable community', has to prove its continued recognition of Aboriginal laws and, 'so far as practicable', observation of customs based on its traditions, as well as proving that its traditional connection with the land has been substantially maintained (Gray 1993:157–8). In these evidentiary requirements alone, there is much scope for debate and conflict when claims are heard. It is unfortunate that the same decision which impels Aboriginal people towards *rapprochement* with white Australians appears already to be eroding Aboriginal unity because of competing claims for land.[9] While it is clear that Mabo and the Native Title Act replace what were principally moral claims with a legal right (Nettheim 1993:104), the very slow pace of granting claims has given rise to increasing frustration and resentment on the part of native title claimants.[10]

Aboriginal strivings for land rights began many decades ago, but since the 1970s the demand for land rights has become a central theme of political struggle and rhetoric. In the Northern Territory and several states, legislation was passed permitting some form of claims to land by indigenous people. The High Court's ruling on native title, however, created an entirely new situation because it acknowledged, for the first time, that in law the indigenous people of Australia were prior owners of the continent. The Mabo decision was taken with respect to a claim brought by Torres Strait Islanders, Australia's other indigenous population. These Melanesian cultivators are culturally distinct from the larger Aboriginal population, whose ancestors were hunter-gatherers. Although it has been argued (Brunton 1992) that this difference was sufficiently great to have invalidated any extension of native title to the rest of Australia, the Court's decision clearly left the way open for Aboriginal claims to proceed. My focus here is primarily on the Australian Aborigines.

Reactions to Mabo

The Mabo decision was given a decidedly mixed reception by the Australian populace. Mabo has been generally supported by indigenous Australians, the federal Labor government and many other groups and individuals, who see it as an important step in bringing about a formal and lasting reconciliation between black and white Australians. However, the fact that both Mabo and the Native Title Act have left unclear several issues of major importance has engendered opposition from certain interest groups and individuals. The uncertainties created by the new legal situation are allegedly threatening investment and mineral exploration.[11] These opponents include state governments (notably, Western

Australia), users of land resources (most notably the mining
industry and pastoralists) and the federal Opposition parties, all
of whom have sought to undermine and circumvent the new
measures. At the local level, too, there are many ordinary rural
Australians, neither rich nor powerful, who see the enactment of
land rights as threatening to their properties and livelihood.
Criticism and objections from these quarters have fostered negative
attitudes in the populace.

Opposition to Mabo by some states, particularly those with the
largest areas of claimable Crown land, has been vehement. Most
state governments tend to resent federal interference, particularly
in land matters, and most have objected to the native title
legislation. One commentator was moved to suggest that, 'The time
is overdue for the Premiers to view Aborigines in their states as
citizens with rights rather than enemies of the state' (Brennan
1993a; quoted in Hocking 1993:179).[12] Western Australia went so
far as to enact legislation extinguishing all native title, but in a
unanimous decision handed down in March 1995 the High Court
declared the state legislation to be invalid.[13] In addition to the issue
of states' rights, anti-Mabo politicians have marshalled support
by appealing to the self-interest of the non-indigenous population.
Many Australians view compensatory and ameliorative measures
as discrimination against them, an attitude grounded in an
ahistorical view of social justice – the 'one nation, one law' stance
that is favoured by the federal Opposition parties (Goot 1994).
Commenting on the aftermath of Mabo, one prominent historian
suggests that something monumental is transpiring: 'a struggle
for the soul of Australia' (Reynolds 1994:19). In this view, unless
Australia achieves a formal and lasting reconciliation with its
indigenous people, its self-image as a fair and just land will
continue to be mocked by the history of its oppression of them.
An Aboriginal version of this perspective was perfectly conveyed
during Australia's Bicentennial celebrations in 1988, when, having
declared an oppositional 'year of mourning', Aborigines adopted
the neatly ambiguous slogan, 'White Australia has a Black History'.

Challenges to Aboriginal Ethnogenesis

From the beginning of colonization in Australia, its indigenous
people were excluded from nation-building activities, and, when

federation occurred in 1901, the constitution specifically excluded them.[14] As a consequence of this exclusion and pervasive oppression and racism, Aboriginal people have increasingly felt a need to forge their own 'nation'. Eriksen (1993:100), writing on ethnicity and nationalism, suggests that nation-states, when establishing links between cultural groups and the state, have tended to 'create abstract communities of a different order from those . . . kinship-based communities which pre-dated them'. This creative process, the construction of a 'common culture,' is what I term 'nation-building' or 'ethnogenesis' (Jones and Hill-Burnett 1982:216). The challenge for Aboriginal nation-builders has been to overcome problems of distance and cultural diversity, and to present a unified front and a positive self-image. Yet even the claim to represent Aboriginal people is in conflict with strongly maintained traditional values surrounding local autonomy, which limit the ability of individuals to 'speak for' others. Thus Michael Dodson, the Aboriginal and Torres Strait Islander Social Justice Commissioner, states: 'I acknowledge to my country men and women that it is not appropriate that my views should be substituted for their own direct voices or that I can presume to speak for any person's particular traditional country.'[15] Another example, from a recent national meeting, is typical of Aboriginal public self-presentation. The speaker, who in skin colour and phenotype is very clearly an Aboriginal person, began by saying, 'I want it clear that I'm talking only for my country, the Yuin nation', and used humour to make a telling point about identity and authenticity: 'The [New South Wales] government's saying there aren't any Blacks in New South Wales' (he then pointed to himself and asked the gathering) 'Am I White? I'd like conferrment [confirmation] from this meeting, so I can go back and tell them!'[16]

Although Aboriginal leaders have effectively used international forums, such as the Working Group on Indigenous Peoples, to embarrass Australia, nation-states remain reluctant to grant separate nationhood to encapsulated indigenous minorities (Nettheim 1994:73). Moreover, Mabo reiterated that Aboriginal sovereignty was not justifiable, and few Aborigines have called for the establishment of a separate nation.[17] The obstacles to sovereignty appear to be formidable, because the Aboriginal population is dispersed and most people have no discrete and clearly bounded land base (Brennan 1994:95). Since Mabo, however, many Australians, including indigenous people, see some form of self-government or self-determination as a politically realizable goal. While the word 'sovereignty' continues to be used by some Aboriginal leaders, this rhetoric is more a message to the dominant society about Aboriginal aspirations than a reflection of convictions concerning future autonomy.

The tendency to talk of Aboriginal people as if they are a homogeneous unity or community of interests masks the reality of a pervasive heterogeneity that continues to pose major difficulties for the forging of a 'common culture'. The category 'Australian Aboriginal' is a colonial creation, originating from the invasion of the continent. It demonstrates the widespread tendency of colonizers to ignore internal cultural variations and simply designate a unitary and highly contrasted (i.e. markedly inferior) other. Traditionally, territorial attachment was a major element in indigenous identity construction, and boundaries were conceptualized largely on the basis of perceived regional cultural differences that were religiously validated. Although there was no national political unit or identity, there were in fact some universally shared elements of a distinctive 'Aboriginal culture'. A few of these elements, particularly the Dreaming concept, plus contemporary slogans, such as 'the land is our mother' and 'we don't own the land; the land owns us', have become popular symbols of Aboriginality.

Following colonization, but particularly since the consciousness-raising era of the 1960s, a pan-Aboriginal identity has developed that is now embraced by most Australians of Aboriginal ancestry. For many Aborigines living where colonial impacts were greatest, elements of identity arose less from 'traditional' culture than from a shared history of oppression and experiences of racism. The political ideologies generated by indigenous leaders have focused intensely on this shameful history, probably because it resonates strongly with a majority of Aboriginal people, and may also carry greater moral weight among non-Aborigines, who would know or care little about shared traditions. In asserting a positive self-image that contests the negative ascriptions imposed on them by the dominant majority, many Aborigines invoke the originally imposed notion of an Aboriginal ethnicity, with its heavy emphasis on blood quotients and descent, as a positive element of shared national identity. Rhetorical themes, exemplified by such statements as 'our Aboriginality is in our blood' and 'we need to establish our links to the land through our blood', are common. As M. Tonkinson (1990) notes, there is a strong strand of essentialism in Aboriginal pronouncements about identity, reminiscent of the racialist ideas that informed legal classifications of Aborigines in the nineteenth and early twentieth century. In the words of one Aboriginal writer, 'it is the Aboriginal "essence" which makes an Aborigine and it is this essence which states, restates, informs and reforms his/her and our culture and social reality' (Nyoongah 1992:157). For most Aboriginal people, 'Aboriginality' tends to be reduced to that essence, or inner something, or distinctive 'spirituality' possessed by everyone who is Aboriginal.[18]

A major challenge to efforts to forge a pan-Aboriginal unity derives from the long duration of the frontier, which began with the arrival of the First Fleet at Sydney Cove in 1788 and ended in the 1960s in the remote Western Desert. This has exacerbated diversity in culture and lifestyles. Thus, for many Aboriginal people in remote areas of central and northern Australia, continuities with the past still underlie major values and behaviours, while Aborigines of mixed descent in southern Australia are generations removed from such direct continuities with a 'traditional' past. Most city-dwelling White Australians, who rarely encounter Aborigines, derive their models for understanding Aboriginality and Aboriginal culture almost exclusively from the 'real blackfellas' of the remote interior. This implied contrast is problematic because it simultaneously affirms the existence of an authentic cultural tradition while calling into question the 'Aboriginality' of the great majority of Aboriginal people whose lifestyles differ from that tradition (Beckett 1988a:6).

What is perceived as the 'traditional' culture of remote Aboriginal Australia has tended to function for other Australians as a kind of baseline, a set of absolutes of colour and culture against which to measure Aboriginal people's fitness to be so designated. The history of the National Aboriginal Consultative Committee (NACC) demonstrates the negative impact of such attitudes. The promulgation of a pan-Aboriginal ideology was accelerated in the 1970s when the Federal Government established an elected national Aboriginal advisory body. The NACC provided a major impetus for an increased national Aboriginal presence, but its eventual demise illustrates some of the major obstacles to ethnogenesis (Weaver 1983). The most prominent NACC leaders and spokespersons were Aboriginal people of mixed descent; they became targets of attacks both from white Australians and some Aboriginal people in remote areas, who invoke criteria such as descent to assert their own authority and question the Aboriginal identity of these leaders (Chase 1981:24). A penchant for associating cultural characteristics with skin colour, shared by many Aboriginal as well as non-Aboriginal Australians, has at times operated to challenge the authenticity of the Aboriginal majority, more than two-thirds of whom are of mixed descent.

Aboriginality and *Kastom*

The diversity, dynamism and contradiction inherent in constructions of 'Aboriginality' suggest parallels with those of *kastom* (customs/tradition) and nationalism in Melanesia. There, *kastom* has been used by indigenous leaders as a unifying cultural symbol or rallying cry. Yet it also connotes distinctive bodies of local lore, such that attempts to specify a body of 'national' *kastom* invite the loaded question, 'Whose *kastom* will be chosen as exemplary?' (Tonkinson 1982). An Australian example concerns the search for an indigenous label that will apply universally to Aboriginal people and replace 'Aborigines', an alien imposition. Leaders in south-eastern Australia have aggressively urged the adoption of the label 'Koori', from a language of that region. Although the term has been embraced by many non-Aborigines, it has not won favour with Aboriginal people elsewhere in the continent, who are opposed to replacing their local 'tribal' labels with one that is foreign and therefore inappropriate.

The Aboriginal rallying cry of 'land rights' also has structural parallels with *kastom* in that the term 'land rights' embodies a wide range of differing meanings, from claims grounded in Australian law to those resting on moral right and assertions of need (cf. Archer 1991:166). Such popular and oft-repeated slogans as 'the land is our mother' and 'the land owns us' would not survive scrutiny on the basis of prevailing patrilineal ideologies and traditional Aboriginal dogmas that, within a framework of dominance by spiritual forces, give precedence to human agency in the regulation of relations with the natural world (Stanner 1966/ 1989; Tonkinson 1991).

Aboriginal activists in urban areas have built a successful

consciousness-raising campaign around the slogan, 'cultural revival is survival'. In areas of the continent where land rights have had significant impact, the claims process itself has been a powerful force contributing to both 'revitalization' and an increasing tendency among Aborigines to objectify their culture (cf. Eriksen 1993). A prominent Aboriginal spokesman, Charles Perkins, recently underlined the vital importance of 'cultural renaissance' in ensuring the survival of a distinctive Aboriginal people and culture. He calls for organized cultural and social exchange programmes between 'traditional and urban Aboriginal people', and the establishment of a national cultural base to enhance confidence and credibility (Perkins 1994:37). Sutton (1988) notes that urban and rural Aborigines are forging (and reforging) links and are thus rapidly narrowing the formerly vast gulf between them. The reuniting of families separated by the operation of past government policies has been accelerated enormously by land claims and associated genealogical and other research. Also, employment requirements have meant a flood of urban Aboriginal people going to work in remote Australia. These shifts, together with an increasing biculturalism among rural Aboriginal people, have important implications for the grounding of an Aboriginal 'nation' status.

Mabo and Nation-building: Obstacles and Promise

In the late 1980s, a severe economic recession was among a number of factors contributing to setbacks in the Aboriginal struggle for self-determination, despite a sizeable minority of non-Aboriginal Australians expressing support for specific measures of redress, over and above Aboriginal citizenship entitlements (Goot and Rowse 1991:11). Despite many improvements in the degree of self-management, especially in rural and remote areas, Aborigines were (and still are) firmly on the bottom of Australia's socio-economic ladder. A severely disadvantaged and economically and socially marginalized minority, they remained relatively powerless in the face of continued prejudice and the tendency of both federal and state governments to act paternalistically in legislating for and about them. For a growing Aboriginal 'elite', avenues to power and influence were confined to the state agencies that employed them. Having to operate from a subsidized power base limited their freedom to criticize continuing injustices without fear of reprisal.[19]

One notable consequence of the movement of Aboriginal people into state bureaucracies may be a transformation of racialized structures of opposition that characterize rural and remote areas of Australia. Rowse (1993a:284) notes that the straightforward dichotomy between Aboriginal people and whites is shifting to one that opposes 'the peripheral agents of the colonial state and their indigenous clients' to the central bureaucrats, both Aboriginal and white. If this is the case, Rowse suggests, political strategies and acts of resistance to the state may or may not include ideologies of Aboriginality, and Aboriginal bureaucrats seeking to legitimize their administrative power likewise may or may not utilize such ideologies. There has long been a perception among some Aborigines that Aboriginal bureaucrats, particularly those in senior positions, are losing touch with their people and are acting more as agents of the state than as advocates for the Aboriginal cause; as Jones and Hill-Burnett (1982:229) note, such discontinuity is 'an integral aspect of the political circumstances of ethnicity'. Labels such as 'Black Mafia' (and, in the case of those accused of only recently 'coming out' as Aborigines, 'instant coffees') have become common in urban Aboriginal critical discourse.

The problem of co-optation has persisted despite the avowed aims of the Federal Government to promote genuine self-determination for indigenous Australians. In 1990, its much heralded reorganization of federal Aboriginal affairs resulted in the creation of the Aboriginal and Torres Strait Islander Commission (ATSIC), whose Councillors and Commissioners are elected throughout Australia by their own people. However, many Aborigines continue to view this body as an arm of the government, staffed largely by 'Kooricrats' (Aborigines from south-eastern Australia). In recent years there have been moves by Aboriginal organizations such as Land Councils to form themselves into larger regional and national entities that can exert greater political pressure and are more independent of government than ATSIC. Several important national meetings and conferences of such bodies have been held, at which consensus has been reached on major issues affecting indigenous aspirations.

These manifestations of national unity have been intensified by Mabo and are indicative of a new political balance. As Hocking (1993:200) suggests, 'Australia's indigenous peoples now speak at the political level with confidence in their legal rights to equal and non-discriminatory treatment and of their original ownership of the lands of the continent.' Evidence of a more assertive espousal by Aboriginal people of their rights under law is coming from all parts of the country as land claims are being lodged under new post-Mabo procedures. Also of signal importance were the events that unfolded in the context of tense negotiations over the content of the Federal Government's enabling legislation, the Native Title Act 1993. A group of prominent Aboriginal and Islander leaders, with the strong support of church groups, non-government organizations and others in the wider community, engaged in an intense lobbying effort.[20] They induced the government to reverse its earlier decision to suspend the Racial Discrimination Act (RDA), which would have been disastrous for Aboriginal aspirations, by protecting it against attempts at extinguishment by state governments.[21] This positive outcome provided, for the first time in Australia, clear evidence that a group of indigenous people were taken seriously as national leaders, and could directly influence decisions at the highest level of government.

A most significant aspect of negotiations over the Native Title Act in 1993 was the emergence, from outside government bureaucracies, of an Aboriginal leadership at a national political level. These leaders made important gains for Aboriginal people as a whole by spirited engagement with the wielders of power rather than repudiating the legitimacy of that power. Aboriginal leadership is a crucial element in processes of nation-building; it exemplifies better than any other indigenous institution the nexus between knowledge and power or, more broadly, that between 'culture' and 'politics'. Leadership in any acephalous society is a complex and difficult issue, and in Aboriginal societies the subtleties involved in assessing who has the right to speak for/about whom and in what circumstances ensure that, even for the actors themselves, it is sometimes difficult to be confident. Claims of legitimacy are based largely on the assumed possession of certain kinds of knowledge, much of which is territorially anchored and bounded; and the right to assume leadership roles is situationally defined. Assertion of leadership thus becomes particularly difficult when Aboriginal people attempt to operate in the wider political arena – whether or not possession of esoteric 'traditional' knowledge still remains a criterion for leadership.

It would be difficult to understate the continuing challenges that confront Aboriginal Australians in the working out of their relationships with the dominant population. The strong commitment of the government to promoting a national self-image as a multicultural society has many critics, indigenous people included. While conservative critiques centre on multiculturalism's alleged emphasis on difference and potential for social fragment-ation, Aboriginal objections are grounded in a desire to remain clearly separated from all other 'ethnic' minorities, since they wish to be regarded as descended from the original inhabitants, distinct from recent immigrants, and to claim special status because of a long history of victimization not shared by immigrants. These and other issues are yet to be resolved as Australia seeks to define itself as a nation exemplifying freedom and fairness.

Conclusion

In this contribution I have intimated that, despite the limitations of Mabo in securing land title for indigenous Australians, its symbolic force is such that it may provide the basis for recon-ciliation between indigenous and other Australians. Once the legal testing is completed – a process that may take several years – Australians will have gained a clearer idea of its ramifications, and the dust of hostility may settle. Resolution of the question of constitutional reform and the move to a republic could also facilitate the forging of a new national identity, freed once and for all from colonial reins and reign, more attuned to Australia's geographical position in Asia, and inclusive of the indigenous symbols that alone can transform a one-hundred-year-old nation into a truly ancient one.

For national symbols to emerge that are grounded in Australia's indigenous history and supported by the descendants of its original inhabitants, the necessary reconciliation has to be real and lasting. Mabo marks a big advance by its affirmation of racial equality before the law and its recognition of native title. There have also been small but positive signs of a national mood swing towards reconciliation. The most prominent manifestations of this change relate to the unprecedented successes of certain Aboriginal artistic forms, for example, the 'rock' band Yothu Yindi, the autobiographical novel *My Place* by Sally Morgan and Aboriginal paintings, for which there is now a rapidly growing international market (Morton 1996). Here I mention briefly several other examples whose significance extends well beyond the event itself.

The first is the protest rally and march organized by Aboriginal people on the day chosen for the major bicentennial celebration in January 1988. Centred around the catch-cry, 'We have survived 200 years', this rally provided the occasion for an unprecedented demonstration of pan-Aboriginal unity, attracting representative groups from all over the country. Not only did the dire predictions of mass violence, made by conservative politicians, prove totally groundless, but thousands of non-Aboriginal people joined the march, which was cheered on by many of the hundreds of thousands of spectactors who attended the Sydney celebration. Through extensive television coverage, the nation witnessed the event and, judging by media reactions, Australians expressed not only patriotic emotions but also empathy and support for the Aboriginal viewpoint. A second exemplary event was when the champion Aboriginal athlete Cathy Freeman carried an Aboriginal flag on her victory lap at the Commonwealth Games in Canada in 1994, and a senior Australian athletic official threatened her with sanctions. This resulted in an unexpectedly strong reaction from the Australian media and public in support of her action. Both the Sydney rally and this event appear to have had a notable impact symbolically.

More ambiguous, but nevertheless in some respects indicative of a significant bridging of the divide between indigenous and other Australians, has been the identification felt by conservationists with indigenous people. There has never been a cult of the 'noble savage' in Australia, where, from the early years of the frontier, assessments of Aboriginal people and culture have leaned much more towards a Hobbesian view. In recent years, however, there has been something akin to a cult of the 'noble environmentalist' (Sackett 1991:242), wherein white environmentalists have attempted to make common cause with Aborigines against resource developers. It must be said, however, that, while some of these alliances have been mutually educational and positive, others, in which Aboriginal people decided in favour of development taking place, provoked some exasperated environmentalists into depicting them as inauthentic, having measured them against an imagined but distorted 'traditional' standard and found them wanting (Sackett 1991; see also Anderson 1989). Also, environmentalists are not alone in embracing aspects of Aboriginal culture; New Age adherents have shown great interest in Aboriginal 'spirituality' in the past few years, with mixed reactions from indigenous people.[22]

Finally, I wish to return to the central issue of Aboriginality and identity, and to my suggestion that the dominant representations in Aboriginal rhetoric appear to be moving from a defensive or reactive tone to one that is more culture-centred, emphasizing commonalities, continuity and survival. This more positive form of self-representation, which is also less confronting to non-indigenous Australians, can be explained in various ways. It may well be related to the growing incidence and strength of cultural revival activities in many parts of the country. Heavily culturally based, these centre on 'land, language and law' and the fact of survival as sources of identity and pride. Aboriginal rhetoric surrounding these community-based movements has less to say about oppression than about Aboriginal culture as enduring and empowering. By this I am not suggesting that discourses of resistance are disappearing; rather, they are couched less in direct opposition to white hegemony and historical abuses and more in terms of survival and the strength of Aboriginal culture as proof of successful resistance.

Another possible motivation for change is a growing realization among Aboriginal people that appeals or demands for rights and justice articulated in terms of historical factors, like racism and brutality, do not induce guilt in the majority of white Australians, who pronounce themselves blameless for what happened long ago and refuse to accept responsibility for past horrors, since *their* consciences are clear. 'Blaming the victim' is a popular Australian sport, not confined to the conservative politicians who rail against the alleged excesses of the welfare state, particularly in relation to Aboriginal people. The strength and ubiquity of such views would convince Aboriginal people that most Australians are impervious to moral argument couched in oppositional terms, so a more conciliatory approach is preferable. A minority of Aboriginal leaders would not agree, particularly those who refuse to accept the legitimacy of British sovereignty. Having given up on the nation-state as a moral agent, they direct their protests to international human rights bodies, and maintain an opposition rhetoric centred on dispossession and genocide (Rowse 1993b:22–4). However, they enjoy little support among Aboriginal people, and seem to have been swept aside by events since Mabo.

To return to my major contention in this contribution, namely, that Mabo's greatest significance lies less in its ability to give Aboriginal people title to land than in providing a nexus between the 'political' and the 'cultural' dimensions of Aboriginality. Legal title may well prove to be of greater commercial than political significance, since Aboriginal councils and associations will most probably remain the primary platform for Aboriginal politics. The legal recognition of what indigenous people have believed and stated, that they are the prior owners of the land, is of course immensely significant. Yet this is not the only reason why the notion of native title has been so rapidly embraced by Aboriginal people. An equally potent reason is that native title specifies – and therefore legitimizes – Aboriginal 'culture', in the form of 'laws and customs', as the key determinant of title. The inscription in law of customary practices as an essential criterion provides a powerful and timely reinforcement, not only of cultural pride and Aboriginal identity, but also of the many activities now undertaken by Aborigines in exemplification of their motto, 'cultural revival is survival'.[23] These activities are virtually inseparable from continuing efforts by Aboriginal people to gain greater political control over their affairs, both internally and in relations with the nation-state. By its explicit synthesis of these two powerful, already interrelated elements, the Mabo decision constitutes a momentous development, having both real and symbolic consequences for the processes of Australian *and* Aboriginal nation-building.[24]

Notes

1. I am most grateful to Myrna Tonkinson for her detailed critique of this article. I also thank Victoria Burbank, Mary Edmunds, Gillian Hutcherson, Tim Rowse, John Stanton, Peter Sutton, Sandy Toussaint, David Trigger and Nancy Williams for their helpful comments. At the time of writing, a federal Labor government, led by Prime Minister Paul Keating, was in power. However, the federal election of March 1996 brought the conservative Liberal-National Coalition to power.
2. Aboriginal people figure daily in the mass media to an extent

that would be unthinkable of, for example, native Americans in the USA.

3. In my use of the term 'nation', I follow Eriksen (1993:100), who defines 'nations' as 'ideological constructions seeking to forge a link between a (self-defined) cultural group and state'. Aboriginal people are increasingly using the term 'nation' to refer both to the indigenous population as an entity, and to their own linguistic communities or regional groups.

4. Speech at the Australian launch of the International Year of the World's Indigenous People, December 1992; quoted in Brennan (1993b:101).

5. Quoted in Riley (1994).

6. In 1991, according to the Commonwealth Census, 27 per cent of the indigenous population was living in cities with more than 100,000 persons.

7. In the case of leasehold title, the issue of extinguishment of title is not everywhere clear-cut, since in three states pastoral leases contain various provisos that guarantee continued Aboriginal access to said lands. Native title is thus certainly impaired but nevertheless, in the view of some commentators, exists to the extent permitted by the conditions set out in the leases (Brennan 1994:2). In December 1996, the High Court of Australia ruled that pastoral leases do not necessarily extinguish native title, in what is now known as the Wik decision (after a north Queensland group that brought the action). In the resulting furore, the federal government and other interest groups have sought to limit – or in the view of some critics, extinguish – the rights and interests of indigenous claimants. The Wik controversy has generated a lot of anxiety and anti-Aboriginal sentiment, which has adversley affected the ongoing national push for reconciliation between indigenous and non-indigenous Australians.

8. Besides the Native Title Act, there is draft legislation to establish a Land Fund and an Indigenous Land Corporation, in recognition that most indigenous people have been long since dispossessed of their land and hence cannot prove continuous association, rendering them ineligible to benefit from the High Court's Mabo decision and the Native Title Act.

9. Edmunds (1994:39), noting that disputes are increasing as the material and symbolic stakes increase, observes: 'It may be . . . that this incorporation of an adversarial legal system [by

Aboriginal groups] as a further resource for contestants not only encourages but almost requires the sacrifice of notions of broader group identity for the pursuit of individual and family interests.'

10. See Commonwealth of Australia (1995:5–6). As Social Justice Commissioner Dodson puts it: 'We do not come to the process by which native title is recognised devoid of misgivings, and the system will have to be sensitive to our situation if the claims process is to meet the necessary human rights standards.' The nature of the legal right conferred by the Native Title Act is subject to further clarification, by either amendment or judicial ruling.

11. These critics do not acknowledge that the legal uncertainties apply as much to those seeking native title as to those wanting it denied. For Aboriginal people, the onus of proof is on them to provide evidence according to the constraints of the legislation.

12. Long before Mabo, it was clear that demands for Aboriginal rights generally and land rights in particular were a most divisive and potentially explosive issue. A major opinion poll taken in 1984 concluded that about one-third of the Australian public was 'intractably opposed to land rights, one third firmly supportive and a third in the middle leaning increasingly to opposition and prejudice through fear, ignorance, misinformation and soft racism' (Australian National Opinion Poll 1984; see also Rowse (1988) for a critique of this poll suggesting that the results may not have been as negative as portrayed by the pollsters). A later poll (1991–2), still prior to Mabo, indicated a continuing lack of enthusiasm for special initiatives concerning the indigenous people: less than one-third of the Australian people favoured special tribunals for Aboriginal people or legal recognition of Aboriginal customs, and less than one- fifth believed that the Constitution should recognize Aboriginal self-government (Galligan 1994).

13. For a summary of this decision, see Commonwealth of Australia (1995; Appendix 4).

14. No laws could be made on their behalf by the central government, and they could not be counted in population censuses (until overturned by referendum in 1967).

15. Commonwealth of Australia (1995:3).

16. National Native Title Induction Course, University of Western Australia, December 1994.
17. The Aboriginal lawyer, Michael Mansell, has been a leading proponent of sovereignty, and was architect of the Aboriginal Provisional Government, a little-known body (Mansell 1993:56). However, more recently he seems to have abandoned the goal of full sovereignty in favour of Aboriginal self-government (Mansell 1994:166).
18. Legal definitions are likewise minimalist, consisting of an element of self-reference plus recognition by 'the Aboriginal community'.
19. See Tonkinson (1989). See also Jones and Hill-Burnett (1982: 224): 'in 1976 not a single visible national-level Aboriginal leader was discovered who did not occupy a position in, or connected with, government or . . . an organization funded by the government'.
20. In the view of Peter Sutton (personal communication), this was a negotiated settlement achieved by people who shared more than rules: some, at least, shared the intellectual fibre and stamina required to achieve a result without serious withdrawal by either party.
21. The RDA is vital to native title because attempts by state governments to weaken or abolish native title would be inconsistent with it and hence invalid.
22. See, for example, Richards (1995), whose account of New Agers' involvement with a recent central Australian Aboriginal dance festival explores 'the fine line between reconciliation . . . and plunder'.
23. However, in its thoughtful discussion of customary law, the Australian Law Reform Commission (1986) suggested that 'recognition' is a rather conservative alternative to establishing political frameworks for Aboriginal autonomy, which may or may not pertain to customary law.
24. That the political and cultural strands in Aboriginal identity construction – resistance and persistence – are analytically separable and yet closely intertwined is one of the few points of general agreement among scholars recently embroiled in heated debates about Aboriginality: how and whether to conceptualize it, the nature and content of resistance and how to problematize it, the legitimacy of various kinds of essentialism expressed emically and etically, and the role and

morality of anthropology in constructing and analysing Aboriginal identity (see, for example, Beckett 1988b; Morris 1988; Hollinsworth 1992; Trigger 1992; Cowlishaw 1993; Langton 1993; Rowse 1993b).

References

Anderson, B. (1983). *Imagined Communities. Reflections on the Origins and Spread of Nationalism*, 2nd edn. New York: Verso.

Anderson, C. (1989). Aborigines and Conservationism: the Daintree–Bloomfield Road. *Australian Journal of Social Issues* 24(3):214–17.

Archer, J. (1991). Ambiguity in Political Ideology: Aboriginality as Nationalism. *The Australian Journal of Anthropology* 2 (2): 161–70.

Australian Law Reform Commission (1986). *The Recognition of Aboriginal Customary Laws*. Canberra: Australian Government Publishing Service.

Beckett, J. (1988a). Introduction. In: J. Beckett (ed.), *Past and Present: the Construction of Aboriginality*, pp. 1–10. Canberra: Aboriginal Studies Press.

—— (1988b). The Past in the Present; the Present in the Past: Constructing a National Aboriginality. In: J. Beckett (ed.), *Past and Present: the Construction of Aboriginality*, pp. 191–212. Canberra: Aboriginal Studies Press.

Brennan, F. (1993a). Undermining Mabo. *The Age*, 4 October 1993.

—— (1993b). Mabo and the Racial Discrimination Act: the Limits of Native Title and Fiduciary Duty under Australia's Sovereign Parliaments. In: J. Flew (ed.), *Essays on the Mabo Decision*, pp. 86–102. Sydney: The Law Book Company.

—— (1994). Pastoral Leases, *Mabo* and the *Native Title Act 1993*. In: *Land, Rights, Laws: Issues of Native Title*. Issues Paper No.1. Canberra: Native Titles Research Unit, Australian Institute of Aboriginal and Torres Strait Islander Studies.

Brunton, R. (1992). *Mabo* and Oral Traditions. In: *Mabo and After*, pp. 13–23. Melbourne: Institute of Public Affairs.

Chase, A. (1981). Empty Vessels and Loud Noises: Views about Aboriginality Today. *Social Alternatives* 2(2):23–7.

Commonwealth of Australia (1995). *Native Title Report (January–June 1994)*. Report of the Aboriginal and Torres Strait Islander

Social Justice Commissioner. Canberra: Australian Government Publishing Service.

Cowlishaw, G.K. (1993). Introduction: Representing Racial Issues. In: *The Politics of Representation and the Representation of Politics. Oceania* special issue 63(3):183–94.

Edmunds, M. (1994). 'Do not Shoot. I am a British Object': Anthropology, the Law and Native Title. In: M. Edmunds (ed.), *Claims to Knowledge, Claims to Country*, pp. 33–42. Canberra: Native Titles Research Unit, AIATSIS.

Eriksen, T.H. (1993). *Ethnicity and Nationalism: Anthropological Perspectives*. London: Pluto Press.

Galligan, B. (1994). Public Attitudes to Aboriginal Issues. In: C. Fletcher (ed.), *Aboriginal Self-Determination in Australia*, pp. 99–105. Canberra: Australian Institute of Aboriginal and Torres Strait Islander Studies.

Goot, M. (1994). Polls as Science, Polls as Spin: Mabo and the Miners. In: M. Goot and T. Rowse (eds), *Make a Better Offer: The Politics of Mabo*, pp. 133–56. Leichardt: Pluto Press.

Goot, M. and Rowse, T. (1991). The 'Backlash' Hypothesis and the Land Rights Option. *Australian Aboriginal Studies* 1:3–12.

Gray, T.A. (1993). The Myths of Mabo. In J. Flew (ed.), *Essays on the Mabo Decision*, pp. 148–77. Sydney: The Law Book Company.

Hocking, B. (1993). Human Rights and Racial Discrimination after the Mabo Cases: No More Racist Theft? In: J. Flew (ed.), *Essays on the Mabo Decision*, pp. 178–204. Sydney: The Law Book Company.

Hollinsworth, D. (1992). Discourses on Aboriginality and the Politics of Identity in Urban Australia. *Oceania* 63(2):137–55.

Jones, D. and Hill-Burnett, J. (1982). The Political Context of Ethnogenesis: an Australian Example. In M.C. Howard (ed.), *Aboriginal Power in Australian Society*, pp. 214–46. St Lucia: University of Queensland Press.

Langton, M. (1993) Rum, Seduction and Death: 'Aboriginality' and Alcohol. *Oceania* 63(3):195–206.

Mansell, M. (1993). Australians and Aborigines and the Mabo Decision: Just Who Needs Whom the Most? In: J. Flew (ed.), *Essays on the Mabo Decision*, pp. 48–57. Sydney: The Law Book Company.

—— (1994). Taking Control of Resources. In: C. Fletcher (ed.), *Aboriginal Self-Determination in Australia*, pp. 163–6. Canberra:

Australian Institute of Aboriginal and Torres Strait Islander Studies.

Morris, B. (1988). The Politics of Identity: from Aborigines to the First Australian. In: J. Beckett (ed.), *Past and Present: the Construction of Aboriginality*, pp. 63–85. Canberra: Aboriginal Studies Press.

Morton, J. (1996). Aboriginality, Mabo and the Republic: Indigenising Australia. In: B. Attwood (ed.), *In the Age of Mabo: History, Mabo, Aborigines and Australia*, pp. 117–25. Sydney: Allen and Unwin.

Nettheim, G. (1993). 'The Consent of the Natives': Mabo and Indigenous Political Rights. In: J. Flew (ed.), *Essays on the Mabo Decision*, pp. 103–26. Sydney: The Law Book Company.

—— (1994). International Law and Sovereignty. In: C. Fletcher (ed.), *Aboriginal Self-Determination in Australia*, pp. 71–84. Canberra: Australian Institute of Aboriginal and Torres Strait Islander Studies.

Nyoongah, M. (1992). Self-Determining our Aboriginality, a Response to 'Discourses on Aboriginality and the Politics of Identity in Urban Australia'. *Oceania* 63(2):156–7.

Perkins, C. (1994). Self-Determination and Managing the Future. In: C. Fletcher (ed.), *Aboriginal Self-Determination in Australia*, pp. 33–46. Canberra: Australian Institute of Aboriginal and Torres Strait Islander Studies.

Reynolds, H. (1994). Land and Customary Law: 1993 Perspective. In: C. Fletcher (ed.), *Aboriginal Self-Determination in Australia*, pp. 19–23. Canberra: Australian Institute of Aboriginal and Torres Strait Islander Studies.

Richards, D. (1995). Whitefella Dreaming. *HQ Magazine*, May–June 1995:61–7.

Riley, R. (1994). Aboriginal Self-Determination: Can State Laws Cope? In: C. Fletcher (ed.), *Aboriginal Self-Determination in Australia*, pp. 167–73. Canberra: Australian Institute of Aboriginal and Torres Strait Islander Studies.

Rowse, T. (1988). Middle Australia and the Noble Savage: a Political Romance. In: J. Beckett (ed.), *Past and Present: the Construction of Aboriginality*, pp. 161–77. Canberra: Aboriginal Studies Press.

—— (1993a). Rethinking Aboriginal 'Resistance': the Community Development Employment (CDEP) Program. *Oceania* 63(3): 268–86.

—— (1993b). *After Mabo: Interpreting Indigenous Traditions*. Melbourne: Melbourne University Press.

Sackett, L. (1991). Promoting Primitivism: Conservationist Depictions of Aboriginal Australians. *The Australian Journal of Anthropology* 2(2):233–46.

Stanner, W.E.H. (1966/1989). *On Aboriginal Religion*. Oceania Monograph 11/36. Sydney: Oceania.

Sutton, P. (1988). Myth as History, History as Myth. In: I. Keen (ed.), *Being Black: Aboriginal Cultures in 'Settled' Australia*, pp. 251–68. Canberra: Aboriginal Studies Press.

Tonkinson, M. (1990). Is It in the Blood? Australian Aboriginal Identity. In: J. Linnekin and L. Poyer (eds), *Cultural Identity and Ethnicity in the Pacific*, pp. 191–218. Honolulu: University of Hawaii Press.

Tonkinson, M. and Tonkinson, R. (1994). Embracing Difference: Australia's Changing Self-Image. In: D. Haskell (ed.), *Tilting at Matilda*, pp. 174–85. Fremantle: Fremantle Arts Centre Press.

Tonkinson, R. (1982). National Identity and the Problem of *kastom* in Vanuatu. In R.M. Keesing and R. Tonkinson (eds), *Reinventing Traditional Culture: The Politics of Custom in Island Melanesia*, pp. 306–31. *Mankind* special issue 13(4).

—— (1989). Aboriginal Ethnicity and Nation-Building within Australia. In: M.C. Howard (ed.), *Ethnicity and Nation-Building in the Pacific*, pp. 136–51. Tokyo: United Nations University.

—— (1991). *The Mardu Aborigines: Living the Dream in Australia's Desert*, 2nd edn. Fort Worth: Holt, Rinehart and Winston.

Trigger, D.S. (1992). *Whitefella Comin': Aboriginal Responses to Colonialism in Northern Australia*. Cambridge: Cambridge University Press.

Weaver, S.M. (1983). Australian Aboriginal Policy: Aboriginal Pressure Groups or Government Advisory Bodies? *Oceania* 54: 1–23, 85–108.

Chapter 13

Knowing the Country: Mabo, Native Title and 'Traditional' Law in Aboriginal Australia

Ad Borsboom

With its decision of 3 June 1992 that Australia was not *terra nullius* when settled by the British in 1788, the High Court of Australia rewrote Australia's law on the impact of colonization. The implications of this change in the common law are potentially vast and no less than revolutionary (Sanders 1994:1). The profound significance of this development has already been acknowledged by governments, by the media, by indigenous people themselves and by the pastoral and mining industries (ATSIC 1993).

The decision is known as the Mabo case. Eddie Mabo, from Murray Island in the Torres Strait, began in 1982 with three other Islanders action in Queensland courts seeking confirmation of their traditional land rights. They sought recognition of continuing traditional rights from the Australian legal system, claiming that Murray Island and surrounding islands had been continuously inhabited and exclusively possessed by their people, the Meriam people. After hearings of the Queensland Supreme Court the claim was finally brought before the High Court of Australia, which, by a majority of six to one, ruled that 'the lands of this continent were not *terra nullius* or "practically unoccupied" in 1788' and that the Meriam people were 'entitled against the whole world to possession, occupation, use and enjoyment of the lands of the Murray Island'. Sadly, Eddie Mabo had died before the Court's decision became final in June 1992, but his name is for ever connected with the recognition of native title in Australia.

In fact the name Mabo now has come to stand for much more than recognition of native title, as is aptly demonstrated by comments of the Aboriginal and Torres Strait Islander Commission (ATSIC):

> Apart from its practical effects, the MABO judgement also has great political and symbolic importance. It has given all Aboriginal and Torres Strait Islander people – the victims of much of Australia's history since 1788 – a measure of dignity and justice, and once again made land rights an important national issue. It has set a new agenda for debate on relations between indigenous and non-indigenous Australians (ATSIC 1993:1).

As this statement demonstrates, Mabo stands for a variety of ideas, attitudes and emotions at once: unlawful disposition of land, denial of indigenous systems of land tenure, dignity, justice, reassessment of historical and future relations with non-indigenous Australians and the right to their own, distinctive way of life within the Australian nation-state.

Therefore Mabo exemplifies what Ortner in another context has called 'summarizing symbols', symbols which operate 'to compound and synthesize a complex system of ideas, to "summarize" them under a unitary form which, in an old fashioned way, "stands for" the system as a whole' (Ortner 1973:1340). These symbols sum up, express and represent for the participants, in an emotionally powerful and relatively undifferentiated way, what the system means to them (Ornter 1973:1339).

The debate on Mabo has been going on since 1992 and has lost nothing of its emotional intensity since then. It truly affects all segments of Australian society, and no wonder: the Court acknowledges that early perceptions of Aboriginal society as disorganized groups wandering the bush were quite wrong and that Australia was not *terra nullius* but occupied by people with traditions, customs and an indigenous system of land tenure (ATSIC 1993:5).

The High Court Mabo decision was followed by the passing of the Commonwealth Native Title Act in 1993. This Act, like the High Court decision on which it is based, transforms the ways 'in which indigenous ownership of the land may be formally recognised and incorporated within Australian legal and property regimes. The process of implementation, however, raises a number of crucial issues of concern to native title claimants and to other interested parties' (Native Titles Research Unit, 1995). These crucial issues refer mainly to the workability of the Act, and Aboriginal representative bodies are, as Altman and Smith conclude (1995:11), faced with a tactical balancing act: on the one hand, expensive and time-consuming legal, research and consultative processes, and, on the other, the fact that political reality dictates that 'outcomes, in terms both of the recognition of native title (from the indigenous perspective) and of commercial development of land where native title has been recognised (from the wider societal perspective) are urgently needed' (1995:11.)

In this chapter,[1] I do not venture to undertake the impossible task of exploring all the uncertainties of this moment about the implications of the Mabo judgment, or to discuss the conflicting views of various parties concerned or to evaluate the avalanche of publications on Mabo since 1992. Here I am merely interested in investigating one example of what the Court considered the basis for native title, namely the 'traditional law and customs of people having the relationship with the land'.

To explore these 'traditional laws and customs' in relation to the land I turn to an area where up till the present day Aborigines have been able to maintain a continuous relationship with the land: north-eastern Arnhem Land. I must immediately stress that the case analysed here, that of the Wurgigandjar clan of the Djinang-speaking people, does not stand for Aboriginal Australia as a whole and that there are many variations of indigenous relationships with the land throughout the continent. In each part of Australia, as Sutton emphasizes (1995:4), there are 'many kinds of indigenous group that can be defined on the basis of interests in, and associations with, land'. In remote Australia these interests are complex and may be mediated by residence, kinship, incidents of personal history and ritual knowledge; they may also vary with age and gender (Peterson 1994:2). In my Arnhem Land example these interests in and associations with land are closely linked with local sets of totemically and ritually linked units. The knowledge and control of songs, myths, rituals and objects related to this local sets of totems is crucial in expressing interests in and association with a clan's estate. Although my study here is confined to just one clan, I must emphasize that clans are not isolated units and that throughout Arnhem Land knowledge and control over a clan's estate and its sacred lore is shared with a number of other clans. I turn to this briefly later in this chapter.

Dreaming Cluster

Wurgigandjar (‚blossom of the stringy bark') country stretches roughly between the township of Ramingining and Gadji lagoon. Throughout Arnhem Land the intrinsic relation between a clan, some natural species and certain localities is mediated through a restricted number of Dreamings (totems), which take concrete shape in religious forms of mythology, songs, dances, objects and ritual enactments. These Dreamings together comprise what I have called a Dreaming cluster (Borsboom 1978a:34) and the Wurgigandjar Dreaming cluster consists of the following species:

1   Wild Honey (Djareware)
2   Stringy Bark
3   Nectar-eating Bird (Geganggie)
4   Crow
5   Spiritual Beings
6   Jungle Bird (Djudo Djudo)
7   Possum
8   Cabbage Palm
9   Mud Cod
10   Bream Fish
11   North-west Monsoon
12   Water

Not all of these Dreamings (prototypes of species) are exclusive to the Wurgigandjar clan, but the composition as presented here is. Other clans in the area have comparable constellations of Dreamings, composed, however, of different species.

At first sight, the elements in this cluster seem a rather random collection of species, but upon a closer look there is a strict logic or 'rationale' to their clustering together. The presentation of these species in this order is based on the mythological route of Djareware, the clan's founder, who travelled roughly from the south-east to the north-west and met with the other Dreamings of this cluster throughout his journey. In the following, I present an abridged and very schematic account of this route and the habitat Djareware gave shape to.

Djareware, the First Wild Honey Being, is the main Dreaming for the Wurgigandjar. Sometimes he is identical with Wild Honey (Dreaming 1) and the honey for which this being is the prototype, but mostly he stands for more than this. He not only brought wild honey but is responsible for the whole habitat and species connected with it: the bees, flowers, stringy barks (Dreaming 2, in which the honeycombs are to be found) and nectar-eating birds such as Geganggie (3). He also brought the stone axe and taught people how to find honey and to open the nests with this axe.

So this part of the Wurgigandjar estate, the drier and higher parts of the Wurgigandjar country, also called 'gravel' country, is the habitat of the first three Dreamings of the cluster. In addition Crow (4) belongs also to this cluster as he is paired with Geganggie in an oppositional relationship. They fought about the ownership of certain rituals, whereby Geganggie ended up with the Maradjiri, a so-called 'birth-pole' ritual in which new life and fertility is the central theme, and Crow with death rituals.

Crow takes up an ambiguous position in the cluster because he also marks the transition to a group of Dreamings connected with death: the Spiritual Beings (5), Jungle Bird, called Djudo Djudo (6), and Possum (7). By now the habitat has changed from dry, open eucalyptus country with blossoming trees, an abundance of honey and nectar-eating birds to a jungle type of environment with dense vegetation and a sinister atmosphere. No one likes to visit these spots, of which several exist in Wurgigandjar country.

The jungle birds living in these places are messengers of the Spirits. Possums live in hollow trees and their prototype, the Dreaming Possum, is connected with hollow-log coffins, which are used for the bones of the dead.

Travelling further westwards, Djareware gave shape to another type of country: the open wetland environment towards Gadji lagoon and further to the north-west. The connection between Possum and the next Dreaming, Cabbage Palm (8), is that Possum feeds on fruits of these trees. In this sense Possum is as ambiguous as Crow as he too marks the transition from one group of Dreamings – those connected with jungle and death – to another, those Dreamings connected with life again. These are the various Fish Dreamings (9 and 10) and also Monsoon (11) and Water (12), which every year give a new lease of life to nature after the long and hot dry season.

So the habitats described here as the homes of the various species are all to be found in the country of the Wurgigandjar clan: from dry 'gravel' places in the eastern, higher parts to jungle to small creeks and billabongs in the lower western areas towards

Gadji lagoon. This lagoon forms the western boundary of the Wurgigandjar estate and is Mother's country to the men of the Wurgigandjar clan.

Levels of Explanation

Let me now try to answer the question about the rationale or logic behind the clustering together of these species, because that is essential for the understanding of the relationship between a specific group of people and its estate. This relationship is mediated by Dreamings, the prototypes of natural species connected with both people and their country. The analysis given below is based on information and observations of mythological accounts, dance performances and other ritual enactments, but above all it is derived from the songs. I emphasize the importance of the songs because, of all the religious forms which are employed to celebrate the exploits of the dreamtime beings, the songs are performed most frequently and on each occasion present a complete picture of the story, whereas (public) myths and dances usually only deal with fragments of it.

In most song sessions all Dreamings (from 1 to 12) are sung in the order presented here, that is from the species associated with the dry and higher stringy bark country in the eastern part of the clan's estate, via those connected with the jungle to the species belonging to the lower, wet areas in the west. Each Dreaming is the theme of a song and each song is composed of a number of verses. All these songs together form the Wurgigandjar song cycle, which is performed not only during rituals to accompany dances and ritual enactments, but also on other occasions: when somebody is sick or dying, when somebody has died and the corpse is still in the camp, when guests are leaving to ensure them a safe trip, and in preparation of ceremonies. The rather strict order in the presentation of the song cycle and the information encoded in its texts is the basis for the following analysis.

The Spatial Aspect

The cluster as a whole breaks down in subclusters and the main connection between the Dreamings of the same subclusters is that they share the same natural habitat. Thus there is a subcluster located at the higher, eastern parts of the Wurgigandjar estate, the dry 'gravel' country with its open eucalyptus forests. This is the habitat of Stringy Bark, Wild Honey and Geganggie. Then there is the jungle type of subcluster of beings living in dark places with dense vegetation: the Spirits and Jungle Birds. Finally there is the subcluster living near or in water in the lower parts of the Wurgigandjar estate: Cabbage Palm, Mud Cod, Bream and Water. As already indicated Crow and Possum are ambivalent as they mark the transition between subclusters.

This structure is reflected in the regular sequence in which the species of the whole cluster are sung; to put it simply, from the dry gravel country via the jungle to the creeks and billabongs, or, as one of the song men once said: 'When we sing, we sing from the top to the bottom.' So one explanation for the regularity in sequence is the close fit between the Dreamings of the Wurgigandjar cluster and the natural features of the clan's estate, as shaped by the travels of Djareware, that is roughly from the south-east to the north-west.

It is obvious of course that the three subclusters, like the corresponding types of landscape in Wurgigandjar country, are not absolutely separate: just as one type of scenery fades out into another, so the species of which these Dreamings are the prototypes interpenetrate one another's habitat. Thus when species of Dreaming clusters are sung it is not only the main types of habitat of the various species that are represented (the subclusters), but also the transition from the one type to the other. Crow marks the transition between the first and second subcluster, and Possum that between the second and third. In both cases these Dreamings are ambiguous in character in that they are connected with death, but also with life and fertility: Crow because he feeds not only on carcasses but also on berries and in certain cases is associated with fire, and Possum because, although he lives in hollow trees like the bones of the dead, he also feeds on nectar and is in certain contexts accredited with great sexual appetite and fertility.

One may conclude that the spatial structure underlying this Dreaming cluster operates on three levels. First, there is the sequence in types of habitat, not as rigid and schematically as depicted here, but definitely present in the Wurgigandjar clan estate. Second, there is the south-east–north-west axis as one of the most important spatial orientations, in significance comparable with our north–south orientation. The two prevailing winds in the Arnhem Land seasonal cycle originate from either of these two directions, namely the north-west monsoon and the south-east winds. In their personal mythologized form, these winds (Bara and Wulma) feature as models for relationships between human groups: just as these Dreamings constantly exchange winds, so do human groups with products and marriage partners.

The third spatial structure is the axis aerial–terrestrial–subterranean. In the first subcluster it is species who fly in the air which feature most prominently: birds and bees. The song text and myths also emphasize other scenes high up in the air: blossoming of flowers in the stringy bark tree, the moving of branches by the wind. In the jungle the emphasis is on the terrestrial level: low vegetation, jungle fowl and spiritual beings who run or, as is the case with one of them, are lame. The habitat of species in the third subcluster is subterranean (the fishes) or halfway between land and water (mud cod).

It is interesting here to note that this relationship between sections of a song cycle and various aspects of the landscape is not only common in Arnhem Land (see, for example, Keen 1994:146–50, 239), but that it also occurs among certain Melanesian horticulturists. An in-depth analysis by Wassmann into the meaning and function of song cycles of a Middle-Sepik society in Papua New Guinea (1991) gives ample illustrations of this. Two of the characteristic features of the songs are very comparable to my Arnhem Land example: the songs always follow each other in the same pattern (1991:55) and they are very closely related to localities. As in the Wurgigandjar song cycle, here too the song cycle as a whole re-creates the primal migration of the founder of the clan in its entirety, but each individual song 'marks a specific station in this migration; that is to say it is precisely localized and occupies a prescribed place in the cycle' (1991:52). This is not the only structural similarity to the Wurgigandjar example from Arnhem Land. The division of the environment into tracts on the upper course of the Sepik and the lower course (1991:198–203) also corresponds to the opposition 'high and dry' (gravel country) and 'low and wet' (creeks and billabongs) in my analysis of the Wurgigandjar Dreaming cluster. In an earlier discussion on Mabo (see also Beckett 1994:8–11) the question was raised whether or not the relationship to the land of the Torres Strait Islanders, who as Melanesians had already adopted agriculture, was basically different from that in mainland Australia. However, from comparisons with Wassmann's analysis, it appears that the similarities of relationship with the land are striking and far more important than the watershed created in cultural evolutionary theories constructed by European scholars between Aboriginal hunter-gatherers and Melanesian horticulturists. The analogies discussed here are in line with other studies on structural resemblances between Arnhem Land and Melanesian cultural systems (van Baal 1963; van der Leeden 1970).

Below I will explain how these environmental divisions, as in Wassmann's analysis, function as metaphors for the social organization of the clan under discussion here.

The Time Aspect

As is the case with the sequence of the songs in relation to spatial characteristics, there is a similar connection between the clustering together of these species and the seasonal cycle in tropical northern Australia. Starting again with species of the first subcluster, the song texts refer frequently to climatic conditions. The Stringy Bark verses describe how the branches of the stringy bark trees 'sing out and move' because of the wind coming from the southern inland. C.H. Berndt described this wind as the 'honeywind': it is the time when 'new bees are starting to fly but their wings are still soft, and when honey is so plentiful that people must eat fast to avoid wasting any. This wind therefore belongs to the honey and the bees' (1970:1313). It is also the time when the grass is burnt down and the stringy bark flowers. On our calendar this period is roughly between June and September, being the first and most pleasant months of the dry season.

Some song texts in the second and in the first part of the third subcluster refer to the period later in the dry season, when the country is much drier and the heat becomes unbearable. The Possum text says that he complains of the heat, which causes such discomforts as headache. The verses in the last subcluster describe the dangerous situation in which the various fish (Mud Cod, Bream and others) find themselves at the very end of the dry season when there is hardly any water left in the creeks and billabongs. The fish are trapped and close to death, but relief is brought soon by the rains of the wet season. This important transition, when nature gets a new lease of life, is described in detail in the verses of North-west Monsoon and Water. The text not only presents a vivid picture of the time preceding the first rains, when the sun is very hot, clouds are building up (but no rain yet) and the heat is oppressive because of the high humidity, but also describes what happens with the arrival of the monsoon. The rains start, the running water pushes fish out of their traps in shallow water into the creeks, now full of water, and the grass is beginning to grow.

So here too the order of presentation is important because of its intrinsic connection with the seasonal cycle. In this way the song cycle serves as a model for the time/space axis, both on a concrete and on an abstract level. This is essential for the functioning of a traditional hunters and gatherers society, because it is of vital importance to know where to find what kind of food at any specific time. On a concrete level there are the various literal descriptions about the condition of nature at any given time. On an abstract level these Dreamings and the species of which they are the prototypes are used as metaphors to organize perceptions of time and space and to contemplate them.

The Cosmological Aspect

A third principle underlying this cluster of Dreamings is the grouping together of species associated with life or with death. The first subcluster celebrates life. Wild Honey and the bird Geganggir, associated with the blossom of the stringy bark flowers, feature as dominant Dreamings in clan rites with a life-symbolic character, such as a rite called Maradjiri in which young children feature prominently. In English Wurgigandjar spokesmen some-times called the rite the 'birth-pole' ceremony. In certain myths Geganggie stands to Crow as life to death. Geganggie lives in and around stringy bark trees and feeds on nectar. According to the song texts he sits on top of these trees at the *matai* place, *matai* being the bud of the stringy bark flower. In the Dreamtime Geganggie became 'boss' for this Maradjiri or birth-pole rite, in which nearly all the enactments point to fertility and life symbolism. Crow frequents places where rubbish is to be found and eats rotten food. The myths, songs and dances about Crow in the context of the Maradjiri rite credit him with having smelt the decomposing flesh of a corpse and with having collected and eaten it so that the bones could be used for second disposal in a hollow log (as said above, Crow's character is ambiguous, as in other contexts he may also be associated with life).

Again Crow marks the transition to the jungle subcluster exclusively composed of beings associated with death. The spirits and their messenger, the bird Djudo Djudo, play important roles in the various death ceremonies. Once the Maradjiri also belonged to this category, but after a fight, as one of the myths narrates, Geganggie obtained this rite from Crow, who already possessed all the death rituals.

The song man of the Wurgigandjar clan explained that this had consequences for the content of the Maradjiri: Djareware instructed the Dreamtime beings that from now on (in the Maradjiri) 'no more Possum, Mere, Mewal [the spirits]; you dance Mewal and Possum, but leave them for Bugabod and Dopan [names of funeral and post-burial rites]. Mo more for Maradjiri; for the Maradjiri you dance and sing that Stringy Bark mob [referring to Stringy Bark, Wild Honey and Geganggie].' This mythological account about the division of life-symbolic and death rituals not only expresses the opposition between life and death but also between the two subclusters, which function as metaphors for this opposition, with Crow as mediator.

The third subcluster emphasizes life again. When many creatures are close to death, Monsoon brings relief with his rains, which guarantee many kinds of food, such as fish and shells, and makes everything grow again. One of the fishes in this cluster, Bream Fish, is an important Dreaming in the life-symbolic Maradjiri rite and its design is frequently painted on the chests of young children. It is generally believed in Arnhem Land that the spirits of unborn children take the form of these fish just before they enter their mother's womb.

So the presentation of the cluster in this order is closely related to the enduring opposition of life–death–life. Perhaps the intermediary role of Crow and Possum between the opposing clusters is meant to stress that life and death, although oppositional stadia of being, form a continuum, along which everything existing constantly moves, a sequence of oscillations (Leach 1971:126).

Subsistence

The next structuring principle underlying the Wurgigandjar
Dreaming cluster is the opposition edible and inedible. This
opposition runs along the same lines as the life–death division.
The importance of wild honey as food (but also as medicine and
love elixir) appears from the Dreamings in the first subcluster.
Djareware brings the bees and honey birds, makes the flowers
blossom and shows not only how to find honey, but also how to
collect it with sticks. He also left behind a most important object,
namely the stone axe, used to cut open the nests of the bees in the
stringy bark tree. These Dreamtime exploits are not only narrated
in the mythology and sung during singing sessions, but also
ritually acted out in great detail in the aforementioned Maradjiri
rite.

The species in the jungle subcluster have nothing to offer in
this field, and, unlike the open forest (of the first subcluster), people
hardly ever visit these rather sinister places.

The songs and myths belonging to the species of the third
subcluster emphasize edible species again: fish, fruits, plants,
shells, etc. One of the song phrases is literally translated as
Djareware generously saying to the human ancestors of the
Wurgigandjar people (after the creeks and billabongs are filled
with water) 'the fish is yours'.

It is interesting to note that it is Possum again who plays a kind
of intermediary role between inedible and edible (respectively the
second and third subcluster): the song text devoted to him explains
that he feeds on cabbage palm fruits. These fruits are toxic and
harmful, that is when eaten raw. Djareware instructed how to
prepare this food, namely by immersion in water for a few days
before eating. These fruits, mentioned in the Possum song, seem
to mark the transition between inedible and edible food.

Social Organization

A final structuring principle concerns the organization of the
Wurgigandjar people into two lineages, for which the environmental division into higher and lower parts of the clan's estate
function as metaphors. To explain this I first turn to a section of
the founding myth of the Wurgigandjar clan. Djareware divided

the country into two parts. That happened at Djimbi Creek, now a landmark of great spiritual significance for all Wurgigandjar. There Djareware changed himself too: from Wurgigandjar-Guragngere (*guragngere* meaning neck, a metaphor for the eastern upper part of the clan's estate) to Wurgigandjar-Nongere (*nongere* meaning ankle, which stands for the lower, western part of Wurgigandjar country). By dividing the estate into a *guragngere* and *nongere* section and changing his identity likewise, he laid the foundation for the division of the clan into two lineages: people from the top, Wurgigandjar-Guragngere, and people from the bottom, Wurgigandjar-Nongere. This part of the myth forms the basis for an elaborated dance in the aforementioned Maradjiri or 'birth-pole rite', where the leading dancer, enacting Djareware, divides a line of male dancers in two lines, and reunites them at the end of the performance.

Thus the choreography of the dance reflects an actual social situation: the clan is composed of two lineages whose members at some times operate independently and emphasize an identity of their own, and at others work closely together as one group and accentuate common ancestry and interests. In the song cycle the text of one of the verses of the Djareware song refers to this partition: Djareware divided the group of bees which travelled with him into two parts. When asked, the song man commented on this by referring to Djareware's exploits at Djimbi Creek, where he not only divided the land in two parts but also changed himself from Guragngere ('from the top', eastern part of the clan's estate), to Nongere ('from the bottom', the western half). As in Wassmann's analysis from the Sepik region (1991:53), here too the texts recited in the songs are small excerpts from long and elaborated myths.

In this final structuring principle there is no mention of the jungle subcluster, which apparently is irrelevant here. Perhaps this is so because the jungle environment, consisting of a few, relatively smaller patches of land around Djimbi Creek, is considered equally important to all Wurgigandjar. It is the environment of the Spirits, where also the souls of the deceased of both lineages move to after death. Socially it is undefined: a kind of no man's land and not specifically associated with either of the two lineages.

In Table 13.1, I try to summarize what has been said about the many levels of meaning in the relationship of a clan with its natural habitat, as mediated by a cluster of Dreaming.

Table 13.1 Levels of meaning in the Wurgigandjar Dreaming cluster

Name	Space	Space	Space	Time	Cosmology	Economy	Social
Djareware Stringy Bark Geganggie	South-east	Dry gravel	Aerial	Start dry season	Life	Edible	*Guragngere*
Crow							
Spirits Djudo Djudo	Halfway	Jungle	Terrestrial	End dry season	Death	Inedible	
Possum							
Cabbage Palm Mud Cod Bream North-west Monsoon Water	North-west	Wetlands	Subterranean	Wet season	Life	Edible	*Nongere*

Discussion

The basis for the recognition of native title in the Mabo judgment is the traditional law and customs of people having a relationship with the land. The case analysed here is an example of such a relationship, but it must be stressed again that in present-day Aboriginal Australia there are significant regional variations as far as traditional law and customs as the basis for native title are concerned.

The relevance of the Arnhem Land example, in my view, is that it comes as close as one can get to a pre-European system of land tenure and that similar systems were functioning in Aboriginal Australia when the first European colonists concluded that Australia was *terra nullius*. I immediately hasten to say that this assumption does not imply that I hold a traditionalist view on tradition, as if present-day Arnhem Landers are the last representatives of an unchanging, pre-European, way of life. In previous writings I have tried to show how new traditions developed in recent years (Borsboom 1978b) and how this idea of unchanging traditions among hunter-gatherers is a European construct (Borsboom 1992). I am also aware of the current anthropological debates on 'invention', 'construction' or 'objectivation' of tradition, debates which have given great impetus to the study of cultural traditions.

However, anthropological research among Arnhem Land Aborigines in the 1930s (Warner 1937; Thomson 1949) demonstrates that the basic principles of totemism and relationship towards land, however much they may have changed on the surface, are very comparable to what we see now. Before the 1930s the impact of the European presence in Arnhem Land was relatively mild compared with the disruptive effects elsewhere in Australia. The seasonal visits of the Macassans from Indonesia, which stopped early this century, had brought new materials and some new ideas into Arnhem Land, but these influences became easily incorporated.

Above all, the complexity of the system of land tenure as discussed here and its intrinsic connection with similar systems of neighbouring groups are such that a recent invention thereof is highly unlikely. So, although changes and developments have occurred in the customs underlying the indigenous system of the relationship to land, there are ample reasons to assume (let's call it 'circumstantial evidence') that the structural core of the systems still functioning in Arnhem Land today precedes the European invasion of Australia.

Trying to interpret the exact nature of the relationship between an Arnhem Land clan and its country is a complex venture. The multiple layers of interconnected explanations and meanings (spatial, seasonal, cosmological, economic, social) imply that one cannot just reduce this relationship to basically one of these fields, for example to the religious or the economic, and consider the other sets of meanings simply as aspects thereof. In this sense the nature of the relationship discussed here differs from Western notions of land tenure in industrial and technological societies, where indeed one angle, namely the economic, is predominant: land as an asset in a market-orientated environment.

To understand the full meaning of this complex, ontological relationship between a clan and its estate in my Arnhem Land example, I propose to turn to an older conceptual framework and apply that as an analytical tool. I am referring to Mauss's concept of 'total social phenomena': 'In these total social phenomena, as we propose to call them, all kinds of institutions find simultaneous expression: religious, legal, moral, and economic. In addition, the phenomena have their aesthetic aspect and they reveal morphological types' (Mauss 1980:1).

The Wurgigandjar Dreaming cluster, just like similar clusters from neighbouring clans, composes such a total social phenomenon. All kinds of institution do indeed find simultaneous expression. Religious, cosmological, economic and social aspects are clearly encoded in this system, which simultaneously reveals morphological types, since the Dreaming cluster and its subdivision in subclusters also deal with forms and structures: of nature and types of environments and of time and space perceptions.

However, in addition to the aspects which I have analysed up till now, Mauss's concept entails a number of other elements, namely the legal, moral, aesthetic and psychological. As these modalities are also included in the concept of 'total social phenomena', I now conclude with a more general discussion about them in relation to indigenous systems of land tenure.

The *legal* aspect is not explicitly referred to in the texts of songs and myths, but the inextricable relationship between an Arnhem Land clan, or a section thereof, and tracts of its country of which the Dreaming cluster narrates is indisputable. Membership of a clan, explains Morphy (1991:48–9),

> gives an individual sets of rights and obligations with respect to the ownership of land and *mardayin*, which according to Yolngu [Aborigines from north-eastern Arnhem Land] ideology are jointly owned by the members of a clan as a whole. *Mardayin*, translated by Yolngu as 'history law', 'sacred law,' or simply 'law, centres around songs, dances, paintings, and sacred objects which relate to the actions of the *wanggar* [ancestral] beings in creating the land and the order of the world.

Thus rights in *mardayin* – as compiled in the Dreaming cluster in my example – and rights in land are, as Morphy concludes, two sides of the same coin. However these rights are not confined to the members of the land-owning clan. Space does not allow to work out here in detail the rather complex system of land tenure and the distinction between the possession of rights and the exercising of those rights (Morphy 1991:57–75). But in matters of land rights before courts it is essential to take into account that the children of the female members of a clan, who by definition belong to another clan, have also rights in and responsibility for the estate of their mother's clan. In Yolngu society these children hold, as Williams explains (1986:52) for the Yirrkala, the right of assent or veto 'to any major decision that affects their mother's land or their mother's mother's land, a right which they regularly exercise'. Also, the sons of female members of the land-owning group have the obligation to make and decorate ritual objects for their real or classificatory mother's brothers (Williams 1986:52–3).

This implies that not only Wurgigandjar men and women have rights and interests in their own clan estate and *madayin*, but also those male members of other clans who married Wurgigandjar women. At present these are men from clans called Djadewitjibi, Mildjingi and Ganalbingu. Some of these men with their families live more or less permanently on the Wurgigandjar estate and exercise their rights in Wurgigandjar land matters and ceremonial activities, just as Wurgigandjar men do in the *mardayin* and lands of their mother's and mother's mother's clans located westwards of the Gadji area. (See also Maddock's distinction between owners and managers (1972) and Keen's discussion (1994:124–30) on disputes over succession to land.)

These indigenous legal aspects pertaining to groups or individuals who have rights and interests in a clan's estate and its *mardayin* must play a vital role in the interpretation of the High Court's definition of 'native title' as 'the communal, group or individual interests of the Aboriginal peoples or Torres Strait Islanders in relation to land or waters' (ATSIC 1993), with the addition in section (a) that 'the rights and interests are possessed under the traditional laws acknowledged, and the traditional customs observed, by the Aboriginal people and Torres Strait Islanders'.

Looking at the *moral* and *aesthetic* aspects of this Dreaming cluster as *a total social phenomenon* has become somewhat delicate since 'traditional' Aboriginal attitudes towards nature have been hijacked by New Age adherents and conservationists, who construct idealized and mystified images of the people in question to serve their own agendas. By writing Aborigines back into the landscape and thus enhancing the romantic view that Aborigines are part of the environment itself, contemporary Aborigines are 'at risk of being judged, to their political disadvantage, a degeneration of such "natural man"' (Head, quoted in Rowse 1993:118). Rowse discusses in a section called 'Black against Green' (1993:11–117) how conservationists, who opposed the construction of a road in the rain forest, were surprised when Aborigines in Queensland welcomed the prospects of a better road. The conservationists had expected fierce support from the Aborigines in question. Chris Anderson (1989) analyses the background of these events. In this respect I agree with Rowse' advice (1993:113) to be cautious with general ideas about Aboriginal culture and world-views, and get to know the local political structures, customs and personalities.

My findings in this respect correspond also with Coomb's opinion (quoted in Rowse 1993:115) that Aboriginal social organization, such as the Arnhem Land clans, can be understood as a means of apportioning collective responsibilities for nature to particular families and individuals belonging to particular tracts of 'country'. Through the dances, songs, ritual enactments and paintings belonging to a particular Dreaming cluster, individuals and families composing a clan give shape to this responsibility. Or, as Morphy (1991:49) emphasizes: '"Looking" after the *mardayin*, then, is a requirement and responsibility of the landowners. However, use of the *mardayin* is also a statement about rights in land, since the *mardayin* represents an ancestral charter to the land.'

Use of the *mardayin* in a morally responsible way presupposes knowledge and, according to Hiatt and Jones, to be knowledgeable (or 'enlightened') is to be able to sing and enact stories of the totems of one's group and one's place (quoted in Rowse, 1993:110). The emphasis is on land and nature, but it is a humanized nature, both in a practical and in a morphological sense: practical because one of the responsibilities is to 'clean up the country' through seasonal fire-stick farming, which permits nature to regenerate and transforms, in Aboriginal terminology, 'wild' country into 'quiet' country; morphological because people, as said before, give form and structure to nature, space and time. Hiatt and Jones call it a 'unified systematic ontology' which is at once religion, philosophy and science (quoted in Rowse 1993:11).

A final aspect of the Dreaming cluster as total social phenomenon concerns its *psychological* domain. Learning the songs, dances and rites through a series of initiations instils attitudes in individuals so as to guarantee the long-term interests and survival of the group and the parts of the country connected with it.

Laudine (1994:111–12) concludes that totemism provides a 'framework for inculcating valued attitudes to nature, for reinforcing in the individual psyche a heightened sense of identification with nature which is ultimately of more use to the survival of the group than any short term individual exploitative pattern'.

Totemism, in Arnhem Land moulded into Dreaming clusters, personalizes the human relation to tracts of country and specific natural species. Munn (1970:157) in her study on central Australia calls it a fundamental 'mode of orientation' towards external objects (parts of the material world, like the country) and seeks to interpret the psychological ground for this orientation. This orientation, she asserts, is not indicative of a 'confusion of categories' or a failure to distinguish the subjective from the objective, the self from the object world. On the contrary, it should be apparent 'that this orientation is grounded in the awareness of subject–object distinctions' (Munn 1970:158). But each person regards himself as having some ancestral components inside him and so he is immediately bound to this external world (Munn 1970:159), being the transformation of this ancestral world. Through learning and performing (as in the Arnhem Land example) its clan's myths, songs, dances and paintings, each individual links, so to speak, the interior subjectivity of his or her person with important tracts of the country, being the external world. Special sites in the country are 'understood to be part of the self. Responsibility for country is not separated from responsibility for self' (Laudine 1994:106).

I have tried here to explore the multiple complexity of what in the Mabo judgment is called 'traditional systems of land tenure'. In the context of Mabo three brief conclusions may be relevant. First, my Arnhem Land example may demonstrate how such a system permeates all realms of Aboriginal cultural traditions and as such is truly a *total social phenomenon*. Second, Morphy's distinction between the possession of rights in *mardayin* and country, and the exercising of those rights, is most important in identifying all those who have a legal interest in land within the indigenous system of land tenure. The religious and economic interests in tracks of the country exceed the interest of the particular clan who happens to own that particular section of the land. Finally it should be stressed that it is necessary to move from general accounts of 'Aboriginality' to an engagement with the land-use wishes of particular Aboriginal people (Rowse 1993:114). Again I emphasize the many variations of indigenous relationships with the land throughout the continent and comply with Merlan's conclusion (Merlan 1994:25) that 'between the concept of native title's abstract existence and loss there exist a whole range of socio-historical possibilities'.

Note

1. The final draft of this paper was revised at the Centre for Aboriginal Economic Policy Research (CAEPR), Australian National University (ANU), Canberra. I am grateful for the hospitality and stimulating comments. I also thank Dr Ian Keen from the Department of Anthropology and Archaeology at ANU for his very valuable comments.

References

Altman, J. and Smith, D. (1995). Funding Aboriginal and Torres Strait Islander Representative Bodies under the 'Native Title Act 1993'. In: J. Fingleton (ed.), *Land, Rights, Laws: Issues of Native Title*, pp. 1–12. Canberra: Native Titles Research Unit, Australian Institute of Aboriginal and Torres Strait Islander Studies.

Anderson, C. (1989). Aborigines and Conservationism: the Daintree–Bloomfield Road. *Australian Journal of Social Issues* 24(3):214–27.

ATSIC (Aboriginal and Torres Strait Islander Commission) (1993). The Mabo Judgment. *Current Issues,* February.

Beckett, J. (1994). The Murray Island Land Case and the Problem of Cultural Continuity. In: W. Sanders (ed.), *Mabo and Native Title: Origins and Institutional Implications*, pp. 7–25. Canberra: Centre for Aboriginal Economic Policy Research (Research Monograph no. 7).

Berndt, C.H. (1970). Monsoon and Honeywind. In: J. Pouillon and P. Marandu (eds), *Echanges et Communications. Mélanges offerts à Claude Lévi-Strauss*, Vol 2, pp. 1306–26. La Hague: Mouton.

Borsboom, A. (1978a). Dreaming Clusters among Marangu Clans. In: L.R. Hiatt (ed.), *Australian Aboriginal Concepts*, pp. 106–21. New Jersey: Humanities Press.

—— (1978b). *Maradjiri. A Modern Ritual Complex in Arnhem Land, North Australia.* Nijmegen: University of Nijmegen.

—— (1992). Millenarianism. Australian Aborigines and the European Myth of Primitivism. *Canberra Anthropology* 16(2):11–27.

Keen, I. (1994). *Knowledge and Secrecy in Aboriginal Religion.* Oxford: Clarendon Press.

Laudine, C. (1994). Aboriginal Environmental Knowledge. Science, Religion or Education for Group Survival? M.A. thesis, Macquarie University.

Leach, E.R. (1971). *Rethinking Anthropology.* London: Athlone.

Maddock, K. (1972). *The Australian Aborigines.* London: Allan Lane, The Penguin Press.

Mauss, M. (1980). *The Gift. Forms and Function of Exchange in Archaic Societies.* London: Routledge and Keegan. (First published in 1925.)

Merlan, F. (1994). Entitlement and Need: Concepts Underlying and in Land Rights and Native Title Acts. In: M. Edmunds (ed.), *Claims to Knowledge, Claims to Country*, pp. 12–27. Canberra: Native Titles Research Unit, Australian Institute of Aboriginal and Torres Strait Islander Studies.

Morphy, H. (1991). *Ancestral Connections. Art and an Aboriginal System of Knowledge*. Chicago: University of Chicago Press.

Munn, N. (1970). The Transformation of Subject into Object in Walbiri and Pitjantjatjara Myth. In: R. Berndt (ed.), *Australian Aboriginal Anthropology*, pp. 114–63. Nedlands: University of Western Australia Press.

Native Titles Research Unit, Australian Institute of Aboriginal and Torres Strait Islander Studies (1995). *Land, Rights, Laws: Issues of Native Title*. M. Edwards (ed.). Issues Paper April 1995.

Ortner, S.B. (1973). On Key Symbols. *American Anthropologist* 75(5):1388–46.

Peterson, N. (1994). How to Recognise the Claimant: Individuals, Representatives and Groups. In: *Proof and Management of Native Title*, pp. 1–5. Canberra: Native Titles Research Unit, Australian Institute of Aboriginal and Torres Strait Islander Studies.

Rowse, T. (1993). *After Mabo. Interpreting Indigenous Traditions*. Melbourne: Melbourne University Press.

Sanders, W. (1994). Introduction. In: W. Sanders (ed.), *Mabo and Native Title: Origins and Institutional Implications*, pp. 1–7. Canberra: Centre for Aboriginal Economic Policy Research (Research Monograph no. 7).

Sutton, P. (1995). Atomism versus Collectivism: the Problem of Group Definition in Native Title Cases. In: J. Fingleton and J. Finlayson (eds), *Anthropology in the Native Title Era*, pp. 1–11. Canberra: Australian Institute of Aboriginal and Torres Strait Islander Studies.

Thomson, D. (1949). *Economic Structure and the Ceremonial Exchange Cycle in Arnhem Land*. Melbourne: Macmillan.

van Baal, J. (1963). The Cult of the Bull-Roarer in Australia and Southern New Guinea. *Bijdragen tot de Taal-, Land- en Volkenkunde* 119:201–14.

van der Leeden, A.C. (1970). Australia and New Guinea. Propositions Regarding Comparative Research. In: *Anniversary Contributions to Anthropology: Twelve Essays. Published on the Occasion of the 40th Anniversary of the Leiden Ethnological Society W.D.O.*, pp. 77–91. Leiden: Brill.

Warner, L. (1937). *Black Civilization. A Social Study of an Australian Tribe*. New York: Harper and Brothers Publishers.

Wassmann, J. (1991). *The Song to the Flying Fox*. Port Moresby: National Research Institute, Cultural Studies Division (Apwitihire: Studies in Papua New Guinea Musics, 2).

Williams, N.M. (1986). *The Yolngu and Their Land: A System of Land Tenure and the Fight for Recognition*. Stanford: Stanford University Press.

Chapter 14

'All One but Different':[1] Aboriginality: National Identity versus Local Diversification in Australia

Barbara Glowczewski

Today Aboriginal people of Australia are different from one another not only as a result of their cultural heritage (the continent used to have more than 500 languages) but also because of their individual history of contact – reserves, separation of the children from the parents, mixed descent, etc. Nevertheless most of them claim the existence of an 'Aboriginality' as a common identity even though its definition is not unanimous.[2] The emergence of this political pan-Aboriginality is accompanied by new affirmations of singular local identities which are only partly defined by tradition. To claim their Aboriginality, rather then opposing themselves as a political entity versus non-Aborigines, Aboriginal people affirm themselves first as different from and eventually opposed to their other Aboriginal neighbours. It is as if pan-Aboriginality itself was creating the emergence of those identity singularities, as if the process of anthropological and social heterogeneization was part and parcel of the creation of political uniformity.

This chapter will present some of the practices and discourses which oppose or draw together various government agencies and Aboriginal organizations (at local, state or federal level). Gender relations, theories of kinship and ritual innovations will also be considered. Aboriginality as a national identity is a construction of post-contact history in relation to non-Aborigines. But autochthonous status in terms of ethnic identity (by name, language or place) always existed as the foundation of the cohesion of each Aboriginal society or at least local group. It included indigenous theories of conception and kinship, social and marital organization, ways of economic survival and religious systems. The affirmation of an Aboriginal 'spirituality' associated with land rights and its political relations with Christian Churches will be discussed. Aboriginality as a melting-pot of collective traditions and militantism is undetachable from individual creations (art, literature, etc.) but also from conflicts of interests, which seem to promote the identity of local groups when they are placed in opposition to one another.

Totemic, Linguistic and Territorial Identities

In the last decade, essentialism, that is everything that has to do with the innate and the biological transmission of any features (physical, psychological or other), became taboo for many scholars. Everything has to be explained by the acquired: culture, social environment, education, etc. It is as if talking of differences in terms of skin colour, genes, blood, but also 'spirit' or any other notion of inherited 'essence' was racist.[3] Such a position denounces as racist all indigenous theories of descent and substances based on the transmission of some physical characters and/or of spiritual essences. It ignores the fact that for many indigenous people the opposition between innate and acquired just as between body and spirit does not make sense. In the name of 'political correctness', the voice of the people that anthropology studies ends up being denied. Instead of listening to what the 'others' have to say, academics pretend to impose on them what they think they shouldn't be allowed to say. To avoid such ethnocentric danger, the critic of essentialism should look at two aspects which are too often ignored: on one hand, the Western ideological effects of the prevalence of the acquired on the innate and, on the other hand, the specificity and the place in identity discourses of the indigenous 'essentialist' theories. In Australia, as for many other Oceanian cultures, essentialism is indissoluble from a certain relation to the environment, which differentiates people according to their places of identification.[4]

The Australian debate about spirit versus semen is famous (Tonkinson 1978). I will not answer here the question if Aboriginal people were aware or not of the relation between copulation and conception. What's important is that they repeated for decades and continue to do so: there is no child without a spirit-child who chooses the mother he wants to be born from. It means that a person is something other than the simple result of a biological transmission. There is no body without a spirit, and this spirit comes from somewhere other than the father or the mother. The spirit-child transmits 'essences' which identify the child in spirit and in flesh with some members of his family group, but also with some animals, plants or natural phenomena – totems – and finally with a place. It is often in a dream announcing the future birth that the mother, the father or somebody else discovers the place and name of the animal and the plant embodied by the spirit-child and that will become the child's totem. For most of the central and northern groups spirit-children as part of the ancestral essence were dropped by some ancestral heroes in different places waiting to be born. At the death of a man or a woman the spirit-child returns to the same spot that he came from, waiting to be born again.

Austrialianists usually call totems 'Dreamings', as in many Aboriginal languages the word for dream is used to refer to the totemic species (Jukurrpa, Alchera, Bugarri, Wangarr, etc.); but these indigenous concepts also refer to spiritual essences, the ancestors, their myths, their geographical itineraries and the whole time–space where these actions happened and can be experienced by the dreamers (Stanner 1965; Glowczewski 1991). The notion of the Dreaming and the articulation between a parallel time–space, its eternal ancestors, totems and places and their system of transmission vary in each society. Even if there is no unanimous definition, all these Aboriginal theories reveal a basic principle: the identity of each person is founded on an exterior agency that internally links him or her to a group, to some mythical ancestors, to different (totemic) species and places.

The development of the foetus is animated by the spirit-child, which comes from a rock, a tree or a water-hole. For the Central Desert groups, this spirit-child gives to the child the power to move and to talk, and it is often identified by a name which is the condensed version of a Dreaming song. The foetus is reacting to all ingested substances; that is why mothers can be submitted to various food taboos during pregnancy and also breast-feeding. In some groups semen through sex was supposed to help the feeding of the foetus and fathers had to also follow food taboos. The eventual resemblance to the father or the mother was explained by the Dreaming, the totemic essence: all people sharing the same Dreaming are supposed to share some physical characteristics, which can differ for men and women.[5] Commonly the child is born with a Dreaming mark, which is explained by the circumstances in which the spirit entered the mother: for instance, a baby has a scar in the same spot as the kangaroo that was killed by the father, who did not know that this animal was the shape taken by the spirit-child. Beyond all their particularities, all Aboriginal theories of conception insist on the fact that the body and its substances, like blood, contain essences (life-forces, images) which transcend humanity and at the same time give to each person his or her singular human condition, a local identity which contributes to the collective identity of the land-owning group and of the larger language group.

The notion of humanity in most Aboriginal groups used to encompass the people who can understand each other, that is who talk a similar language or with whom the language group exchange goods or rituals. People with whom one has nothing in common were more or less assimilated to 'non-humans'. Traditionally the boundaries of the 'tribal' identities were much more fluid because they were redefined with new alliances that drew together different groups for exchanges of goods or rituals. Marriages were most often endogamous in the language group but regular marriages between groups of different languages were one way to renew or inaugurate alliances.

Mythic Filiations and Ritual Alliances

If alliances are embodied in marriages, first of all they are ritually and mythologically founded. People of different groups can share common non-human ancestors if they share the same totemic names. Itineraries of the travels of those mythical ancestors – the Dreamings – connect the individuals and the groups, making them share a common totemic identity: Kangaroo Dreaming, Goanna Dreaming or Rain Dreaming. Some of those roads extend over several thousand kilometres, connecting groups from different language groups (tribes). It is through the celebration of rituals associated with those mythical travels that classificatory kinship is constantly reproduced, as each of the mythical heroes is defined by a name in the system of two moieties, four sections and six or eight subsections (Glowczewski 1991). Aboriginal people call their subsection, section or moiety name their 'skin' or their 'body'. People who are not related by blood call themselves 'brothers' or 'sisters' when they share the same moiety, section or subsection name, and they use another kin term (mother, father, brother-in-law, sister-in-law, etc.) to address anybody else.

Basically this system aims at the distribution of ritual roles (marriages are arranged according to more complex kin considerations). During any ceremony – initiation, funeral, totemic ritual – everybody receives his or her role according to the relation between the name of his category (moiety, section or subsection) and the name of the category of the initiate, the deceased or the ancestor celebrated. It is the position of 'brother', 'father', 'mother', 'spouse' or 'mother-in-law', etc. which will determine the role to play: for instance, only a 'father-in-law' (by his category) can initiate a boy. In other words, the roles change for the same person according to the ceremony which is performed; he or she ends up playing in turn all the possible roles. Outsiders are automatically placed in the kin system by being identified with one or other of the categories: there are never more that eight roles (the eight subsections). This system, which is still applied in the communities or towns whose inhabitants have maintained a ritual life, explains how various totemic identities can be constructed.

A man or a woman is not only identified by the totemic essence and place of its conception (his conception Dreaming) but he also acquires the totemic essence (Dreaming) of his father's line, mother's line or some other group. This is not innate but acquired through rituals. Gaining through rituals many classificatory fathers and mothers, a man or woman does not systematically share the totemic essence of all those people. But in some totemic ceremonies all the men or women, according to their kin category, can be identified with the Dreaming essence of the celebrated totemic ancestor for the time of the ceremony. Rituals constantly reaffirm singular Dreaming filiations shared between men, non-human ancestors and places and by such they maintain those singularities between all the allies. Aboriginal people call this in English the Law. Traditionally all men and women had to become Law men or Law women by following different Laws (rituals), receiving Law messages through dreams (songs, paintings) and participating in the circulation of those rituals among different groups.

The circulation of different Laws strengthens kinship and

alliance links while reaffirming the differences of identities. With colonization the circulation of rituals has been accelerated: the coastal or river groups who were violently touched by European enterprises, welfare and missions elaborated and exported new rituals in the desert; in return desert groups exported some of their cults. This has created not so much a uniformity of beliefs but a mythico-historical continuity that sometimes has given rise to messianic cults (Glowczewski 1983; Swain and Rose 1988). Some Dreamings are shared by different linguistic groups; for instance the Two-Men Dreaming line runs from the Central Desert to the north-west coast and back south past more then ten groups (Warlpiri, Kukatja, Ngarti, Wangkajungka, Mangala, Nyigina, Karajarri, Yawuru, Mardu, etc.): in each group one or two local groups who are the 'descendants' of these two ancestors own the land marked by them and the songs and rituals that celebrate their travels. In such a case, the groups having the most active ritual life – for instance in the desert – are seen by others as the custodians of the authenticity of a Dreaming order in the river or coastal regions where many Laws have been abandoned; on the other hand, Dreaming ancestors connected with the coastal regions are acknowledged by the desert groups.

Replacing one's own ceremonies by new ones means a partial change of identity. In the Kimberley, groups insist on the fact that they are different if they descend from groups speaking a different language (even when they do not talk this language any more) because they come from a different land. But they also underline the fact that they are 'one mob' when they share the same Laws. Some families who do not participate in any ceremony believe that Aboriginal identity has to be marked on the body of their sons through circumcision. Some parents send their sons to be initiated in another group who still practise initiation. Others have the operation performed in the hospital. Interestingly, while circumcision was traditionally (and still is in some places) the sign of the affiliation to a totemic group and the sign of the alliance with others, it has now become a sign proving pan-Aboriginality. But some Aborigines do not circumcise, claiming their identity on a different base.

Interdiction on Mixing the Colours

Until recently, administrators and settlers spoke of 'full-blood', 'half-caste' or 'quadroon'. Considering that Aborigines do not have recessive genes in the colour of their skin, the idea of a racial 'whitening' was developed: the 'half-caste' girls were separated from their family to be married to 'quadroon' boys, so that in a generation or two any trace of Aboriginal blood would disappear. In this process the men were not to be married to a lighter girl. At the turn of the century, Bischofs (1908), a German Pallotine father who was in charge of an Aboriginal mission in the Kimberley, wrote that all the children of an Aboriginal woman who had only one relation with an Asian man will be 'half-caste' (even if the father is 'full-blood').[6] Chief protector of the Aborigines of the north-west, he recommended that Aborigines be kept away from Europeans and from the indentured Asian labourers. Mixed unions were a crime, the women accused of prostitution were put in jail and the children taken away.

Many life stories talk of the strategies adopted to resist the segregationist policy. Today many Aboriginal parents or children are looking for their lost families. From the Aboriginal point of view, the unions with white or coloured men were not necessarily seen as a bad thing. Of course, there were many situations of rape but women also talk of their love stories. On the northern coast, 'yellow fellow' designates Asians or Aborigines of mixed descent (with Asians or Europeans). On the west coast, the expression 'coloured' is more often employed for Aborigines of mixed Asian descent who developed their own communities after many Asians were sent back to their countries. The Australian administration assimilated them to other Aborigines unless the 'whitening' policy gave them the status of Europeans.

Discrimination that did not allow Aboriginal people to be paid wages for their work pushed many families of mixed descent to ask for a certificate of exemption (which meant stopping any relation with Aboriginal people who were not exempted). Aborigines use the expressions 'full-blood' and 'half-caste' sometimes to oppose not so much the colour of the skin but the way of life: a 'full-blood' living in town can be called a 'half-caste'. Urban militants have denounced the use of those terms and popularized the expression 'part-Aboriginal'. The Australian law now states that any person of Aboriginal descent, whatever the colour of his or her skin, could identify as an Aboriginal. The claiming of an Aboriginal identity is partly due to the fact that, after having been depreciated by the whites for decades, it gained a positive aura with the 1967 referendum, which gave citizenship to all Aboriginal people, followed by various social advantages: scholarships and more recently the restitution of land.

Even though all people of mixed descent are officially recognized as Aboriginal, it happens that, when conflicts burst out in Aboriginal families or organizations, the opposition 'full-blood/ half-caste' reappears but with a different meaning: the reference to blood does not refer to a racial purity but a life-style. Anybody is accused of being a 'half-caste' whose behaviour is perceived as treason to the Aboriginal cause; but 'full-blood' can also be used as an insult, suggesting an incapacity to understand the new issues of Aboriginality.

Living according to two Laws – the Aboriginal one and the Government one – has been the way in many Aboriginal communities. For the Warlpiri the term for human, *yapa*, is used for all Aboriginal people in contrast with *kardiya*, used for the Europeans, that is all the migrants and their descendants. Aboriginal Law refers to Aboriginal identity in terms of locality, language, totemic essence (the Dreamings), classificatory kinship or ritual life. The question arises of the relation of such a definition to our Western categories, which very schematically oppose the identity of the self (for psychology or psychoanalysis) and the cultural identity (for classical anthropology and sociology). I believe that this dichotomy does not exist in Aboriginal societies, not because, as some suggest, the notion of the self would be only social – the individual identifying himself with the society – but because the society is entirely grounded on a notion of the self defining each individual as involved in a network of identifications and self-references which vary according to the context. In a context of social destructuration, Aboriginal identity can still be defined at a family or individual level through elements of the traditional notion of the self. People show their attachment to places and develop local Creoles. In towns extended kin networks and the obligation of assistance are very strong; people often interpret natural catastrophes and accidents by the fact that some Aborigines or non-Aborigines transgressed some aspect of the Law, for instance destroyed a Dreaming site by building a dam. The diagnosis of paranormal powers to kill or cure and the interpretation of visions, dreams or other signs are still common, especially to attribute a totemic and localized spirit-child to a newborn.

Christian Churches and Aboriginal Spirituality

At the conclusion of a women's conference held in March 1993, Aboriginal women recommended that Aboriginal Spirituality with its Dreamtime stories should be nationally registered as the Aboriginal religion because 'Aboriginal Spirituality gives to everybody from childhood to old age a sense of "who I am" . . . It is the Aboriginal identity. It is the respect of the elders, caring and sharing and a strong relation to and love of land.' It was advised that Aboriginal kids should be given Aboriginal names to strengthen their Aboriginality.[7] After decades of anthropological discussions on the religious or non-religious status of Aboriginal spirituality and at the time where deconstructivist tendencies blame traditional cultural references for fixing Aboriginality in an ideal and passé image of a mythical Dreamtime, it is an interesting challenge that the same elements are claimed by Aboriginal people, here women, as the basis of a religion to officialize and as the foundation of Aboriginal identity. Many young or older Aborigines who claim their Aboriginality do not rely on religious beliefs, or even reject them. But the expression 'caring and sharing', here used to define the religion, is also used in a secular way to define Aboriginal identity. Health organizations, for instance, use the slogan 'caring and sharing' to oppose risks and deviant behaviour (alcoholism, domestic violence, etc.).

Aboriginal Spirituality being part and parcel of the link with the land, claiming land necessarily involves proof of people's spiritual associations with the land and their responsibilities as custodians. Even when these responsibilities are not practised any more, it is in reference to the past culture as a heritage that Australian law recognizes the protection of Aboriginal sites. In other terms, religion has become synonymous with culture, not necessarily in the way it was traditionally practised but in a way acceptable to the national and international cultural norms: such as the status of recognized religions, school teaching, art market or legislation which is supposed to confirm the ancestral link between Aborigines and the land.

Aboriginal religion lies both in the individual and in a network of connections between individuals and their respective lands and myths. Each individual only exists because he (or she) embodies ancestral spirits of the land, those which are celebrated in the ritual life. Spirituality is thus indissoluble from the notion of person and place. From a traditionalist point of view the Aboriginal people who refuse this link of the individual to a spirit and to a specific place have 'lost' the knowledge of their link, but this link is still present through their ancestors and in their being because there is no individual without a territorialized spirit.

Is this to say that non autochthonous people would be without a spirit? A text of Stanner (1979) was called *White Man Got No Dreaming*, according to the expression of many Aborigines, for whom 'lacking Dreaming' (especially having no link to land) is the sign of not being Aboriginal. In Central Australia, when non-Aborigines live for a long time with Aborigines, their children who are born in that place are granted with a Dreaming, sign of their implantation. Some Aborigines also consider that Christianity or rather the story of the Bible and Christ is the Dreaming of the white people. Nevertheless, most of them notice a fundamental difference: the Australian Dreamings are inscribed in the land, while this European 'dreaming' pretends to be everywhere and nowhere. In reaction, some groups of the Kimberley say that Noah's ark has its secret place in the Australian desert to save them from a new flood (Kolig 1989).[8] For some Warlpiri the translation of the Bible into Warlpiri will allow the Christian God to 'learn their language' so that he recognizes the Warlpiri places and his representatives on earth – the government – give them the land back (Swain 1988).

Ancestral religion was indissoluble from the social and political organization – especially the principles of land using and land owning. Today the spiritual approach consists in defining the place of Aboriginal people in the Australian society, through the respect of their land rights in the context of development. Some Aboriginal people think they will achieve this through an alliance with the Christian God. Traditional elements – such as rhythms of songs, corporal painting, use of dreams – have sometimes been adapted to celebrate the Christian message. Indigenous Churches emerge with their specific cult. The official Churches, contrary to the new evangelical sects, tend to promote the spiritual importance of the attachment to the land.[9]

The Impossible Alliance: Paternalism and Self-determination

Christian conversion allows some groups to maintain their 'tribal' identity, but in many cases the ancient local and linguistic singularities are erased in the process (Swain and Rose 1988). Christianization was often violently imposed in the missions which took the children from their parents to teach them in English. Native languages were often lost. Missionaries prevented bestowal, polygamy and the big difference of age between the spouses. By opposing the marital prescriptions, the missions destroyed the social cohesion of the traditional alliances. And by forbidding the performance of most of the rituals that marked all the life cycle before, they weakened the models for becoming a man or a woman. Finally, by refusing non-Aboriginal paternity, they prevented the emergence of new forms of family structures.[10]

The mission paternalism has been criticized. In a way, the failure of many communities to manage their own affairs according to new structures of authority is related to decades of infantilization. The destitution of the authority of the father induces the multiplication of matrifocal domestic units, the men being left without any responsibility and drowning in grog (Hunter 1993). With the lack of family models, many young people, boys or girls, are also seduced by drinking. Christianity often finds its converts among the young or older drinkers: being a Christian becomes synonymous with 'not drinking'. For many Aborigines, because Christianity is based on a notion of evil (foreign to Aboriginal thought), it appears to be the only way they can protect themselves from all the evils – violence, destructuration, etc. – introduced by the settlers. Funerals are always celebrated by the Church today, but sometimes a traditional ritual is organized afterwards to find out who is responsible for the death. In the Fitzroy region a hairstring rope is passed around the gathering and when it shakes it indicates the culprit: it is the power of the Dreaming which is supposed to manifest itself.

Is the alliance of Christianity and Aboriginal spirituality compatible with the claim of two separate Laws (the Dreaming and the government as connected with the Bible)? Not really if we consider the inclusive character of the monotheist religion as well as of Western economics and politics. The same is true when traditional elements are recognized by Western institutions: art, school or the written justice. Aboriginal writers, artists, musicians or film makers, by showing images of Aborigines yesterday and today, participate in the promotion of Aboriginality and in defining this concept according to international cultural norms. Aboriginal school curriculums and bilingual programmes also have their double-sided aspect: the creativity and dynamism of the oral literature is threatened by the pretended 'authenticity' of written versions of the mythical stories, which then become laic (desacralized) in this process, or they are even transformed into children's tales instead of being initiatory knowledge for adults.

A young Aboriginal boy, who was a brilliant student in the Broome school and had been initiated by the Bard, thought that this knowledge of the bush did not belong in the school. The necessity of keeping the two modes of knowledge separate can also be seen in the way the elders protect their secrets: some books had to be withdrawn from shops because they were revealing things the old people did not want the young ones to discover in that way. Some refuse to transmit anything to the young people when they judge that they are not able to keep this knowledge.

In the north of Australia, a series of myths talk about the first contact. In all cases the white men either steal from the Aboriginal people or give them gifts that they refuse. This mythical interpretation of the contact should be compared with the fact that since Aboriginal people have been receiving money – salaries, allowances, pensions, royalties, etc. – they are often accused of wasting it (in cards, alcohol, etc.) as well as of breaking very quickly the cars and houses which are given to them. Aboriginal leaders are trying to change the image of the Aboriginal as a victim into one of achievement. But many families of Aboriginal men or women who constitute the new political élite or become artists of international renown find it hard to escape a certain pressure of their surroundings which draws them into fourth-world conditions even though they can earn a lot of money. In these circumstances, Aboriginal culture is perceived as more profitable to the non-Aboriginal dealers than to the Aboriginal artists. It is in a way the conjunction of the two myths: Aboriginal people refuse the gifts of the white men who steal their culture. In such a context can reconciliation be thought of in terms of an alliance? Alliance supposes that each partner keeps his differences both culturally and socially, that is keeps his autonomy and power of decision to manage his affairs. But all the Western gifts (money, food and others goods) and even the Australian laws relative to Aboriginal people continue to present a vice. If they do not destroy, they assimilate or do not leave any room for self-determination.

Some non-Aborigines claim that Aborigines develop a racism against them. It could be explained in the following way. Day and night, Aboriginal people are confronted with a bureaucratic machine that constantly frustrates their attempts at self-determination; they can only regard with suspicion any non-Aboriginal that they identify with this dominant order: an order that excludes them by stigmatizing them and alienates them while pretending to seduce them. This climate of suspicion and rejection is not restricted to relations with non-Aborigines: it is also observed between Aboriginal family groups. In such conflicts, the accusations are often that the other made a bad alliance with non-Aborigines or that they are like coconuts (black outside but white inside). When the achievement is big, the accusation is that the person is too different to have a legitimate place with the others. Such accusations encumber everyday life with tensions and conflicts. They show that the traditional ways of resolving conflicts do not operate any more. They also underline that cohabitation of different groups on the same spot is now permanent and not seasonal like before. It is because there are no new structures allowing the self-management of all those people that the Aboriginal population is always depending on a bureaucratic welfare that imposes on it its own contradictions. But it is also possible to see these conflicts in a positive way. They call for new ways of conciliation. When the opponents constantly redefine their position, they reinforce the local singularities and through this process Aboriginality is constructed.

Towards Reconciliation

One can roughly define five phases in the Australian Aboriginal policies:

1 After the violence of the contact of the nineteenth and early twentieth century, a policy of protection was installed. Ration depots and reserves were set up to keep the Aborigines away from the settlers unless contracts were established so that the

settlers could employ Aborigines (especially on cattle stations) without having to pay them.

2 The Native Administration Act in 1936 marked the beginning of the 'assimilation policy' based on the idea of skin whitening and the system of exemption. By forbidding Aboriginal people from different categories to mix together, the policy of assimilation only justified a form of apartheid which was already operating in many public places.

3 The referendum of 1967 extended the right to vote and citizenship to all Aboriginal people. It started the policy of 'integration'. For many Aborigines it was been summarized as 'the right to drink'. The obligation to give equal pay resulted in the massive dismissal of the free Aboriginal labour from the stations. A workless population was then forced to settle in reserves or on the fringe of the towns. The notion of a pluricultural Australia developed in relation to new migrants and helped in a way to give room to the specificity of the Aboriginal cultures.

4 In the 1970s, self-determination and self-management became the official priorities. It was expressing Aboriginal desire, but the complexities of Australian bureaucracy led to a failure (Tonkinson and Howard 1990; Hunter 1993). A committee of non-Aborigines and an ex-body of nationally elected Aboriginal representatives of the National Aboriginal Conference ((NAC) militated in favour of a treaty with the federal government.[11] In 1985, the NAC was dissolved to be replaced by a body of public servants: the Aboriginal Development Commission (ADC), which had a budget to buy land for Aborigines. The notion of a treaty was replaced by the one of reconciliation.

5 In 1990, the ADC and the old Department of Aboriginal Affairs were replaced by the Aboriginal and Torres Strait Islander Commission (ATSIC), formed as a federal hierarchy with nominated members (Aboriginal and non-Aboriginal)[12] and as regional councils with elected Aboriginal members. ATSIC was supposed to decentralize all the Aboriginal departments and decisions (for development, health, housing, etc.). Soon it was accused of not being decentralized enough, of not taking into account the decisions of its elected local councils, and even of not answering the real needs as expressed in the field.

In 1992, the Mabo case was won: it recognized a native title on the island of Murray for its inhabitants. This precedent changed the constitution, which until then did not recognize the ownership of land by Aboriginal people. The federal government had heated discussions with the State governments, mining trusts and other organizations, and after two years finally established a Mabo Law. This Law allows indigenous groups to claim a native title, region by region. Many non-Aboriginals see it as a threat for their backyards and the economy. The real issue, in my opinion, is not to oppose the interests of Aborigines to those of the whole nation. Recognizing Aboriginal people as the traditional owners of the land should allow them to participate in the decisions relative to the development of the nation so they can benefit from it not only on an individual basis but also collectively. After decades of control and welfare, money or services are not enough. A complete social restructuration with a development decided for themselves is needed. In the Kimberley, 51 per cent of the land used for cattle stations is already managed by Aboriginal people. This was possible because these stations were abandoned by the Europeans when the cattle industry started to fail. From the Aboriginal point of view the stations allow their survival. It is an example of a double-speed economy.

For the judges who passed the Mabo Law the understanding of native title is not the same: for Brenan the links to the land have to be customary, for Toohey it is only the occupation of land since 1788, without a constant presence but regular visits proving the possession. The High Court has excluded from the native title all land used for permanent public establishments, roads, etc. But native title can be claimed on national park or reserve lands. It has not been defined what will be the status of the land sold to private people or under lease – most cattle or fishing enterprises – or when some activities of development – mining or tourism – are started on them; the different conditions for compensation also have to be discussed. In the Northern Territory, the land handed over to Aboriginal Trusts through the Land Rights Act (1976) gives to the trustees a right of veto in relation to development and a right to royalties (4 per cent maximum) on the mining benefits. Most of the mining companies, supported by some local governments, refuse to generalize this system to the hundreds of native titles in request that are to be judged in special tribunals set up since the Mabo legislation.

In this complex situation, many lawyers and anthropologists are called to work to define the local content of eventual native titles. Aborigines themselves confront each other on the question of traditional inheritance of rights: for instance, with the transmission of land, is it a traditional mode that has to be followed, is it to be a patrilineal, matrilineal or other mode? Or should the colonial trauma be taken into account and the right to land given to all the descendants? In the 1970s, with the first land claims of the Northern Territory, some anthropologists started to question the systematization of the model of unilinear transmission and patrilocality. It was shown that in the Western Desert the links to land are first of all determined by the conception of Dreaming, which often differs from the father's Dreaming. And even in the Central Desert groups, who follow a patrilineal transmission of land, ownership cannot be detached from other rights on land that are systematically acquired by the matrikin and other allies: the question is of course especially sensitive when mining royalties are involved. As for the north-western groups of the Broome region, I am currently working, through oral history and analysis of ritual exchanges, at showing that the traditional system of land ownership and land use was much more complex than the patrilocality postulated by Radcliffe-Brown (Glowczewski 1998).

The current attitude on this issue – giving an anthropological content to the native titles – insists on the importance of this moment of Australian history where Aborigines consolidate their Aboriginality not as a political ideology but as a force of local cohesion, region by region.[13] Beyond common tendencies, localization means an identity singularization which is reproduced in two ways: first, through the continuity with the local ancestral heritage – such as renewing ceremonies, creating cultural festivals or reconstituting local history; secondly, the creation of new social structures, such as tribal or family corporations, having the aim to resettle on their land or to negotiate their participation in the development of towns or national parks, women's groups, refugees, etc.

It looks as if the polarization between local identities and a pan-Aboriginal identity is a very dynamic element in the creation of new alliances with non-Aboriginal local powers. The national alliances with national powers tend to balance the local ones. They also involve an international solidarity with indigenous groups from other parts of the world. Exchanges have developed both politically – at the United Nations – and culturally – for instance with the Festival of the Pacific. In such manifestions traditional Aboriginal dancing and painting are next to new Aboriginal talent in plastic arts, literature, theatre, music and cinema. The international recognition of these artists and the recent fame of some Aboriginal champions promote a cultural respect which erects them as symbols of a new political force. Aborigines who are close to their land, language and customs, just as the ones who have lost it, tend to identify with such a multiple-sided Aboriginality.

Notes

1. 'All different but one mob' is another expression often used by Aboriginal people to talk about their diversity and commonality (cf. documentary on the Kimberley, Milli Milli, 52 min., by Wayne Barker, Aboriginal film-maker).
2. Beckett (1988), Keen (1988), Thiele (1991). Keeffe (1988) opposes two types of identities: the identity of persistence is based on the identification by language, beliefs and religious practices, and any elements that characterize the way of life and a vision inherited from before the contact with non-Aborigines; the identity of resistance is orientated towards the revision of the contact history, the valorization of a national identity symbolized by a flag and land rights, the denunciation of the bad conditions of life, all analysed in terms of exclusion, exploitation, etc. In fact, persistence and resistance are often interwoven together and with other elements.
3. A special issue of *The Australian Journal of Anthropology* (Thiele 1991) has been dedicated to this problem in Australia.
4. For Watson (1990:39) ethnic differences culturally inherited can only be maintained if there is a conjunction between people and land.
5. For instance, among the Warlpiri of Lajamanu where I worked, the men of the Possum clan have their feet shaped like this animal, but the women have their lips which become darker in the season of the black plums *yawakiyi* (connected with the Possum Dreaming (Glowczewski 1989)).

6. This theory of impregnation, common for animals, was used by the Nazis: it was considered that an Aryan women was contaminated after having one sexual relation with a Jewish man so that all her future progeny would bear signs of this (Conte and Essner 1995:119–50).

7. 'Safe Keeping: Women's Business', Australian Indigenous Women and Museums National Conference, 6–8 March 1993, Adelaide; unpublished statement.

8. Also Jesus (Jinimin) showed himself to some Woneiga (Warnayaka Warlpiri) in Central Australia: he had a black and white skin and announced that Aboriginal people will have a white skin once they win their fight against the Europeans; he promised to protect their culture, which he took with him into the sky, under the form of two cults – Wanadjarra and Worgaia – which have since spread in all the Australian West (Petri and Petri Odermann 1964).

9. A manifesto on land rights was published by the Australian Council of Churches and the World Council of Churches supported Aboriginal land rights. In January 1988, the Australian Heads of Churches made a declaration 'Towards Reconciliation in Australian Society – Reconciliation and Aboriginal Australians' (unpublished paper) asking the Parliament to formally recognize the Aboriginal prehistory and its heritage; and the counsellor of the Catholic priests submitted a project to all political parties to negotiate the terms of a 'compact': this is when the term reconciliation was adopted.

10. Some descendants of Aborigines and Malays, Filipinos or Indonesians were Muslims: a mosque was even built in Broome, but the Christian authorities baptized the children.

11. In fact, many Aborigines were not keen on this idea of a treaty; for them no organization could pretend to sign in the name of all the groups concerned. But it became popular as a symbol, especially thanks to the song 'Treaty' of the Aboriginal Rock 'n' Roll Band Yothu Yindi from Arnhem Land.

12. The inhabitants of the Torres Strait, whose ancestors came from Melanesia to live on those islands long before the arrival of the Europeans, are now integrated in all the Aboriginal policies; similarly the Australian Institute for Aboriginal Studies (AIAS) has become the Australian Institute for Aboriginal and Torres Strait Islander Studies (AIATSIS).

13. Koori, a traditional name for the tribes of the south-east, has now entered the everyday language to refer to Aboriginal people of the Sydney/Melbourne region but Aborigines from other regions prefer to use their own local names, such as Nyoongar in the south-west (region of the town of Perth).

References

Beckett, J. (ed.) (1988). *Past and Present. The Construction of Aboriginality*, Canberra: Aboriginal Studies Press.

Bischofs, P.J. (1908). Die Niol Niol, ein Eingeborenenstamm in Nordwest-Australien. *Anthropos* 3:32-40.

Conte, E. and Essner, C. (1995). *La Quête de la race – Une anthropologie du nazisme*. Paris: Hachette.

Glowczewski, B. (1983). Manifestations symboliques d'une transition économique: le 'Juluru', culte intertribal du 'cargo'. *L'Homme* 23(2):7–35.

—— (1989). *Les Rêveurs du désert, Aborigènes d'Australie.* Paris: Plon.

—— (1991). *Du rêve à la loi chez les Aborigènes d'Australie*. Paris: Presses Universitaires de France.

—— (ed.) (1998). *Liyan-Yarndu Yawuru Oral History*. Broome: Magabala Books.

Hunter, E. (1993). *Aboriginal Health and History – Power and Prejudice in Remote Australia*. Cambridge: Cambridge University Press.

Keeffe, K. (1988). Aboriginality: Resistance and Persistence. *Australian Aboriginal Studies* 1:67–81.

Keen, I. (ed.) (1988). *Being Black: Aboriginal Cultures in 'Settled' Australia*. Canberra: Aboriginal Studies Press.

Kolig, E. (1989). *Dreamtime Politics – Religion, World View and Utopian Thought in Australian Aboriginal Society*. Berlin: Reimer.

Petri, H. and Petri Odermann, G. (1964). A Nativistic and Millenarian Movement in North West Autralia. In: T. Swain and D.B. Rose (eds), *Aboriginal Australians and Christian Missions*, pp. 391–6. Adelaide: Australian Association for the Study of Religions.

Stanner, W.E.H. (1965). The Dreaming. In: W.A. Lessa and E.Z. Vogt (eds), *Reader in Comparative Religion. An Anthropological Approach*, pp. 158–67. New York, Evanston and London: Harper and Row. (First published in 1958.)

—— (1979). *White Man Got No Dreaming, Essays 1938–73*. Canberra: Australian National University Press.

Swain, T. (1988). The Ghost of Space – Reflections on Warlpiri Christian Iconography and Ritual. In: T. Swain and D.B. Rose (eds), *Aboriginal Australians and Christian Missions*, pp. 452–69. Adelaide: Australian Association for the Study of Religions.

Swain, T. and Rose, D.B. (eds) (1988). *Aboriginal Australians and Christian Missions*. Adelaide: Australian Association for the Study of Religions.

Thiele, S. (ed.) (1991). *Reconsidering Aboriginality. The Australian Journal of Anthropology*, special issue 2(2).

Tonkinson, R. (1978). Semen Versus Spirit-Child in a Western Desert Culture. In: L.R. Hiatt (ed.), *Australian Aboriginal Concepts*, pp. 81–92. Canberra: Australian Institute of Aboriginal Studies.

Tonkinson, R. and Howard, M. (eds) (1990). *Going it Alone: Prospects for Aboriginal Autonomy*. Canberra: Aboriginal Studies Press.

Watson, J.B. (1990). Other People Do Other Things: Lamarckian Identities in Kainantu Subdistrict, Papua New Guinea. In: J. Linnekin and L. Poyer (eds), *Cultural Identity and Ethnicity in the Pacific*, pp. 17–41. Honolulu: University of Hawaii Press.

Chapter 15

Essentially Black, Essentially Australian, Essentially Opposed: Australian Anthropology and Its Uses of Aboriginal Identity

John Morton

Introduction

In 1986 Gillian Cowlishaw stated the following in a paper on 'Aborigines and Anthropologists': 'It is my contention that it is not the task of social scientists to define who is and who is not an Aborigine, or to pronounce on how far a community conforms to some typical or traditional form of Aboriginal society' (1986:10). She had in mind a form of anthropology which most anthropologists now deem to be out of date, an anthropology which, at least implicitly, aligned 'true' Aboriginality with certain markers of 'authentic tradition' (dreamings, hunting and gathering skills, particular types of kinship and marriage patterns, etc.) which have aided in creating currently popular ideas about 'the oldest living culture in the world' in contemporary Australia. Such alignment is usually now interpreted as hegemonic, with academic represent-ation being characterized (in Saidian terms) as 'Aboriginalist' (Hodge 1990; Hodge and Mishra 1991; Attwood 1992), producing authoritative truths about indigenous Australians within a context of the extension of colonial powers. However, according to Cowlishaw, there is now a break in the production of such knowledge, since Aboriginal people 'are themselves defining what Aborigines are . . . And part of the Aborigines' struggle today is over who is to define the very category "Aboriginal"' (1986:10). This leads her to pose the following rhetorical question: 'Will

anthropologists continue to attempt to [define this category]?'
(1986:10; cf. Cowlishaw 1987, 1988a, 1990a, 1992).

The relationship between anthropology and its traditional
subject-matter (its generalized 'Other') is certainly pressing in
Australia (as elsewhere) at the current time, and no more so than
in connection with the representation and identity of indigenous
Australians (Aborigines and Torres Strait Islanders), Fourth World
peoples routinely characterized as belonging to the ranks of the
colonized and the dominated.[1] To some extent, the Australian
situation is consistent with Adam Kuper's view that, within the
contemporary theoretical climate of pluralism and 'cacophony of
voices, the best lines are always given to the oppressed' (1994:543).
This is why Cowlishaw poses her rhetorical question to
anthropology within a context which emphasizes the recent
challenge of the Aboriginal production of knowledge. While
Cowlishaw does not say that 'only natives should study natives'
(Kuper 1994:545), she clearly accepts the view that Aboriginal
people know best when it comes to matters of their own identity.
This creates the situation where anthropologists no longer have
the authority to define the category 'Aboriginal'.

While I am partly sympathetic to this point of view, I, like Kuper
(1994), want to argue against certain forms of this logic, and I wish
to do so within a framework formed by recent debates about the
role of essentialism in academic representation. Cowlishaw's
argument is, I believe, part of an anti-essentialist trend in
anthropology which eschews explanatory recourse to 'race' or
'tradition', sometimes explicitly characterizing essentialism as a
sin which diverts us from dynamic conflicts and variations in
people's historical trajectories (see Rowse 1990 and Thiele 1991
for Australian examples). This trend is naturally related to the
'cacophony of voices' mentioned by Kuper, since the exorcism of
essences leads directly to pluralism and to the climate of opinion
which emphasizes that any anthropological text cannot be the final
word on the matter of identity. Paradoxically, however, at the same
moment that we are enjoined to deliver 'partial truths' (Clifford
1986), we are also expected to bear objective witness to 'the native's
point of view' (Geertz 1983; cf. Kuper 1994:542). Thus, if the claim
is made to adequately represent an indigenous point of view, and
that point of view is primary in the definition of identity, at what
point can the anthropologist refrain from serving to define
Aboriginal people?

This paradoxical situation appears to be motivated by anthropology's postcolonial predicament (Friedman 1994:67–77), and I would argue that it takes shape through a systematic process of denying ethnographic authority, even though that authority is, and has to be, covertly preserved. Moreover, I maintain that this authority is preserved precisely to the extent that it continues to be wedded to forms of essentialism which implicitly prescribe peculiar brands of Aboriginal identity fitted to postcolonialist conditions. That identity is usually framed positively by the idea of resistance, which is seen as a response to colonial domination, and negatively by the idea of tradition, which is often seen as the concern of conservative anthropology (or of 'foreign, metropolitan, exoticizing ethnography . . . equated with the experience of colonialism' (Kuper 1994:544)). In addition, this ongoing (but covert) presence of essentialism raises the question of appropriation. If older styles of anthropology in some sense took over the primitive and the exotic to use them in the service of Occidental identity (see Diamond 1981; Torgovnik 1990), to what extent would ongoing forms of essentialism under postcolonial conditions continue this process of assimilation?

I aim to broach such questions through an examination of the work of three writers who are drawn to a broad resistance model in Aboriginal studies – Cowlishaw herself, Andrew Lattas and Patrick Wolfe. The work of these three authors is, I suggest, broadly consistent in approach, notwithstanding some important differences in range, emphasis and critical understanding. Discussion of their work will thus allow me to demonstrate the coherence of the disparate themes with which they deal. In particular, I want to show how the explicit resistance ('oppositional') model of Aboriginal culture developed by Cowlishaw is linked, firstly, to a critique (developed by Lattas) of the intellectual appropriation of Aboriginality by white Australians and, secondly, an analysis (carried out by Wolfe) of the relationship of such appropriation to anthropological writing and the operation of the Australian nation-state.[2] I will begin by dealing further with the arguments put forward by Cowlishaw.

Lost and Found

It is now routinely asserted that Aboriginality is a discursive construction that is wholly an effect of colonial history. As a category of people, Aborigines did not exist before Europeans arrived in Australia to use that category and formulate the truths that it entailed (Attwood 1992). Cowlishaw (1987) has claimed that anthropology from its outset cooperated with this 'Aboriginalism' by continuously engaging with the largely compatible paradigms of 'race' and 'culture' (Kahn 1989), thus making purity of blood isomorphic with unsullied tradition. Being black and being traditional became the marks of authentic Aboriginality, thus bolstering the mutually interpenetrating images of 'an ancient race' and 'a 50,000-year-old culture', clichés that have retained their force to the present day, particularly in Australia. With Aborigines widely recognized as the most 'primitive' people on earth, anthropology, by concentrating virtually exclusively on quasi-pristine examples of Aboriginal society, came to implicitly authenticate a dark, exotic and traditional world, thus relegating those who were not dark, exotic and traditional to some other place essentially non-Aboriginal. This other place could be geographic-ally located in the more populous regions of Australia, where the presence of Euro-Australians was greatest, but it could also be located in time, with Aborigines in those same regions being referred to as 'contemporary' as opposed to 'traditional'. These space–time coordinates were correlated with 'race' and 'culture' to produce 'inauthentic' Aborigines as whites *manqués* – 'half-castes' who had 'lost their culture'.[3] So distorted is this picture that one is entitled to suspect that the deployment of such forms of racial and cultural essentialism are framed by some kind of wishful thinking or desire (a point I return to below).

Broadly speaking, the thrust of Cowlishaw's work, as expressed most expansively in her book, *Black, White or Brindle* (1988b), is to fill the functionalist void of 'settled' Australia (Keen 1988) with a largely novel, postcolonial appreciation of Aboriginality as an 'ongoing recreation of a distinct cultural heritage which also has its own vocabulary, its family form, pattern of personal interaction and even its own economy' (Cowlishaw 1988b:283; cf. Langton 1981). As Cowlishaw says elsewhere: 'One source of this culture has been the specific everyday experiences . . . which have given rise to common-sense . . . ideas which conflict with whites' common-sense concerning normality, propriety and the sanctity of private property' (1987:234). In a wider situation conditioned by 'the intrusion and hostility of whites' (1987:234), Aboriginal people have become 'better known for breaking the dominant taboos and not understanding the totems than for having totems and taboos of their own' (1987:232). In other words, theirs is a culture of resistance (or an oppositional culture). This statement is, of course, proffered as part of a definition of who Aborigines 'really' are.

Cowlishaw is explicit in her aim: she wants to counter the view that Aboriginal people in 'settled' Australia have 'lost their culture'. This she deems to be absurd, saying: 'One could as well lose one's biology' (1987:10). Such rhetoric is informed by a reading of anthropology's recent *rapprochement* with history, which seems to be closely allied to its suspicion of essentialism. So, for example, Cowlishaw quotes Eric Wolf's ironically titled *Europe and the People without History* (1982):

> In the rough and tumble of social interaction, groups are known to exploit the ambiguities of social forms, to impart new evaluations or valences to them, to borrow forms more expressive of their interests, or to create wholly new forms to answer to changed circumstances . . . 'A culture' is thus better seen as a series of processes that construct, reconstruct and dismantle cultural materials (in Cowlishaw 1988b:282).

This, she says:

> is a quite different way of viewing culture from the old tradition-retained-or-lost one. If culture is a creation, an expression of a human group's responses to their social existence, then the changing conditions of that existence do not mean a loss of culture . . . Rather there occurs a cultural response to a different situation. That is, the Aboriginal response to change is cultural by definition. While Aborigines have not chosen the weapons or the arena on which the struggle is played out, nonetheless they have . . . continually responded to and resisted the hegemony of white society (1986:10).

Essentializing anthropology thus appears incompatible with historical truth. But is it?

While Cowlishaw (1987) has made the point that, when functionalism took over from evolutionism, culture replaced race partly by maintaining a metaphorical equivalence, I would argue that history now often replaces culture in a similar way.[4] What is at stake in such anthropological transformations cannot, I think, be settled entirely by reference to empirical evidence, although I

admit that Cowlishaw's depiction of Aboriginal life in western
New South Wales, where she conducted her fieldwork, is largely
consistent with the facts there and elsewhere in Aboriginal
communities. That there is widespread resistance to white
authority cannot be doubted and I partly agree with Lattas when
he says that Cowlishaw makes a convincing case for 'atomised
and individualised resistances to police power and white culture'
being 'shared cultural experiences for Aborigines' which 'can form
the basis of their collective identity' (Lattas 1993:242; cf. Morris
1989). But, while contemporary moves in the direction of history
have brought to light much that is new about such countercolonial
experience, to what extent are these moves dependent upon the
same processes of partiality and essentialist theorizing that have
characterized the paradigms of earlier anthropological generations?

One relevant point has been taken up by Tim Rowse (1990; cf.
Morton 1989), who has claimed that Cowlishaw's work is spoiled
by a form of political essentialism which forces her into acts of
negative recognition, particularly in relation to non-resisting
Aborigines – those who, in one form or another, take up respectable
or semi-respectable positions in schools, bureaucracies and other
institutions. Cowlishaw refers to such people as 'interstitial' and
'not representative', thus making Rowse conclude:

> For her, Aboriginality equals resistance, and other strategies and styles
> of life (such as those of the interstitial group) are aberrations from
> Aboriginality's basic historical trajectory. Though Cowlishaw often
> shows us the dispersed and heterogeneous quality of contemporary
> Aboriginal responses to colonialism, like the anthropologists she
> criticises she has her own conception of what is truly and essentially
> Aboriginal (Rowse 1990:190).

Of course, nowhere does Cowlishaw ever directly say that
'interstitial' Aborigines are not 'real' Aborigines, and she has cited
this fact in her defence (Cowlishaw 1993:193). However, this does
nothing to allay the suspicion that Rowse is correct in identifying
her particular brand of essentialism, which is entailed by a kind
of ideological drift. After all, many of those conservative
anthropologists working in the functionalist era did not explicitly
say that 'non-traditional' Aborigines were not really Aboriginal
either, although this is all too easily read into their commentaries.
Surely, if an older anthropology contributed to the idea that

Aborigines in 'settled' Australia had lost their culture simply by overwhelmingly emphasizing (and therefore authorizing) the idea of the traditional black, a newer anthropology overwhelmingly emphasizing opposition contributes equally to the idea that those persons whom Aboriginal people sometimes refer to as 'yellafellas', 'flash blacks', 'coconuts' or 'up-town niggers' have lost their history.

There is, in fact, nothing in history which makes it intrinsically anti-essentialist (Meikle 1985). Indeed, there is nothing in any historical perspective which, in itself or by itself, militates against the construction of archetypes and the projection of these into the life worlds of others. For example, Steve Hawke, son of Australia's ex-prime minister, recently wrote a piece whose trailer read: 'Black history and tradition . . . can fill the hole at the core of white Australia's code of values' (1991–2). Here, Hawke manages to counter the drift of Cowlishaw's pronouncements by readily combining a conception of traditional culture with colonial history and further tells us about the famous Kimberley resistance hero, Jandamarra or Pigeon, whom he characterizes as 'the black Ned Kelly' – 'probably the figure in Australian history closest to Geronimo and the other great warriors of America' (1991–2:13). In his estimation, the Aboriginal people of the Kimberley 'have history coming out of their ears', since 'they have a sense of identity' and 'a sense of purpose' (1991–2:14). Obviously, a good deal of this surfeit of history lies in the theme of Jandamarra's resistance passing over into the myth of the hero (Muecke, Rumsey and Wirrunmurra 1985:81ff.; cf. Narogin 1990:165–78). I do not, of course, claim that Hawke and Cowlishaw have an identical agenda: they do not (and the nature of Hawke's should become clearer below). However, I do believe there are more than superficial similarities in their projects.

Some have claimed that Cowlishaw has adopted a romantic approach to Aboriginal resistance and I agree with that assessment. Rowse, for example, says that while an 'oppositional culture is meant to bestow some dignity on its participants, . . . some young men seem now to be falling into suicidal despair', and he suggests that an oppositional culture among Aboriginal people could equally well be interpreted as 'a culture without interests, eschewing the political process to celebrate an Otherness without future, sustained economically by welfare cheques without end' (1990:190). This image is, of course, intended to be a degrading one, and responsibility for such degradation in colonial and postcolonial history is precisely the matter in question at this point. While Lattas (1993:241–4) has defended Cowlishaw against the charge of romanticism, his claims do not deal with the straight-forward fact that concentrating on resistance and opposition as 'culture' valorizes certain practices which may in fact hardly be worthy of the name. Cowlishaw's rhetorical statements about 'loss of culture' being comparable with absurd ideas about 'loss of biology' obscure the fact that one can indeed lose one's biology – in sickness and in death.

This leads us directly to the unfashionable and paradoxical idea of a 'culture of poverty', which is consistent with the view that 'some forms of oppositional behaviour . . . may be highly destruct-ive both to their participants and to those closest to them, and may have the effect of further disrupting and immobilising the powerless' (Pettman 1991:191).[5] It may well be true that 'the charge of romanticism against Cowlishaw [is] made by those who would like to retain their role as experts' (Lattas 1993:242) in the analysis of Aboriginal politics and identity, but this is not necessarily an unhealthy anthropological state of affairs. After all, it is informed expertise which places one in a better position to judge, and it is in a matter of judgement that Cowlishaw and her critics disagree. Naturally, Cowlishaw's valorization of an Aboriginal culture of opposition (Lattas 1993:251–61) is consistent with Kuper's idea that in contemporary anthropology 'the best lines are always given to the oppressed', but it is obvious, I think, that this only partially corresponds with 'the native's point of view'. The force behind this drive to identify with a culture of resistance seems to be a desire to be viewed as 'radical'.

In fact, Aboriginality is simply too complex to wrap in an oppositional strait-jacket, and Cowlishaw has said as much herself (1994:82). In the first place, for many Aboriginal people who would count as 'interstitial' in Cowlishaw's terms, their mainstream success and respectability in Australian society is taken as a *measure* of their resistance, in so far as they may regard their elevation in status as a struggle against the odds which has actually permitted them to carry their fight into institutional domains which were previously exclusively white. Such Aborigines are clearly only 'coconuts' from a very particular point of view, although they certainly are often seen as being co-opted by mainstream society. Strangely, this marks the partiality of Cowlishaw's depiction at the same time that it affirms the general application of her terms.

Indeed, it strikes me that *any* anthropology which depicts Aboriginal people as persistently resilient and historically active serves to collaborate with an overall image of resistance consistent with the contemporary political slogans 'White Australia has a black history' and 'We have survived'. Perhaps, then, it is anthropologists, as well as Aborigines, who have history 'coming out of their ears'.

Secondly, while resistance is not incompatible with accommodation (Trigger 1992; cf. Cowlishaw 1993:184–5), it is certainly not necessarily inconsistent with the affirmation of tradition either. Cowlishaw has spent some considerable time exposing essentialist biases in the antiquarianism of salvage anthropology, and yet her criticisms, while largely valid, are perhaps too systematic. Aborigines are, in fact, sometimes *rightly* better known for their relatively exotic totems and taboos rather than their violation and studied ignorance of perceived white standards; yet this can often be taken as further evidence of resistance in the face of genocidal and ethnocidal threats. Cowlishaw does not explicitly deny this, but her damning treatment of those who pursue a 'traditionalist' agenda (Cowlishaw 1986:7–8) suggests that she is investing considerable effort in the protection of her oppositional preferences. As much was confirmed in her review of Ian Keen's edited volume *Being Black* (1988), when she accused the editor of being unqualified to deal with the complexities of Aboriginal identity in 'settled' Australia on the grounds that he had no expertise 'in the extensive literature and theories concerning Fourth World peoples, colonialism, and racism' and that his only claim to fame was to have solved 'the "Murngin problem," an abstruse anthropologist's conundrum' (Cowlishaw 1990b:246).[6] Once again, then, in this explicit devaluation of 'traditionalist' anthropology, the essentialist partiality of Cowlishaw's resistance model is brought to view, although the anthropological vision of the authentic, primitive black, and its extension into colonial and postcolonial discourses in the wider world have been more systematically explored and judged by others.

Appropriate Subjects

Cowlishaw is certainly correct in seeing the conservative anthropological obsession with (more or less) 'pristine' Aboriginal societies as embarrassing at the present time. Directly linked to this embarrassment is the public use of positive stereotypes of Aboriginal people based upon ideas of authentic tradition, many gleaned from standard anthropological textbooks (e.g. Elkin 1938; Berndt and Berndt 1964; Maddock 1972).[7] Broadly speaking, there is a veritable industry in 'authentic' Aboriginality in Australia, with a variety of commentators conspiring to construct a distinctively Australian national identity out of a new noble savagery and an indigenous sense of place (Morton 1996). The basic terms of this project have already been indicated by the words of Steve Hawke (quoted above): they are essentially redemptive, much in line with the famous saving of the white (American) soul portrayed so clearly in the immensely successful film, *Dances with Wolves* (Alexeyeff 1994:11–28). The Australian version of this theme (*Dances with Dingoes?*) has been extensively explored by Lattas (1990, 1991, 1992a).

Lattas pays particular attention to the popularity of the idea that 'white settler Australians are alienated from and hence need to be reconciled with their environment', particularly in certain 'discursive forms – art criticism, literary criticism, Christian theology, conservationism, and political commentary' (1990:51). While this alienation is portrayed as general in relation to the natural landscape, it has peculiar resonances in relation to Aboriginal people, who are routinely portrayed as having possessed a kind of harmony with the Antipodean conditions that non-indigenous Australians have found so hard to come to know. Colonization itself exemplifies the disjunction. While Aborigines, prior to the European invasion of Australia, are said to occupy a timeless, ritual space, a 'primordial scene of unity against which contemporary White Australian alienation is measured' (Lattas 1990:57), non-indigenous Australians are deemed responsible for all departures from this scene. In this way, colonization is metaphorized as a pseudo-Christian fall from grace, but, at the same time, Aboriginal suffering is also assimilated to the fate of Christ himself: 'In the place of the killing of Christ, the nation is invited to place its slaughter of Aborigines at the symbolic centre of its identity so as to give itself spirituality' (Lattas 1991:312). Hence, the reconciliation of indigenous and non-indigenous Australians becomes a national(ist) project (as is now formally the case).[8]

Lattas describes the operation of this redemptive logic in a variety of discursive movements, but typically characterizes it as an issue of appropriation, with 'Aboriginal beliefs and practices . . . being ascribed a western sacred quality; a sacred quality which comes not so much from Aboriginal beliefs but more from the significance of spirituality for a western soul' (1990:59). To save this soul, non-indigenous Australians must make amends for the sins of colonization and acknowledge the value of emulating an indigenous outlook. For Lattas, however, this liberal agenda – a version of what Rosaldo has aptly called 'imperialist nostalgia' (1989:69) – is pure fiction. It arises because Australian intellectuals socially produce the sense of lack that is taken to be axiomatic of Australian national identity in order to gain for themselves the role of experts in relation to a 'true' sense of self.

> These intellectuals create and require a sense of spiritual crisis in order to create a need for personal and national redemption. Through creating the emptiness we supposedly carry within us, they empower themselves with the custodial role of caring for a wounded national psyche, in much the same way as priests empower themselves through the wounds of Christ's crucifixion. A whole set of pastoral powers comes to be invested in these secular figures who have shifted spirituality from the care of priests and God and tied it much more closely to the projects of nationalism. This ascribed emptiness is, then, a space of power, a cultivated empty wound or bite that popular intellectuals inflict so that they can nurse these existential wounds with their redemptive truths and histories (Lattas 1992a:51).

Since Lattas (1993) has explicitly aligned himself with Cowlishaw's views of resistance and oppositional culture, it is worth noting a structural transformation between his and her work. While Cowlishaw downplays the significance of 'traditional' Aboriginal society in her depiction of Aboriginality, Lattas elevates this same 'tradition', although only in relation to an ideological climate he criticizes and disowns. In fact, then, their depictions of Aboriginality are two sides of the same coin, with the endorsement of black resistance to white authority being a corollary of the critique of the image of traditional Aborigines being in harmony with themselves and their environment. This latter identity, coextensive with (if not quite identical to) functionalist and structuralist premises concerning social solidarity and reciprocity, is evidently seen by Lattas (and perhaps Cowlishaw as well) as inauthentic, in so far as it is said to embody an inadequate analysis of the relationship between knowledge and power in a context of cultural appropriation. Of course, as with Cowlishaw, this leads to problems with Lattas's position: do the pastoral powers of public intellectuals cease to operate once they have reached Lattas's doorstep, or is he, like Cowlishaw, oblivious to his own role as anthropological policeman?

A clue to the answer to this question can be found in Lattas's (1993) problematic attempts to reconcile his adherence to a resistance model with the embracing of traditionalist logics by Aboriginal people. His position here is singularly uneasy and, seemingly paradoxically, follows on from an earlier critique of David Hollinsworth's attempt to argue that a resistance model of Aboriginality (rather than one based on discourses of genetic inheritance and cultural persistence) 'is preferable because it is the most inclusive, dynamic and least readily domesticated by state co-option' (Hollinsworth 1992a:151). This, of course, seems close to the spirit of Cowlishaw's work, although it is much more explicit in its prescriptive tone; yet Lattas criticizes it strongly for precisely the same reason that he criticizes 'imperialist nostalgia' – on the grounds that it is 'the politics of a white person . . . seeking to police the collective memories through which Aborigines invent and reclaim a measure of their authenticity' (Lattas 1992b:160). Lattas then extends precisely the same critique to all other white academics (notably Keeffe 1988 and Thiele 1991) who would, by way of a 'tyranny of [academic] theory', condemn Aboriginal people's essentialized identities. Finally, he proceeds to analyse Mudrooroo's *Writing from the Fringe* (Narogin 1990), in the process praising the Aboriginal author's acute recognition and analysis of an Aboriginal 'culture of poverty' and his corresponding embrace of cultural and racial essentialisms creating 'a mythic space and a primordial identity capable of providing a community with a sense of continuity and a sense of groundedness' (Lattas 1993:254).

There are some enormous intellectual contortions here, with Lattas constructing another structural transformation by way of inversion: a 'bad' employment of the resistance model is contrasted with a 'good' employment of holistic traditionalism. The constant feature which links this opposition with the earlier one between imperialist nostalgia and oppositional culture is, of course, the master polarity between black/Aboriginal and white/non-

Aboriginal. Indeed, in the end, his argument can be reduced to a simple formula: if one is black, any form of self-definition is legitimate; if one is white, one's definition of the Aboriginal other is at fault. Indeed, so keen is Lattas to be seen not to prescribe and police any form of Aboriginality from his standpoint as a white anthropologist that he angrily dismisses more explicit attempts by others to do this. Yet, in the process, he fails to notice how he implicitly valorizes, and therefore authorizes from his position as an academic, the work of Mudrooroo, putting it forward as a 'subtle and sympathetic reading of the identity politics of Aboriginality' (Lattas 1993:261). It is not surprising that writers like Hollinsworth (1992b:170–1) and Thiele (1993:77) react in astonishment in the face of Lattas's angry accusations, since the latter are a measure of his use of the same pastoral powers which he criticizes. In other words, the problem is as much his as theirs.

This is a very strong case of what Kuper (1994) calls giving the best lines to the oppressed. Indeed, Lattas's explicit aim is to give them the *only* lines, and this consideration looks as if it overrides all others. So, for example, while essentialism and appropriation are condemned as aspects of the reconciliation agenda at the heart of contemporary Australian nationalism, those same processes are praised when they are used by Aboriginal writers, at least when those writers appear to resist white hegemony. But, while I would agree with Lattas that essentialism is not something to be routinely dismissed, his understanding of this proposition remains distorting and inconsistent. In the first place, his discourse is baldly 'Occidentalist' (Carrier 1992), setting up a rigid opposition between a generalized Aboriginality, characterized fundamentally by its origin in oppression, and a uniform white institutional framework, defined by its correlative predatoriness. The contradiction generated by this particular form of essentialism is that it places Lattas in the latter category, and the only way he can deal with this is by vehemently denying and resisting his coevals, at the same time affirming and embracing the radical other as fellow fighter. Naturally enough, this is a redemptive project of reconciliation. As such, it entails identification with, and appropriation of, a particular form of Aboriginality. In short, notwithstanding any empirical problems with the Occidentalist framework, it implicitly endorses the same essential Aboriginal identity endorsed by Cowlishaw.

Inappropriate Anthropology

While both Cowlishaw and Lattas are concerned with the general character of anthropological scholarship in relation to the question of Aboriginal identity, this question has been most vigorously, interestingly and comprehensively pursued by Patrick Wolfe (1991, 1994a, b), who traces the relationship between knowledge and power within the twin contexts of institutional anthropology and the state. His analyses pertain to the 'tradititonalist' (particularly evolutionist and functionalist) styles of ethnographic depiction criticized, in their original form, by Cowlishaw and, in their appropriated derivatives, by Lattas. Of particular interest to Wolfe are: first, the concept of 'the Dreamtime' or 'Dreaming', as it originated in the work of Frank Gillen (1896); second, the hotly debated idea of Aboriginal ignorance of physiological paternity, originating partly in the work of Gillen's partner, Baldwin Spencer (Spencer and Gillen 1899); and, third, the general paradigm of structural-functionalism which Radcliffe-Brown (1930–1) introduced into Aboriginal studies, particularly in relation to social and local organization. In each of these instances, Wolfe finds that anthropological discourse is compatible with, and appropriated into, practices performed by various arms of the state.

At one point in his discussion of white appropriation of Aboriginal sacredness, Lattas (1990:63) suggests that it would be interesting to pursue the influence of Emile Durkheim and his book *The Elementary Forms of the Religious Life* (1915) in the creation of Aboriginality as a mythic or ritual space. Wolfe takes this suggestion beyond Durkheim alone to account for the (largely) anthropological creation of the Dreaming in terms of its place in a 'hegemonic language' (Wolfe 1991:198), where the 'concept encodes and sustains the subjugation and expropriation of the Koori [Aboriginal] population' (1991:199). Tracing the idea's history (most significantly) through Spencer and Gillen, A.P. Elkin and W.E.H. Stanner, he argues that the idea was conceived and sustained in anthropological discourse because of the general association of dreams and irrationality, typically portrayed, in the first instance, in Tylor's evolutionist theory of animism. From the moment of the Dreaming's first reception in anthropology, Aboriginal people were projected into vagueness. The Dreaming in turn became popularized in Australia, where it served to support the idea of *terra nullius*.[9] Aboriginality came to be defined as an aimless, somnambulant 'walkabout', with Aboriginal people being fantasized as having been 'asleep' prior to Europeans coming to wake them from their slumber. Hence, the European invasion was legitimized as the instigation of rational mindfulness, work and property. Anthropologists have continued to serve this colonial image whenever they have sought their exotic subjects at or beyond the frontier of white settlement, where ritual presence symbolizes economic and legal absence. Aborigines, having no history and occupying a timeless realm, have an authentic presence that is (or was) 'always somewhere else' (Wolfe 1991:215),[10] and to the extent that Aboriginal people have appropriated this usage for themselves in the reinvention of their traditions, they have acquiesced to the dominant discourse.

Animistic, sacred space is also implicated in the debate, still ongoing, over Aboriginal conception beliefs and knowledge of physiological paternity (or lack thereof). Wolfe shows how this debate has its origins in early debates about 'mother-right' and 'primal promiscuity', and about the link between both of these and 'supernatural impregnation' (1994a:168). Ignorance of phsyiological paternity was, it was supposed, the result of early forms of 'sexual chaos' (1994a:171) in human society, which made the 'obvious' tie between mother and child the primary kinship bond. In addition, the physiological distance between father and child(birth) allowed free reign for animistic thinking, which both broadly projected human agency into the environment and specifically attributed human conception to ancestral spirits dwelling in the landscape. Spencer and Gillen's work in Central Australia, from which also came the concept of the Dreaming, was to become the great confirmatory textual authority for this picture, although ethnographic reports in Australia had already for some time been veering in the same direction.

But it so happened that Spencer also came to give advice to government at a time when its (now notorious) assimilation policy was being framed. This time was also one when white Australians became increasingly concerned about the so called 'half-caste menace' – the increasing numbers of children with Aboriginal mothers and white fathers, who lent the lie to the idea that the Aboriginal race was dying out. Spencer's proposed solution to this problem (although it was not exclusively his own) was to disallow half-caste children to stay with their mothers in Aboriginal camps, effectively putting in place a 'eugenic expedient', now often known as 'breeding them [Aborigines] white' (Wolfe 1994a:167). For Wolfe, assimilation and evolutionist anthropology are consistent to the extent that each depended on an identical bipolar logic: ignorance of physiological paternity belonged to the evolutionary past; contact with the evolutionary present would naturally make this past fade away (and, one might add, in the process affirm white paternity as a metaphor for the conquest of 'virgin' black land). Suitably enough, Spencer marked this transition with a profession of Aboriginal people's ignorance of white paternity, albeit uncharacteristically posed in pidgin English: 'Too much me been eat em white man's flour' (Wolfe 1994a:194)[11] – which Wolfe interprets as 'a textual symptom of the primary linkage between his ethnography and the politics of assimilation' (1994a:194). Such linkage was, in fact, general.

For Wolfe, a further instance of this general phenomenon was the use of Radcliffe-Brown's ideas about local, social and totemic organization in Australia, which set the scene for anthropology's treatment of Australian tribes as 'contained social isolates which were impervious to historical change and dominated by ritual and kinship discourse' (Wolfe 1994b:109) and which 'did not conflict with the practical [economic] exigencies of settlement' (1994b:110). Wolfe calls this image 'repressive authenticity', which

> represents a complex set of relationships as a simple dichotomy. Shared features are anathema. Since the feature most crucially shared by Aborigines and colonisers was an exclusive economic interest in the same land, it is only to be expected that the symbols of Aboriginality which figure most prominently in repressive authenticity are precisely those which least conflict with settler-colonial economics (1994b:111).

The genetic equivalent to this authentic Aborigines was the so-called 'full-blood', whose counterpart, the 'half caste', was discussed in relation to the framing of the debate over ignorance of physiological paternity.

Radcliffe-Brown's construction of the 'real' Aborigine, and various variations thereof, eventually came to be embodied in the criteria for 'traditional ownership' of land according to the Aboriginal Land Rights (Northern Territory) Act of 1976, in spite of the classic model having been shown to be partially inadequate to ethnographic reality in the famous Gove (Yirrkala) land rights case of 1971. Moreover, Wolfe even goes so far as to suggest that little has changed with the Mabo judgment of 1992 (and the subsequent Native Title Act of 1993), in spite of the much vaunted 'overturning' of *terra nullius*, since, in order 'to qualify for native title, Aborigines have to prove "traditional connection" with the claimed land' (1994b:122). In other words, native title is most clearly available to Aboriginal people who have been least affected by *terra nullius* and who are still to be seen as occupying 'traditional' space and time (as opposed to other Aboriginal people whose rights are cast more in terms of those of the 'ordinary citizen'). The pay-off for the state lies in the symbolic capital (identical to that outlined by Lattas) it reaps from the reconciliation agenda, which has been firmly attached to Mabo, with Aboriginality coming to signify 'the real Australia'. At the end of the day, anthropology has provided the constructs out of which the invasion of 'Australia' is completed.[12]

When Rowse reviewed Cowlishaw's work, he stated that she seemed to have 'difficulty establishing an assured or stable position of enunciation' (Rowse 1990:186). We have seen, too, that Lattas's ground is equally problematic. It is interesting to note, therefore, that Wolfe, at the end of his account of the operation of 'repressive authenticity', appears similarly and self-consciously vulnerable, although this is not surprising given that he has on other occasions exhaustively worked through some of the contradictions involved in the non-Aboriginal academic's right to speak about Aboriginal issues (Wolfe 1992a, b; Hodge and Mishra 1992). In assimilating current waves of 'repressive authenticity' to a series of instantiations of a logic of elimination going back to the original invasion of Australia in 1788, Wolfe realizes that he could theoretically be charged (like Cowlishaw and Lattas) with foisting a resistance identity upon Aboriginal people:

> given the analysis of the central role that imposed definitions of Aboriginality have played in the Australian state's attempts to eliminate Aborigines, it would discredit – indeed, completely invalidate – my position if my own analysis were itself to dispense a definition of Aboriginality, yet another normative subject-position for Aborigines to be contained in. To this it may be objected that, in replacing one external or essential determination of Aboriginality (colour, genetic status, etc.) with another (invadedness) this analysis has fallen into the same trap. But I am not stipulating that Aborigines'

collective identity is contingent upon their sharing a sense of invadedness . . . *I have nothing to say about what makes people Aborigines to themselves and to other Aborigines . . . [My] procedure is entirely different from the invasive practice of prescribing proxy Aboriginalities, however gratifyingly oppositional these may seem* (Wolfe 1994b:129, my emphasis).

In addition to this, Wolfe also addresses the question of Aboriginal agency, 'which has been deliberately kept out of this analysis' (1994b:129), which is of a persisting structure (invadedness) rather than of varying events: 'My purpose has been to categorise the colonising strategies deployed in Australia [since first settlement]. It has not been to categorise Aboriginal strategies of resistance, survival or anything else' (1994b:130). Yet this statement seems problematic, because the net effect of the analysis is to demonstrate how 'Aboriginal and settler-colonial discourses remain distinct' (1994b:130). If this is indeed the case, and settler-colonial discourse remains intrinsically hegemonic and invasive, one might be tempted to assume that Aboriginal discourse *must* be oppositional, since, if it is not, then the agency of Aboriginal people has merely been co-opted to a regime which contains resistance and pursues assimilation – a position that would recapitulate that of Cowlishaw.

Wolfe, like both Cowlishaw and Lattas, does maintain a profile that is oppositional *for himself*: he is, like most of us in the postcolonial era, 'opposed' to conservative anthropology and its alliance with the history of invasion. In Wolfe's case, this operates as a systematic denial of the fact that he is in any sense scrutinizing 'the other'. From the outset, his 'tribe' is the anthropologists – Spencer, Gillen, Elkin, Stanner, Radcliffe-Brown and the like. In itself, this is naturally unproblematic, but to claim that one can examine anthropological discourses with no reference to, or judgement of, the posited empirical content of those discourses (Aboriginal people) seems to me singularly strange. Yet Wolfe does not make a single assessment of the ethnographic reality of the Dreaming, ignorance of physiological paternity or social and local organization in Aboriginal Australia, and in this way he quarantines any objective notion of anthropological truth in order to protect a more Foucauldian approach to knowledge. Hence, both Aboriginal agency and indigenous Australian 'reality' can be bracketed, so that, on the face of it, Wolfe is not even talking about real Aboriginal people: his only concern is with (white) discourse.

This strategy is, I believe, tied to his use of the opposition between structure and event. For, if the flux of events in Australian history displaces the reality of 'the more it changes, the more it stays the same', this implies that one may legitimately treat the dominant discourse as wholly self-contained, except in so far as it imposes itself upon 'others' – a position which reproduces again the idea that Aboriginal discourse, in order to be distinctive, must be oppositional. As Wolfe avers elsewhere, assimilationism is still with us, even in the era of reconciliation and self-determination, as part of the 'sustained Australian state project of dissolving Aboriginal sovereignty into the larger Australian polity – a project whose contemporary bureaucratic incarnation relies heavily upon channelling Aboriginal resistance into officially detoxified arenas' (1992b:886). One of these arenas, Wolfe suggests, is the liberal academic establishment, with its antiracist agenda and its commitment to pluralism.

Here, then, we are back to the problem faced by Lattas – how to extricate oneself from a position of white dominance. Wolfe's answer is to say nothing at all about either 'the natives' or their 'point of view'. By the same token, others, like Hodge and Mishra (1991), who do engage with that point of view in the contemporary context, are deemed to be 'inescapably assimilationist' (Wolfe 1992a:335), on the grounds that they continue to be 'reluctant invaders' by appropriating Aboriginal voices, with academic power becoming 'the other's disempowerment' (1992a:337). Admittedly, this critique is heavily weighted towards a certain *kind* of academic work – the semiotic project, which Wolfe characterizes as peculiarly 'invasive' in its 'panoptic scope', leading to a 'dialogic frogmarch' in which 'invaded subjects are refused the option of not speaking' (1992a:337) and a 'hegemonic economy of communications' where the 'invader can even claim to be having a meaningful cross-cultural conversation' (1992a:338).

> For reluctant invaders, this critique entails a methodological injunction: speak when you're spoken to. It requires us to renounce . . . all that ethnographic ventriloquism that presumes to put words into the mouths of the colonized. . . . To call for an epistemological no-go zone might seem to offend the basic requirement for freedom of investigation. Yet it constitutes a prerequisite to free investigation, since without it the space where the other might speak will always be already filled . . . It enables an extratextual space to evade the

envious reach of the colonizing academy. In so doing, it acknowledges the alterity that is presupposed in the very notion of dialogue (1992a:338).

This, I would venture, is a sophisticated conception of the contradictions to be managed in any contemporary anthropological project. Indeed, an 'epistemological no-go zone' seems to be exactly what Wolfe has created in his own work on the relationship between anthropological knowledge and the creation of the Australian state; hence his refusal to become involved in the kind of 'ventriloquism' indulged in by earlier (and perhaps later) anthropologists. However, as he further remarks, this refusal should not be seen as an injunction to exclude Aboriginal voices: it is meant to draw a distinction between appropriation and response (Wolfe 1992b:887–8). My problem, though, is that the distinctiveness of this pair is hardly obvious, since, while we may aim to respond to what is said, the moment it is delivered it must become ours, which is to say *appropriated*. Arguably, all communication entails this *assimilation* of someone else's meaning and in certain respects it matters not a whit whether we are called or not called into dialogue. We can, as Wolfe suggests, 'speak when we're spoken to', but the initiation of conversation may not be the point, any more than the right to remain silent. The point is whether we believe we are right or wrong to say what we say, or whether it is right or wrong to not say it. Such decisions should not be determined by a view of discourse which allows no freedom to move outside a persistent and unchanging 'structure'.

Unlike Wolfe (1992b:887–8), as well as Hodge and Mishra (1992:881), I do not believe that guilt comes with the (academic) territory. It follows that I also do not believe that it is necessary to remain silent until called into conversation by some 'wholly other'. The opposition between invader and invaded is too situational for that and the right to speak becomes a matter for judgement in different situations. Wolfe's position does not seem to allow him that right, and yet there is a clear assumption that he has the right to judge his own kind (the anthropologist/historian/semiotician). That judgement finds academic discourses wanting in so far as they contribute to a definition of Aboriginality that is the object of a logic of elimination. While no explicit prescription is made in relation to Aboriginal people, an implicit one will be realized by readers, who infer that the only way to survive a completely systemic logic of elimination is to resist. In Hegelian terms one might say: if elimination is ceasing to be, resistance can be the only form of being. Politics follows logic in this case – unless, of course, one countenances the possibility of synthesis, which raises the spectre of assimilation. As Wolfe himself avers, 'one's position on binarism cannot be innocent' (1994b:94). It is thus necessary for me to conclude with a declaration.

Conclusion

Naturally enough, Australian anthropology has contributed extensively to historical events involving Aborigines, *and it must continue to do so, even when it says that it does not.* Indeed, I believe that the particular unions of black and white traced above measure the degree to which Cowlishaw, Lattas and Wolfe all identify with particular Aboriginal constituencies; but they also measure the degree to which 'Aboriginal and settler-colonial discourses' *cannot* 'remain distinct'. While it is clearly not Cowlishaw's, Lattas's or Wolfe's intention to prescribe any one identity for Aborigines as a whole, the matching of their oppositional strategies with those of others suggests that a form of appropriation and assimilation is inadvertently taking place. If, as Wolfe suggests, Aboriginal people dealing in the Dreaming are perforce 'speaking English' (1991:218), then this formula also applies when they deal in 'the struggle'. But is 'speaking English' synonymous with 'assimilation'?

Carrier has pointed out that anthropological essentialism cannot and should not be avoided.

> Essentialization appears to be inherent in the way Westerners, and probably most people, think and communicate. After all, to put a name to something is to identify its key characteristics and thereby essentialize it. Certainly essentialization is common in sociology and history . . . Further, some anthropological essentialization is the result of conscious intent . . . [and] anthropologists who are motivated to make or refute a point will shape their representations appropriately. The problem, then, is not essentialism itself. Instead, the problem is a failure to be conscious of essentialism, whether it springs from the assumptions with which we approach our subjects or the goals that motivate our writing (1992:207).

The wish that anthropology and cognate disciplines could ruthlessly expunge essentialism from academic discussions of Aboriginality is therefore absurd. If we eschew all ('racial' or 'cultural') definitions of Aboriginality (Thiele 1991:197) and refuse to take such definitions 'as a starting point for enquiry' (Thiele 1991:196), then the very phenomenon of Aboriginality disappears. It is not so much that Aborigines are necessarily repressed by such theorizing (Lattas 1993:249), but that it leaves anthropologists nothing to write about (from whatever point of view and to whatever effect). This critique is, of course, Weberian 'old hat' and is embodied in our routine strategic use of ideal types, which we now correctly recognize to be political as well as descriptive semiotic devices. And as far as Cowlishaw, Lattas and Wolfe are concerned, there is also a Marxist legacy to take into account: if Aborigines become a 'class' in and for itself through consciousness of oppression, then the role of the intellectual (the holder of some 'truth') must surely be to serve this becoming.

A recent attempt (Mahmood and Armstrong 1992) to rescue the concept of ethnicity from sustained attack has emphasized that a category or class is not necessarily formed in a classically Aristotelian way, by all its members sharing a common or identical trait. Rather, categories are often formed through what Wittgenstein called serial likenesses or family resemblances, 'where there need be no single attribute shared by all members of a category, as long as each member shares some feature with some other member' (Mahmood and Armstrong 1992:5). Related to this is the idea that categories are also formed through prototypes. Here a category is said to function

> in terms of a special set of features called the prototype features. These features are not necessarily shared by all the members but are shared by a substantial number of them, and they are weighted in virtue of how much they are shared. A member of the category that embodies the weighty features is considered a prototypical member, membership in general being determined by the extent to which a member embodies the prototype features (Mahmood and Armstrong 1992:5).

According to this view, ethnicity is not a useless category because of its inherent fuzziness when confronting the diverse realities of group membership, since this fuzziness is an inherent part of the very way we attain group membership as such.

However, something is missing here, and it relates very closely to the dilemmas faced and inadequately resolved by Cowlishaw, Lattas and Wolfe. Prototypes are facets of human action. Being 'ideal types', they carry judgement and are projected with force, which is to say that they are also both stereotypes and archetypes. Ethnic groups like Aborigines have, as it were, constantly been 'up for grabs' in terms of their prototypical features, with individual members maintaining their ethnic consciousness practically and typifying others as more or less like themselves according to their strategic interests. Aboriginality is not simply varied, and thus without any essential feature: it is variable precisely to the extent that Aboriginal people and others vary in their judgements and practices concerning what constitutes 'real' Aboriginality. As a judicious joining of Durkheim and Freud might suggest, a group is only formed through a stereotypical idealization, but this, being an archetypal projection, appears to come from without and take on the character of an external fact. We call this process 'recognition', and it is, of course, 'things' that we recognize. While it is fashionable in the current theoretical climate to speak about flux and indeterminacy, and to bemoan reification, this sometimes has the effect of making us forget that *identity, by its nature, is a 'thing in itself'*. Thus, we all (Aborigines and non-Aborigines) know what 'real' Aborigines are 'really' like – and this 'all' must include anthropologists, some of whom would surely quite rightly lack credibility if they were unable to display expertise by making statements about the very nature and essence of Aboriginality. We cannot escape this kind of project(ion): we can only try to make it credible *and* creditable.

As Cowlishaw, Lattas and Wolfe show well enough, anthropologists and other 'experts' have never simply described Aboriginal people in terms of anything other than ideal types, where these types, although revisable, can consistently be shown to reflect the values of particular people and the climates of their times. Essentializing Aboriginality is also to appropriate it and assimilate it as part of one's own identity, where it then acts as the basis for future projections. This means, of course, that our descriptions are always 'available' (Muecke 1992), although past and present relations between anthropologists and indigenous peoples have made this availability now highly problematic. 'Postcolonialism' has led some anthropologists to the widespread idea that 'the best ethnography is created through dialogue rather than being extracted or imposed on people from outside' (Mahmood and Armstrong 1992:13); yet many still negotiate a position of ethnographic authority with some ambivalence, being careful not to be seen to take self-determination from the hands of an indigenous self. In extreme cases, as with Wolfe, anthropologists assume authority only for their own kind.

Yet the definition of one's 'own kind' is, as we have seen, highly problematic, since, whatever differences might exist between anthropologists and their Aboriginal subjects, identifications are also made. These identifications, as in the evolutionist and functionalist pasts, are muted: after all, is not the subject-matter of anthropology 'the other' in opposition to 'the self'? But they are none the less powerful enough to render any straightforward emic/etic or insider/outsider distinction highly problematic – although, in any case, difference (the process of 'othering') has never been entirely incompatible with similarity (the process of 'assimilation'). In this sense, the history of anthropology parallels the history of the nation-state even more thoroughly than Wolfe might imagine, because it is evident that Australia's pluralist reconciliation agenda is mirrored in the contemporary relationship between Aborigines and academics. Adherence to a resistance model of Aboriginality is, in this sense, a redemptive project, making amends for an anthropology which contemporary practitioners would like to forget, so long as they can be forgiven, or remember, so long as they place sufficient distance between it and themselves. And the one thing we seem to imagine most is that the postcolonial other will not forgive being told who and what it might be.

However, as Durkheim might have said, autonomy (or self-determination) is not incompatible with relatedness; neither is it incompatible with constraint and inequalities of power. If there is a narrative reconstruction of anthropology occurring at the present time in Australia, the success or failure of 'reconciliation' will have to be judged not on the simple presence or absence of logics of appropriation, assimilation and redemption, which, divested of their negative connotations, are simply aspects of all self/other relations, but on the operation of those logics in particular situations. The task, therefore, is piecemeal and 'requires strategic engagement with "Aboriginalism" in its particulars ..., not a generalising ethical dismissal of its "complicity with colonialism"' (Rowse 1993:133). One difference we might look for constantly in this enterprise is between prescribing and informing judgements about what and who Aboriginal people might care or not care to be. I suggest we might find this difference in both the past and the present of Australian anthropology, not least in the ongoing unstable identifications between Aboriginal people and academics.

Notes

1. While indigenous Australians are now officially classified into two racial or cultural groups (Aborigines and Torres Strait Islanders), I am here primarily concerned with the depiction of Aboriginal people (and not their Melanesian counterparts).
2. This chapter has been pieced together from two conference presentations at sessions organized by Cowlishaw and Lattas, and some additional material mainly pertaining to the work of Wolfe. While my arguments are largely critical of these three authors, I freely acknowledge the partial accuracy and importance of their writing. My criticisms will, I hope, be accepted as a measure of that importance, as well as the engaging stimulation which I have derived from their publications. Thanks are due to Cowlishaw and Lattas for the opportunity to publicly rehearse some of the arguments, and to Wolfe, who generously responded to an earlier draft of the chapter, for helping me clarify others.
3. The most stark example of this attitude is found in the fairly recent words of N.J.B. Plomley, who wrote of the Tasmanians: 'Structurally, physiologically and psychologically hybrids are some mixture of their parents. In social terms, they belong to neither race (and are shunned by both), and lacking a racial background they have no history. If they wish to obtain a history, they must wholly identify themselves with the culture of one or other of their parents' (1977:66).
4. One might be reminded here of the fact that Boasian anthropology has in any case always conflated culture and history. As Plomley's remarks in the previous note suggest, race and history can likewise be conflated.
5. The question of the applicability of a culture of poverty argument to Aboriginal conditions is ongoing, having been explicitly raised by scholars like Langton (1981) and Brunton (1993). Similar arguments are currently being rerun in relation

to the views of Maori writer Alan Duff, whose fictional book *Once Were Warriors* (1990) has been made into a highly successful film, to some extent popularizing his political programme laid down elsewhere (Duff 1993). While Duff's views have come across as vigorous and shocking, they are far from novel. In the Australian context, Aboriginal writer Kevin Gilbert's indictments of myth-making blacks and sympathetic whites (1977:1–2) and blacks who live in squalor in the name of resistance (1973:198–9) come readily to mind.

6. The Murngin are now better known as the Yolngu: their 'problem', of course, pertains to kinship and marriage. Keen did his main ethnographic work with Yolngu people (see especially 1994). The 'Murngin problem' is not, of course, any more 'abstruse' than academic debates about race and culture. Cowlishaw is fond of accusing those with 'conservative' anthropological interests of being uninformed about these latter issues (for example, see her response to my (Morton 1989) review of her book; Cowlishaw 1993:193; cf. de Lepervanche 1993:10–11). Undoubtedly, concentrating on what people supposedly do not know makes it easier to ignore what they actually say.

7. See also the many later editions of these three books.

8. The Council for Aboriginal Reconciliation was set up in Australia by the federal government in 1991. Its stated aim is to achieve, through education, a situation where Aboriginal culture can maintain itself and peacefully coexist with non-Aboriginal culture.

9. *Terra nullius*, or 'unowned land', was the legal fiction upon which the Australian state was founded. At the present time, the doctrine is best known for having been officially rejected in the so-called 'Mabo judgment', which established for the first time that indigenous people in Australia can possess native title over their ancestral lands.

10. This 'somewhere else', as an unconscious space, is also discussed in Lattas's papers on the appropriation of Aboriginality.

11. As Wolfe points out, to affirm their expertise, Spencer and Gillen invariably rendered Aboriginal discourse in terms from indigenous languages (Wolfe 1994a:193), notably the Alice Springs dialect of Arunta (Aranda/Arrernte).

12. This summary of Wolfe is not intended to be complete. The

paper in question is a lengthy and involved excursion into the history of state discourses about Aborigines since 1788. Structural-functionalist anthropology completes a section of that history, although, in so far as that same section of history recapitulates its past and foreshadows its future in the reproduction of an ongoing structure of invadedness, it is continuous with the *whole* of the colonization of Australia.

References

Alexeyeff, K. (1994). Travels in Postcoloniality: Race, Gender and the Politics of Identity. Unpublished M.A. thesis, Monash University.

Attwood, B. (1992). Introduction. In: B. Attwood and J. Arnold (eds), *Power, Knowledge and Aborigines*, pp. i–xvi. *Journal of Australian Studies* special issue 35.

Berndt, R.M. and Berndt, C.H. (1964). *The World of the First Australians: an Introduction to the Traditional Life of the Australian Aborigines*. Sydney: Ure Smith.

Brunton, R. (1993). *Black Suffering, White Guilt? Aboriginal Disadvantage and the Royal Commission into Deaths in Custody.* Melbourne: Institute of Public Affairs.

Carrier, J. (1992). Occidentalism. *American Ethnologist* 19:195–212.

Clifford, J. (1986). Introduction: Partial Truths. In: J. Clifford and G.E. Marcus (eds), *Writing Culture: the Poetics and Politics of Ethnography*, pp. 1–26. Berkeley: University of California Press.

Cowlishaw, G. (1986). Aborigines and Anthropologists. *Australian Aboriginal Studies* 1:2–12.

—— (1987). Colour, Culture and the Aboriginalists. *Man* 22: 221–37.

—— (1988a). Australian Aboriginal Studies: the Anthropologists' Accounts. In: M. de Lepervanche and G. Bottomley (eds), *The Cultural Construction of Race*, pp. 60–79. Sydney: Sydney Association for Studies in Society and Culture.

—— (1988b). *Black, White or Brindle*. Cambridge: Cambridge University Press.

—— (1990a). Helping Anthropologists. *Canberra Anthropology* 13(2):1–28.

—— (1990b). Review of I. Keen (1988). *American Anthropologist* 92:246.

—— (1992). Studying Aborigines: Changing Canons in Anthropology and History. In: B. Attwood and J. Arnold (eds), *Power, Knowledge and Aborigines*, pp. 20–31. *Journal of Australian Studies* special issue 35.

—— (1993). Introduction: Representing Racial Issues. In: G. Cowlishaw (ed.), *The Politics of Representation and the Representation of Politics*, pp. 183–94. *Oceania* special issue 63(3).

—— (1994). Policing the Races. *Social Analysis* 36:71–92.

de Lepervanche, M. (1993). Women, Men and Anthropology. In: J. Marcus (ed.), *First in their Field: Women and Australian Anthropology*, pp. 1–13. Melbourne: Melbourne University Press.

Diamond, S. (1981). *In Search of the Primitive: a Critique of Civilization*. New Brunswick: Transaction Books.

Duff, A. (1990). *Once Were Warriors*. Auckland: Tandem Press.

—— (1993). *Maori: the Crisis and the Challenge*. Auckland: Harper Collins.

Durkheim, E. (1915). *The Elementary Forms of the Religious Life*. London: George Allen and Unwin.

Elkin, A.P. (1938). *The Australian Aborigines: How to Understand Them*. Sydney: Angus and Robertson.

Friedman, J. (1994). *Cultural Identity and Global Process*. London: Sage.

Geertz, C. (1983). 'From the Native's Point of View': on the Nature of Anthropological Understanding. In: C. Geertz, *Local Knowledge*, pp. 55–70. New York: Basic Books.

Gilbert, K. (1973). *Because a White Man'll Never Do It*. Sydney: Angus and Robertson.

—— (1977). *Living Black: Blacks Talk to Kevin Gilbert*. Ringwood: Penguin Books.

Gillen, F.J. (1896). Notes on Some Manners and Customs of the Aborigines of the McDonnell Ranges Belonging to the Arunta Tribe. In: W.B. Spencer (ed.), *Report on the Work of the Horn Expedition to Central Australia: Part IV, Anthropology*, pp. 159–96. Melbourne: Mullen and Slade.

Hawke, S. (1991–2). Poor Fellow White Country. *The Independent*, December/January:13–14.

Hodge, B. (1990). Aboriginal Truth and White Media: Eric Michaels Meets the Spirit of Aboriginalism. In: T. O'Regan (ed.), *Communication and Tradition: Essays after Eric Michaels*, pp. 201–25. *Continuum* special issue 3(2).

Hodge, B. and Mishra, V. (1991). *Dark Side of the Dream: Australian*

Literature and the Postcolonial Mind. Sydney: Allen and Unwin.

—— (1992). Semiotics and History: Entering a No-Go Zone with Patrick Wolfe. *Meanjin* 51:877–83.

Hollinsworth, D. (1992a). Discourses on Aboriginality and the Politics of Identity in Urban Australia. *Oceania* 63:137–55.

—— (1992b.) Coagulating Categories: a Reply to Responses. *Oceania* 63:168–71.

Kahn, J. (1989). Culture: Demise or Resurrection? *Critique of Anthropology* 9:5–25.

Keeffe, K. (1988). Aboriginality: Resistance and Persistence. *Australian Aboriginal Studies* 1:67–81.

Keen, I. (ed.) (1988). *Being Black: Aboriginal Cultures in 'Settled' Australia*. Canberra: Aboriginal Studies Press.

—— (1994). *Knowledge and Secrecy in an Aboriginal Religion: Yolngu of North-East Arnhem Land*. Oxford: Clarendon Press.

Kuper, A. (1994). Culture, Identity and the Project of a Cosmopolitan Anthropology. *Man* 29:537–54.

Langton, M. (1981). Urbanizing Aborigines: the Social Scientists' Great Deception. *Social Alternatives* 2(2):16–22.

Lattas, A. (1990). Aborigines and Contemporary Australian Nationalism: Primordiality and the Cultural Politics of Otherness. In: J. Marcus (ed.), *Writing Australian Culture: Text, Society and National Identity*, pp. 50–69. *Social Analysis* special issue 27.

—— (1991). Nationalism, Aesthetic Redemption and Aboriginality. *The Australian Journal of Anthropology* 2:307–24.

—— (1992a.). Primitivism, Nationalism and Individualism in Australian Popular Culture. In: B. Attwood and J. Arnold (eds), *Power, Knowledge and Aborigines*, pp. 45–58. *Journal of Australian Studies* special issue 35.

—— (1992b). Wiping the Blood off Aboriginality: the Politics of Aboriginal Embodiment in Contemporary Intellectual Debate. *Oceania* 63:160–4.

—— (1993). Essentialism, Memory and Resistance: Aboriginality and the Politics of Authenticity. In: G. Cowlishaw (ed.), *The Politics of Representation and the Representation of Politics*, pp. 240–67. *Oceania* special issue 63(3).

Maddock, K. (1972). *The Australian Aborigines: a Portrait of their Society*. Ringwood: Penguin.

Mahmood C.K. and Armstrong, S.L. (1992). Do Ethnic Groups Exist? A Cognitive Perspective on the Concept of Cultures. *Ethnology* 31:1–14.

Meikle, S. (1985). *Essentialism in the Thought of Karl Marx*. London: Duckworth.

Morris, B. (1989). *Domesticating Resistance: the Dhan-Gadi Aborigines and the Australian State*. Oxford: Berg.

Morton, J. (1989). Crisis? What Crisis? Australian Aboriginal Anthropology, 1988. In: J. Rhoads (ed.), *Australian Reviews of Anthropology*, pp. 5–16. *Mankind* special issue 19(1).

—— (1996). Aboriginality, Mabo and the Republic: Indigenising Australia. In: B. Attwood (ed.), *In the Age of Mabo: History, Aborigines and Australia*, pp. 117–35. Sydney: Allen and Unwin.

Muecke, S. (1992). Available Discourses on Aborigines. In: S. Muecke, *Textual Spaces: Aboriginality and Cultural Studies*, pp. 19–35. Kensington: New South Wales University Press.

Muecke, S., Rumsey, A. and Wirrunmarra, B. (1985). Pigeon the Outlaw: History as Texts. *Aboriginal History* 9:81–100.

Narogin, M. (1990). *Writing from the Fringe: a Study of Modern Aboriginal Literature*. Melbourne: Hyland House.

Pettman, J. (1991). Racism, Sexism and Sociology. In: G. Bottomley, M. de Lepervanche and J. Martin (eds), *Intersexions: Gender/Class/Culture/Ethnicity*, pp. 187–202. Sydney: Allen and Unwin.

Plomley, N.J.B. (1977). *The Tasmanian Aborigines: a Short Account of Them and Some Aspects of Their Life*. Launceston: Adult Education Division.

Radcliffe-Brown, A.R. (1930–1). The Social Organization of Australian Tribes. *Oceania* 1:34–63, 206–56, 322–41, 426–56.

Rosaldo, R. (1989). *Culture and Truth: the Remaking of Social Analysis*. Boston: Beacon Press.

Rowse, T. (1990). Are We All Blow-ins? *Oceania* 61:185–90.

—— (1993). *After Mabo: Interpreting Indigenous Traditions*. Melbourne: Melbourne University Press.

Spencer, B. and Gillen, F.J. (1899). *The Native Tribes of Central Australia*. London: Macmillan.

Thiele, S. (1991). Taking a Sociological Approach to Europeanness (Whiteness) and Aboriginality (Blackness). In: S. Thiele (ed.), *Reconsidering Aboriginality*, pp. 179–201. *The Australian Journal of Anthropology* special issue 2(2).

—— (1993). Response to Lattas. *Oceania* 64:77–8.

Torgovnik, M. (1990). *Gone Primitive: Savage Intellects, Modern Lives*. Chicago: Chicago University Press.

Trigger, D. (1992). *Whitefella Comin': Aboriginal Responses to*

Colonialism in Northern Australia. Cambridge: Cambridge University Press.

Wolf, E. (1982). *Europe and the People without History*. Berkeley: University of California Press.

Wolfe, P. (1991). On Being Woken Up: the Dreamtime in Anthropology and Australian Settler Culture. *Comparative Studies in Society and History* 33:197–224.

—— (1992a). Reluctant Invaders. *Meanjin* 51:333–8.

—— (1992b). Reply to Hodge and Mishra. *Meanjin* 51:884–8.

—— (1994a). 'White Man's Flour': Doctrines of Virgin Birth in Evolutionist Ethnogenetics and Australian State Formation. In: P. Pels and O. Salemnik (eds), *Colonial Ethnographies*, pp. 165–205. *History and Anthropology* special issue 8.

—— (1994b). Nation and MiscegeNation: Discursive Continuity in the Post-Mabo Era. *Social Analysis* 36:93–152.

Part IV

Questioning Western Democracy?

Chapter 16

Culture and Democracy among the Maori

Toon van Meijl

> When the control of social and economic forces in a society shifts from
> one section of the community that had traditionally monopolized it
> to another section, it is inevitable that the newly empowered unit
> will begin to assert itself by demanding a share of institutionalized
> authority commensurate with its strength (Hau'ofa 1994:415).

Since democracy has become one of the most popular political
ideologies in the world, many Pacific societies, too, have in recent
years become concerned with the introduction of political structures based, not only on descent, ascribed rank and chieftainship,
but also on political charisma, popular elections and representative
government (Institute of Pacific Studies 1992; Larmour 1994). In
Western Samoa, for example, the first election under universal
adult suffrage was held in 1991 after a referendum in 1990 lifted
the restriction of franchise to *matai*, those men holding ceremonial
titles as elected heads of a limited number of high-ranking families
(Tagaloa 1992; Yamamoto 1994; see also Tcherkézoff, this volume).
At the same time, there is an intensifying drive for a more
democratic system of government in Tonga. It is guided by a group
of intellectuals and church leaders known as the 'Pro-Democracy
Movement', which aspires to transform the archipelago's current
theocracy into a constitutional monarchy with people electing
parliament and the members of the executive or cabinet chosen
from it (Helu 1992; Latukefu 1993; Hau'ofa 1994).[1]

While the political changes in Samoa and Tonga are clearly
inspired by a Western, if not Westminster, model of representative
democracy, elsewhere in the Pacific the so-called liberal-democratic
tide has turned the other way. Thus, in Fiji the chiefly aristocracy

changed the postcolonial constitution and entrenched an indigenous Fijian majority in government after the descendants of the indentured labourers, which the British transported from India to work the Fijian sugar plantations in the nineteenth century, converted their demographic majority into a political majority in Parliament in 1987. The subsequent coups that were designed by a coalition of Fijian chiefs and the military, and which aimed at deposing the mainly Fijian Indian government led by represent-atives of the 'non-indigenous' population, do not require elaboration in this context (see Lawson 1991, 1993; Thomas 1990).

The coups in Fiji were condemned worldwide, although, interestingly, in the Pacific itself not everyone was unequivocally opposed to the moves of Lieutenant-Colonel Sitiveni Rabuka and his companion behind the scenes, the present Prime Minister of the new Republic, Ratu Sir Kamisese Mara. In New Zealand, for example, the coups were supported by a group of Maori nationalists, who described the Fijian stance for 'indigenous rights' as an example of 'assertive action' (Grant 1987; Young 1987). Returning from a visit to Fiji after the first coup, one of the Maori sympathizers commented: 'We were proud of [Rabuka], not only for Fiji but also for what he represented among Maori people . . . We feel that this is our country and migrant cultures are here on our terms . . . We say that if they don't respect our wishes . . . they had better leave this country' (quoted in Grant 1987:47).

Although this relatively radical view is not representative of Maori opinions about the coups in Fiji and certainly not about the position of immigrants in New Zealand, it does illustrate widespread Maori discontent with democracy. As an indigenous minority which has been eclipsed by a foreign majority on their own lands and which now make up an underdeveloped enclave within a liberal-democratic nation-state, Maori people share misgivings about democracy with other Fourth World peoples in the Pacific and elsewhere, notably Hawaii, Australia and North America (e.g. Tagupa 1992). The disadvantaged situation in which most indigenous minorities find themselves exemplifies the potentiality for a 'tyranny of the majority', which is latent in democracy, and, accordingly, that the protection of diverse interests and identities is not automatically guaranteed by democratic politics.

Needless to say, Maori and other indigenous peoples do not simply disfavour democracy *per se*. The argument against democracy in Fourth World societies is directed primarily at parliamentary forms of government which fail to check and balance majority rule and which insufficiently safeguard minority rights and indigenous identity. This conception of democracy is viewed as based on a foreign ideology that was introduced by imperial powers for ruling indigenous peoples in colonial settler states. As such, it is claimed to be radically opposed to the – democratic – values which are represented as characteristic of sociopolitical organization within indigenous societies. It is often argued that internal Maori politics, for example, are guided by the principles of consultation and consensus, ensuring that each and every individual is involved in all decision-making processes (see van Meijl 1994). Particularly in contrast with Western societies, Maori society is frequently represented as a direct and radical democracy enabling all individuals to exercise their rights, to protect their interests and to constitute their own identity. Indeed, the ideal-typical contrast between 'traditional' Maori society and liberal democracies, in which majorities might dominate minorities, is only one step removed from the argument that Maori society is essentially more democratic than European societies (see Vasil 1990:78).

The comparative question which society is more democratic is, of course, inappropriate since different conceptions of democracy are at stake. In my opinion, that is also the main reason why the 'Great Pacific Democracy Debate' is so elusive (Goldsmith 1994). Most reflections on the impact of democracy in the Pacific are, in spite of lip-service paid to 'culture', restricted to an analysis of its operation in political dimensions, or even more specifically to the parliamentary sector of political dimensions (e.g. Institute of Pacific Studies 1992).[2] Such a conception of democracy, however, is in my view excessively narrow and therefore unsuitable for the study of democracy in the Pacific, its relation to indigenous cultures and identities and the way in which the connection is locally articulated. After all, democracy is a multivalent concept with not only political, but also cultural, ideological, moral and even emotional connotations. In consequence, democracy may have different meanings in different cultural contexts. By the same token, democracy may be used to legitimize widely divergent political and cultural practices within the same social situation. The conceptual confusion surrounding the discourse of democracy is further compounded by the fact that the articulation of a political ideology in terms of democracy does not necessarily bear on political practice, while, paradoxically, a discourse on democracy may be absent in areas where sociopolitical developments are taking place which have been clearly influenced by the global dissemination of democracy.

In this chapter, several interpretations, usages and applications of the concept of democracy in Maori society will be discussed. The focus will be on seemingly inharmonious meanings of democracy, on the one hand, in counterhegemonic discourse arguing against the dominance of the European majority within the liberal-democratic New Zealand nation-state, and, on the other hand, in the debate about the recently reinforced position of tribal organizations, in which the need to elect representative or regional (pan-tribal) organizations to complement tribal organizations in (semi-)urban environments is advocated more frequently. My argument will be that the apparent ambivalence toward democracy in Maori society is not simply the result of a contradictory ideology, but due to the multivalence of democracy, which, in turn, is related to differences in sociocultural identities and political interests between various sections of the Maori population. I begin, however, with a reflection on the broader meaning of the concept of democracy in social sciences and the humanities.

De Tocqueville and 'the Democratic Revolution'

Etymologically democracy is derived from the Greek *demos*, 'people', and *kratos*, 'rule' or 'authority'. Thus, literally the word 'democracy' means 'the rule (or authority) of the people'. In ancient Greece the concept of democracy was coined to describe a new form of government in the *polis* or 'city-states', in which the whole citizen body formed the legislature. This form of government was made possible by the fact that a city-state's population rarely exceeded 10,000 persons, while women and slaves enjoyed no political rights.

Greek democracy was a brief historical episode that had little direct influence on the practice of modern democratic states. Nowadays, the word democracy is generally used to describe a form of government in which the supreme power is still vested in the people, but they no longer exercise the same rights in person as in ancient Greece, but do so indirectly through representatives chosen by them at periodically held free elections. In addition, democracy usually implies that the powers of the majority are exercised within a framework of constitutional restraints designed to guarantee all citizens the enjoyment of certain individual or collective rights, such as freedom of speech and religion. Although many different varieties of democracy exist, the one described here is by far the most common; it is known as liberal or constitutional democracy (Pinkey 1993:5–17).

Contemporary views of democracy have been shaped by profound intellectual and social developments taking place in Western societies since the Middle Ages. Particularly significant was the emergence of concepts of natural rights and political equality during the Enlightenment and the American and French revolutions. The development of democracy in the eighteenth and nineteenth century, particularly in the countries that were shaken up by revolutions, was studied in a seminal way by the French political scientist and historian Alexis de Tocqueville, who is now widely known as the founder of liberalism and to some extent also of modern sociology (Buiks 1979). Being one of the great thinkers and theoreticians of democracy, it is remarkable that a discussion of his work is absent in contemporary debates on democracy. His broad approach of democratization processes, notably in the United States, may still contribute to enlightening our understanding of the ambivalence surrounding democracy in Maori society.

De Tocqueville is best known for his book *De la démocratie en Amérique* (1961) (*Democracy in America*), which was first published between 1835 and 1840. It contained a perceptive analysis of the political and social system of the USA in the early nineteenth century. On the basis of observations, readings and discussions with a host of eminent Americans, de Tocqueville attempted to penetrate directly to the essentials of American society and to highlight that aspect which became crucial in his analysis of democracy: equality of conditions (*égalité de conditions*). In the perspective of de Tocqueville democracy was not limited to a political system, but associated primarily with what he labelled an *état social*, the social conditions in a society. In his view, democracy is above all a type of society which is characterized by a relatively egalitarian social structure and equal conditions of existence for all citizens.

Equality of conditions in a democratic society is specified to mean that all groups and individuals are not only equal before the law, but that in practice they also have equal opportunities in education and other sectors of society. Equal opportunities for all citizens eventually result in a levelling of living standards and imply that economical, political or social privileges no longer exist for anyone. Structural inequality is absent in democratic societies, as is any form of hierarchical stratification. Differences that may exist in democratic societies are not structural but individual.

The extension of democracy beyond the realm of law and politics in De Tocqueville's analysis is consistent with his view of democracy as a pattern of culture in which both material and spiritual elements are integrated. It also explains the key role of the now antiquated concept of *moeurs* in de Tocqueville's approach to democracy.[3] Nowadays we prefer the holistic anthropological concept of 'culture', which equally makes it possible to take into account in analysis all material and non-material aspects of an *état social* that may be described as democratic.

While in *De la démocratie en Amérique* de Tocqueville concentrated on a synchronic analysis of democracy in the USA, in his other main book, entitled *L'Ancien Régime et la révolution* (1952) (*The Old Regime and the Revolution*), which first appeared in 1856, he focused on a diachronic analysis of the emergence of democracy in France. The prime purpose of this publication was political: he sought mainly to demonstrate the continuity of political behaviour and attitudes that made postrevolutionary French society as prepared to accept despotism as that of the old regime.[4] The theoretical implication of de Tocqueville's political viewpoint in *L'Ancien Régime* was that democracy cannot be achieved by an instant revolution, such as the French Revolution in 1789. The institutionalization of democracy in a certain society is necessarily the result of a long-term process.[5]

De Tocqueville's analytical point of departure was, accordingly, the sociopolitical situation in the Middle Ages, which he described as *l'état social aristocratique* ('aristocratic social conditions'), and which he contrasted with the ideal type of *l'état social démocratique* ('democratic social conditions'). While the first is characterized by hierarchical stratification, democratic societies are relatively egalitarian. This crucial difference is particularly expressed in the social isolation of groups or classes in so-called aristocratic societies, membership of which is ascribed by birth. In democratic societies, on the other hand, the social lifestyle and the living standards of all people are more or less uniform, and there is a high degree of status mobility. As a result, social relations in democratic societies are more specific and open to individual initiative, whereas in situations characterized by a rigorous distinction between aristocracies and commoners social relations are usually diffuse and collectivist or group-orientated.

Needless to say, the transformation of aristocratic social conditions into democratic social conditions is a long and capricious process, the outcome of which depends to a large extent on the interplay between material conditions and the cultural pattern of a certain society. For similar reasons, the democratic revolution develops rather unevenly in different societies, although the structural character and tendency of developments is, according to de Tocqueville, universal.

Thus, de Tocqueville outlined a number of general features of the process of democratization, which leave sufficient space for local variations. This also makes his model for the analysis of democratization more suitable for the analysis of the relationship between democracy and culture in the Pacific than the narrow perspective of political science. The point may be illustrated with an analysis of democracy at various levels of society in New Zealand, with particular reference to the place of the Maori population therein.

Maori People and the New Zealand Nation-state

In view of the enlightening distinction between synchronic and diachronic analysis in the *oeuvre* of de Tocqueville, it may be useful to make a similar distinction in the analysis of culture and democracy in Maori society. Let me first describe the current state of the Maori nation, before elaborating on developments within New Zealand society, more specifically within Maori society.

Maori people make up an underdeveloped ethnic minority in the New Zealand nation-state. New Zealand counts a population of approximately 3.4 million people; of those 9.6 per cent identify their origin as Maori only, while 12 per cent indicate that they belong to more than one ethnic group, including Maori (Department of Statistics 1993). What characterizes the situation of Maori people in New Zealand most is their structural overrepresentation in negative social statistics. Research into the socio-economic position of the Maori has consistently revealed that they are locked into a vicious circle of underdevelopment: low educational achievement, lower-skilled jobs, high unemployment rates, low income, deprived status, low self-esteem, poor health and high crime rates (Department of Maori Affairs 1989).

Although Maori people are overrepresented in negative statistics of New Zealand, they are underrepresented in the political system of the country. Whilst it is generally acknowledged that in a democratic society special consideration is to be given to minority rights, there has been a notable absence of concern about the political representation of minorities that are clearly distinguisable on the basis of ethnonational criteria. The New Zealand settler colony, too, has a unitary, unicameral, cabinet form of government, although since 1867 the Maori people have been allocated four seats in Parliament. For several reasons, however, this form of ethnic representation has been grossly inadequate.[6]

The four Maori seats were introduced when few Maori people qualified to enrol on the basis of the then existing property provisions. For that reason, too, they were intended only as a temporary expedient until such time as the individualization of Maori land tenure would make it practical for Maori people to qualify for enrolment in terms of the European property qualification (Ward 1973:208–10). The Maori Representation Act of 1867 had a finite life of five years, but in 1872 it was re-enacted for a further five years, and in 1876 it was granted in perpetuity (Vasil 1990:173).

On a purely population basis, Maori people were clearly underrepresented in Parliament from the outset. If the government had granted the Maori people the right of proportional represent-ation in 1867 they would have been entitled to 20 seats, instead of which they gained only four, three in the North Island and one in the South Island. The government, however, was reluctant to increase the number of Maori seats. It seemed to introduce Maori representation only to ease public conscience until the seemingly inevitable occurred: the demise of 'the Maori race' (Stokes 1981:6). In this context, it is equally significant that the number of Maori seats has remained constant at four whereas the number of European seats has since increased to reflect population growth.[7]

Maori politicians are routinely elected by those registered on the Maori roll in arbitrarily defined electorates and on the basis of sheer party politics. Since they are serving extremely large electorates comprising many tribes, they have more difficulties than other Members of Parliament (MPs) in keeping in touch with their electors. As a result they are continually subjected to criticism of remoteness, on the one hand, and favouring their own tribe, on the other. The main criticism levelled at the four Maori MPs, however, is that they seem more concerned with loyalty to their political party than with the predicament of the Maori:

> The four Maori Members of Parliament are the pet rocks. They make statements – grandstanding, posturing, window-dressing. They play their role quite effectively for their Pakeha [European] masters. For their own self-respect they have to present themselves as the representatives of the Maori people and doing things for them. The Maori people, however, have no illusions about that. They have a clear notion of what they are. They are *politicians*, Maori politicians (cited in Vasil 1990:51; author's emphasis).[8]

This statement unequivocally exemplifies the fact that, since the four Maori MPs are considered encapsulated within the New Zealand democratic political system based on majority rule and without special provisions for Maori – minority – rights, they are not accepted singly or collectively as spokespeople for the Maori population. For that reason, too, the institution of the four Maori seats has been the subject of debate for the last twenty years (e.g. Stokes 1981; Lind-Mitchell 1985). New Zealand nationalists propounding the 'we are all one people' myth have argued that there is no justification for the continuation of special represent-ation since the four seats were granted to the Maori at a time when they held a disadvantaged position, which is now no longer believed to be the case. European bigots, on the other hand, have rejected the separate representation in parliament as a form of 'apartheid', but Maori opinion leaders themselves have rejected this as inappropriate and even manipulative, since 'apartheid' was enforced legally while New Zealand Maori people have the option to register either on the Maori or the non-Maori electoral roll (Lind-Mitchell 1985:19).

The more serious contributors to the debate on separate Maori parliamentary representation make a case either for abolition of the Maori seats, or for a significant increase in the number of seats. The advocates of abolition refer to the low number of Maori enrolments, leaving two-thirds of the eligible voters either not registered or enrolled on the general roll. In consequence, they pose the question at what level of majority it will be accepted that the Maori people wish the Maori seats to be dissolved. Their opponents have periodically argued for a significant increase in the number of Maori seats in order to ensure adequate represent- ation. The most recent proposal was formulated by the 1986 Royal Commission on the Electoral System recommending a mix between the existing system of single-member constituencies with single non-transferable votes, and proportional representation with single transferable votes. This system was described as mixed member proportional (MMP) system. The main objective of the new electoral system was to ensure that parties are represented in parliament in proportion to their support at the polls. To that end the number of parliamentary seats would be increased to 120, with half (sixty) elected on the present constituency basis, and the remaining sixty from lists provided by the political parties. An additional aim of the proposal was to provide for fair Maori representation; under the MMP system there could be up to twelve Maori seats in parliament, depending on the number of Maori people registered on the Maori roll. Maori people were also exempted from any threshold requirement (Henderson 1992: 179–80).

In 1993 a referendum was held on the MMP electoral system, which was voted in by a clear majority. Subsequently, a large-scale campaign was held to encourage Maori people to register on the Maori roll. Early in 1994 247,000 Maori voters were registered, but only 101,000 were registered on the Maori roll and as many as 146,000 Maori electors were registered on the general roll. At the same time, 39,000 Maori people were not registered at all (*New Zealand Herald* 17 January 1994).

The deadline for registration under the new electoral system was 14 April 1994. In spite of the efforts of Maori leaders to persuade Maori voters to switch from the general electoral roll to the Maori roll, however, only 21,598 voters responded to the Maori roll drive, ensuring just one extra Maori seat when the electoral boundaries were redrawn; another 16,000 voters were needed for a sixth Maori seat to be created (*New Zealand News UK* 27 April 1994, 2411:9). Needless to say, Maori leaders are disappointed with this result and they are currently in the process of challenging the government about the outcome of the procedure. They argue that the Minister of Justice failed to comply with the Electoral Act by neglecting to inform Maori properly about their rights and how to exercise their option over Maori seats (*New Zealand News UK* 15 June 1994, 2417:11). At the moment of writing it is still unclear whether the legal actions of Maori leaders have been successful,[9] but it is nevertheless beyond doubt that Maori people will not be represented by the twelve MPs to which they are proportionally entitled under the new electoral system.

Reasons for Maori reluctance to register on the Maori electoral roll can only be speculated about. It has often been argued that as Maori people had to confirm their electoral preferences at every Census, which in New Zealand is taken every five years, the system of electoral registration was simply an administrative mess. Another reason that has been given is that because the Maori seats have been regarded as safe Labour seats since the 1930s, many Maori have chosen to vote strategically and make their vote count in the general electorates. In my view, however, what also requires examination is to what extent Maori people are critical of their own leadership, for a recent Maori poll on Maori political issues suggests that approximately 40 per cent of the respondents simply saw no point in registering for the elections since a close correlation between nationally recognized Maori leaders and the Government was assumed (*New Zealand News UK* 18 May 1994, 2413:13). And many Maori people simply have no confidence in the ability of New Zealand's democratic system to terminate the Maori predicament. In a Maori perspective democracy is synonymous with colonization (Vasil 1990:39). In addition, confidence in Maori leadership does not seem to be outstanding in Maori society. Before elaborating on this hypothesis, however, it is necessary to provide a diachronic perspective on Maori sociopolitical organization and Maori leadership.

Changing Sociopolitical Relations in Maori Society

Changes in Maori sociopolitical organization cannot be understood without a perspective on the transformation of Maori society since the beginning of the nineteenth century when colonial settlement began, but it is obviously beyond the scope of this article to analyse these changes in any detail. The transformation of Maori society in colonial history, however, may to some extent be summarized by drawing a comparison with the model of the transformation of

Western society outlined by de Tocqueville. The French visionary of modernity drew a portrait of societies in which differentiated institutions are assigned the performance of specific, specialized tasks in a social system with a highly developed and complex division of labour, which he contrasted with kin communities in 'traditional' societies, which are at once the unit of production, consumption, socialization and authoritative decision-making. Rather than attaching rights or prerogatives to particular groups or persons, the differentiated institutions in modern societies tend to be governed and guided by general rules and regulations that derive their legitimacy from a high level of legal objectification. In principle, at least, they are not the agents of particular individuals such as a divine king, shaman or hereditary chief, who are generally endowed with prescriptive authority, but they act rather according to objectified precepts.

These contrasts by no means complete the characterization of modern and non-modern societies, nor are they the only ones that might be drawn. Nevertheless, they do indicate a striking similarity between modern and Maori society in the directions of change in a long-term perspective. Again I hasten to add, however, that in spite of the striking similarities between de Tocqueville's description of the 'democratic revolution' in Western societies and the transformation of Maori society, there are also important differences. While changes in Western societies were primarily generated by internal processes of industrialization, changes in colonial and postcolonial Maori society have principally been generated in interaction with external colonial forces.

Colonial history in New Zealand may for analytical purposes be divided into two phases that largely correspond with the nineteenth and twentieth century, respectively. The first stage may be described as the period in which the Maori were dispossessed of their lands, while the second may be characterized as the era of urbanization.

At the beginning of colonization, around the year 1800, Maori people were still in full control of their lands, but towards the end of the nineteenth century many Maori people had lost recognition of their interests. It began with obscure deals between Maori individuals and European settlers, of which either party had a different understanding: the first had the impression they were only leasing out the right of occupation, whereas the latter assumed they would acquire permanent title to the land that was the subject of the informal agreements made. As a corollary, several conflicts erupted, particularly after the signing of the Treaty of Waitangi in 1840 (see Orange 1987). Ultimately, these conflicts degenerated into a full-blown war, which lasted from 1859 until 1863. Following the wars of the 1860s one and a quarter million acres of land were confiscated. After the wars the New Zealand government consolidated its position on the confiscated lands, while outside the appropriated areas the sale of land was facilitated by the individualization of land titles. Thus, in the end, many Maori people were dispossessed of their tribal lands (Sorrenson 1956; Kawharu 1977).

Towards the end of the nineteenth century it was widely believed that the Maori as a people were doomed to extinction in the near future. The number of Maori counted at the Census reached an absolute low and the *fin de siècle* was characterized by widespread despondency. Hopes for a restoration of Maori sovereignty were non-existent and many Maori people had no option but to enter paid employment (Metge 1976:35). The massive movement of Maori people into the money economy of European society accelerated at the time of the Great Depression in the 1930s. Although land development schemes were introduced in areas where tribes had retained vast tracts of their land and these helped to mitigate the effects of the depression, elsewhere the only option Maori people had was to migrate from rural areas to the cities. The proportion of Maori people living in cities and boroughs increased from 9 per cent in 1936 to 15 per cent in 1945. Since then the Maori population in urban areas has increased at an average rate of 16 per cent a year (Metge 1964). Urbanization partly resulted from a deliberate government policy to create a cheap labour market. Many Maori people were persuaded to move to cities and enter new occupations in industries.

At present, approximately 80 per cent of the Maori population is residing in urban environments. This raises the issue of the implications of urbanization for traditional sociopolitical organization in Maori society. On the basis of the model of 'modernization' outlined by de Tocqueville, dramatic consequences for the sociopolitical structure of Maori society would be a logical, if not inevitable, outcome.[10] Indeed, the tribal organization of Maori society might formally be still intact, but I would argue that it is necessary to examine the impact of traditional forms of sociopolitical organization on cultural identity and social practice. In my view the dispossession of tribal lands in the course of colonial history has resulted in a situation in which most tribes continue to exist only as nominal organizations without an infrastructural foundation and concomitant influences on social interaction and the construction of a cultural identity. Maori chiefs are still distinguished from people of lower rank but their chiefly titles no longer involve any authority on political matters, except perhaps in the ceremonial field. The dwindling authority of Maori chiefs is mainly due to the wave of urbanization, which has entailed fundamental changes in modes of self-identification among the urban Maori population. Nowadays many Maori people no longer identify in terms of their tribal affiliation, but favour a pan-tribal, national identity as Maori. As a result, the influence of tribal organizations and their chiefs is declining structurally. I shall illustrate this hypothesis with two case studies of political developments in New Zealand, which clearly indicate the influence of democratic views, even though paradoxically they are not substantiated in terms of democracy because of its close association with colonialism in Maori political ideology.

The Maori Congress and Proportional Representation

In spite of indications that in a long-term perspective on changing sociopolitical relations in New Zealand the influence of tribal organizations has been waning since the beginning of the twentieth century, tribal organizations characterized by chiefly hierarchical mechanisms of power have paradoxically re-emerged as powerful interest groups in New Zealand's political arena in the 1980s. The recent reinforcement of tribes has principally resulted from a new government policy of 'devolution'. In New Zealand devolution is commonly defined as the process of identifying specific administrative functions which should be retained at the centre of government with all other functions being devolved as far as possible. Devolution is distinguished from decentralization which involves a mere transfer of executive duties, while devolution involves a transfer of decision-making power, which is constrained but not so restricted as to allow Maori tribes to make trivial choices while leaving all important decisions to the government (Hawke 1988:28).

The policy of devolution was introduced in New Zealand by

the Labour Government, which was elected to office in 1984. As part of the austerity programmes which the government, led by Lange, implemented for economic reasons, several government departments were forced to review the organization of their administration, which resulted in a decentralization and to some extent devolution of central government functions regarding health, social welfare, education, justice, labour and housing, as well as Maori affairs.

In the response to the government proposal for devolution of the Department of Maori Affairs there was a marked distinction between urban and rural groups. The initial concern for the abandonment of the Department of Maori Affairs gradually diminished among tribes in rural areas since it became clear, at least to Maori chiefs, that devolution would revamp tribal organizations and, concomitantly, enhance the influence and authority of tribes and their chiefs (van Meijl 1997).

In urban areas the critique of devolution was of a different nature and therefore persisted. Among pan-tribal Maori communities in urban areas the main objection to the government policy of devolution concerned the restriction that only tribal authorities could enter into contracts with government departments.[11] It seemed as though the many Maori people who since the 1930s have migrated to urban environments no longer feel represented by tribal authorities. In consequence, they claimed a proportional percentage of resources from the Department of Maori Affairs in order to deliver social services to the Maori 'proletariat' living in towns and cities. Maori organizations in cities with significant concentrations of Maori people advocated the distribution of the budget of the Department of Maori Affairs not on a tribal but on a regional basis. Their main argument to review the tribal orientation of the devolution policy was the presumption that, by acknowledging only tribal authorities and bypassing urban organizations, the government aimed at assimilating most Maori people, who were no longer represented by tribal authorities, into the European majority of the New Zealand population.

The division between tribal, predominantly rural communities, on the one hand, and pan-tribal, predominantly urban communities, on the other, surfaced even more clearly when the government decided to proceed with devolution regardless of the massive lobby against it (Maaka 1994). Thus, it also became one of the most controversial issues at the historic national conference aiming to establish a Maori Congress uniting all Maori people in 1988. Unity has ranked high on the agenda of tribal gatherings since the 1850s, but towards the end of the 1980s it was principally debated in the context of devolution, which had brought to light a deepening division among Maori people. While in the past tribal traditions had inhibited unity from being accomplished, since the large-scale migration to urban centres tribal divisions were compounded by the segregation of tribally and non-tribally orientated sections of the Maori population.

The progressive division between tribal and pan-tribal groupings in Maori society came to overshadow the historic divisions between traditional tribes at the foundation conference of the Maori Congress, which was entirely dominated by a difference of opinion regarding devolution and the question whether government resources should be distributed on a tribal or regional basis. Against those in favour of a tribal-based structure of organization stood those in favour of the creation of regional authorities. They were led by the leader of the Mana Motuhake political party, the well-reputed opinion leader Matiu Rata (Hazlehurst 1993). He proposed the setting up of seven Maori regional authorities, each to be elected by voters on the Maori electoral roll in its region. The regional authorities were planned to administer and manage devolution programmes to be delivered to those Maori people living in urban environments and whose identities are no longer believed to be constituted within traditional tribal organizations. Rata never envisaged the regional organizations as replacing tribal organizations, but, instead, they were meant to complement the tribal authorities. In the Maori Congress, too, the regional authorities were proposed to balance the tribal authorities, with three or four representatives from each region and four or five respected elders or chiefs from each tribe (*New Zealand Herald* 14 August 1989).

The most conspicuous characteristic of the proposal to set up regional authorities involved its democratic element. The uncompromising proposition of tribal authorities and paramount chiefs was criticized for being undemocratic in so far as it postulated the traditional right to represent people who could no longer identify in terms of their organization. In addition, the experiments with devolution in the form of Mana and Maccess programmes had raised the awareness of what chiefly authority practically involved. Many people had come to realize that tribal structures of organization were in practice not streamlined from the bottom up, as many chiefs had maintained in the justification of their tribal strategy for development. Instead, the experiments with devolution had made painfully apparent that the theoretical model for the implementation of devolution on a tribal basis was more based on an inversion of European forms of hierarchy to validate the necessity of devolution to Maori tribes, than on an adequate reflection of traditional Maori sociopolitical practices, in which chiefs laid down the law.

It is not surprising that the issue whether to organize the Maori Congress on a tribal or regional basis remained unresolved at the foundation conference of the Maori Congress (Cox 1993). Eventually, the issue was left to be sorted out by a working party of twenty tribal elders, which until today has not come up with a solution potentially able to satisfy everyone. More importantly, however, it has brought to light an innovative drive towards the complementarization of traditional sociopolitical structures of organization with structures based on proportional representation. That this example does not stand alone may be illustrated with another case study.

Partly Proportional Distribution of Fishing Quotas

In 1986 the New Zealand government introduced the Quota Management System to protect the fish resources in the country's inshore, and particularly its offshore, waters. This had become necessary following the extension of New Zealand's economic fishing zone to the 200-mile limit in 1977. Since then, fishing had developed into a substantial commercial resource, as a result of which some species were facing extinction. While conservation was the scheme's rationale, its most radical feature was the creation of property interests in an exclusive right of commercial fishing, which were called individual transferable quotas (ITQs). These were based on allocating allowable levels of catches of any one species to fishermen on the basis of their reported catches over the previous years. In practice, therefore, the system clearly favoured large commercial operators, while at the same time Maori people were painfully reminded of the individualization of titles to land by the Native Land Court and its consequences in the nineteenth century. It was felt, moreover, that the New Zealand government had failed to gain Maori permission to fish the resources of which they were guaranteed the 'full exclusive and undisturbed possession' by the Treaty of Waitangi (Orange 1987). For that reason, the New Zealand Maori Council and the Muriwhenua Maori tribe sought a review of the ITQ system in the High Court, which in 1988 ruled in a landmark decision that Maori people had to be given a fair deal. The Court ordered the government to negotiate with Maoridom over the use of New Zealand's fisheries, which are worth about $1,500 million a year.[12]

Negotiations about Maori fisheries lasted for five years, and the issue became one of the most complicated subjects in Maori colonial history. In the end the so-called 'Sealord deal' was struck in 1992, providing that the New Zealand government would pay to the Maori $150 million over three years as part of Sealord Products Ltd., the largest fishing and fish processing company in the country. In addition, 20 per cent of fish species which were not yet part of the quota system would be allocated to Maori tribes. At the same time, however, it was agreed that in return Maori people would discontinue all court actions and claims to the Waitangi Tribunal concerning commercial fisheries,[13] and also extinguish all Maori commercial fishing rights. The deal was agreed to be the 'full and final settlement' of Maori fishing claims. Legal protection for Maori rights in the Fisheries Act would also be withdrawn, although Treaty of Waitangi rights covering fishing for personal or tribal consumption were retained and even new *mahinga kai* reserves ('traditional fishing grounds') would be designated around the coast (*New Zealand News UK* 30 September 1992, 2330:1).

The deal was, of course, extremely controversial. New Zealanders of European origin accused the government of racist behaviour, particularly for establishing recreational fishing areas which excluded the majority of the New Zealand population. For many Maori people the most objectionable part of the deal was the clause which made it binding on all Maori people, regardless of the question whether they had authorized the Deed of Settlement or not. This criticism must be viewed against the background that the negotiations for the deal were conducted by only four Maori leaders, whose representativeness for all Maori people is highly doubtful: the tribal leaders of the Tainui, Muriwhenua and Ngai Tahu tribes, whose vested interests in fisheries was the most significant, and the chairman of the New

Zealand Maori Council representing all other Maori groupings in New Zealand. Although in the past, too, the government made deals with a limited number of Maori chiefs that were later generalized in law, while Maori mythology abounds with examples of individuals attempting to outplay each other, the social basis of the Sealord deal is extremely small.[14]

The settlement was challenged in New Zealand courts by fourteen Maori groups opposing the agreement, but they were not successful. Subsequently, they went to the Waitangi Tribunal, arguing that the deal contravenes the Treaty of Waitangi. In its response, the Tribunal recommended making the fish regulations and policies reviewable in the courts against the Treaty's principles, and, more importantly, imposing a 25-year halt to Maori commercial fishing claims. The government, however, insists that extinguishing all Maori fishing claims for ever is a non-negotiable part of the deal.

The Waitangi Tribunal also assessed the level of Maori support for the deal and concluded that there was indeed a mandate for the settlement, provided the Treaty was not compromised. This, however, is precisely the overriding concern among the Maori groupings that have been challenging the deal. They are not interested in discussions whether the deal is good or bad as a commercial venture. They are concerned principally about the processes of decision-making in which the government negotiated settlements of historic importance with only four Maori leaders, who did not acquire a mandate from the entire Maori population and yet who agreed to waive all Treaty rights in exchange for money.

Interestingly, now, the Maori groupings resisting the Sealord deal are appealing to Maori forms of direct democracy based on principles of consultation and consensus, which in the case of the negotations about the fisheries were not adhered to, as only tribal organizations were consulted, leaving out the vast majority of the Maori population living in urban, pan-tribal environments. The principles of consultation and consensus should not be taken at face value as characteristic of internal Maori politics, since in the past they guided decision-making processes only within relatively small tribal groupings, whereas at present they are particularly prominent in counterhegemonic discourses of Maori tradition that are usually articulated in opposition to stereotypical represent-ations of European forms of hierarchy. Nevertheless, it is intriguing that the Maori groupings disputing the Sealord deal are indirectly accusing some of the most influential Maori chiefs of being 'undemocratic'. Although they do not couch their criticisms in terms of democracy, they explicitly reject chiefly authority by appealing to the principles of democratic decision-making processes.

Tension between chiefly authority and the influence of 'the people' is inherent in Maori sociopolitical organization, in which asymmetrical alliances between chiefs and tribes are often balanced with a rhetoric of egalitarianism aiming to put some reciprocal restraints on the power and authority of chiefs (van Meijl 1994). In this case, I would argue, however, that we are not simply witnessing attempts to reintroduce traditional principles of democracy or to remind chiefs of their obligation to consult with the people they are supposed to represent. Instead, chiefly authority is disputed because only four chiefs represented the entire Maori population, whereas a significant number of Maori people who have migrated to urban areas have lost touch with their tribal roots. Thus, chiefly authority is not disputed *per se*, but the mandate of the chiefs to negotiate on behalf of people who no longer belong to a certain tribe is contested. This can only be interpreted as another clear indication that internal Maori politics are moving towards the introduction of proportional representation within Maori society.

The drive towards the introduction of proportional representation into Maori political structures is not coincidental but is the outcome of the row among tribes about a division of fishing quotas. After the Sealord deal was signed, Maori tribes failed to reach agreement on allocating fishing quotas to the various parties involved. Two opposing positions dominated the debate, causing roughly a division between northern and southern tribes. The sourthern Ngai Tahu tribes, supported by east coast North Island tribes, argued for allocation of quotas on the basis of the Maori dictum *mana whenua mana moana*: the right to fish the sea off their tribal land area. This would obviously be a big financial windfall for the tribes with smaller populations but large coastal areas. Most northern tribes with little or no coastal boundary could on the basis of the traditional point of departure put forward by Ngai Tahu and companion tribes expect little or no quota and were therefore pushing for the quota allocation to be determined on a population basis.

After a year of negotiations, a compromise was reached on the vexed question of Maori fishing quota allocation. The compromise was based on both traditional fishing areas and tribal numbers. All 15,000 tonnes of inshore quota are now distributed according to *mana whenua mana moana*. The 42,000 tonnes of deep-sea quota are distributed 50 per cent on the basis of *mana whenua mana moana* and 50 per cent on the basis of population numbers using 1991 Census data.

The introduction, albeit partly, of a per capita distribution of resources is unprecedented in Maori history. It shows that not only the principles of chiefly authority but also the value of tribal *mana* in Maori society is changing, undoubtedly as a result of the transformation of Maori society over the past two centuries. Tribes have lost most of their land and continue to exist primarily as nominal organizations. Accordingly, they can no longer claim authority and influence only on the basis of *mana whenua*. It is becoming increasingly necessary to complement tribal prestige as rooted in traditional territories with the democratic principles of proportional representation and a per capita distribution of resources, which are emerging as new codes to streamline Maori sociopolitical organization. That these new principles are not couched in terms of the ideology of democracy is not surprising given the intrinsic association of democracy with colonization in Maori society.

Concluding Remarks

The analysis of democracy in Maori society confronts anthropology with an interesting paradox. On the one hand, democracy is viewed as a Western political system which has been used to disenfranchise the Maori population of their customary rights, common law and indigenous identity in New Zealand and for that reason it is unconditionally rejected in Maori society. On the other hand, there are clear indications that transformations in Maori society over the past two centuries have diminished the authority of tribal organizations and chieftainship to such an extent that some dimensions of democracy are now being proposed or introduced into Maori society. Because of the intrinsic relation between democracy and colonization in Maori political perspectives, however, the democratic innovations in Maori political culture are not explicitly articulated in terms of an ideology of democracy. But de Tocqueville drew attention to the fact that democracy extends beyond parliamentary structures and is intertwined with all dimensions of a society. From a Tocquevillian perspective the emergence of democracy in Maori culture can therefore not be disputed.

Notes

1. For a comparison of Western Samoa and Tonga, see Hills (1993).
2. This seems also the case in other regions, e.g. Pinkey (1993) and Diamond *et al.* (1990). The latter acknowledge in the introduction that social and economic issues cannot be separated from the question of governmental structure, but argue that for methodological reasons only a political analysis is feasible. In their opinion a broad definition of democracy would make empirical research very difficult (Diamond *et al.* 1990:6). It almost reads like a task description for holistic anthropology.
3. It should be realized, however, that in French the meaning of the term *moeurs* is not restricted to morality or spirituality, but that in a broad sense it refers to a way of life. It has been derived from the Latin *mores* and is close to the English 'mores', the meaning of which also encompasses 'custom', 'habit', 'usage', 'way', 'manner', 'rule' or even 'precept'. The word 'mores' is a *plurale tantum* and it was therefore often used in characterizations of certain societies.
4. The traumatic events of the years 1848–51 were clearly the source of his emphasis on the relative durability of centralization and class hostility in French history. For de Tocqueville they reaffirmed the libertarian example of the Anglo-American world.
5. This is not to say that the process itself is not revolutionary, and to avoid that misunderstanding de Tocqueville described it as *la révolution démocratique* ('the democratic revolution').
6. This point is relevant regardless of the question whether parliamentary solutions could possibly resolve the issue of Maori underdevelopment.

7. The number of Maori seats in Parliament has not increased because it is calculated on the basis of the adult population only. Since 50 per cent of the Maori population is under the age of twenty-one, the number has remained at four, the same given in 1867 when the Maori people numbered only 52,000 (Levine and Henare 1994:199).

8. This statement must be understood in the historical context of Maori parliamentary representation. When at the beginning of this century it became evident that Maori MPs were effectively powerless to transform the main trends in the colonial history of New Zealand, many turned from an interest in parliamentary representation to the prophet leader Ratana, who, however, had a clear political mission as well (Henderson 1963). He aligned himself with the poor during the Depression and offered, in return for aid, his support to the Labour Party. In 1932 the first Ratana member was elected in Parliament, and by 1943 all four Maori seats were held by Ratana members. This liaison between the Ratana Church and the Labour Party was to last for 40 years. It was the first time in which the seats were unified in a systematic way to achieve political ends. The close alliance between Maori MPs and the Labour Party, however, has not brought about any significant political changes.

9. Since the time of writing the Court of Appeal has dismissed the legal challenge to the way in which the Maori roll option was run after the referendum on the MMP electoral system (*New Zealand News UK* 4 January 1995, 2445:7). As a result, there are currently five Maori seats.

10. Unfortunately, examinations of changes in Maori society are few and far between. Elsewhere I have argued that this is mainly due to the rhetorical devices which are characteristic of contemporary discourses of Maori politics, and which represent Maori traditions, including forms of sociopolitical organization, as timeless (van Meijl 1990).

11. This basis of the devolution policy, which also explains the support of it by Maori chiefs, has recently been described as a form of 'tribal fundamentalism' (Levine and Henare 1994).

12. The report of the Waitangi Tribunal on the Muriwhenua fishing claim provides an excellent overview of the extremely complicated issue of Maori fisheries (Waitangi Tribunal 1988).

13. The Waitangi Tribunal was established in 1975 to investigate Maori claims of being 'prejudicially affected' by any policy or practice of the Crown which was believed to be in violation of the Treaty of Waitangi; see Sorrenson (1989).
14. See *Pacific News Bulletin* (1993) and Walker (1994).

References

Buiks, P.E.J. (1979). *Alexis de Tocqueville en de democratische revolutie: Een cultuursociologische interpretatie*. Assen: Van Gorcum.

Cox, L. (1993). *Kotahitanga. The Search for Maori Political Unity*. Auckland: Oxford University Press.

Department of Maori Affairs (1989). *Te Hurihanga o Te Ao Maori. A Statistical Profile of Change in Maori Society*. Wellington: Department of Maori Affairs.

Department of Statistics (1993). *New Zealand Official Yearbook 1993. Te Pukapuka Houanga Whaimana o Aotearoa*. Wellington: Department of Statistics/Te Tari Tatau.

de Tocqueville, A. (1952). *L'Ancien Régime et la révolution*. Paris: Gallimard, Oeuvres Complètes, Tome 2.1. (First published in 1856.)

—— (1961). *De la démocratie en Amérique*. Paris: Gallimard, Oeuvres Complètes, Tome 1.1. (First published in 1835–40.)

Diamond, L., Linz, J.J. and Lipset, S.M. (eds) (1990). *Politics in Developing Countries: Comparing Experiences with Democracy*. Boulder/London: Lynne Rienner.

Goldsmith, M. (1994). The Great Pacific Democracy Debate. Paper presented to the Pacific Islands Political Studies Association Conference, Rarotonga, December 1993 (revised version).

Grant, A.K. (1987). Fantasies of Power. *New Zealand Listener* 3 September-October 1987, p. 47.

Hau'ofa, E. (1994). Thy Kingdom Come: The Democratization of Aristocratic Tonga. *The Contemporary Pacific* 6(2):414–28.

Hawke, G.R. (1988). *Report of the Working Group on Post Compulsory Education and Training in New Zealand*. Report prepared for the Cabinet Social Equity Committee.

Hazlehurst, K.M. (1993). *Political Expression and Ethnicity: Statecraft and Mobilisation in the Maori World*. Westport (Conn.): Praeger.

Helu, I.F. (1992). Democracy Bug Bites Tonga. In: Institute of Pacific Studies (ed.), *Culture and Democracy in the South Pacific,* pp. 139–52. Suva: University of the South Pacific, Institute of Pacific Studies.

Henderson, J.M. (1963). *Ratana: the Origins and the Story of the Movement.* Wellington: Polynesian Society (Memoir No. 36).

Henderson, J. (1992). Culture, Ethnicity and Political Represent-ation in New Zealand. In: Institute of Pacific Studies (ed.), *Culture and Democracy in the South Pacific,* pp. 171–90. Suva: University of the South Pacific, Institute of Pacific Studies.

Hills, R. C. (1993). Predicaments in Polynesia: Culture and Constitutions in Western Samoa and Tonga. *Pacific Studies* 16(4):115–29.

Institute of Pacific Studies (ed.) (1992). *Culture and Democracy in the South Pacific.* Suva: University of the South Pacific, Institute of Pacific Studies.

Kawharu, I.H. (1977). *Maori Land Tenure: Studies of a Changing Institution.* Oxford: Oxford University Press.

Larmour, P. (1994). A Foreign Flower? Democracy in the South Pacific. *Pacific Studies* 17(1):45–77.

Latukefu, S. (1993). The Pro-Democracy Movement in Tonga. *Journal of Pacific History* 28(3):52–63.

Lawson, S. (1991). *The Failure of Democratic Politics in Fiji.* Oxford: Clarendon.

—— (1993). The Politics of Tradition: Problems for Political Legitimacy and Democracy in the South Pacific. *Pacific Studies* 16(2):1–29.

Levine, H. and Henare, M. (1994). Mana Maori Motuhake: Maori Self-Determination. *Pacific Viewpoint* 35(2):193–210.

Lind-Mitchell, E. (1985). The Maori Seats: Retention or Abolition? Hurupaa: Undergrowth. *Student Journal of Anthropology* 3: 13–24.

Maaka, R.C.A. (1994). The New Tribe: Conflicts and Continuities in the Social Organization of Urban Maori. *The Contemporary Pacific* 6(2):311–36.

Metge, J. (1964). *A New Maori Migration; Rural and Urban Relations in Northern New Zealand.* London: Athlone Press and Melbourne: Melbourne University Press (London School of Economics Monograph in Social Anthropology No. 27).

—— (1976). *The Maoris of New Zealand: Rautahi.* London: Routledge and Kegan Paul. (First published in 1967.)

New Zealand Herald (1982–3; 1987–90; 1994, January-June).

New Zealand News UK (1991–94).

Orange, C. (1987). *The Treaty of Waitangi*. Wellington: Allen and Unwin.

Pacific News Bulletin (1993). Sealord: A Deal Full of Fish Hooks. *Pacific News Bulletin* 8(3):12–13.

Pinkey, R. (1993). *Democracy in the Third World*. Buckingham: Open University Press.

Sorrenson, M.P.K. (1956). Land Purchase Methods and their Effect on Maori Population, 1865–1901. *Journal of the Polynesian Society* 65(3):183–99.

—— (1989). Towards a Radical Reinterpretation of New Zealand History: the Role of the Waitangi Tribunal. In: I.D. Kawharu (ed.), *Waitangi: Maori and Pakeha Perspectives of the Treaty of Waitangi*, pp. 158–78. Auckland: Oxford University Press.

Stokes, E. (ed.) (1981). *Maori Representation in Parliament*. Hamiltom: Centre for Maori Studies and Research (Occasional Paper No. 14).

Tagaloa, A.F.L. (1992). The Samoan Culture and Government. In: Institute of Pacific Studies (ed.), *Culture and Democracy in the South Pacific*, pp. 117–38. Suva: University of the South Pacific, Institute of Pacific Studies.

Tagupa, W. (1992). Confronting Democracy in Hawaii: An Informal Assessment of an Island Political Culture. In: Institute of Pacific Studies (ed.), *Culture and Democracy in the South Pacific*, pp. 191–204. Suva: University of the South Pacific, Institute of Pacific Studies.

Thomas, N. (1990). Regional Politics, Ethnicity and Custom in Fiji. *The Contemporary Pacific* 2(1):131–46.

van Meijl, T. (1990). *Political Paradoxes and Timeless Traditions: Ideology and Development Among the Tainui Maori, New Zealand*. Canberra: Australian National University, unpublished PhD thesis (reproduced by the Centre for Pacific Studies, University of Nijmegen, the Netherlands).

—— (1994). Maori Hierarchy Transformed: The Secularization of Tainui Patterns of Leadership. In: M. Jolly and M. Mosko (eds), *Transformations of Hierarchy: Power and Process in the Austronesian World*, pp. 279–306. *History and Anthropology* special issue 7.

—— (1997). The Re-emergence of Maori Chiefs: 'Devolution' as a Strategy to Maintain Tribal Authority. In: G. White and L. Lindstrom (eds), *Chiefs Today: Traditional Pacific Leadership and the Postcolonial State*, pp. 84–107. Stanford: Stanford University

Press and Honolulu: East West Centre. (Contemporary Issues in Asia and the Pacific Series).

Vasil, R. (1990). *What do the Maori Want? New Maori Political Perspectives.* Auckland: Random.

Waitangi Tribunal (1988). *Muriwhenua Fishing Report (Wai-22).* Wellington: Waitangi Tribunal.

Walker, R. (1994). Maori Issues. *The Contemporary Pacific* 6(1): 183–5.

Ward, A. (1973). *A Show of Justice: Racial 'Amalgamation' in Nineteenth Century New Zealand.* Auckland: University Press and Oxford University Press.

Yamamoto, M. (1994). Urbanisation of the Chiefly System: Multiplication and Role Differentiation of Titles in Western Samoa. *Journal of the Polynesian Society* 103(2):171–202.

Young, D. (1987). Living with Diversity. *New Zealand Listener.* 26 September 1987, p. 11.

Chapter 17

Is Aristocracy Good for Democracy? A Contemporary Debate in Western Samoa

Serge Tcherkézoff

Introduction

In the independent State of Western Samoa, a large debate is involving politicians in town as well as villagers from the 300 villages of this country. Translated into our words, it could be expressed in this rather paradoxical way: Is aristocracy good for democracy? Is the *faamatai* (the system of chiefs) good for the *alofa* (social mutual help, gift-giving and sympathy) between people and for ensuring that everyone is equally represented in the collective decisions?[1]

In Samoa, the traditional system of sacred chiefs has never been discontinued.[2] The arrival of Christianity did not cause much of a contradiction, because the main aspects of the traditional religion and its taboos were in the system of genealogies, rank and status between chiefs, and not in some objects or temples. The first missionaries were welcomed by local chiefs, who used the traditional Polynesian logic of war: bringing in a new divinity brings new *mana* that may be superior. Since then, Christianity and the system of chiefs coexist harmoniously. The same person cannot be a pastor and a chief. The pastor is to the village like a sister is to her brother: a sacred link to the origin; the chiefs are the fathers/brothers of the village. The new God took the place of the pre-Christian one and is still considered as the apex (in the logic of status) and the origin (in the cosmogony) of all the titles of chief in Samoa.

The German colonial time was very brief (1899–1914) and the

administration tried to control but not to overthrow the chiefs' system. Their control was exercised through a court deciding on rivalries about succession to chiefly titles, in this way ending the frequent local wars. The main interest of the German power was to create large copra-producing estates. But the short amount of time allowed them to spoliate only 15 per cent of the land; the rest has remained, up to now, as was the custom, land held jointly by the community forming an extended family, *aiga*; it is land that cannot be sold.[3]

The time of the New Zealand Protectorate on Western Samoa (1920–62) did not change much in the political life of the villages. The administration never envisaged establishing colonists on Samoan land and tried mainly to organize a school and health system, and central juridical and police powers.

At the time of independence (1962), the people of Samoa (through Constitutional Assembly and referendum) insisted on setting up a parliamentary system where only the chiefs would be the electors and the eligible people, where only they would vote and be elected to represent a district (at the time, the country was divided into some forty districts) and sit in Parliament. In 1990, another referendum broke up a part of that system and established universal suffrage for electors, the candidates for parliament remaining the chiefs only.

Since the announcement of that referendum (the question was whether to keep the system of 1962 or to have universal suffrage for electors – but not for eligibility) and up to this day, the debate has been very lively in Samoa, because the result of the referendum was not significant (a very small majority voting yes and a large abstention).

One might think that the debate follows the normal path of history and globalization in Westernized terms. Some people still favour the traditional system, where the decisions affecting the life of the local groups were in the hands of the sacred chiefs, and this is to be expected. A certain number favour universal suffrage and that number will grow as education and openings towards the 'global' world improve. Gradually, the country will evolve from aristocracy to democracy and achieve what is already emerging, the imposition that the candidates could also be non-chiefly people, eligibility then becoming a universal suffrage system as well.

But, actually, this is not what is going on and what is talked about. All proponents, those in favour of the 1962 system, those in favour of the 1990 system (universal suffrage for electors only) and those in favour of complete universal suffrage, seem to have the same goals and values. They all hold that the way they propose is the only way to save and preserve for ever the *faamatai*, the 'chief system' as it is usually but unfortunately translated, and they all hold, too, that their way is more 'democratic' than the others. The paradox is striking. The traditionalist political party and the progressive party, which oppose each other fiercely in Parliament (although the division is more complex than a dichotomy), fight for the same goal: to save aristocracy (the chief system). Simultaneously, both of them say that in doing so they will better preserve 'democracy' in the country.

To understand what is behind the paradox, we must look more closely at what seem to us to be 'aristocracy' or 'chief system' as well as at what Samoans call 'democracy' (or *temokalasi* as they also say).

About 'Aristocracy'

The so-called (by foreigners) 'chief system' is a kind of aristocracy where there are no families who are not aristocratic. All Samoan families (*aiga*) are noble: a country of nobility without peasantry.

Actually, the chief – the *matai* – is the head of an extended family defined as a worship community, a genealogical group, with a joint land ownership. Members worship the name of a founding ancestor. To be 'alive', this name must always be the name of (at least) one member of the family. Through a ceremony, this name is bestowed on this person who then, immediately, becomes known as and called *XX* (the name of the founding ancestor). This office of bearing the family name, after a ritual investiture, is called *matai*. The literature calls those names thus transmitted and bestowed 'titles'. But the word can be misleading with its reference to an oligarchy: on the contrary, in Samoa, there are no families without a 'title' since the 'title' is the name of the family (with the obligation to keep it alive through the ritual bestowal on it at each generation). When the person entitled to the name dies, another one is chosen to receive the name and to become the *matai* of the family. The whole community forming the extended family (and that may mean dozens and sometimes hundreds of people) decides who must be chosen, and the same community can, at any time, take away the title from the person who has been chosen (if this person is considered unable to represent with 'dignity' the family in the face of the other families in the village) and bestow it on somebody else.

Genealogically speaking, the family groups together all those people who can say that they are related (in any way) to at least one of the past *matai* of the family. The system thus allows much flexibility. All those people are said to be 'heirs' to the founding name and there is no genealogical rule to restrict the possibility to be chosen by the community to become the next *matai* of the family.

Each ancestral name which has thus become a title (the source of identity of a group a people) is associated with a piece of land (where ideally there is the burial or birth site of the founding ancestor): the land of the family. These pieces of land form the 80 per cent 'customary-held land' of the total land of the country, the rest being private or State property – a heritage of the German colonial time. One understands why this land cannot be sold: it is another materialization of the common identity of the group, just as an ancestral name cannot be sold. Such a name can only incorporate – and so it is for the land. Polynesian cultures are well-known for the extensive use of what we call adoption. In Samoa, the person coming (having been invited or accepted) to live on one's family land quickly becomes a 'child of the land' and as such a 'brother', a new member of the group, and hence a true 'heir' to the name. There are no Samoan families without a title, there are no Samoan families without their customary land (even if this piece of land is sometimes smaller than it was in the nineteenth century). Hence, there are no Samoan families who are not noble.

Samoans do have expressions which distinguish between noble and 'rustic' behaviour: *tu faatamalii*, 'in the manner of chiefs',[4] versus *tu fanua*, 'in the manner of earth [creatures]'. The latter expression does not include any depreciation regarding working the land – all Samoans are gardeners and planters and are very proud of their taro fields. Rather, it is part of the cosmological opposition, common to all Polynesian cultures, between sky and earth, day and darkness, life and death.[5] Very significantly, this differentiation between noble and rustic behaviour has nothing to do with one's birth. Anybody can be said to be one or the other. Samoans say that all non-*matai* people should always behave in the *faatamalii* way; and, conversely, any *matai* who commits 'unworthy' acts may be talked about as beginning to behave in a *tu fanua* way – and, in this case, if he continues, he can expect that the whole extended family will soon meet and decide to take away the *matai* title from him and bestow it on another member of the family.

Another important aspect is the multitude of chiefs, since they are nothing else than (elected) family heads. Linked to that is the idea that the social hierarchy is an overall system of differentiated but common belonging of all chief names to one and the same history of Samoa. There are as many *matai* as there are families (and even more, because a name can be split to acknowledge different 'sides' in large extended families). The result is this: In a country of 160,000 people (where more than half are under 21), there are 15,000 *matai*, and the whole system of chiefs or *faamatai* is in a way an overall (but very fluid and flexible) ranking of all the families, through the ranks of the ancestral names.

This idea of ranking, or more exactly of respect, precedence on all ceremonial occasions, is, in short, a projection of the difference of ancientness of the different names, a difference in length of the genealogies (of the succession of the *matai*s of a family, from the founding ancestor up to now); the longer the genealogy, the more proximate to the origin (the divinity) the name. But this gradation of status operates within the common belonging of all families, of all ancestral names and hence of all *matai*s to a common 'sacred circle', *alofi sa*, ideally represented when one thinks at the level of the whole country, but quite materially existing and acting at the level of a village *nuu*. Each Samoan village, more exactly 'polity', is a circle of founding ancestral names, re-enacted any time the village council meets: all the *matai*s of the village sit in a circle to hold council. They all belong to the same circle and, at the same time, they each of them have a different position on the circle – since these circles are organized through a system of axes (centre of village/periphery) and each seat or groups of seats (materialized by a post of the round house) are ranked on the circle.

What may seem to an outsider to be the 'aristocratic' system of Samoa is, on the one hand, the fact of common belonging and ranking between families and, on the other hand, the distinction between *matai* and non-*matai* within the family. But this second distinction is one between the ancestor embodied in the *matai* and all his 'heirs'. It is not traditionally a class distinction between all the *matai* of the country, on the one hand, and all the non-*matai* of the country, on the other hand. And, as already stated, there is no rule to exclude any category of people from becoming *matai* if the family thinks that this person is able to 'represent' the family *vis-à-vis* the other families of the village and the district. The two distinctions merge into the same idea of hierarchy: the *faamatai*, the *matai* system. God is the origin of the first people, the first ancestors, the first names. Other names have as their origin a semi-god, product of the union of the god with a human female. Other names of *matai* have been created by existing *matai*. Here lies the essence of a very ancient and still important rule. Any *matai*, with the assent of his family, may always give a piece of land to an individual and attribute to both of them a name that they will carry and transmit, and there begins a new line of *matai*. In the old time, the characteristic occasion was in exchange for having served in war. In this way, the winning party was creating its own and new pool of *matai* names.[6] At the end of this holistic chain from divinity to humanity, the relation between *matai* and non-*matai* (within the family) is one between 'father' and 'children',[7] continued by the relations between non-*matai* people of the same sex, who are 'elder/younger brothers'.[8]

Within this wide and continuous hierarchy (gods, semi-gods, founding ancestors, lines of *matai* embodying the founding names, and all the 'heirs' of each name who are 'children of the land' and 'children' of their respective *matai* name), the idea of competition is very present but the goals of the competition are again the *matai* names. By taking advantage in ceremonial exchanges, in oratorical debates, etc., the family name is raised within the village. To raise a name is to have the right to express (and the ability to persuade of the historical existence of) more of the genealogical links that can exist between the origin of the name and other *matai* names, and are more ancient. In doing much of the work involved in these exchanges, one is said to 'serve', *tautua*, his family and his *matai* name. And it is not surprising to hear Samoans explaining that the route that brings one to be chosen as a *matai* by his fellows is precisely the ability of 'serving', shown during many years. 'Serving' is in a way a cultural act (serving the *matai* is in a way making offerings to the ancestor), and, in doing so, one shows that he is able to be the first in serving: he can be the priest of the group, if one can put it so – and this is also the definition and duty of a *matai* (who leads and organizes the daily prayers today as he did 160 years ago, when the prayers were adressed to Tagaloa-a-Lagi).

In the end, it becomes clear that we have a system different from what it may first appear to a Westerner. Differentiation is not inequality but hierarchy, hierarchy operates within a common belonging to the same 'circle'.[9] There are no families who are not 'chiefly' families. In other words, 'aristocracy' is universal in Samoa – which explains why, when Samoans heard about 'democracy', they said that they 'already have it'.[10]

About 'Democracy'

The idea of democracy, which has been very much brought into the culture of the recent generations through the school and which is indeed seen as a value by Samoans, can be approached and is approached in the debate in two ways: one is the idea of representation and its relationship to the idea of universal suffrage, the other is – and it comes as more of a surprise in respect to Western ideology – the very idea of voting, as contrasted to the process of reaching consensus.

The Level of the Democratic Choice

Because the *matai* is elected and can be removed from his office by the same people, because the electors are all the members of the family, the election of the *matai* is said by many Samoans to be a strongly democratic system. But this idea leads to two different views. People in favour of complete universal suffrage (eligibility and electors) or a semi-universal one as it has been since 1990 (all adults choose between *matai* candidates) do not contest that view but consider that a direct democracy (people elect parliament) instead of an indirect one (people elect *matai*, who elect among themselves) is still better, since the second system does not allow all individuals to have a say in the choice of the parliamentarians. Opponents answer that, given the contemporary state of political knowledge and consciousness in the country, the idea that every adult has free choice is absolutely demagogic and opens the way to mass manipulation. Of course, supporters of total universal suffrage add that that the second system is not democratic because it does not allow everybody to compete for a parliamentary seat. The opponents answer that, as there is no barrier to becoming a *matai*, there is no barrier to eventually becoming a Parliament member. The reply to that goes: the way is much longer, because, in order to become a *matai* in the family, a person must prove over many years his inclination to give his time to the welfare (and good representation) of the group (and, in most cases, the *matai* not being discharged, the candidate for *matai*-ship must wait for the *matai* in charge to pass away – although there is often the possibility of splitting a title between several people). Again, the answer to this from the pro-*matai*-system group is that there is always the possibility of extending the number of *matai* by creating new ones, which still allows people elected as *matai* to be controlled by their electoral (familial) basis. The rejoinder to that is: 'You are killing the *matai* system from inside in thinking to extend it to many young people.' This discussion brings us to another part of the debate.

Politics versus *matai* System

Although, for the present, the question of democracy is a decision between the *matai* system of elections (only *matai*s vote and are eligible) and the semi-universal one of 1990, the real debate is between the *matai* system and the full universal one. It is clear that the latter will advance rather rapidly if the semi-universal system is definitely considered by all Samoans as a better one than the old system, establishing then an idea of political progress towards 'democracy' and the idea of democracy being then understood primarily as meaning 'universal suffrage'. Thus, the debate is between the following:

1 Opening the way for everybody to compete on a path where the possibility to become a Parliament Member can be quickly achieved – instead of waiting to become a *matai* in the family.
2 Maintaining the necessity of the first step, to be first a *matai*, the main argument being that a *matai* has to feel responsible at all times *vis-à-vis* his electors (his extended family) while a parliamentarian, once elected for five years, has no further institutional control exercised over him.

This obligation of the *matai* to feel responsible every minute is said to be the best school for learning the duties of group representation. This is where those of the pro-*matai* system of elections add that, if needed, the creation of *matai* names could be greatly increased, using the traditional possibility of any existing *matai* to create new *matai* names (see above and below); in this manner, it will reduce the problem of waiting half a lifetime or more in order to become *matai* and only then being allowed to stand for Parliament, while keeping the main idea of controlling (the person representing the group) through family ties (which cannot be bought through bribery) instead of political ties.

These exchanges of ideas on the system of representation explain why all sides of the contemporary Samoan debate say they defend democracy, the difference being the level at which they think that the democratic choice should be exercised: within the family (when electing the *matai*) or at the district level (when all adults vote to choose between *matais* the one who will represent the district in the Parliament) or at the individual level (anyone over 21 years of age may vote and be a candidate). But what about the fact that all sides of the contemporary debate also say that their respective programme aims at preserving the continuation of the very existence of the *faamatai*, the *matai* system (or 'mataïsm' as some Samoans say in English)? This brings us back to the proposition of extending the number of *matai*.

The argument of the pro-universal suffrage group who say that this universal suffrage is (a paradox to the ear of the outsider) a better way to preserve the *faamatai* (the *matai* system in all its aspects of village and national life) is the following. The *matai* system always (or, anyway, since the nineteenth century) had the possibility to extend by itself: an individual *matai* has the right to create new *matai* names and to donate a piece of land to be attached to that name – and, even today, he may bestow a name without land, those names being then directly attached to the main name. The persons invested with those names become sometimes chiefs of subgroupings of the extended family (and sometimes are just counsellors to the main chiefs). This possibility is the very one the pro-*matai* voting-system group wants to use in order to allow many more people to quickly become *matai* and hence voters, but still maintain the first step of control where the individual is judged by those who know him closely (and who agree or do not agree to give him the title of *matai* – which opens for him the way of national politics if, as the next step, he is elected by the district, by all the *matai* of the district, to become the representative of that district).

But the problem is that this possibility had already been overused by existing *matai*, not with the idea of opening the way for bright people so that they would have faster access to politics, but with the idea of creating for oneself a pool of electors who, grateful for having received that new status of *matai*, will vote, on the day of district election, for the *matai* who created them. The tendency started in the 1970s and reached a peak at the end of the 1980s, when the number of *matai* became twice the usual one. Of course, this tactic contains a possibility for people who have means to hand out money, to organize beautiful feasts for the bestowal of those 'small' new *matai* names, and to thereby win the election. Actually, the main argument of the pro-universal-suffrage group is not so much the inequality of chances, created by this possibility of bribery, but the fact that the *faamatai* deteriorates with the creation of hundreds of 'false' *matai*. In order to preserve (for the family and village everyday life) the authority of the (real) *matai*, one must abolish what created an incentive for declaring new *matai*. In absolutely separating the political life from the *faamatai*, the latter will be preserved: there will no longer be any need to create hundreds of 'false' *matai* if, through universal suffrage, the question of parliamentary elections is disconnected from the *matai* system.

The answer of the opponents is that, quite rightly, when they create numerous new *matai*, they modify the traditional *matai* system by considerably expanding it. But if the expansion is made not for and through bribery (creating new electors to serve the ambition of existing *matai*) but only to open the way more quickly for people who deserve to one day be a politician, the modification is good (for democracy) but will be limited and will not destroy the spirit of *matai*-ship. On the contrary, the solution proposed by the other side, i.e. to separate politics and *faamatai*, creating the realm of politics through universal suffrage and limiting the *faamatai* only to family and village tradition, will be more certain to kill the *faamatai*, because this traditional authority rests heavily on the idea that the *matai* represents the group in the face of the whole (village, district, nation) and certainly not on the idea that the *matai* is only a guardian of legends and genealogies.

Apart from this – and here is crucial matter that needs investigation – the pro-*matai* system of elections group says that such a separation will hasten the division of the country, already on its way, between, on one side, the town and its periphery and, on the other side, the rest of the country, the 'outer villages'. As a matter of fact, one-third of the population of the country now lives in the urban and peri-urban area, which is still a string of villages, each village having its *matais*, but where there are more houses than plantations, with increasing dependency on paid labour, the well-being of the family depending more on the salary received by a few individuals than on the communal organization of agriculture and fishing, organization that was headed and inspired by the *matai*. Opposed to that area are what are now called the villages 'outback' (the rest of the country).[11]

In the end, this way of promoting 'democracy' will establish a wide gap and inequality between a part of the country living with Westernized politics (but which will suffer from the lack of ways to control the politicians) and another part where the knowledge of ways of controlling politicians (when politicians were the *matais*) will be useless because, anyway, the *matai* will have become the local guardians of the village folklore, a lore kept to be recited on evenings around the fire and performed for tourists sent out to 'villages' from the hotels (which, indeed, are rapidly emerging in the town area). If the progress of universal suffrage means the separation of the *faamatai* from the 'real' politics, if the 'preserving' of the *faamatai* in the end becomes its 'folkorization', and if that result brings about a new division in the country between a town which knows how to cope with Western-style politics and, on the other side, the villages which will only be manipulated by these politics, then some Samoans say that 'democracy' will not be achieved and will even go backwards. The fear that this scenario may become true is one of the main reasons in the attitude of those Samoans who protest against developing the universal-suffrage system in their country.

The Idea of Voting

It is clear that the full realization of the non-*matai* system of 'democracy' in Samoa is total universal suffrage, and the real debate is clearly between that system and the *faamatai*. If the country follows this logic, the semi-system of 1990 will only be a transition. Symmetrically, the full and coherent ideological system of the *matai* system of 'democracy' (and those who are the advocates of it deliberately avoid the English word and use its

Samoanized form *temokalasi*) goes further than only to the fact of having an electoral system limited to the *matai*. The full programme evoked by several influential members of that side is to abolish the whole idea of electoralism, brought in with the Constitution in 1962, and to return to the traditional Samoan form of group decision, the consensus *faatasi* (literally 'as one', used in everyday language like our word 'together').

Those people explain to the visitor that the real 'democracy' in 'the Samoan way', the *temokalasi faaSamoa*, is to suppress the very possibility of voting, even in a system limited to the *matai*, because the process of voting is built on the logic of 'force', *malosi*, and creates a winning side, *malo* (the word was used for the winning side in a war), and a defeated side, *vaivai* (besides its past use in the context of war, the word means also 'weak'); the result is only divisions among people. On the contrary, the *faatasi* mode of choosing, which was and – it is essential to note – still is the mode of choosing a new *matai* within a family, allows reaching decisions while maintaining unity.

For those people, the difference between the *faamatai* political system and the Western political system is not a question of 'chiefly election' vs. universal suffrage, not only because *matai* are not what Westerners call 'chiefs' – as we have seen in the first part of this chapter – but because behind the question of who can vote or be elected lies the question of the mode of group decision and the whole world-view of the relation between individual and group.

How can we approach and translate this idea of consensus? For us Westerners, consensus is, politically speaking, an idealistic or utopic concept. Of course, if, in council, everybody agrees on the issue at stake, there is unanimity – but the voting system can express this unanimity as well. And if there is disagreement, only the voting system can show where the majority is to reach a decision. Viewed from this logic, any 'consensus', if it is realized on an issue where there is disagreement, shows only that some people, at a certain point, were afraid or unable to continue expressing their position and made it possible for the voices of influential people to win the case. Consensus is only a blur put on pragmatic inequality and does not help to improve democracy.

Samoans do not deny that a consensual decision, *faatasi*, does not mean that there was total unanimity from the start. Why is it so important then for them 'to discuss the matter, during days and weeks if necessary, until everybody agrees on one decision'? Because, in this traditional way, the meeting ends with everybody drinking the *kava*, the divine beverage (decoction of *Piper methysticum*), this act binding every participant in a decision which is now guaranteed by the ancestors and the divine. It means that any action which would be taken later by someone against the decision would be breaking a taboo and taking the risk of unavoidable sanction (sickness, etc.). A consensual decision obliges people to stick to it until the issue is reopened in another meeting. But the main consequence of this is not that everybody is 'obliged' to follow the decision but that everybody shares in it.

Everyone, those who proposed the point or agreed to it from the start, as well as those who disagreed with it but in the end temporarily abandoned their disagreement to allow a consensus to take place, everyone shares in the decision and feels that way. Those who, seen from a voting system point of view, would have been the defeated side do feel as well as the others that they belong to that decision, that they had their share in it (if only in letting it happened), and that, drinking with the others, they are not excluded in any way from the process following the decision. All this, of course, does not bar them from trying to prepare the minds of all the community so that an inversion of the balance of power could take place in the next meeting. But, in such a system, the division between sides is always only prospective, and the decisions are alway 'unanimous', even if their variation shows the variation in time of the balance of power in the village.

It so happens that this was the only Samoan way of reaching decisions. Out of that circle of togetherness, *faatasi*, the only possible action was war. It did happen frequently, but one understands easily that, when the only way to reverse a decision outside of the scenario of unanimity in meetings is war, people do think twice before crossing the gap and becoming violent.[12]

This tradition of consensus still operates in the choices of *matai* in a family, with the corrective added by the Germans at the beginning of the century: a Land and Titles Court which people can always appeal to when the different sides in a family, each presenting their own candidate to be *matai*, are unable to reach consensus. The possibility of appealing to the Court replaced the traditional wars (and the existence of local wars did end at that time), but the necessity of appealing is considered, as was the declaration of war, something 'bad' and 'shameful' for the family, since it shows the inability of the family to reach consensus.

The presence of the Europeans introduced, already a long time ago, the invention of voting. The first instances the Samoans witnessed were the assemblies of white missionaries of the London Missionary Society in the 1830s, where they were taking decisions on the organization of the Church.[13] Later on, the white community of merchants, assembled in what gradually became the town of Apia, did the same. The German and the New Zealand administration of course used that system, through the 'advisory' councils of Samoan *matai* that they set up to approve the work of the administration, and the United Nations brought in the process of referendum when time came for independance. The first elections of parliamentarians were held by consensus. Rapidly, the number of candidates, *matai*, wishing to sit in Parliament necessitated making choices, and the system of voting was adopted. We have described some of the later consequences of this adoption. Today, as some Samoans say, maybe utopically, the time has come to gauge the negative effect of the institution of voting – mainly the creation of divisions between a 'winning' and a 'defeated' side – and to contrast them to the traditional idea of communal sharing in the decision through consensus which binds together people having opposed ideas.

In sum, the contemporary debate in Samoa between the promoters of the semi-universal suffrage system of 1990 and the pro-*matai* voting system of 1962 is only the forefront of the deeper debate between the whole idea of universal suffrage and the total *faamatai* system which includes consensus and ignores the very idea of voting.

It seems that the choice between democracy and aristocracy in Western Samoa is not as simple as one might have thought, even if one wants to promote only the ideas attached to democracy. These ideas are very much present in Samoa and the problem is certainly not how to explain to a 'traditional' 'ethnic group' who would still worship sacred chiefs what are the values and virtues of democracy. The problem is that Samoa has the chance to built its future on ideas and experiences that come both from the *faamatai* tradition and from the Western tradition of democracy and to maybe create a new synthesis where the advent of democracy will not just be the replacement of hierarchy (in the *faamatai*) by inequality (in the Western-style politics). There lies the real question of the future of the country. If the opening of the electoral system to all individuals at the same time means a new distinction, becoming immediately an inequality, between 'town people' and 'villagers', 'professional politicians' and 'people', between – as Samoan say more and more – the people of the town and 'the people of the back [of the country]', it is not sure that it will really mean a progress in democracy.

If the outsider had anything to say in the debate, he would put forward the argument that hierarchy is always able to encompass a great number of its contraries, inequality as well as equality (and thus the *faamatai* allows much space for equality between individuals). But when one is left only with inequality, when inequality is no longer contained within hierarchy, then the only social logic at work is the process of setting apart.[14] One scenario is that the direct and total replacement of *faamatai* by universal suffrage would use a theoretical equality (of access to vote) but could create many inequalities that, in the end, will not serve democracy. There is a need to look for a new synthesis.

Notes

1. For reasons connected to the ethical outside position in which the observer must remain, I will only define and oppose the different ideas expressed by Samoans (individuals, groups, political parties) without naming these groups or individuals or describing the political arena they belong to.
2. See Tcherkézoff (1997a, b).
3. See Tcherkézoff (1992b).
4. All chiefs (family heads) are called *matai*. But *matai* can be *alii* (this is the word present in the expression *faatamalii*) or *tula*, properly sacred chiefs or 'orators', the latter usually being linked in some ways to an *alii* name.
5. There are many symbolic relations between *alii* and the sky.
6. The constant interplay between genealogy and war in the dynamics of the Polynesian title system is well known (see Sahlins 1985; Valeri 1985).

7. This does not mean that women are excluded from the hierarchy, but, as 'sisters and daughters', their sacred role is more within the transmission of the *matai* name and the relation to the ancestor and to God, while the *matai* ship is the duty of the 'brothers and the sons'. But the *matai* only embodies the name. To make decisions, he often relies on the sisters, who can 'know and see' the truth; regarding the whole debate on gender roles in Samoa, see Schoeffel (1979), Shore (1981), Tcherkézoff (1992a, 1993, n.d.).

8. The relation between sisters and brothers is different and, in a way, encapsulates the whole chain: it is a kind of whole/part relationship (see Tcherkézoff 1993).

9. All this ideology does not preclude in any way that inequality can play an important rule within the strategies of competition, more and more every day as the importance of having financial means to invest in traditional exchanges increases. But the point is that the competition is still today in Samoa within the politics of 'raising *matai* names' and not in capitalizing resources in order to gain power and the right of exploitation of other people (this applies only partly to the small merchant community of the town, which plays a more and more important role in national politics, and this evolution could, in a near future, bring about drastic changes in the global ideology which I describe here).

10. I summarize in this way the numerous talks with Samoan intellectuals, who say that the traditional Samoan system is, for the reasons just mentioned, a 'democratic' one.

11. It was, in large part, with the vote of the people of that part of the country that the referendum of 1990 was made, the rest of the country showing a somewhat higher percentage of non-participation (abstention or also because the access to register on electoral rolls was much easier for people in the urban and peri-urban area).

12. A violence which, as is all violence in Samoa, has no rule and no limits, precisely because it always takes place 'outside' society, 'society' being defined as a hierarchy of 'circles' of decisions (see Tcherkézoff 1997a, b).

13. See Tcherkézoff (1997a, b).

14. On the difference between notions of 'hierarchy' and 'inequality', see Tcherkézoff (1994, 1995a, b).

References

Sahlins, M. (1985). *Islands of History*. Chicago: University of Chicago Press.

Schoeffel, P. (1979). Daughters of Sina: A Study of Gender, Status and Power in Samoa. PhD thesis. Canberra: Australian National University.

Shore, B. (1981). Sexuality and Gender in Samoa: Conceptions and Missed Conceptions. In: S. Ortner and H. Whitehead (eds), *Sexual Meanings: The Cultural Construction of Gender and Sexuality*, pp. 192–215. Cambridge: Cambridge University Press:

Tcherkézoff, S. (1992a). La question du 'genre' à Samoa. De l'illusion dualiste à la hiérarchie des niveaux. *Anthropologie et Sociétés* 16(2):91–117.

—— (1992b). Les enfants-de-la-terre à Samoa. Tradition locale et développement imposé. In: J.F. Baré (ed.), *La Terre et le Pacifique*, pp. 15–40. *Etudes Rurales* numéro spécial 127–8.

—— (1993). The Illusion of Dualism in Samoa: 'Brothers-and-Sisters' are not 'Men-and-Women'. In: T. del Valle (ed.), *Gendered Anthropology*, pp. 54–87. London: Routledge and Kegan Paul.

—— (1994). Hierarchical Reversal, Ten Years on (Africa, India, Polynesia). Part I: the Hierarchical Structure and Part II: Rodney Needham's 'Counterpoints'. *Journal of Anthropological Society of Oxford* 25(2):133–67, 25(3):229–53.

—— (1995a). L'inclusion du contraire (L. Dumont), la hiérarchie enchevêtrée (J.P. Dupuy) et le rapport sacré/pouvoir. Relectures et révision des modèles à propos de l'Inde. Part I: un modèle asymétrique et Part II: statut et pouvoir en Inde: la logique concrète de l'inclusion du contraire'. *Culture* 14(2):113–34, 15(1):33–48.

—— (1995b). L'autocar à Samoa ou la hiérarchie au quotidien. *Gradhiva* 18:47–56.

—— (1997a). Introduction. In: S.Tcherkézoff and F. Douaire-Marsaudon (eds), *Le Pacifique-sud aujourd'hui. Identités et transformations culturelles*, pp. 9–36. Paris: CNRS Editions (serie 'Ethnologie').

—— (1997b). Culture, nation, société. Changements secondaires et bouleversements possibles au Samoa Occidental. In: S. Tcherkézoff and F. Douaire-Marsaudon (eds), *Le Pacifique-sud aujourd'hui. Identités et transformations culturelles*, pp. 309–37. Paris: CNRS Editions (serie 'Ethnologie').

——— (n.d.) Qu'est-ce qu'un acte sexuel, au Samoa Occidental? Paper presented at the Symposium 'Horizon de l'anthropologie et trajets de Maurice Godelier', Cerisy, June 1996. Manuscript.

Valeri, V. (1985). *Kingship and Sacrifice. Ritual and Society in Ancient Hawaii.* Chicago: Chicago University Press.

Notes on the Contributors

Ad Borsboom (PhD University of Nijmegen) is Professor at the Centre for Pacific Studies, Department of Anthropology, University of Nijmegen. Since 1972, he has conducted fieldwork in Australia investigating religion and social change in Aboriginal societies, identity and land rights. His writings include *De Clan van de Wilde Honing: Spirituele Rijkdom van de Aborigines,* and he is, together with Ton Otto, editor of the reader *Cultural Dynamics of Religious Change in Oceania* (1997, Leiden).

Ben Burt (PhD University of London, 1990) is Education Officer for the Ethnographic Department of the British Museum (formerly Museum of Mankind) in London. He has carried out fieldwork in Kwara'ae, Solomon Islands and is author of *Tradition and Christianity: The Colonial Transformation of a Solomon Islands Society* (1994, Harwood Academic Publishers) and co-author of *Falafala ana Ano 'i Kawara'ae: The Tradition of Land in Kwara'ae* (1992, University of the South Pacific, Suva, with Michael Kwa'ioloa *et al.*) and of *Living Tradition: A Changing Life in Solomon Islands* (1997, British Museum Press, with Michael Kwa'ioloa).

Bronwen Douglas (PhD Australian National University, 1973) is Fellow in the Research School of Pacific and Asian Studies at the Australian National University. Being a historian by training, she has done archival and library research in Paris, Rome, Nouméa, Sydney and Canberra and conducted ethnohistorical fieldwork in New Caledonia and Vanuatu. Her writings include numerous articles in international journals and *Across the Great Divide: Journeys in History and Anthropology* (1998, Harwood Academic Publishers).

Thomas K. Fitzgerald (PhD University of North Carolina, 1969) is Professor of Anthropology at the University of North Carolina at

Greensboro. He conducted extensive fieldwork in New Zealand (among Maori university graduates and about the aspirations of Cook Islanders) as well as in North Carolina, Sweden, Finland and Monserrat (West Indies). He is author of *Education and Identity: A Study of the New Zealand Maori Graduate* (1977, New Zealand Council for Educational Research, Wellington), *Aspirations and Identity of Second Generation Cook Islanders in New Zealand* (1988, Department of Education, New Zealand, Wellington) and *Metaphors of Identity: A Culture–Communication Dialogue* (1993, State University of New York Press).

Jonathan Friedman (PhD Columbia University, 1972) is Professor for Social Anthropology at the University of Lund, Sweden. He has conducted twenty-three months of fieldwork in Hawai'i. His writings include numerous articles published in international journals and *Cultural Identity and Global Process* (1994, Sage), *System Structure and Contradiction in the Evolution of 'Asiatic' Social Formations* (1972, new edition forthcoming, Altamira Press/Sage); he has edited *Consumption and Identity* (1994, Harwood Academic Press) and is co-editor of *Melanesian Modernities* (1996, Lund University Press, with James Carrier).

Barbara Glowczewski (PhD 1988, Panthéon-Sorbonne, Paris), is Researcher at the Centre National de la Recherche Scientifique, Laboratoire d'Anthropologie Sociale, Paris. She has carried out several field researches in Central Australia since 1979 and in the Kimberly (between 1991 and 1998). Her books include *Yapa – Aboriginal Painters from Balgo and Lajamann* (1991, Baudoin Lebon), *Du rêve à la loi chez les Aborigènes* (1991, Presses Universitaires de France) and *Adolescence et sexualité: l'entre-deux* (1995, Presses Universitaires de France).

Berit Gustafsson (PhD Institute for Advanced Studies in Social Anthropology, University of Gothenburg, 1993) is currently Visiting Research Fellow at the Papua New Guinea Research Institute. She has carried out extensive fieldwork on M'buke Island, Manus Province, Papua New Guinea and fieldwork among M'Buke families in Port Moresby is ongoing. Her writings include *Houses and Ancestors. Continuities and Discontinuities in Leadership among the Manus* (1992, IASSA, University of Gothenburg).

John Morton (PhD Australian National University, 1986) is Senior Lecturer at the School of Sociology and Anthropology, La Trobe University, Melbourne, and Senior Curator, Museum Victoria, Melbourne. Between 1981 and 1998, he carried out eighteen months' fieldwork with Arrernte people in various Central Australian communties. Apart from numerous articles published in books and international journals, he has co-edited Géza Róheim's *Children of the Desert II* (with Werner Muensterberger) and *Persons, Bodies, Selves, Emotions* (1995, with Martha Macintyre).

Ton Otto received his anthropological training at the University of Nijmegen and his PhD in 1991 from the Australian National University. He is Chair of Ethnography and Social Anthropology at the University of Aarhus in Denmark. Between 1986 and 1995, he carried out field research in Papua New Guinea, mainly in Manus and Lavongai, for a total period of thirty-three months. His publications include the edited volume *Pacific Islands Trajectories* (1993, Canberra and Nijmegen) and the two co-edited works *Narratives of Nation in the South Pacific* (1997, with Nicholas Thomas) and *Cultural Dynamics of Religious Change in Oceania* (1997, with Ad Borsboom).

Philippe Peltier (DEA 1981, Sorbonne University) is Curator of the Oceanic collections at the Musée National des Arts d'Afrique et d'Océanie, Paris. Between 1984 and 1992, he carried out twenty-six months of fieldwork among the Adjirab, East Sepik Province, Papua New Guinea. His writings include *David Malangi. La Galerie des Cinq Continents* (1995, Paris).

Jens Pinholt received his academic training from the Institute of Anthropology, University of Copenhagen, where he obtained his MSc (magisterkonferens) in 1971. He is Associate Professor at the Department of Ethnography and Social Anthropology, University of Aarhus. Since 1973, he has carried out repeated and extended fieldwork in the Solomon Islands, Santa Cruz and Reef Islands. He is co-editor of *Livsformer og Kultur* (1992, Copenhagen, with Esther Fihl).

Gerhard Schneider received his anthropological training at the Free University of Berlin (MA 1988) and at the University of Cambridge, where he obtained his PhD in 1997. He has conducted eighteen months of fieldwork in the Munda Roviana Lagoon, New Georgia Island, Western Solomon Islands. He is contemporarily teaching at the Institute of Ethnology, University of Göttingen.

Gunter Senft (PhD University of Frankfurt, 1982, Habilitation Technische Universität Berlin 1992) is Senior Research Fellow at the Cognitive Anthropology Research Group, Max-Planck-Institute for Psycholinguistics in Nijmegen, the Netherlands. Being a linguist by training, he has been doing twenty-eight months of (anthropological-) linguistic research on Kilivila, the Austronesian language of the Trobriand Islands of Papua New Guinea. He has written numerous articles and has authored *Kilivila. The Language of the Trobriand Islanders* (1986, Mouton de Gryter), *Classificatory Particles in Kilivila* (1996, Oxford University Press), and edited *Referring to Space: Studies in Austronesian and Papuan Languages* (1997, Clarendon).

Nigel A. Stephenson received his anthropological training at the University of Basel, where he obtained his PhD in 1993. He has conducted extensive fieldwork in Papua New Guinea among the Wam people in the East Sepik Province. He currently holds a position as Lecturer at the Institute of Ethnology of the University of Basel. His writings include *Wotal – A Year in the Life of a Youth Group* (1987, The National Research Institute, Papua New Guinea) and *From Kastom to Komuniti: A Study of Equality and Inequality in a Changing Society. The Wam of East Sepik Province* (forthcoming, Basel).

Serge Tcherkézoff (PhD 1981, Paris) is Maître de Conférences, Ecole des Hautes Etudes en Sciences Sociales and co-founder of the Centre de Recherche et de Documentation sur l'Océanie in Marseille. Between 1975 and 1987, he carried out fieldwork in East Africa and, since 1981, he has worked in Western Samoa. His writings include, besides numerous articles, the co-edited volume *Le Pacifique-sud aujourd'hui* (1997, Paris, together with Françoise Douaire-Marsaudon).

Robert Tonkinson (PhD University of British Columbia, 1972) is Professor of Anthropology, University of Western Australia. His fieldwork sites are Western Desert, Western Australia, with a total of thirty-eight months' fieldwork since 1963, and Vanuatu, with twenty-eight months' research since 1966. His most recent writings include the co-edited works *Social Anthropology and Australian Aboriginal Studies* (1988, Aboriginal Studies Press, Canberra, with R.M. Berndt), *Going it Alone? Prospects for Aboriginal Autonomy: Essays in Honour of Ronald and Catherine Berndt* (1990, Aboriginal Studies Press, Canberra, with M.C. Howard), and he is author of *The Mardu Aborigines: Living the Dream in Australia's Desert* (1991, Holt, Rinehart and Winston).

Toon van Meijl is a graduate from the University of Nijmegen, the Netherlands, and the Australian National University, from which he obtained his PhD in 1991. At present he is a Senior Research fellow of the Royal Netherlands Academy of Arts and Sciences and is based at the Centre for Pacific Studies, University of Nijmegen. He conducted twenty-five months of fieldwork among the Tainui Maori. His writings include the co-edited works *Politics, Tradition and Change in the Pacific* (1993, Bijdragen tot de Taal-, Land- en Volkenkunde), and *European Imagery and Colonial History in the Pacific* (1994, Saarbrücken, both with Paul van der Grijp).

Jürg Wassmann (PhD 1979, Habilitation 1992, both University of Basel) is Professor for Anthropology and Head of the Institute of Ethnology, University of Heidelberg. He has carried out fieldwork in Papua New Guinea (since 1972 sixteen months among the Iatmul people, since 1986 twenty-two months among the Yupno people) and in Bali, Indonesia (ten months since 1992). His writings include numerous articles published in international journals and *The Song to the Flying Fox* (1991, Port Moresby), *Das Ideal des leicht gebeugten Menschen* (1993, Berlin), *Historical Atlas of Ethnic and Linguistic Groups in Papua New Guinea, Part 4 New Britain, Part 5 New Ireland, Part 6 Bougainville* (1995, Basel).

Index

Aboriginals *see* Australia
Alasa'a, Samuel 17, 104–12
Allan, Colin 202–3
Anderson, Benedict 5, 14
Aotourou 131
Arese, life story 18, 25, 213–28
aristocracy
  Tonga 17, 20–1
  Western Samoa 30–1, 419–23
Armstrong, S.L. 376
Australia
  Aboriginal and Torres Strait
    Islander Commission
    (ATSIC) 298, 312, 348
  Aboriginals 15–16, 27–9
  Aboriginality 29, 295–7,
    335–51
  anthropological writings
    355–79
  Arnhem Land 313–30
  Christianity 344–5,
    352(nn9, 10)
  colonial attitudes 357–8
  culture 358–63
  definition 355–7
  Dreamings 314–24, 329,
    337–8, 339–40, 344,
    368–9
  essentialism 336, 356–7,
    367, 375–6
  half-castes 341–3, 358,
    369–70, 379(n3)
  history of government
    policies 347–8

identity construction
  288–9, 292–6, 300–3,
  306(n24), 335–51,
  351(n2)
kastom 296–7
kinship 338–40, 369
Koori 353(n13)
land rights 28–9, 289–91,
  304(nn7, 8), 305(n12),
  311–13, 327–8
political power 297–300
relationship with land
  325–30
religion 343–5, 352(n8)
traditional laws and
  customs 313–30,
  339–40, 342
Warlpiri 344, 351(n5)
Wurgigandjar clan
  313–30
Yolngu people 380(n6)
Arnhem Land, Aboriginal
  customs 313–30
Council for Aboriginal
  Reconciliation 380(n8)
Mabo decision 15, 27–9,
  289–91, 311–12, 349, 371
  reactions 291–2
nation-building 16, 287–8,
  303–4(n3)
National Aboriginal
  Consultative Committee
  (NAAC) 295–6
Native Title Act (1993)

290–1, 299, 304(n8, 10), 312–13
Racial Discrimination Act (RDA) 299, 306(n21)
terra nullius 15, 27, 28, 29, 290, 371, 380(n9)
Avatip people *see* Papua New Guinea

Bader, Sabine 131–2
Baeanisia, Abraham 103–4, 113
Baker, Roger 124–5
Barter, Jane and Peter 125
Bauman, Zygmund 10
Bell, William 112
Bensa, Alban 72, 76–7
Borsboom, Ad 16, 28, 311–30
Bougainville, L.-A. de 120, 131
Buka Island *see* Solomon Islands
Burt, Ben 17, 22, 97–115

Carrier, J.G. and A.H. 230
chiefs
    New Caledonia 71–2
    Western Samoa 30–1, 417, 419–23
Christianity
    Australian Aboriginals 344–5
    dispute mediation, Papua New Guinea 159–60
    Hawaii 52–4
    missionaries 12
    New Caledonia 73
    Solomon Islands 111, 282–3(n10)
Clifford, J. 280
colonialism
    cultural effects 12–13, 16–17
    legal systems 5–6

New Caledonia 70–87
Pacific 12
plantation life 222–8
Western Samoa 417–18
Cook, Captain, Hawaii mythology 44–52, 55–7
Cook Islanders, New Zealand 18, 257–61
copra production 282(n4)
Court, Charles 290
Cousteau, Jean-Michel 127
Cowlishaw, Gillian 355–63, 375–9
Crawford, Peter 277, 281(n1), 282(nn8, 9)
cricket, warfare analogy 176
cultural identity, migrants 257–64
cultural relativism 255–7
cultural traditions, film-making 27, 270, 279–81
culture
    concepts 11–13
    definition 253–5, 265(n2)
    identity distinction 26, 255, 262
    traditional or modern 12–13

de Tocqueville, Alexis 393–5, 400
democracy
    concepts 391–5
    Maori society 30, 395–410
    Tonga 20–1, 389
    Western Samoa 30–1, 389, 417–31
Deplanche, E. 82
descent lines
    Papua New Guinea 232–5
    Solomon Islands 192–3, 195–6, 197, 201–3, 204–5

Dodson, Michael 293
Douarre, G. 78–9, 80
Douglas, Bronwen 17, 21–2, 67–87
Duff, Alan 379–80(n5)
Dunning, E. 175–6
Durkheim, E. 377, 378

education, multiculturalism 261–4
Eriksen, T. Hylland 272
Errington, F. 101–3, 115
essentialism 15–16, 336, 356–7, 367, 375–6
ethnogenesis, Aboriginals 292–6

Fenualoa people *see* Solomon Islands
Fiji, political coups 389–90
film-making, Vaiakau cultural traditions 19, 27, 270, 279–81
fishing rights
New Zealand Maori 405–9
Papua New Guinea 25–6, 242–50
Solomon Islands 206
Fitzgerald, Thomas K. 26, 253–64
football
Papua New Guinea 19, 182–5
warfare analogy 175–6
Frazer, Ian 114
Friedman, Jonathan 10, 16, 20–1, 37–64, 271

gambling, Papua New Guinea, trade analogy 178, 187–8
Geertz, Clifford 2
Gewertz, D. 101–3, 115

Ginsburg, F. 280
global village 8–9
globalization 2–4
local actors 9–11
market place 6–8
Glowczewski-Barker, Barbara 15, 28–9, 335–51
Guiart, J. 82–3
Gustafsson, Berit 19, 24, 169–88

Harrison, Simon 173, 176
Harvey, David 8
Hau'ofa, Epeli 9, 17, 20–1, 38, 273–4
Hawaii
Captain Cook stories 44–52, 55–7
Christianity 52–4
exchange not reciprocated 60–2
exchange or theft 54–8
hanai adoption practice 58–9
Keanae 61–2
ohana social organization 59–60
Hawke, Steve 361
headhunting
Papua New Guinea 172–3
Solomon Islands 193, 198–9
High Court of the Western Pacific, Native Land Appeal Case no. 9 (1971) 201–4
historical interpretations
Hawaii 37–64
New Caledonia 70–87
Solomon Islands 97–115
Trobriand Islands 119–34
historical truths 68–70
Hocart, A. 197, 198, 204–5, 208–9(n1)

hockey, Papua New Guinea
179–82
Hollinsworth, David 366
Huxley, Aldous 135(n6)

identity
Aboriginals 288–9, 292–6,
300–3, 306(n24), 335–51,
351(n2)
colonial 22, 67–87, 274
culture distinction 26, 255,
262
migrants 18, 257–61
modernism 40–2
Papua New Guinea
personal 213–28
social groups 24, 177–8,
182
Wam people 143–66
political focus 261, 265(n3)

Jackson, Jean 262
Jandamarra 361

Kanak people *see* New
Caledonia
kastom 6, 17, 271
Aboriginals 296–7
Papua New Guinea 18–19,
148–9
Kazukuru people *see* Solomon
Islands
Keen, Ian 363, 380(n6)
Keesing, Roger 14–15, 100–2,
112, 271
kinship, aboriginals 338–40,
369
komuniti, Papua New Guinea
18–19, 148–9, 158–9, 161, 166
Körner, Regine 128
Kuper, Adam 356

Kuschel, Rolf 114
Kwaio people *see* Solomon
Islands
Kwara'ae people *see* Solomon
Islands

Lambert, P. 91(n22)
land disputes, Solomon
Islands 24–5, 191–208
land rights
Australian Aboriginals 15,
28–9, 289–91, 304(nn7, 8),
305(n12), 311–13, 327–8
Papua New Guinea 238–41
Laracy, Hugh 100
Lattas, Andrew 357, 360, 362,
364–7, 375–9
Lavongai Island *see* Papua
New Guinea
leadership types, Papua New
Guinea 236–8
legal systems, colonialism 5–6
Linnekin, J. 61–2, 76, 77
local actors 9–11, 18–19
Ludwig, Harald 126–7

Mabo decision, Australia 15,
27–9, 289–91
McLuhan, Marshall 8
Mahmood, C.K. 376
Malaita *see* Solomon Islands
Malinowski, Bronislaw 121–3,
135–6(nn 6, 7), 136(n15)
Mannheim, K. 43
Mansell, Michael 305(n17)
Maori *see* New Zealand
Mara, Ratu Sir Kamisese 390
marine resources, Papua New
Guinea 25–6, 242–50
market, global 6–8
Matankor people *see* Papua

New Guinea
Mather, L. 155
matrilineal descent
 Papua New Guinea 232–5
 Solomon Islands 24–5,
  192–3, 195–6, 197, 201–3,
  204–5
M'Buke Island *see* Papua New
 Guinea
media
 cultural effects 256–7
 globalization 7
mediation
 definition 143
 Wam people, Papua New
  Guinea 152–66
Meyrowitz, Joshua 256
migration
 cultural identity 257–64
 transnational 8–9
modernism, identity 40–2
modernization, Papua New
 Guinea 173–5
Morphy, H. 327
Morris, Desmond 175
Morton, John 15, 29, 355–79
multiculturalism 261–4,
 265(n4)
Murdoch, Rupert 7
Murngin problem 363, 380(n6)

nation building, Australia 16,
 287–8, 303–4(n3)
nation-state 5
New Caledonia
 Balade 71–4, 79–80, 85
 Belep 72, 73
 chiefs' power 71–3, 74
 clan names 80–1,
  89–91(nn16–20)
 colonial texts 70–87

la Coutume 85–6
 historical invention 70–87
 Hoot/Waap relationship
  82–4
 house-mound lineages 77,
  78, 89–90(nn17–18)
 Kanak people 71–87
 legislation 75
 place-names 78–81
 Pou,bo 71, 75, 79, 85
 settlement patterns 71, 73,
  88(n6), 88–9(n9)
New Georgia Island *see*
 Solomon Islands
New Ireland *see* Papua New
 Guinea
New Zealand
 colonization 400–1
 Cook Islanders, cultural
  identity 18, 257–61
 Department of Maori
  Affairs 403
 devolution 402–5
 electoral system 398–9
 Maori
  democracy 30, 395–410
  fishing quotas 405–9
  parliamentary
   representation 396–9,
   411(nn7, 8)
  socio-economics 395–6
  sociopolitical changes
   399–402
  tribal organization 402–5
  urbanization 401
 Maori Congress 404–5
 Treaty of Waitangi 401, 406
 Waitangi Tribunal 406, 407,
  412(n13)
'noble savage' myth 16, 22–3,
 119–20, 123

Oertl, Marianne 125–6, 130
Omai 131
oral traditions 97–9
    Hawaii 44–52
    Solomon Islands 22, 103–12,
        213–28
Ortner, S.B. 312
Otto, Ton 19, 25–6, 229–50

Pacific
    colonization 12, 16
    sea of islands 9, 17, 21, 38,
        273–4
Papua New Guinea
    Arese, life story 18, 25,
        213–28
    Avatip people 173, 176
    cargo movement 228
    Chambri 101–3, 115
    colonialism
        first contacts 216–19
        plantations 222–8
    fishing rights 26, 242–50
    headhunting 172–3
    Japanese relationship
        220–2
    land rights 238–41
    languages 231
    Lavongai Island 230–50
        clan groups 232–5
        land rights 238–41
        leadership 236–8
        marine resources
            management 242–50
    lingua franca 137(n17)
    Manus Province
        ethnic groups 169–73
        gambling 178, 187–8
        sport 178–88
        warfare 172–3
    marine resource

management 25–6, 242–50
Matankor people 169–70,
    174, 179
M'Buke Island, Bismarck
    Hockey League 179–82,
    186–7
modernization 173–5
New Hanover *see* Lavongai
    Island
New Ireland
    baitfish payments 26,
        246–8
    Lavongai and Tigak
        Islands 230–50
Ponam, fishing rights 230
Second World War oral
    history 220–2
social groups 169–88, 225–7,
    232–5
song cycles 318–19
sport as identity 24, 175–88
Tigak Islands 231–50
    clan groups 232–5
    land rights 238–41
    leadership 236–8
    marine resource
        management 242–50
Titan people
    football 182–5
    gambling 187–8
    social identity 169–88
trade 171–2
    gambling analogy 187–8
Usiai people 169–70, 172,
    174, 182
Wam people
    ethnography 145–8
    kastom and *komuniti*
        148–9, 158–9, 161, 166
    power dispute mediation
        23, 152–66

sorcery claims 23, 143–4, 152–3, 160–1
wantok system 170, 188(n1), 225
Warengeme village, power dispute 146, 150–66
Yupno people 12–13
Pasolini, Pier Paolo 2
Peltier, Philippe 18, 25, 213–28
Perkins, Charles 297
Phillips, B. 203
Pinholt, Jens 19, 26, 269–81
Pittroff, Ursula 128
place names, colonial, New Caledonia 78–81
Plomley, N.J.B. 379(n3)
Poyer, L. 76, 77

Rabuka, Lieutenant-Colonel Sitiveni 390
Radcliffe-Brown, A.R. 368, 370
Rata, Matiu 404
Ratana 411(n8)
Reef Islands *see* Solomon Islands
Reich, Wilhelm 121–3
religion
    Australian Aboriginals 343–4
    Western Samoa 417
    see also Christianity
research, ethics 133–4
Richards, Mose 127
Rivers, W.H.R. 203
Rowse, Tim 360
rumours 143–4, 155–7

Sahlins, M. 43
Santa Cruz Islands *see* Solomon Islands, Reef Islands

Schiefenhövel, Wulf 130, 131–2
Schneider, Gerhard 19, 24, 191–208
Second World War, oral history 220–2
Senft, Gunter 16, 23, 119–34
sexual behaviour, Trobriand Islands 121–34
soccer *see* football
Solomon Islands
    Buka Island, plantation life 224–7
    Dunde village 193–6
    Fenualoa people 269–81, 281–2(n2)
    fishing rights 206
    headhunting 193, 198–9
    Kazukuru people 192–208
        court case 201–4
        descent lines 24–5, 192–3, 195–6, 197, 201–3, 204–5
        traditional culture 196–200, 204–6
    Kwaio people, oral history 102–3
    Kwara'ae people, oral history 104–12
    land disputes 24–5, 191–208
    land tenure, oral traditions 108–10
    local history 22, 97–115
    Malaita, oral history 22, 103–12
    Munda, land ownership disputes 24–5, 191–208
    New Georgia Island, land disputes 24–5, 191–208
    oral history 102–12
    Pijin 113–14

publication of oral histories
113–15
Reef Islands
cultural heritage 275–9
film-making 270, 279–81
red-feather rolls 276, 277,
278, 282(n8)
trading networks 275–7,
282(n5)
Roviana 193, 197–8, 204–5
stories of Samuel Alasa'a
104–12
timber rights 19, 204, 206–7
trade networks 275–7,
282(n5)
Vaiakau people 269–81,
281–2(n2)
Christianity 282–3(n10)
puki trading 26–7, 275–7,
282(n5)
song cycles
Aboriginal 316–19
Papua New Guinea 318–19
sorcery, Wam people, Papua
New Guinea 143–4, 152–3,
160–1
spaghetti principle 42
Spate, O. 45
Spencer, Baldwin 368, 369–70
sport
as social identity 175–88
warfare analogy 24, 175–6,
185–7
Stephenson, Nigel 18, 23,
143–66
Strathern, Andrew 101

Tahiti, 'noble savages' 120
Tavake, Basil 277, 282(n7)
Tcherkézoff, Serge 30–1,
417–31

texts
colonial 70, 88(n3)
definition 87(n2)
Theroux, Paul 128–30
Thomas, N. 271–2
Tigak Islands *see* Papua New
Guinea
timber rights, Solomon Islands
19, 204, 206–7
Titan people *see* Papua New
Guinea
Tjibaou, J.-M. 86
Tomalala, visit to Germany
130, 131–3, 136–7(n16),
137(n18)
Tonga
aristocracy 17
democratization 20–1, 389
Tonkinson, Robert 15, 16, 27–8,
287–303
Torres Strait Islanders
352(n12)
land claims 291, 311–12
tourism, sexual 125–7
trade
gambling analogy 24, 178,
187–8
Vaiakau people 26–7, 275–7,
282(n5)
transnational migration 8–9
Trobriand Islands
cricket as warfare 176
'Islands of Love' myth
123–30
'noble savage' 16, 22–3, 123
sexual tourism 125–7
Tomalala's visit to Germany
130, 131–3, 136–7(n16),
137(n18)
writings of Malinowski and
Reich 121–3

tuna fishing, baitfish
payments 246–8

USA
African-American culture
265(nn3, 5)
Alternative Dispute
Resolution (ADR) 6
Usiai people *see* Papua New
Guinea

Vaiakau people *see* Solomon
Islands
van Meijl, Toon 16, 30, 389–410
Vieillard, E. 82

Waleanisia, Joseph 99
Wallis, Mary 72, 82, 88(n7)
Wam people *see* Papua New
Guinea
warfare
Papua New Guinea 172–3

sport analogy 24, 175–6,
185–7
Western Samoa
chief system 30–1, 417,
419–23
democracy 30–1, 389,
417–31
gender roles 432(n7)
German colonialism 417–18,
430
matai 31, 419–31, 431(n4)
political system 418–19,
423–31
religion 417
voting 427–31
Wolfe, Patrick 357, 368–79,
380–1(n12)

Yngvesson, B. 155
Young, Michael 99
Yupno people *see* Papua New
Guinea